FAIR COP:
LEARNING THE ART OF POL

Janet B.L. Chan with Chris Devery

Police forces around the world have been undergoing major social
and organizational changes in recent years. In this unique longitudinal study, Janet Chan, Chris Devery, and Sally Doran analyse the
complexity of police socialization in response to changing conditions.
Following 150 new police recruits through two years of training and
apprenticeship, the authors question the traditional model of socialization that assumes a degree of stability and homogeneity in the
organizational culture. They suggest that recruits' developmental
paths are often quite diverse and the overall police culture is increasingly subject to change.

Drawing on interviews, observations, and questionnaires, the
authors depict the complex processes by which recruits adapt, redefine, cope with, and make sense of the positive and negative
aspects of their training and apprenticeship. Bringing together
rigorous quantitative analysis with rich ethnographic description,
Fair Cop provides new empirical data and theoretical understanding
regarding change and the reproduction of police culture.

JANET B.L. CHAN is a professor in the School of Social Science and
Policy at the University of New South Wales.

CHRIS DEVERY teaches at New South Wales Police College.

SALLY DORAN is a research assistant at the School of Social Science and
Policy at the University of New South Wales.

JANET B.L. CHAN
with Chris Devery
and Sally Doran

Fair Cop:
Learning the Art of Policing

UNIVERSITY OF TORONTO PRESS
Toronto Buffalo London

© University of Toronto Incorporated 2003
Toronto Buffalo London
Printed in Canada

ISBN 0-8020-3663-5 (cloth)
ISBN 0-8020-8491-5 (paper)

Printed on acid-free paper

National Library of Canada Cataloguing in Publication

Chan, Janet B.L. (Janet Bick Lai), 1948–
  Fair cop : learning the art of policing / Janet B.L. Chan ; with
Chris Devery and Sally Doran.

  Includes bibliographical references and index.
  ISBN 0-8020-3663-5 (bound).   ISBN 0-8020-8491-5 (pbk.)

  1. Police training.   2. Police – Attitudes.   I. Devery, Chris
II. Doran, Sally III. Title.

  HV7923.C43 2003   363.2'071   C2002-904349-2

This book has been published with the help of a grant from the Humanities
and Social Sciences Federation of Canada, using funds provided by the
Social Sciences and Humanities Research Council of Canada.

University of Toronto Press acknowledges the financial assistance to
its publishing program of the Canada Council for the Arts and the
Ontario Arts Council.

University of Toronto Press acknowledges the financial support for
its publishing activities of the Government of Canada through the
Book Publishing Industry Development Program (BPIDP).

Contents

Acknowledgments

This study was funded by an Australian Research Council (ARC) Collaborative Research Grant (1995–7) as a joint venture between the University of New South Wales (UNSW) and the New South Wales Police Service (NSWPS), with Janet Chan as the chief investigator and Chris Devery as the chief collaborator. The success of the grant application was due partly to the support and assistance of the then assistant commissioner, Jeff Jarratt of the NSWPS, the then dean of studies at the NSW Police Academy, David Bradley, and the then Director of the UNSW Research Office, Merrilee Robb.

Many people in the NSW Police Service contributed to the success of this study. I would like to give my special thanks to the class of police recruits who generously agreed to participate in the study. The project would not have been possible without their consent and cooperation. More than anything else, we are grateful for their appreciation of the value of research. Thanks are due also to the many academy staff, patrol/local area commanders, education development officers, field training officers, shift supervisors, and other police officers who cooperated with and facilitated our fieldwork over the two years. I would also like to thank Julie Stewart for facilitating the negotiation of the publishing agreement.

Chris Devery acted as our first point of contact at the police service, and the project benefited from his ability to convey the importance of the research to a wide range of people within the service and secure their understanding and support. Chris also undertook some of the fieldwork, provided valuable comments on the manuscript, and wrote chapter 4.

Sally Doran provided the pillar of strength for this complex and at times difficult project. Besides helping design the research instruments, interviewing and observation, managing and analysing data, maintaining financial accounts, and conducting library research, she managed the onerous task of organizing the data collection activities – all of this with efficiency, enthusiasm, and meticulous attention to detail. Her ability to orchestrate the project's complex research tasks around an inflexible timetable while meeting other demands of the research (all this while working half-time!) was truly remarkable. It is not an exaggeration to say that the project would not have succeeded without her strong and capable hands. Sally is also the junior author of chapter 2 and the senior author of chapter 8.

For their assistance with the interviews and observations, I thank (in alphabetical order) Lyn Barnes, Liz Bowen, Jody Camden, Lise Carroll, Fay Davidson, Sara Graham, Marion Horsky, Frank Leonard, Kim McKay, Michael Murphy, Deirdre Shields, Lisa Simone, Richard Thorowgood, and Darren Viscovich. Frank Leonard deserves special thanks for his thoughtful contributions to the project and his willingness and ability to meet some of the more demanding aspects of fieldwork. Sadly, Marion Horsky passed away before the end of the project. She was a source of inspiration to us: even when she was too ill to contribute, she never lost her enthusiasm for the project. I also thank Lise Carroll and Deirdre Shields for assisting with the data analysis of some of the surveys. For their help transcribing the interviews, I thank Beverly Loughton, Karen Monkerud (who also assisted with data entry), Fran Smithard, and Janelle Stevens.

I am grateful for the administrative support given to the project by the University of New South Wales, especially Susan Byrne at the School of Social Science and Policy, who handled the paperwork, and Warwick Dawson at the research office, who dealt with various aspects of the industry partnership arrangements. For their persistence and hard work in negotiating with the NSW Police Service a licence to publish, I thank Peter Dowdall and James Walsh of the UNSW Research Office.

I would also like to thank my colleagues at the School of Social Science and Policy for their support over the years. I benefited from my study leave at the University of British Columbia in the second half of 1997. My appointment as Walter S. Owen Visiting Chair at the Faculty of Law and as visiting scholar at Green College provided a stimulating environment for my work on this project. Thanks are also due to David Dixon, Richard Ericson, Peter Manning, Peter Saunders, and two anonymous reviewers of the *Australian and New Zealand Journal of Criminology* for their comments on the paper 'Negotiating the Field,' in which I explored some of the theoretical arguments of this book.

Virgil Duff deserves special thanks for his support of this book. The comments of three anonymous reviewers for University of Toronto Press and the Humanities and Social Sciences Federation of Canada (HSSFC) were invaluable in helping me sharpen the focus of the book. The manuscript benefited from the careful editing by Matthew Kudelka. I also gratefully acknowledge the subsidy granted by the Aid to Scholarly Publications Program of the HSSFC.

Finally, I would like to thank my partner Peter Saunders and my children Karen Beilharz and Kenneth Chan, who have supported me through years of trying to balance the demands of work with meeting their needs. I also thank Karen for preparing the index.

Preliminary results of this study were presented as papers at learned conferences over the years. These include: J. Chan, 'Learning the Craft of Policing.' Paper to the Annual Conference of the Australian and New Zealand Society of Criminology, Wellington, NZ, 1996; J. Chan, '"Good" and "Bad" Policing: Views of Recruits.' Paper to the Annual Conference of the Australian and New Zealand Society of Criminology, Brisbane, 1997; J. Chan. 'Learning the Culture: The Effect of Age, Gender, Education and Ethnicity on the Socialisation of Police Recruits.' Paper to the American Society of Criminology Annual Conference, San Diego, 1997; J. Chan and S. Doran, 'Learning in the Field: The Transmission of Cultural Knowledge in Police Organisations.' Paper to the Australian and New Zealand Society of Criminology Annual Conference, Surfers Paradise, 1998; and J. Chan, 'Negotiating the Field: New Observations on the Making of Police Officers.' Paper to the Australian and New Zealand Society of Criminology Annual Conference, Perth, 1999. A substantially expanded and revised version of 'Negotiating the Field' was published in 2001 in the *Australian and New Zealand Journal of Criminology*.

FAIR COP
LEARNING THE ART OF POLICING

1

Organizational Socialization and Professionalism

This book is a study of police socialization at a time of change. Traditionally, socialization is conceived as the process through which a novice learns the skills, knowledge, and values necessary to become a competent member of an organization or occupation. In policing this involves not only learning the laws, procedures, and techniques of law enforcement and order maintenance, but also acquiring a range of organizational skills, attitudes, and assumptions that are compatible with those of other members of the occupation. Successful socialization often involves a personal metamorphosis – and not always a positive one. Research has consistently shown that most recruits join the police with high expectations and lofty ideals, but by the time they graduate as police constables, many have become disillusioned and cynical about police work and the police organization, although they remain firmly committed to their vocation and bonded with their work mates. Why does this happen? Central to past assumptions about police socialization is the notion of police culture – a system of shared values and understandings that is passed from one generation of police to the next. The conventional wisdom is that as recruits become integrated into the operational ('street cop') culture, they adopt conservative, cynical attitudes as well as deviant practices. Police culture is thus seen as a breeding ground for unprofessional practices, as evidenced by various high-profile inquiries into police corruption in Australia and elsewhere (Fitzgerald Report 1989; Mollen Report 1994; Wood Report 1997).

Just as police culture is linked with police misconduct, professionalism is regarded as the antidote to misconduct (Brogden and Shearing 1993: 107–8). In recent years there have been attempts to rescue policing from its tarnished image by elevating the occupation to a profession – by reforming training programs, developing police-specific tertiary qualifications, and establishing ethical and practice standards (see, for example, Etter 1992). Police training is one of the most direct ways available to foster police professionalism. By designing training curricula to promote professional values and 'best practices' among new recruits, reformers hope to bring cultural change to the occupation. The success of these training reforms is uncertain. The available evidence suggests that no matter how enlightened the training program is intended to be, once recruits come face to face with the realities of operational police work, they fall under the negative influence of the 'street cop' culture that undermines professionalism (Centre for Applied Research in Education [CARE] 1990). The problem with professional police training is thus one of 'training decay,' which begins with field training and continues as recruits become full-fledged police officers.

This book challenges this pessimistic view of police socialization. It questions the fundamental framework within which police socialization is understood, starting with the conventional wisdom that police culture is all-powerful and unchanging, that recruits automatically and uncritically adopt corrupt values or bad practices during their socialization period, and that police culture is always the antithesis of professionalism. By analysing the experience of a cohort of 150 police recruits in an Australian state over a two-year period, we show that their developmental paths are often much more varied and much less determined than the conventional wisdom would have us believe. More important, by relating the cohort's experience to contemporary changes in the organizational and political conditions of policing, we demonstrate that police culture is much less homogeneous and much more open to change than was once assumed. Finally, we use the case study to refine and extend the Bourdieuian theoretical framework adopted in Chan (1997) in order to provide a more general understanding of the socialization process within organizational cultures in transition.

In the following sections we set out the theoretical context for our study of police socialization. We examine concepts such as professionalism, culture, and socialization, and we discuss the findings of the literature. We then critique the existing framework for understanding socialization, and summarize the reconceptualization of police culture first developed in Chan (1997) and its application to socialization.

Professionalism in Policing

Professionalism has been termed 'the third logic' for organizing and controlling work. While *market* focuses on costs and is controlled by consumers' preferences, and *bureaucracy* emphasizes predictability and efficiency and is governed by rules and managers, *professionalism* values specialized knowledge and quality of service and is regulated by members of the occupation (Freidson 2001). In practice, however, professionalism means different things to different people at different times and serves various purposes. Historically, police professionalism has been about establishing policing as a lifelong career devoted to public service (Sturma 1987), independence from political control (Vollmer 1971: 237), concern for administrative efficiency and technological innovations (Walker 1977: 167), raising recruitment and training standards (Reiner 1978; Bradley and Cioccarelli 1989), or adopting a results-oriented, problem-solving approach to policing (Goldstein 1979). As a result of recent moves to 'professionalize' policing, a credentialist definition of professionalism has come to dominate the public debate; even so, police professionalism should be seen as a multifaceted and dynamic concept.

The term professionalism is often perceived as a rhetorical device used by occupational groups to legitimate their power and authority. According to Manning, the police use this term as their most important 'presentation strategy' in the process of 'defend[ing] their mandate and thereby ... build[ing] self-esteem, organizational autonomy, and occupational solidarity or cohesiveness' (1997: 12). For Manning, professionalism is an ideology aimed at both internal and external control:

> Externally, professionalism functions to define the nature of the client, to maintain social distance with the clientele, and to define the purposes, the conventions, and the motivations of the practitioners; internally, it functions to unify the diverse interests and elements that exist within any occupational or organizational group ... Efforts made toward achieving professionalization of an occupation are, above all, efforts to achieve power and authority. (1997: 121; see also Price 1977: 86)

The meaning of professionalism varies with a member's function and status in the organization. As Manning has warned, the term professionalism is by no means uniformly understood by police:

Rhetoric can take on different meanings even within the organizational hierarchy. To patrolmen,[1] the term 'professionalism' means control over hours and salary and protection from arbitrary punishment from 'upstairs'; to the chief and the higher administrators, it relates to the public-administrations of efficiency, technological expertise, and standards of excellence in recruitment and training. (1978a: 10)

The concept of professionalism is universally embraced, yet there is evidence that some lower-ranking police officers see professionalization as an academic exercise that isn't relevant to the practice of 'locking up crooks' (Etter 1992: 22). Indeed, at a time when reformers are promoting professionalism as a philosophical and ethical commitment, some police regard it as a vehicle for career advancement.

Historical studies of occupations suggest that professionalization does not always result in better services; in fact, it has sometimes resulted in a 'systematic disabling' of 'clients' (Illich 1977: 28). There is good reason to be sceptical – the new push for police professionalism may have arisen from the need to control 'police work' in a climate of jurisdictional competition and interagency rivalries (cf. Abbott 1988). The movement is taking place at a time when the legitimacy and expertise of traditional police forces are increasingly being challenged. Findings of police corruption, malpractice, and incompetence by government commissions, the proliferation of specialist policing agencies, and the expansion of the private security industry have meant that the traditional roles and responsibilities of police forces are more and more being questioned and eroded. A revealing statement of the driving force behind the need to professionalize Australia's police forces is found in Etter:

If, in the future, policing cannot deal with the more complex and intellectually demanding aspects of police work, then the 'cream' of police work may well be skimmed off and supernumerary bodies similar to the National Crime Authority (NCA), the Australian Securities Commission (ASC) and the Independent Commission Against Corruption (ICAC) will continue to proliferate. If action is not taken to halt this trend, Police may be left with only the routine and more mundane aspects of their present role. (1992: 21)

In the policing of organized crime, distrust and rivalry have led to constant friction between agencies (Fitzgerald Report 1989: 169; also see Corns 1992). Corns has argued that apart from the 'territorial imperative,' which generates intense interstate and interagency conflicts, a great deal of the rivalry revolves around claims of expertise (1992: 179). It may be that the recent trend toward professionalization is as much about reforming the profession internally as it is about the control of work and the division of expert knowledge (cf. Ericson 1993).

But perhaps we need not be so sceptical about police professionalism. Whether or not policing becomes a 'profession' like the law and accountancy, the concept of professionalism – in the sense of high standards of practice – is necessary for police reform and police education. As Bittner pointed out more than two decades ago, without meaningful discussions of what constitutes 'good police practice,' professionalism is likely to remain an abstract ideal:

> Presently good and bad work practices are not distinguishable, or, more precisely, are not distinguished. Worst of all, we have good reasons to suspect that if some men are possessed by and act with professional acumen, they might possibly find it wiser to keep it to themselves lest they will be found to be in conflict with some departmental regulation. The pending task [has to do with] discovering those good qualities of police work that already exist in the skills of *individual practitioners*. It is not enough to discover them, however, they must be liberated and allowed to take their proper place in the scheme of police organization. By making the possession and use of such skills the controlling consideration in the distribution of rewards, we will have a beginning of a professional system for controlling police practices. (Bittner 1978: 50)

One writer who gave much thought to the practical meaning of police professionalism was William Ker Muir. He accepted the premise that the capacity to use coercive force if necessary is central to the police role (cf. Bittner 1978), and he proposed (1977: 50) a model of good police practice in terms of Weber's professional politician – one who combines the virtues of passion ('a capacity to "integrate" coercion into morals') with perspective ('intellectual "objectivity"'). Hence, police professionalism is reflected in a mature practitioner who has the strength to 'endure the antagonisms' aroused by the paradoxical use of coercive power 'for the general welfare,' combined with an inner 'knowledge of tragedy' – 'a comprehension of the suffering of each inhabitant of the earth, a sensitivity to man's yearning for dignity, and, ultimately, "some kind of faith" that no individual is worthless' (50–1). In Muir's model, the professional police officer is one who is neither cynical about society nor troubled by moral conflicts over the use of coercion.

The development of a sound and detailed concept of police professionalism is obviously an important step. But even assuming there is a widely accepted definition of police professionalism (which there is not), the questions remain: How can professionalism be taught? And how can it be learned by recruits so as to be reflected in their subsequent practice? The key issue in recruit training is whether formal training has any lasting influence on practice, given the inevitable tensions between theoretical knowledge and practical experience. One common theory is that once recruits are confronted with 'real' police work and become assimilated into the police occupational culture, their formal (usually academy-based) training turns out to have limited impact on how they carry out their duties. We now turn to the apparently corrupting influence of police culture.

Police Culture and the Limits of Training

The concept of 'police culture' was first developed by social scientists. Ethnographers studying routine police work uncovered an informal system of 'recognizable and distinct rules, customs, perceptions, and interpretations of what they see, along with consequent moral judgments' among police officers (Skolnick and Fyfe 1993: 90). These rules are often unrelated to – and may even contradict – formal laws, regulations, and guidelines. Skolnick (1966) suggested that this distinctive way of interpreting and responding to the world gave rise to a police 'working personality.' Furthermore, the occupational culture operates at a level of shared customs, values, and assumptions:

> The occupational culture constructed by the police consists of long-standing rules of thumb, a somewhat special language and ideology that help edit a member's everyday experiences, shared standards of relevance as to the critical aspects of the work, matter-of-fact prejudices, models for street-level etiquette and demeanor, certain customs and rituals suggestive of how members are to relate not only to each other but to outsiders, and a sort of residual category consisting of the assorted miscellany of some rather plain police horse sense. (Manning and Van Maanen 1978: 267)

Reiner (1992: 111–29) lists the key characteristics of police culture as follows: a sense of mission, an orientation toward action, a cynical or pessimistic perspective on the social environment, constant suspiciousness, an isolated social life coupled with a strong code of solidarity with other police officers, a sharp distinction between good guys and bad guys (i.e., between the rough and the respectable), a conservative stance in politics and morality, a machismo outlook that permits sexism and alcoholic and sexual indulgence, prejudice toward ethnic minorities, and a pragmatic view of police work that discourages innovation and experimentation.

In recent years the term 'police culture' has entered public discourse as a convenient label for a range of negative values, attitudes, and practice norms among police officers. For example, police culture was identified in Queensland as responsible for police misconduct and as a major obstacle to successful police reform (Fitzgerald Report 1989: 200–12; see also Wood Report 1997). Fitzgerald saw the Queensland police culture at the time of the inquiry as primarily negative and as reflecting 'contempt for the criminal justice system, disdain for the law and rejection of its application to police, disregard for the truth, and abuse of authority' (Fitzgerald Report 1989: 200). In particular, Fitzgerald suggested that an unwritten 'police code' operated within the culture that condoned misconduct and corruption. Young, inexperienced, and impressionable recruits were susceptible to the influences of the culture:

> Naturally, after a very short time in the Police Force, young people lose any sense of perspective on the culture of which they have become part. Fellow police and police work define their self-image, their attitude to society and their place within it. Peer pressure becomes overwhelming and is supported by other factors. (1989: 211)

Fitzgerald suggested that 'new recruits must be protected from absorption into the culture' (212), and recommended that recruit training be upgraded to include 'ethical standards as an essential integrated aspect of all matters taught' (382).

Operational police culture tends to undermine formal training. This has long worried police enducators. In an American police force in the early 1970s, Van Maanen found a culture of complacency and disenchantment. His famous quote from a police veteran neatly sums up both the futility of formal training and the lack of incentive for work performance: 'There's only two things you gotta know around here. First, forget everything you've learned in the academy 'cause the street's where you'll learn to be a cop; and second, being first don't mean shit around here. Take it easy, that's our motto' (Van Maanen 1973: 415).

Research in Australia provides evidence that police recruits do indeed embrace negative values commonly attributed to the police culture. For example, recent longitudinal studies of police recruits in Queensland and New South Wales found that as officers became 'socialized' into the policing occupation, their attitudes became more conservative (Christie et al. 1996) and more ethnocentric (Wortley 1992). The evidence from Wortley (his study was carried out on 412 NSW police recruits between 1988 and 1991) suggests that the academy succeeded in 'reducing or containing racist and authoritarian attitudes of recruits,' but once the probationers went into the field, these 'gains were reversed.' In particular, recruits who were sent to areas with large Aboriginal populations became more racist than other recruits. An evaluation of the NSW recruit training program refers to this problem as one of 'training decay,' which occurred during the field training period, in the course of which 'operational and occupational realities serve to undermine both the formal curriculum ... and the development of reflective and critical understanding' (Centre for Applied Research in Education [CARE] 1990: 54). The same report cites recruits' accounts that during field training, proper procedures were substituted by conventional shortcuts – a practice 'promoted by the FTOs [Field Training Officers] and other Patrol personnel and serve to undermine the confidence of the probationer in the Academy-based training he or she has received' (55). In this vein, the academy was dismissed as 'Bullshit Castle' and its curriculum as 'Alice in Wonderland stuff.'

The notion of 'training decay' is consistent with the popular view that police culture undermines professionalism. For example, the code of solidarity means that in their assessments, field training officers and experienced constables are often reluctant to criticize recruits' practices; this undermines the formal training process (CARE 1990: 62–71). The corollary of this is that professionalism can be used as a 'device for limiting the influence of police culture' (Brogden and Shearing 1993: 108). Yet efforts to 'professionalize' police through education, professional ethics, and accountability measures have traditionally met with limited success. This has prompted the suggestion that in order to 'work,' professionalism must come down from its lofty height and be more relevant to practice:

More realistically, for professionalism to be effective as a device that will restrain police culture, it must resonate with rank-and-file experience and not be imposed from the top by police elite. It must be connected to the operational reality of policing, be relevant to the specificity of policing, and experientially based. Professionalism in policing should not be removed from the hurly-burly of rank-and-file work. Rather it should seek to elevate, in skill and commitment, the 'best practice' of ordinary police persons. Doing this, like so many things in police reform, is easier said than done. (Brogden and Shearing 1993: 109)

This counsel creates theoretical confusion and at the same time provides a way out of it. Treating professionalism as something distinct from – and the antithesis of – police culture creates confusion because it assumes that the influence of police culture is all negative, when in fact there is plenty of evidence that police culture does a great deal to help police officers survive in a dangerous, unpredictable, and alienating occupation (Reiner 1992; Goldsmith 1990). In effect, this way of thinking negates the possibility of reform by ruling out the possibility of a professional police culture. It is also important to emphasize that notwithstanding the apparent similarities in police culture across jurisdictions, police organizations are internally culturally diverse (Manning 1978b: 244; Chan 1997). So it is misleading to assume there is a single culture operating at any one time.

Brogden and Shearing's comment that professional ideals must be made practical points to a way out of this theoretical confusion. The challenge is not to 'restrain police culture' from its negative influence on practice, but rather to make professionalism (in the sense of 'good practice') part of the operational police culture – the accepted 'values, norms, perspectives and craft rules' that inform police conduct (Reiner 1992). As Brogden and Shearing caution, this is 'easier said than done'; even so, this way of thinking recognizes that 'bad' practice models should have no more privileged access to, and direct impact on, officers than 'good' ones if the good ones work just as well (if not better) in practice. To paraphrase Fielding (1988: 135) in the context of recruit training, both 'good' and 'bad' models have to make a pitch for the recruit's support: any model that fails to maximize desirable outcomes is likely to be dismissed.

So it is unhelpful to think of police culture as the culprit that 'corrupts' practice and leads to 'training decay.' Furthermore, it is not useful to compare formal and informal influences (cf. Fielding 1988) when trying to understand police practice. It is simpler to consider that within police organizations, recruits will encounter both 'good' and 'bad' practice models during formal instruction and in less formal occupational settings. How often 'good' or 'bad' models are encountered will depend on the prevailing culture of the police organization and on how training is organized. More generally, how recruits' conceptions of 'good' and 'bad' policing develop in the course of their training is a crucial component of their socialization process. The transmission of occupational culture – including notions of 'good' and 'bad' policing practice – is a complex phenomenon that we discuss in the next section.

The Transmission of Police Culture

There have not been many systematic studies of police socialization (see Van Maanen 1973, 1975; Fielding 1988), although there is a substantial literature on professional or organizational socialization in other fields (see, for example, Saks and Ashforth 1997; Ashforth, Saks, and Lee 1998; Ashforth and Saks 1996; Adkins 1995; Morrison 1993; G.R. Jones 1986; Van Maanen and Schein 1979). As mentioned earlier, organizational socialization is the process by which a person learns the values, attitudes, and acceptable behaviours he or she requires in order to participate as a member of an organization (Van Maanen 1976: 67; Van Maanen and Schein 1979). Through socialization, new members acquire various types of cultural knowledge – the assumptions, values, cognitions, and behavioural norms of the organization (Schein 1985; Sackmann 1991). In policing, the various dimensions of cultural knowledge have been labelled loosely as 'police culture.'

New members go through various stages of socialization (Van Maanen 1976). Often there is a phase of *anticipatory socialization* during which people prepare themselves before entering an organization by taking on its values, attitudes, skills, and knowledge. This is followed by an initial period of *encounter* with the organization, which can be a difficult phase if new members' expectations of their job and the organization were unrealistic. The newcomer's experience at this phase is mediated by environmental, organizational, relevant-group, task, and individual factors (Van Maanen 1976). Finally, continued membership in the organization demands some form of *metamorphosis* on the part of the newcomer. The extent of individual change is 'situationally determined and dependent upon both organizational and individual characteristics' (115).

The consequences of socialization often depend on the 'socialization tactics' (Van Maanen and Schein 1979) adopted by the organization.

Socialization tactics can be 'institutionalized' or 'individualized' (G.R. Jones 1986). The socialization of police recruits is institutionalized in that it is typically *collective*, *formal*, *sequential*, and *fixed* in duration at the academy stage, and *serial* (where experienced members groom newcomers) at the field training stage. Typically, it involves *divestiture* processes that strip away certain personal characteristics of the newcomer.[2] Institutionalized socialization tends to encourage conformity rather than innovation (G.R. Jones 1986), although this depends on whether innovation is expected of organizational members (Ashforth and Saks 1996).

Schein, who has written extensively on organizational culture, has reviewed the theories explaining how culture develops among groups. These theories are also useful for explaining how organizational culture is reproduced or transformed. Schein (1985: ch. 7) suggests that theories of culture formation fall into three broad types: *sociodynamic theory*, which is concerned with group dynamics and shared understandings; *leadership theory*, which describes the role of leaders in creating and embedding their assumptions in organizations; and *learning theory*, which deals with cognitive learning and explains how some cultural features become entrenched while others disappear. Though leadership theory is useful for understanding cultural formation and cultural change in organizations, sociodynamic theory and learning theory are more relevant for understanding how police culture is transmitted to new recruits. These two are briefly discussed below.

Sociodynamic Theory

This type of theory focuses on the 'underlying interpersonal and emotional processes' that explain how and why 'shared' solutions, understandings, and world views develop written a group:

> ... how each individual comes to feel that he is a member of the group in the first place and how each member resolves the core conflict between the wish to be enveloped by and fused with the group, thereby completely losing personal identity, and the wish to be completely autonomous and free of the group, thereby potentially becoming estranged from and losing potential membership in the group. (Schein 1985: 149–50)

The hypothesis is that people have three primary needs in a social context: the need to be included and to 'develop a viable role or identity within the group' (inclusion); the need to 'master the environment' (influence and control); and the need to feel accepted and secure (acceptance and intimacy). When thwarted, these needs generate strong anxiety; when fulfilled, they generate 'positive energy': 'The first and most powerful experience of "sharing" thus comes with the discovery that every member has similar feelings of anxiety and alienation' (151).

Studies of police socialization have found similar processes operating among new recruits. Van Maanen (1973: 410) described how the 'harsh and often arbitrary discipline' encountered at the police academy gave rise to a collective consciousness among recruits of being 'in the same boat,' and helped develop group solidarity among members of the same class and increased distance from old acquaintances:

> The main result of such stress training is that the recruit soon learns it is his peer group rather than the 'brass' which will support him and which he, in turn, must support. For example, the newcomers adopt covering tactics to shield the tardy colleague, develop cribbing techniques to pass exams, and become proficient at constructing consensual ad hoc explanations of a fellow-recruit's mistake. Furthermore, the long hours, new friends, and ordeal aspects of the recruit school serve to detach the newcomer from his old attitudes and acquaintances. In short, the academy impresses upon the recruit that he must now identify with a new group – his fellow officers. (411)

Fielding makes a similar observation about the role of drill training in building up group consciousness among recruits (1988: 61–2).

However, individuals working in the same environment bring into the job different emotional coping styles and cognitive styles, which they have developed in past cultural settings. Over time, members learn to accommodate one another's styles, especially when working together is essential for survival in the organization. Some may decide to leave because their needs are not being met; those who remain 'gradually develop common conceptual categories and a language geared to mutual understanding and acceptance' (Schein 1985: 154). For example, Fielding (1988: 92) observes that recruits who confront 'how great their ignorance of practice is' in the field are strongly influenced by experienced officers, who pass on 'subversive knowledge' about coping strategies and an 'operating ideology' justifying these practices, which may or may not be in line with 'approved procedures.' Recruits begin to see the limitations of 'formal, by-the-book' knowledge, compared with the useful, practical procedures they learn from experienced officers. In time, recruits develop a degree of contempt for 'academic knowledge,' as contrasted with practical, commonsense knowledge (140). Similarly, Van Maanen (1973: 415) describes how recruits cope with the realities of police work by learning to 'stay out of trouble' and follow 'the line of least resistance' for organizational survival. As Fielding points out, a recruit after joining the police begins renegotiating his sense of self-identity through interaction with others, so that eventually 'he leaves society behind to enter a profession that does more than give him a job, it defines who he is' (Ahern 1972: 3, quoted by Fielding 1988: 41).

These processes of negotiating self-identity in a new occupational setting are not driven entirely by needs satisfaction and organizational survival. Rather, members in organizations develop shared understandings and defence mechanisms in both conscious and unconscious ways:

> The process of 'getting acquainted,' 'testing the waters,' and 'finding one's place in the group' can ... be seen as a highly complex interaction involving both conscious and unconscious elements, both rational assessments of the situation and irrational projective identifications elicited by one's own unconscious needs and the characteristics of particular other people in the group. (Schein 1985: 156–7)

Learning Theory

Schein proposes that culture is learned in organizations through a complex process that involves absorbing not only 'overt behavior patterns' but also cognitions and emotions (1985: 174). According to Schein, culture is transmitted by a group-based learning process either through positive reinforcement of successful solutions to problems ('problem solving') or through successful avoidance of painful situations ('anxiety avoidance'). This distinction between problem-solving learning and anxiety-avoidance learning is an important one for understanding police culture. Problem-solving learning is considered positive and rewarding, whereas anxiety-avoidance learning is negative and defensive: 'Avoidance learning is often *one*-trial learning. Once something works, it will be repeated indefinitely, even if the source of pain is no longer active' (177).

Many of the negative aspects of police culture seem to have developed as anxiety-avoidance mechanisms rather than as innovative problem-solving strategies. For example, perceptual stereotypes and operational shortcuts enable officers to place people and situations they encounter into ready-made categories, and to apply standard operational methods. Schein considers 'cognitive overload and/or an inability to decipher and categorize the multitude of stimuli impinging on the senses' as a major source of anxiety (*cognitive* anxiety) for people; thus, a stable system of cognitions is 'absolutely necessary' for their own protection and survival (179). Furthermore, police officers' work involves considerable potential for risk and danger, which are sources of *role-related* anxiety. Hence, operational 'rules of thumb' reduce the level of uncertainty and anxiety in police work and make unfamiliar situations seem more predictable. Police officers are often required to 'form a rapid first impression, to group people quickly according to whether they were likely to behave rebelliously or cooperatively' (Muir 1977: 157). Fielding (1988: 42–5) suggests that 'making work' – 'converting boredom to excitement by generating one's own activity' such as car stops and high-speed car pursuit – is another way of coping with the danger and boredom of police work. Besides dealing with external risks related to street work, officers also learn to deal with the anxieties generated by 'paperwork' requirements within the organization. This often involves 'back-covering' activities. One of Fielding's probationers observed that producing 'appropriate paperwork' to satisfy the demand for accountability became an end in itself and a significant factor in determining action:

> You've got a crime report to fill in as soon as a crime's happened and if you're not very careful, you start thinking of the paperwork before you think of what you're doing. There could be an offender there and you're getting your paperwork out before you've assessed the job. In the long term the paperwork is more important because I'm in my probation and you can get in trouble over your paperwork a lot easier than if you arrest somebody unlawfully. (in Fielding 1988: 118)

Similarly, occupational solidarity helps officers reduce their *social* anxiety by offering recipes for avoiding trouble and preventing isolation within the police force. For example, by observing the 'code of silence,' officers avoid the threat of being ostracized by colleagues as well as the danger that assistance will be withheld during emergencies.

As noted earlier by Schein, the consequence of anxiety-avoidance learning is that the group tends not to question any original assumptions, even if those assumptions were incorrect. This is because such questioning would itself be anxiety-provoking or painful. For example, Muir found that police officers preferred to be overly suspicious rather than overly trusting when approaching citizens. Officers used a 'minimax' strategy to minimize the maximum risk in their work:

> In the event that an assumption was erroneously suspicious, the policeman ended up unhappy but at least had the consolation that he was alive to appreciate his unhappiness. In the instance where the mistaken assumption was initially trusting, the policeman's mistake was not redeemed by the fact of personal survival. The mistaken oversuspicion meant wasting a citizen; the mistaken overtrust meant death. (1977: 166–7)

As Muir points out, this type of strategy offers no incentive for checking the correctness of the initial assumption; such checking would be considered a waste of time. Anxiety-avoidance learning can also result in the group being overprotective of their accepted rituals, beliefs, and assumptions. The group may eventually lose any ability to change and innovate. As Sparrow and colleagues (1990) point out, mistake avoidance and resistance to change seem to go hand in hand.

The Influence of Culture on Practice

There is overwhelming evidence that police recruits learn the craft of policing through the cognitive filters of the occupational culture 'with numbing regularity' (Van Maanen 1975: 215). Yet questions remain. Do all police end up with a fairly uniform set of attitudes and practice orientations? And do these attitudes and orientations necessarily lead to a particular pattern of practice?

The literature offers some evidence that police attitudes and work orientations do vary even within a single organization. Muir (1977), for example, classifies officers into four groups according to their moral attitude toward the use of coercive force and their intellectual view of human pain and suffering. Similarly, Shearing (1981) classifies officers according to their responses to the subculture and to departmental policy. Reiner sees these categories as corresponding to functional and rank structures within the organization:

> The same underlying types are postulated: an alienated cynic, a manage-

rial professional, a peace-keeper and a law-enforcer. These correspond with the basic organizational division of labour between management/ rank and file, and CID/uniform patrol. But the differing orientations are already discernible in samples of uniform patrol officers, prefiguring future career developments. (1992: 132)

Fielding argues, however, that among constables there is no single 'final perspective' (Becker et al. 1961, quoted in Fielding 1988: 203); rather, there are a number of 'competing value positions' forming a repertoire of resources to be drawn from as necessary (204). As Manning and Van Maanen point out, the processes of occupational socialization should be seen as contingent and continuous rather than uniform and only occurring at the early stages:

> The assignment of recruits, for instance, to different precincts, shifts, and beats will provide for different recruit experiences, as will the assignment of recruits to different supervisors, colleagues, and patrol partners ... The various task and structural arrangements within police organizations promote considerable segmentation in the perceptions of policemen toward such aspects of their work as task predictability, danger on the job, organizational production pressures, autonomy from supervision, and even encounters with citizens ... Nor is the occupational socialization of policemen confined strictly to the early 'breaking-in' period of a police career ... The socialization of police is a continuous process that occurs at least to some degree, every time an individual crosses hierarchical, functional, or social boundaries within an organization ... Potentially, any police career can take many twists and turns, periodically requiring an individual to adapt to novel circumstances and surroundings. (Manning and Van Maanen 1978: 271–2)

Even if the influence of the occupational culture is overwhelming, officers' practices are not necessarily totally guided by it, especially when decisions are made by the officers on their own:

> All that the emphasis on work-based culture implies is that priority is given to influence arising from the work setting rather than officer biography. Further, decisions made on individual grounds, those divergent from the occupational culture, are necessarily less visible; they are likely to be taken when the officer is alone. (Fielding 1988: 18)

Fielding's research suggests that recruits do discern differences in the practice models presented during training and are more reflective than they are generally given credit for:

> Recruits do not pass through training like automatons but reflect on their experience and evaluate the programme according to practical use on the street. The occupational culture, functioning as a repository for the collective wisdom of police, is an intervening source of evaluation ... But one must not forget that entry to the police is not automatically entry to the culture, that some officers will not and never will wish to fit into that culture, that there is more than one police culture, and that individual decisions are always an expression of the individual's perspective at the time as he or she uniquely makes sense of all perceived influences. (Fielding 1988: 54)

Adherence to the dominant culture may simply be another skill that novices learn in order to survive in the organization:

> What constables do varies, and once 'inside' the culture, no one is more aware of that than the officers themselves. It may be necessary to 'go along with' what one senses to be the dominant value ... But aspirants do this in full awareness that it is a tactic. Once confident of their place, and ability to use the necessary justifying rhetoric in relation to their own complex of values, officers begin to move in and through the culture to secure their own ends. (Fielding 1988: 185)

One of the recruits told Fielding: 'As you get on in this job you get more and more guarded and keep yourself more and more to yourself. You keep your opinions and your attitudes to yourself' (93). Recruits, Fielding finds, become more 'evaluative' about the police culture as they gain confidence in the job (190), and some have acknowledged the inaccuracy of some of the stock 'stories' of the culture (135).

Re-examining Police Culture and Socialization

The foregoing analysis of the available literature on police socialization points to the complexity of the socialization process: new members may acquire various skills, knowledge, and values relevant to their participation in the organization, but they do not necessarily end up with a uniform set of attitudes and practice orientations. The socialization process is not necessarily linear, and it does not stop at the early stages of a member's entry into an organization. Far from being shaped totally by a particular occupational culture, recruits are active and reflective participants in the socialization process. These findings call for a more dynamic and complex theoretical framework for understanding organizational socialization than is currently available.

In a study of police reform in Australia, Chan (1997) raised various criticisms of the concept of police culture as it is traditionally understood. Her concern was that an adequate theory of police culture should be able to account for variations in culture instead of assuming its uniformity; recognize the agency of police actors instead of treating them as passive recipients of the culture; situate cultural practices in the structural conditions of policing; and provide a theory of cultural change (Chan 1997: ch. 4). Similar considerations ought to apply to theorizing on police socialization: a useful theory of socialization should be able to account for variations in culture and for the processes and outcomes of socialization; recognize the active part played by recruits; situate the socialization process within the sociopolitical conditions of policing; and reflect the impact of any cultural change. Yet most models of socialization found in the literature do not meet these criteria. They typically assume the existence of a relatively homogeneous and stable organizational culture into which newcomers become acculturated. Processes of socialization are portrayed as dependent on the socialization tactics employed by the organization and the learning and adaptation on the part of the newcomers (Van Maanen and Schein 1979; Ashforth and Saks 1996), yet few models take into account the *proactive* role played by newcomers in the socialization process (Morrison 1993). Even though it has been acknowledged that environmental conditions – broader societal values, economic conditions, characteristics of the community in which the organization is located, regional norms, the status of the occupation or organization within the social structure, the relationships among organizations, and so on – do influence the socialization process, these factors are seen 'for the most part ... [to be] relatively stable and beyond the immediate day-to-day control of either the organization or the individual' (Van Maanen 1976: 85). In the present era of globalization, marketization and new accountability (see Ericson and Stehr 2000), however, the stability of organizational environment and organizational culture can no longer be assumed. Certainly, dramatic changes have taken place in the policing environment in recent years, not only in terms of social, demographic, and economic conditions, but also in terms of policing rhetoric and strategies (O'Malley and Palmer 1996), legal regulation (Dixon 1997), recruitment and training (Chan 1997), technology (Manning 1992; Ericson and Haggerty 1997; Chan 2001b; Chan et al. 2001), and management and accountability (Leishman et al. 1996; Chan 1997, 1999; Ericson and Haggerty 1997). Any model that ignores such changes will not be able to adequately account for the dynamism and complexity of socialization in modern organizations.

Chan's (1997) framework for understanding police culture seems well suited for theorizing about police socialization. By combining the insights of organizational theorists (Schein 1985; Sackmann 1991), the critique of culture by Shearing and Ericson (1991), and Bourdieu's concepts of 'field' and 'habitus' (Bourdieu 1990a; Bourdieu and Wacquant 1992), Chan's framework takes into account the structural conditions and cultural knowledge of policing and emphasizes the central importance of agency in linking field and habitus with practice (Chan 1997: ch. 4). The following is a summary of the relevant concepts.[3]

A Reconceptualization

Several useful ways of theorizing about culture can be found in the literature. In particular, Schein's and Sackmann's cognitive perspectives of culture provide for the existence of multiple cultures within a police organization. Shearing and Ericson's phenomenological treatment of culture recognizes the active and creative role played by members of the police force. Finally, Bourdieu's relational theory, which explains cultural practice as the result of interaction between cultural dispositions (habitus) and structural positions (field), situates culture in the social and political context of police work. All three perspectives provide for some theorizing of change. Each of these perspectives will be discussed in turn.

CULTURE AS KNOWLEDGE

Organizational theorists provide a useful framework for conceptualizing police culture. For Schein, culture is the property of a stable social unit that has a shared history. It is also a 'learned product of group experience' (1985: 7). His definition of organizational culture is especially appropriate when applied to police organizations:

[Culture is] a pattern of basic assumptions – invented, discovered, or developed by a given group as it learns to cope with its problems of external adaptation and internal integration – that has worked well enough to be considered valid and, therefore, to be taught to new members as the correct way to perceive, think, and feel in relation to those problems. (1985: 9; italics removed)

Sackmann, adopting Schein's definition, describes the essence of culture as 'the collective construction of social reality.' Her model of culture encompasses all forms of shared, organized knowledge: 'the form of things that people have in their minds; their models for perceiving, integrating, and interpreting them; the ideas or theories that they use collectively to make sense of their social and physical reality' (1991: 21). She assigns cultural knowledge in organizations to four dimensions: *dictionary knowledge*, which provides definitions and labels of things and events within an organization; *directory knowledge*, which contains descriptions about 'how things are done' generally in the organization; *recipe knowledge*, which prescribes what should or should not be done in specific situations; and *axiomatic knowledge*, which represents the fundamental assumptions about 'why things are done the way they are.' Axiomatic knowledge, often held by top management, constitutes the foundation for the shape and future of the organization. It may be adjusted or revised from time to time as a result of critical evaluations or growing experience. Like Schein, Sackmann sees cultural cognitions as being held by groups rather than individuals. These cognitions are socially constructed, and may be changed or perpetuated by organizational processes through repeated applications. In time, these cognitions are imbued with emotions and acquire degrees of importance; they also become 'habits' of thought that translate into habitual actions.

The significance of this formulation of culture as knowledge lies in its ability to account for multiple cultures. Schein (1985) suggests that whether an organization has a single culture or multiple subcultures is an empirical question. Much depends on the existence of stable groups with shared experiences (1985: 7–8). Though top management may have imposed or negotiated a consensus about the rationale of the organization (axiomatic knowledge), there is no reason to assume that the other dimensions of cultural knowledge are invariant throughout the organization. Sackmann's own case study found that both dictionary and recipe knowledge varied according to members' responsibilities and positions in the hierarchy.

Yet this cognitive model of culture leaves a number of questions unanswered. For example, how does knowledge lead to action, and under what conditions does it happen? Also, there is little discussion in Sackmann about how the various dimensions of knowledge are related to the power relations external to the organization, or to relations between the organization's members and their environment.

CULTURE AS CONSTRUCTION

Not all formulations of police culture treat officers as passive objects moulded by the almighty culture. Shearing and Ericson (1991) have argued that in their work activities, police officers are not simply socialized into and guided by the police culture; rather, they actively construct and make reference to that culture. For police officers, the police culture is a 'tool-kit' for producing a sense of order, and the constant 'telling' of the culture serves for them to 'factualize' and make objective that culture. This culture is transmitted not through a process of socialization and internalization of rules, but rather through a collection of stories and aphorisms that instruct officers on how to see the world and act in it. Stories prepare officers for police work by providing a 'vehicle for analogous thinking' and by creating a 'vocabulary of precedents' (Ericson et al. 1987). Stories, and the silences that surround those stories, create a way of seeing and being.

This approach to interpreting police culture removes the deterministic framework of a rule-based theory of action and allows for variations in how police cultural knowledge is applied:

> It recognizes that police stories provide officers with tools they can use to get them through the business of police work without minimizing the fact that this still requires individual initiative and daring. It also recognizes that officers differ in their competence in using this cultural tool-kit ... Finally, it recognizes that what they do will be retrospectively constituted as ordered via the reflexive methods that are part of this doing. (Shearing and Ericson 1991: 506)

Thus, cultural knowledge in the form of police stories presents officers with ready-made schemas and scripts. These in turn help individual officers in particular situations to limit their search for information and organize information in terms of established categories. They also constitute a sensibility out of which a range of actions can flow, and provide officers with a repertoire of reasonable accounts they can use to justify their actions. However, this model of police culture is silent about the social and political context of police work, even though police stories undoubtedly contain implicit or explicit expressions of power relations within police organizations.

CULTURE AS RELATIONS

Researchers no longer view culture solely in terms of informal influences that seek to undermine or subvert the formal goals or rules of organizations; more and more, thet are looking to sources of irrationality in the formal structure itself (see Powell and DiMaggio 1991: 13). Ericson (1981), for example, found that departures from due process protections of the accused were not 'extra-legal' rules at all; they were decisions legitimated by the criminal law itself. The question remains: How do formal structures influence cultural practice? A useful approach to understanding how cultural practices develop is found in the social theory of Pierre Bourdieu. Two key concepts of relevance here are the *field* and the *habitus*:

> A field consists of a set of objective, historical relations between positions anchored in certain forms of power (or capital), while habitus consists of a set of historical relations 'deposited' within individual bodies in the form of mental and corporeal schemata of perception, appreciation and action. (Wacquant 1992: 16)

For Bourdieu, society comprises an ensemble of relatively autonomous fields. A *field* is a social space of conflict and competition whereon participants struggle to establish control over specific power and authority, and in the course of the struggle, to modify the actual structure of the field. Thus a field 'presents itself as a structure of probabilities – of rewards, gains, profits, or sanctions – but always implies a measure of indeterminacy' (Bourdieu, in Wacquant 1992: 18). Central to the concept of the field is the notion of *capital*. There are various forms of capital, which operate in different social fields. These include economic capital, cultural or informational capital, social capital, which relates to connections and membership in groups, and symbolic capital, which is the form that other types of capital assume when they are regarded as legitimate (Bourdieu 1987: 3–4). Bourdieu compares a field to a game in which players possess tokens of different colours representing different types of capital. A player's position, strategic orientation, and relative force in the game all depend on both the volume and the composition of the tokens in hand. Participants can play to increase their capital, or they can play to change the rules of the game; thus the field can also be a field of struggle (Bourdieu and Wacquant 1992: 98–100). In policing, the field reflects the social, political, and legal capital available to police – both *individual* resources such as rank, experience, physical strength, skills, knowledge, discretion, autonomy, information, connection and reputation; and *organizational* resources such as promotional opportunities, public support, budget allocation, legal powers, and political independence.

Habitus, on the other hand, is a system of 'dispositions' that integrate past experience and enable individuals to cope with a diversity of unforeseen situations (Wacquant 1992: 18). Agents acquire these dispositions either individually, through family and the education system, or as a group, through organizational socialization. These dispositions are similar to what has been described as 'cultural knowledge,' except that they include physical and emotional dispositions as well as cognitions and values. Instead of seeing culture as a 'thing' – for example, a set of values or rules, or an informal structure operating on actors in an organization – Bourdieu argues for the primacy of *relations*, so that habitus and field function fully only in relation to each other. Habitus generates strategies that are coherent and systematic but also 'ad hoc because they are "triggered" by the encounter with a particular field' (19). The relationship between field and habitus operates in two ways: on the one hand, the field *conditions* the habitus, which is the 'product of the embodiment of the immanent necessity of a field'; on the other hand, habitus *constitutes* the field as it provides the cultural frames for making sense of the field (Bourdieu and Wacquant 1992: 127).

Like the police stories discussed earlier, habitus allows for creation and innovation in police work. It is a 'feel for the game'; it enables an infinite number of 'moves' to be made in an infinite number of situations. It embodies what police officers often refer to as 'common sense' (see Manning 1997) and what is commonly known as 'policing skills' (see Brogden et al., 1988). Long-term members of an organization tend to take their habitus for granted, because 'when habitus encounters a social world of which it is the product, it is like a "fish in water"' (Bourdieu and Wacquant 1992: 127). When recruits join a new organization, however, they carry with them the habitus that is a product of the field they previously inhabited. To reverse Bourdieu's analogy, in their initial encounter with the organization they are likely to feel like 'fish out of water.' Where there exists a stable organizational culture, most recruits learn consciously or otherwise to adapt to the sensibilities and cognitions of peer groups, in order to reduce their sense of alienation and anxiety (Schein 1985).

In this way, Bourdieu's theory succeeds in relating policing 'dispositions' to the social and political context of policing. It also allows for the existence of multiple cultures, since officers in different organizational positions operate under different sets of field and habitus. This framework can be criticized for overemphasizing the 'unconscious' or automatic connection between habitus and practice and for not accounting for rational action (see, for example, Alexander 1995). Bourdieu has argued that rationality rarely plays a part in practical action:

> The conditions of rational calculation are practically never given in practice: time is limited, information is restricted, etc. And yet agents *do* do, much more often than if they were behaving randomly, 'the only thing to do.' This is because, following the intuitions of a 'logic of practice' which is the product of a lasting exposure to conditions similar to those in which they are placed, they anticipate the necessity immanent in the way of the world. (1990a: 11)

Hence, even though police practices may *appear* rational, the 'cop code' is more the result of 'codification' by researchers and police officers than a set of rules that generate practice. Nevertheless, Bourdieu concedes that habitus can have its '"blips," critical moments when it misfires or is out of phase,' so that some degree of 'practical reflection' is necessary in some situations to evaluate action or to correct mistaken or imperfect moves (2000: 162). Furthermore, the capacity to rely on the automatic guidance of habitus depends on the situation and position the actor occupies:

> The degree to which one can abandon oneself to the automatisms of practical sense obviously varies with the situation and the area of activity, but also with the position occupied in social space: it is likely that those who are 'in their right place' in the social world can abandon or entrust themselves more, and more completely, to their dispositions (that is the 'ease' of the well-born) than those who occupy awkward positions, such as the *parvenus* and the *déclassés*; and the latter are more likely to bring to consciousness that which, for others, is taken for granted, because they are forced to keep watch on themselves and consciously correct the 'first movements' of a habitus that generates inappropriate or misplaced behaviours. (2000: 163)

This is an important insight for understanding the situation of recruits, who are likely to be conscious and cautious about their 'first movements' because their habitus is the product of a different world. Until they have adjusted their habitus to one that is appropriate to their new environment, it is in their interest to constantly evaluate their actions and correct any mistaken moves.

CULTURAL CHANGE

The three perspectives outlined all allow some scope for cultural change. Shearing and Ericson have the least to say about change, but their model provides for human action that is both 'guided and improvizational' (Shearing and Ericson 1991). With Bourdieu, cultural change is possible through changes in the field or in the habitus, although he does not outline an explicit theory of change. According to Bourdieu, habitus is 'an *open system of dispositions* that is constantly subjected to experiences, and therefore constantly affected by them in a way that either reinforces or modifies its structures' (Bourdieu and Wacquant 1992: 133). Thus, changes in the field affect the habitus, because the field 'structures the habitus' (127). Sackmann's work offers the most explicit theorizing about the processes of change. Cultural knowledge, Sackmann observes, acts as a link between strategy and organizational processes. Thus changes in organizational culture occur when axiomatic knowledge is changed; this in turn sets off other changes:

> Existing cultural knowledge, strategy and organizational processes began to be questioned when top management group perceived threats in the internal and external environments of the firm. As a first step they debated and negotiated axiomatic knowledge. Once in place this axiomatic knowledge defined the firm's purpose, its strategic intention, its design, and characteristics of preferred members ... In the process of negotiating axiomatic knowledge, existing dictionary and directory knowledge was altered. This knowledge then guided the thoughts, attention, and actions of organizational members both in terms of organizational processes and in terms of strategic concerns and their implementation. Their actions, and the outcomes of their actions, in turn, maintained, reinforced, and further adjusted directory, dictionary and axiomatic knowledge. (Sackmann 1991: 156)

The idea that axiomatic knowledge is the starting point for cultural change is important, and we will return to this observation later in the book. In terms of policing, cultural change involves re-examining the rationale and purpose of policing, then formulating a new strategic direction and setting in place the organizational processes for implementing change.

FIELD, HABITUS, AND POLICE PRACTICE

The close relationship between police cultural knowledge (habitus) and the structural conditions of police work (field) has long been recognized in the literature: police culture is seen as having been developed as a mechanism for coping with the dangers and unpredictability of police work. Also, it is commonly assumed that there are close links between cultural knowledge and police practice, although those links have not been clearly established. The danger of ignoring the links between structural conditions, cultural knowledge, and police practice is that a simple-minded model of linear causality can easily be implied. Such a model ignores the key fact that police officers participate actively in the construction and reproduction of cultural knowledge and institutional practice. It also gives a misleading impression that cultural knowledge and police practice can be changed simply by changing structural conditions.

Thus, in a revised model of police culture, the *active role* played by 'police actors' – who include all members of the police organization – is a crucial link between these elements. This link is often missing from discussions about police culture and institutional practice. The main point being made here is that structural conditions do not completely determine cultural knowledge and that cultural knowledge does not totally dictate practice. Police officers, working within the structural conditions of policing, play an active role in developing, reinforcing, resisting, and/or transforming cultural knowledge. They are not passive carriers of police culture. In a similar vein – to borrow the game analogy used by Bourdieu (1990) – officers who have learned 'a feel for the game' (cultural knowledge) are not restricted to a limited number of 'moves' (modes of practice). Hence in their practice they take into account any changes to structural conditions. Whether a structural change results in any change in cultural knowledge or institutional practice depends on the nature of the change and the capacity of officers to adapt to the change. The relationships between the elements are neither unidirectional nor deterministic.

This perspective on organizational culture and institutional practice has been recognized by organizational theorists (see Powell and DiMaggio 1991). Theorists at one time viewed institutional behaviour as the product of the internalization of values and attitudes; more recently they have been finding other models more useful and more powerful. For example, instead of explaining corrupt police practice in terms of the inculcation of corrupt values among officers through a vaguely understood process of socialization, we can view officers as active decision makers who are nevertheless guided by the assumptions they learn and by the possibilities of which they are aware. The cultural knowledge they acquire generates schemas and categories; these in turn both help them to organize information and lead them to resist evidence contrary to these schemas. Their awareness of structural possibilities provides 'menus of legitimate accounts' (Powell and DiMaggio 1991: 15), or a 'vocabulary of precedents' (Ericson et al. 1987), which they can use to justify their actions. It follows that institutional practice is partly the product of a 'practical consciousness' (Giddens 1984), or a 'logic of practice' (Bourdieu 1990b: 11) that is based not on rational calculations but rather on learned 'common sense' and skills. However, practice is also guided partly by the actor's awareness of how action can be retrospectively justified rationally – that is, what types of justification are organizationally permitted.

This type of analysis can be extended to the level of groups or organizations. It is well recognized in organizational theory that organizations do not simply react to their environments – they *enact* them (Weick 1979). This means that organizations – more precisely, *people* within organizations – are not passive entities; rather, they take an active part in the construction of their environments. When applied to policing, this has significant implications for understanding how structural conditions affect organizational practice. For example, Smith's (1994) analysis of the Queensland police bureaucracy prior to the Fitzgerald inquiry illustrates how a police organization could enact its political environments to ensure its own survival. For many years the Queensland Police Force was able to strongly influence law enforcement policies and obstruct reforms. It also used propaganda quite successfully to promote a favourite public image, even though the force as an institution had been corrupt for many years. Recognizing the active role played by police actors (and groups of actors) is an important antidote to the simplistic view that deviant institutional practice is *caused* by a deviant police culture, which is in turn a necessary product of the structural conditions of police work.

The Habitus of Policing

What do we know about the habitus of policing? The research literature has described some of the basic characteristics of the 'street cop'
culture. These characteristics are best considered as elements for constructing an ideal type; they are not necessarily universal or unchanging. In fact, recent reforms and developments in policing have been
constantly challenging these ideal-typical features of police culture. A
convenient approach to summarizing the habitus of policing is to apply
Sackmann's (1991) four dimensions of cultural knowledge: axiomatic
knowledge (which constitutes the basic rationale of policing), dictionary knowledge (which sets up categories about the people and events
police come into contact with), directory knowledge (which informs
officers on how to go about getting their work done), and recipe knowledge (which prescribes the menu of acceptable and unacceptable practices in specific situations). Yet this typology misses an important
dimension of the policing habitus that relates to the physical or bodily
dispositions. Following Bourdieu, we will call this fifth dimension
'bodily knowledge.'

Axiomatic Knowledge: The Doxa of Policing

This refers to the fundamental assumptions about 'why things are done
the way they are' in an organization. Axiomatic knowledge is self-
evident knowledge, or what Bourdieu calls *doxa*, 'so as to distinguish it
from an orthodox or heterodox belief implying awareness and recognition of the possibility of different or antagonistic beliefs' (1977: 164).
The doxa of policing is the taken-for-granted 'truth' about police work
that is never disputed and never needs defending. Police traditionally
see their work in terms of waging a 'war against crime,' maintaining
order, and protecting people's lives and property. Reiner points out
that officers often bring a sense of mission to their work: 'their sense of
themselves as "the thin blue line," performing an essential role in
safeguarding social order, which would lead to disastrous consequences
if their authority was threatened' (1992: 112).

According to Manning, the public generally imagines police work to
be exciting, dangerous, and efficient (1978a: 12–13). The public image
of the police as heroic 'crook catchers' and 'crime fighters' is encouraged by officers themselves. The public in turn demands 'more dramatic crook-catching and crime prevention.' Police organizations then

convert these demands into 'distorted criteria for promotion, success and security' (1978a: 13). As a result, police often make a distinction between 'real' police work and the work they routinely perform. For the young American officers Van Maanen observed, 'real' police work was about exercizing their special occupational expertise: 'to make an arrest, save a life, quell a dispute, prevent a robbery, catch a felon, stop a suspicious person, disarm a suspect, and so on' (1978a: 121). Yet police officers spend very little time on the street carrying out what they consider their 'primary function.' 'Real' police work, then, becomes both 'a source of satisfaction and frustration' (1978a: 122).

Another important aspect of the doxa of policing is related to the domination of masculinity. The need to use coercion in some situations (Bittner 1978) is often equated with the need to use physical force, aggressive crime fighting, and toughness. Through the association between physicality and masculinity, policing is generally regarded as men's work (Heidensohn 1992: 73; Martin 1999). This, even though the bulk of police work is about order maintenance, service, and conflict resolution, all of which require a range of interpersonal and problem-solving skills. The introduction of 'community policing' and the recruitment of female officers to many police forces in recent years (Manning 1997) may have challenged this dimension of cultural knowledge, but the doxa of police as crime fighters continues to dominate, and consequently, so does the belief that police work is still essentially a 'man's job' (Appier 1998). The strength of this doxa is such that even female officers accept the physicality of the job, and see it as the natural order, which needs no further justification.

Manning's (1978c: 73–4) research suggests that police officers generally see their work as uncertain and unclear ('You never know what to expect next'). Hence, they base their decisions on experience, common sense, and discretion rather than on 'an abstract theory of policing, the law, or police regulations.' Decisions can only be justified situationally ('You can't police by the book'). They take it for granted that experience is the foundation of policing and essential to occupational competence.

Dictionary Knowledge: Police Categories

Dictionary knowledge provides definitions and labels for persons, things, and events the police encounter in the course of their work. Research studies suggest that 'police work requires officers to summarise complex and ambiguous situations in a short period of time and to take some action' (Holdaway 1995). Hence, officers develop routine ways of categorizing their environment and the people they encounter in the community. American researchers found that police officers develop notions of normal and abnormal appearance in relation to the public places they patrol. These notions of normality and abnormality are context dependent: 'What is normal for a place is normal for the place at a time' (Sacks 1978: 194). In a study of a suburban Canadian police force, Ericson noted a similar tendency for patrol officers to develop indicators of abnormality: these included '1) individuals out of place, 2) individuals in particular places, 3) individuals of particular types regardless of place, and 4) unusual circumstances regarding property' (1982: 86).

Reiner has also commented on the distinction police make, with regard to the general public, between 'the rough and respectable elements, those who challenge or those who accept the middle-class values of decency which most police revere' (1992: 117–18). Muir described a similar 'separation of people into the governables and the rebels ... those who might revolt against police authority from those who would not' (1977: 156–7). Police in Australia have been accused of forming stereotypical opinions about the criminality of certain ethnic groups (Australian Law Reform Commission 1992: 201) and of regularly linking Aboriginal people with crime and social disorder (Cunneen and Robb 1987). Ericson's study in Canada found similar: police stereotyped racial and ethnic minorities and young people with disorderly appearance and conduct as 'the scum of the earth' (Ericson 1982: 66–7). Ethnic stereotyping reinforces police notions of respectability, and is 'a stable feature of the occupational culture' (Holdaway 1995).

Dictionary knowledge also applies to police work itself. The doxa that policing is about crime fighting and physicality means that sexual differences are immersed in the sets of oppositions that organize police work: physical versus emotional, outside (on the street) versus inside (in the office), real police work (arresting criminals) versus other work, use of force versus other means of dispute resolution, and so on (Martin 1999; cf. Bourdieu 2001).

Directory Knowledge: Police Methods

Directory knowledge tells police officers how operational work is routinely carried out. To a certain extent these operational methods flow out of the definitions and categories provided by dictionary knowledge. For example, in proactive policing, officers are 'chronically suspicious' and are forced 'to make snap decisions about the appropriateness of what people are doing' (Bayley and Mendelsohn 1969: 93). Having developed indicators of normality and abnormality, roughness and respectability, police officers tend to target the unusual and the disreputable. Following these 'cues' may be routine police work, but the impact on minorities can be profound (Bayley and Mendelsohn, 1969: 93). For example, in the Redfern district of Sydney, an individual 'out of place' is an Aborigine driving a red Laser (as mentioned in the television documentary *Cop It Sweet*). Young people congregating in parks, shopping malls, pinball parlours, and the like, are also obvious targets for proactive stops.

As mentioned earlier, an important feature of police work is the capacity and authority to use coercive force if necessary. Bittner considers this capacity to use force as 'the core of the police role': 'every conceivable police intervention projects the message that force may be, and may have to be, used to achieve a desired objective' (1978: 36). The use of force or the threat of force by police is often seen as a legitimate means of taking charge of situations to maintain authority, to control suspects, to obtain information, or even to dispense 'street justice' (Westley 1970; Baldwin and Kinsey 1982; Van Maanen 1978b; Chan 2000b). Nevertheless, in the vast majority of situations, police do not resort to force. Far more often, they restore order by applying well-developed interpersonal skills to gain compliance, resolve conflicts, and provide support to victims and fellow officers (Martin 1999). Yet the crime-fighting, masculine doxa of policing 'celebrates physical prowess, and demands emotional control in the face of danger and injury,' and devalues interpersonal skills and emotional support (116).

Recipe Knowledge: Police Values

This refers to the normative dimension of cultural knowledge. It suggests what should or should not be done in specific situations. It provides recommendations and strategies for coping with police work. Van Maanen's research of an American police force provides some significant observations. For example, officers learn to 'stay out of trouble' by doing the minimum amount of work required; 'gung-ho' officers are routinely ridiculed by their peers (1978a: 125). Officers also develop a sceptical attitude toward police supervisors and managers and learn not to expect much from the organization; their rewards come in the form of camaraderie and 'small favours' granted by sergeants (127). In addition, officers learn to 'cover their ass' to avoid disciplinary actions. To this end they often manipulate their written records of events in order to protect themselves (Manning 1997: 168–9).

Another well-documented aspect of police recipe knowledge is the 'code of silence' and solidarity that police officers resort to when faced with allegations of misconduct (Westley 1970). Reiner sees solidarity as a response to the working conditions of policing, 'a product not only of isolation, but also of the need to be able to rely on colleagues in a tight spot, and a protective armour shielding the force as a whole from public knowledge of infractions' (1992: 116). According to Skolnick and Fyfe, the code is typically enforced 'by the threat of shunning, by fear that *informing* will lead to exposure of one's own derelictions, and by fear that colleagues' assistance may be withheld in emergencies,' rather than by violent means (1993: 110; original emphasis).

The masculine doxa of policing also supports a norm of 'emotional self-management'; this equates the control of emotions with occupational competence: 'Even talking about pain, guilt, or fear is rare since officers who reveal their feelings to other officers may be viewed as weak or inadequate' (Martin 1999: 116). Recruits are taught early on to hide their emotions and to maintain emotional detachment when dealing with the public. Male officers must hide fear and 'act like a man'; women are allowed to show fear and emotions and to apply for exemptions from difficult duties. Legitimate ways of managing emotions include the use of humour, the release of tension through physical exercise, drinking alcohol, and having sex (Martin 1999).

Bodily Knowledge: Policing Hexis

This refers to the physical or corporeal dispositions that police officers carry as members of the occupation. The doxa of police as crime fighters requiring physical strength justifies the physical requirements for entry into the occupation and the drill and endurance training that police recruits are subjected to. Police training, like military training, involves 'the disciplining, controlling, and occasional mortification of the body' (Morgan 1994: 167). Involved in this dimension of habitus are many aspects of physical appearance: uniforms, regulations regarding hair length and style and body piercing, and also 'ways of walking, talking, standing, looking, sitting, etc' (Bourdieu 2000: 141). The point is always to convey authority and discipline. As Fielding observes, physical training and drill are ways of building character – obedience, compliance, tolerance of physical discomfort, and so on (1988: 60–1). The doxa of police as crime fighters and the taken-for-granted equivalence between police work and physicality result in sexual differences being used to justify the notion that policing is 'men's work.' Thus, in order to survive in the occupation, female officers have to learn to take on masculine deportment and 'new behavior regarding verbal, facial, and bodily displays that convey their authority to citizens,' including 'learning not to smile ... and to avoid postures that indicate hesitation or unreadiness to act' (Martin 1999: 122).

The Field of Policing

In Bourdieu's framework, the field of policing, like any other field, is a social space of conflict and competition that is structured by hierarchies of rewards (capital) and sanctions (negative capital). The field is dynamic in that its structure is 'determined by the relations between the positions agents occupy in the field' (Johnson 1993: 6). It is important, however, to distinguish between the position of policing – the policing occupation or a police organization – in the *field of power* (the power relations in society) and the positions of agents *within the field of policing*.

The policing field exists in a subordinate or dominated position within the field of power: it is a relatively low-prestige occupation in terms of economic capital, but it enjoys a high degree of public and government support (political and symbolic capital). This is because policing is inherently political: it is an institution 'created and sustained by political processes to enforce dominant conceptions of public order' (Skolnick 1972: 41, quoted in Reiner 1992: 2). As Manning (1978a: 18–19) points out, the law is itself a political entity, being the 'product of what is right and proper from the perspective of different politically powerful segments within the community.' Because of their highly symbolic position in society's defence of power and morality, police officers are vested with wide discretionary powers to stop, question, arrest, search, and detain suspects (Dixon 1993; McBarnet 1979; Ericson 1982). Nevertheless, with the advent of the 'new public management' and several dramatic revelations of police misconduct in some Western democracies, police organizations are being subjected more and more to performance-related accountability requirements that are placing their management and operational activities under closer scrutiny and evaluation (Chan 1999).

Within the field of policing itself, agents compete for the control of various types of resources or capital. To survive in the occupation, officers require both social capital and cultural capital. Officers need social capital, in the form of support networks, to protect themselves not only against the external dangers or hostilities associated with police work, but also against arbitrary supervisory or management practices. Most police forces are still organized along military lines, with uniforms, chains of command, progression through the ranks, strong disciplinary rules, and formalized training. The military metaphor usually translates into a disciplinary regime that insists on a high number of rules and regulations: 'What sorts of rules and regulations exist in such a setting are in some ways less important than that there be plenty of them and the personnel be continually aware that they can be harshly called to account for disobeying them' (Bittner 1978: 42). In police organizations, accountability traditionally takes the form of explicitly and continually paying attention to internal discipline, such as dress code, departmental procedures, and so on, rather than auditing how officers make decisions and deal with citizens. Officers are rewarded for staying out of trouble and for 'good pinches' (46). Bittner describes the typical relationship that emerges between police officers and their superiors as one in which 'supervisory personnel are often viewed by the line personnel with distrust and even contempt'; yet to secure loyalty from their subordinates, supervisors often resort to 'whitewashing bad practices involving relatively unregulated conduct' or covering officers' mistakes (48). Van Maanen (1983: 280) similarly noted a 'high degree of mutual dependence and reciprocity' between officers and their sergeants. Thus, the accumulation of social capital requires the cultivation of mutually supportive relationships with fellow officers, including one's supervisors or subordinates.

Policing also values cultural capital in the form of information, knowledge, and competence. Since much of police work at the operational level calls for individual judgment, localized responses, and discretionary decisions, policing is characterized by 'situationally justified actions' (Manning 1997) – that is, actions are taken as the situations demand, and then rationalized later in terms of the available rules. Officers who can establish good networks of informants, who know their way around legal and bureaucratic rules, or who build an impressive record of arrests and convictions, are highly valued. Rank is a well-recognized and visible form of cultural capital, and so is experience. Also, detectives and specialist officers possess more cultural capital than general-duty or community officers. With the large-scale introduction of information technology into policing, police with 'IT' expertise have become highly valued (Chan et al. 2001).

Physical capital – strength, physique, and tolerance of harsh conditions – is another valuable form of capital in the field of policing. In recent years, many police forces have lowered their physical requirements for entry (such as height) in order to encourage the recruitment of women and some minority groups; even so, physical strength and agility is still an important criterion for entry into the occupation. As noted earlier, physical training is seen as a crucial part of character building and of constructing a 'disciplined' force. Within the crime-fighting model of policing, physical strength and endurance is taken for granted as part of what it takes to be a police officer. So women, who are typically less physically 'tough,' are in a position of negative capital here.

Symbolic capital – which is based on 'reputation, opinion and representation' (Bourdieu 1990a: 93) – is defined by the predominant habitus, but can also be established by law or policy. In the crime-fighting model of policing, the officers who carry the most symbolic capital are those who bring in the 'good' arrests, who can be trusted to protect others, and who have experience or rank. New visions of policing such as community policing and problem-oriented policing are seeking to change this by introducing alternative sources of symbolic capital based on the ability to solve problems, work with members of the community, and provide service. Although police misconduct has always been a violation of legal and regulatory requirements, honesty, integrity, and professionalism in police work were not a valued form of symbolic capital until revelations of corruption and malpractice in some jurisdictions in recent years caused governments to introduce tough measures for controlling corrupt or unprofessional officers. 'New' policing models and anticorruption measures are seeking to 'legalize' professionalism and integrity as forms of symbolic capital, but success in this will depend on the symbolic power to change the habitus to the extent that officers accept the validity of these changes (Bourdieu 1990a: 136–8). With new policing models, success will require a change in axiomatic knowledge or the doxa of policing as described above. With anticorruption measures based on deterrence, success is premised on a high probability of detection and a high certainty of sanction; in effect, this approach changes the recipe knowledge of maintaining a code of silence. Where anticorruption measures are based on compliance, success can only be achieved through comprehensive risk management and harm minimization efforts – in effect, building accountability into the dictionary and directory knowledge by requiring officers to fill out compulsory fields and mandatory forms as part of their work (cf. Ericson and Haggerty 1997; Chan et al. 2001).

Socialization in a Changing Field

The field of policing has been changing since the globalization of markets and communications, advances in information and biotech, the commercialization of policing and security services, changing legal regulation and managerial control of police conduct, and the emergence of alternative models of policing. If socialization is the learning of policing habitus on the part of the recruits, what happens when the field of policing itself is changing? Bourdieu's framework suggests that shifts in the field – such as changes in systems of rewards and sanctions – lead to adjustments of the habitus. How does this happen? Put simply, changes in the field create a new 'necessity,' which may require the creation of new strategies for coping. For Bourdieu, 'social conditions *activate* in the agents certain acquired qualities and capacities of the mind and the body' (Hage 1994: 430). Under changing conditions, organization members with habitus shaped by the 'old culture' may be as ill at ease as the newcomers because the organizational habitus they acquired no longer fits current conditions:

> In situations of crisis or sudden change ... agents often have difficulty in holding together the dispositions associated with different states or stages, and some of them, often those who were best adapted to the previous state of the game, have difficulty in adjusting to the new established order. Their dispositions become dysfunctional and the efforts they may make to perpetuate them help to plunge them deeper into failure. (Bourdieu 2000: 161)

While the organization is adjusting its habitus, newcomers are likely to encounter a diverse rather than a homogeneous culture; at the same time, they are having to adjust their own individual habitus to the changing field. Newcomers are more likely to be conscious of or reflective about their own adjustments. Like the new tennis player who reenacts a missed shot, the recruit needs to rethink his or her movements and strategies to make early corrections to any initial mistakes. Unlike the experienced player, the novice cannot 'abandon' himself or herself to the (newly learned) habitus to guide practice (Bourdieu 2000: 163). In policing, perhaps more than in other occupations, every action takes place in full view of either members of the public or one's colleagues. The cost of a mistake can range from mild humiliation, to being the butt of office jokes, to losing fellow officers' trust or public respect.

When a field is changing, socialization is a less predictable, more diverse, and more open process than when conditions are relatively stable. Also, recruits are much more aware of their own adaptations to the new environment, and as a result their learning process is much less automatic and much more reflective.

Organization of This Book

In this chapter we have outlined the theoretical context for understanding police socialization. We suggest that it is unhelpful to perceive 'professionalism' and 'police culture' as opposing influences on recruits, or to equate 'good' practice with formal instruction and 'bad' practice with informal socialization. We argue instead that recruits may encounter both 'good' and 'bad' practice models in both formal and informal settings. Past research has made it clear that recruits eventually adopt conceptual categories, attitudes, and strategies of the occupational culture through conscious and unconscious processes of learning; it does not follow from this that there is but a single conception of 'good' practice within the occupational culture, that recruits are no more than passive receivers of cultural influences, or that cultural norms necessarily completely dominate practice. Traditional theorizing about organizational socialization tends to assume the existence of a stable organizational culture, in which newcomers play a passive or reactive role. A suggested framework using Bourdieu's concepts of field and habitus provides a more useful approach to understanding the socialization process, especially when structural conditions are changing and organizational culture is neither stable nor homogeneous.

The rest of this book is organized as follows. Chapter 2 describes the research questions addressed in this study and offers a brief account of the recent history of the police organization that participated in the research. The chapter goes on to detail this project's research design and data collection processes. The methodological, legal, and ethical issues that arose in the study are also highlighted. In the chapters that follow, we detail the experience of a cohort of recruits in the first two years of joining the police, tracing how their ideas of 'good' police practice developed in the academy and in the operational field, who influenced them, and how they resolved issues and negotiated their identities at various stages of their development. In particular, chapter 3 describes the sociodemographic characteristics of the cohort and analyses their expectations and preparations for joining the police. Chapters 4 and 5 focus on their experiences of academy training and field training respectively, and analyse how these training experiences shaped their conceptions of professionalism. Chapter 6 analyses the attitudinal and personal changes that occurred over the training period. In the two chapters after that, we explore how changes in the field may have impacted on the socialization of recruits: chapter 7 examines the adaptations of recruits to the new reforms, and chapter 8 investigates women's adaptations in a male-dominated culture. The final chapter summarizes the research findings and discusses their theoretical and practical implications.

2

Research Organization and Methods

JANET CHAN AND SALLY DORAN

There have not been many systematic studies of police socialization. Van Maanen in the United States (1973, 1975) and Fielding in Britain (1988) conducted significant and groundbreaking research in their own time, but their findings need to be tested on more recent data.[1] The research that forms the basis of this book examines the experience of a cohort of recruits during their first two years in a police organization. In particular, this research focuses on how recruits learn to become competent in their work and how they develop concepts of professionalism. Of special interest are the importance of training and regulatory structures relative to occupational culture. The main research questions addressed are as follows:

- How do police recruits learn the 'craft' of policing?
- What are their conceptions of 'professionalism' in police work and how do these conceptions change as they develop as police officers?
- How does 'police culture' manifest itself during the first two years?
- To what extent do recruits embrace or resist influences from 'good' and 'bad' models? How are these influences resolved?

The Case Study Organization

The New South Wales Police Service (NSWPS) – the organization that participated in the study – is the oldest and largest police force in Australia, with over 13,000 sworn police officers and a yearly budget of over a $1 billion. It was founded in 1862 (Finnane 1999). It serves the state of New South Wales, which has a population of around 6 million and covers an area three times the size of the United Kingdom. The functions of the state police include preventing, detecting, and investigating crime; responding to citizens' calls for police service; traffic control and road safety; conducting emergency and rescue operations; and analyzing intelligence.

It is the more recent history of the NSWPS that most concerns us. The 1980s and 1990s were decades of rapid and constant change for the service, although the pressure for change had been building up since the 1960s (Chan 1997: ch. 6).

The Lusher Inquiry into the NSW police administration marked an early turning point in this history: the report made more than 200 recommendations in a wide range of areas, including management, recruitment, training, promotion, working conditions, and police corruption (Lusher Report 1981). The establishment of the NSW Police Board and the appointment of John Avery as police commissioner in 1984 heralded a number of significant and fundamental changes to the philosophy, organization, and operation of policing in New South Wales. Avery was committed to fighting corruption and to introducing more accountable, community-based policing practices. At the same time, the police organization moved toward a flatter, more decentralized structure, in keeping with the managerial orthodoxy of the times. Promotion by merit replaced the old system of promotion by seniority (Chan 1997: 124–7). Recruitment and training practices also underwent radical transformation. The service committed itself to attracting more women and more people from ethnic and Aboriginal communities. Changes were introduced to recruitment criteria such as educational and physical requirements. Training systems adopted new curricula and policies and a totally new educational philosophy (see Chan 1997: 129–36; see also chapter 4).

Avery retired in 1991 and was succeeded by Tony Lauer, who continued to support and implement many of the reforms initiated under Avery. The rhetoric of managerial success and impeccable accountability became pervasive in the organization's presentation of itself, both to its own members and to the outside world (Chan 1999; Dixon 1999: 2). Ironically and unexpectedly, at the height of its self-confidence, the NSWPS fell under the scrutiny of a Royal Commission into police corruption, established as a result of a parliamentary motion by an independent MP (Dixon 1999: 1). This commission, headed by a Supreme Court judge, undertook covert investigations and held public hearings that were widely reported in the media. Following a number of damaging revelations of corrupt police activities and the dramatic 'roll-over' of witnesses, the commission concluded that a state of 'systemic and entrenched corruption' existed in the police service (Wood Report 1997: 84). The list of corrupt activities unearthed included process corruption, such as fabrication of evidence; the accepting of gratuities; improper associations; fraudulent practices; drug abuse; assaults and abuse of police powers; theft and extortion; protection of drug dealers, vice operators, and illegal gaming interests; drug trafficking; and interference with internal investigations (1997: ch. 4).

The Royal Commission's findings provoked widespread public outrage and had political repercussions. The government was eager to show its determination to clean up the police service. In response to the commission's findings, major reforms were introduced. A Police Integrity Commission was established as a permanent and well-funded independent authority for investigating serious corruption and overseeing an 'external strategic audit' of the reform process. Peter Ryan was imported from the United Kingdom as the new police commissioner. The command and accountability structure was reorganized yet again. There was a tightening of corruption prevention procedures; for example, 'Commissioner's Confidence' provisions[2] were introduced 'to remove corrupt, inept, lazy officers' (Ryan 1998: 3). Also restructured was the office of Internal Affairs, which conducts integrity testing to target corrupt officers and random alcohol testing of police. A new employee management system was tried out for dealing with complaints and minor misconduct '*swiftly* and *fairly* at the *local level*' (4, original emphasis). Operations and Crime Review, a 'hard-nosed accountability system to ensure that commanders and managers are more directly accountable for their performance,' was implemented (6).

This brief account of the recent history of NSWPS shows that the organization has undergone nearly two decades of continuous and often radical change. The fieldwork for our project spanned a period that roughly coincided with the term of the Wood Commission. It is important to understand this study in the context of that history.

Recruit Training in New South Wales

Recruit training in New South Wales has undergone a number of changes in recent years. As part of the sweeping reforms introduced in the mid to late 1980s, the training of police recruits was modified according to the recommendations of the Lusher Report (1981). The Police Recruit Education Programme (PREP), introduced in 1988 and still operating during this research project, was an eighteen-month training program with the following components: an eight-week residential training (Phase 1) on policing, law, and police practice at the police academy; a four-week observation period in patrols (Phase 2); another 14-week residential training (Phase 3); a forty-nine-week on-the-job training (Phase 4) under the supervision of field training staff; and a final two-week assessment (Phase 5). PREP was based on a 'full professional model,' as opposed to a 'limited expert model,' of policing (Bradley and Cioccarelli 1989). Its approach 'called for police training and education to be built upon progressive adult education principles including experiential learning, case study, educational contextual studies and the importance of practicum' (NSW Police Service 1992: 11).

The aim of PREP was to produce 'reflective practitioners' who make effective decisions based on policing by consent, operational independence, and accountability (CARE 1990: 8). Professionalism was defined in terms of the qualities possessed by a 'master police practitioner': knowledge of policing, effective communication skills, commitment to ethical standards, respect for individual rights, self-awareness, empathy, and problem-solving skills (NSWPS 1989: 3–4).

Two years after its introduction, PREP was evaluated by a team of independent researchers from the United Kingdom (CARE 1990). The evaluation documented the program's strengths and also identified some of its weaknesses. One of the most serious of the latter was found in the field training component (Phase 4), during which probationary constables became 'assimilated in the traditional policing culture,' and rejected the 'reflective professional' model of policing taught at the academy (NSW Police Service 1993: 25). A number of changes to Phase 4 were implemented as a result of this evaluation. For example, demonstration patrols were introduced during which probationers were provided with training support and a period of induction (see chapter 5).

PREP was also scrutinized by the Wood Commission (Wood Report 1997). In its final report, the commission echoed the Lusher Report's criticism of the stance that the police service should be the sole provider of police training. Although it left final decisions to the appropriate advisory bodies on police education, the commission spoke 'strongly' in favour of a system in which officers could enter the police service only after acquiring qualifications from approved tertiary institutions. Practical skills training would be delivered at the police academy and through a field training program closely integrated with the academy (276).

At present, the recruit training program (called the Constable Education Program) consists of six 14-week sessions over two years at Charles Sturt University; these lead to the Diploma of Policing Practice. Sessions 1 and 3 are taken at the Police Academy; sessions 2, 4, 5, and 6 involve field-based education along with distance learning. Students are not considered for recruitment into the police service until they have satisfactorily completed the first three sessions of study. University graduates in appropriate disciplines are given advanced standing in the course. Although the current training program is very different from the system that was operating during our research project, many of the issues raised in this book are still relevant.

Research Design

The research design drew on the rich tradition of systematic studies of police work since the 1970s (Black 1971; Reiss 1971; Ericson 1981/1993; Ericson 1982; Ericson and Haggerty 1997; Mastrofski et al. 1998). Using a longitudinal approach (cf. Van Maanen 1973, 1975; Fielding 1988), we followed the progress of a cohort of approximately 150 police recruits at regular intervals for two years. We employed a variety of research techniques, including face-to-face interviews, questionnaires, and observation. In addition, we used documentary materials such as course outlines, police internal documents, and official reports as supplementary data. Table 2.1 provides an overview of the research timetable and outcomes.

Surveys

Questionnaires were administered to all recruits at four points:

1. In the first week of Phase 1 of PREP, the beginning of an eight-week residential course at the academy.
2. At the end of Phase 3, after approximately six months of training, before recruits began their forty-nine-week field training in Phase 4.
3. During Phase 5, roughly eighteen months after entry to the academy.
4. Six months after the completion of PREP, when recruits had begun working as police constables.

TABLE 2.1
Overview of the research design, schedule, and outcomes

Month	Stage of police training	Population (survey)	Completed questionnaires	Population (interview)	Completed interviews	Completed observation
1	Phase 1 (academy)	149	Survey #1 (147)	74	Round #1 (73)	
2						
3	Phase 2 (field observation)					Observation #1 (19 shifts)
4						Observation #2 (debrief)
5	Phase 3 (academy)	143	Survey #2 (127)	66	Round #2 (59)	
6					Academy instructors (10)	
7	Phase 4 (field training)					Observation #3 (total 58 shifts)
8						
9	Demonstration patrols					Demonstration patrols (30 shifts)
10						
11						
12						
13						
14	Training patrols					Training patrols (28 shifts)
15						
16						
17						

TABLE 2.1
(*concluded*)

Month	Stage of police training	Population (survey)	Completed questionnaires	Population (interview)	Completed interviews	Completed observation
18	Phase 5 (academy)	139	Survey #3 (134)	61	Round #3 (54)	
19						
20						
21	22 as constable	Work 146	Survey #4 (87)	(Mail) 61	Round #4 (53)	Observation #4 (38 shifts)
23						
24						
25						
26						
27						
28						
29						
30						
31						
32						
33						
34						
35						
36					FTOs (18)	
37						
38						
39					Relegated officers (7)	

The questionnaires collected basic demographic data about the recruits, as well as information about their initial expectations, their
experiences at various phases of training, their training and field experiences, their views of the organization, and their orientation toward
police work. In particular, we examined respondents' conceptions of
professionalism in policing.

Response rates[3] for the first three surveys, which were administered
at the academy during class time, were very high: 98.7, 88.8 and 96.4
per cent respectively. Survey 4 was conducted by mail, as the cohort
had by then graduated and been deployed in local area commands
throughout the state. The response rate for survey 4 was 59.6 per cent –
much lower than the previous rounds but generally considered acceptable for mail-out surveys, although sample bias remains a problem
(see, for example, Babbie 1992: 267).

Interviews

Face-to-face interviews were conducted with an initial random sample
of about seventy-five recruits,[4] who were re-interviewed at three other
stages as outlined above. These interviews were designed to obtain
detailed and contextualized accounts of recruits' experiences at each
stage of their development. The first three rounds of interviews were
conducted at the academy. In the third round, however, only thirty-
four interviewees showed up at the prearranged times. This was a very
busy period (Phase 5) for the probationers; apparently our interview
schedule clashed with some of the study groups organized by tutors.
By contacting the missing interviewees later on in the field, we were
able to complete a further twenty interviews. All interviews for round 4
were conducted in the field; officers stationed in rural areas were interviewed by telephone.

At each stage, various factors affected the number of successfully
completed interviews. These factors included resignation, relegation,
or termination of interviewees; failure to attend the interview; difficulties organizing interviews in the field (round 3); and refusal. Two of the
seventy-five selected recruits were never interviewed (one never commenced training, the other failed to attend the first two rounds and
then refused rounds 3 and 4). Nine subjects refused to be interviewed
in at least one of the four rounds. Only forty-six recruits were successfully interviewed in every round.

Two attempts were made to interview the four recruits in the interview sample who had left the service. The first was around ten months after the commencement of training, the second some eighteen months after the cohort had graduated. In each case, no interviews were conducted; the subjects either refused the interview or failed to respond to the request. Eight of the nine relegated officers (those who did not graduate with the cohort class) agreed to be interviewed when invited near the end of the project. However, only seven of these interviews were completed, as one person had resigned by the time the interviewer made contact with the local area command to arrange the interview. This person was not followed up.

Most interviews were tape recorded and transcribed. Where transcription was not possible because of technical difficulties or because interviewees refused to allow taping,[5] interviewers' notes were used to write up the interviews.

To complement the longitudinal study of recruits, we interviewed ten academy instructors and eighteen field training officers[6] (FTOs) about a range of issues: how they saw their role, the training they received, their views on PREP, and how the PREP model was applied in practice. Academy instructors were chosen on the basis of availability and were interviewed at the same time as the second round of recruit interviews. FTOs were nominated by the education and development officers (EDOs) at ten selected local area commands (LACs) across Sydney.

Observation

The research team also spent more than 900 hours in the field observing a sample of recruits at various stages of their training: during Phase 2, when recruits spent four weeks at a police patrol[7]; during the debriefing session at the end of Phase 2; during the forty-nine-week field training period; and during the six-month period following Phase 5. To obtain a reasonably representative picture of field experience, we sampled nineteen shifts (eight-hour work periods, even though patrols are now moving to twelve-hour shifts) in Phase 2, fifty-eight shifts in Phase 4 (thirty in demonstration patrols and twenty-eight in training patrols), and thirty-eight shifts during the six-month period following graduation. The purpose of the observation was to obtain first-hand understanding of some of the recruits' experiences, as well as information on their actual practices.

Different methods were used to select patrols for each round of observation. In Phase 2, students were placed in patrols near their homes. To minimize costs, only metropolitan patrols were selected for observation. We tried to gather data for a range of geographic locations and socioeconomic and workload characteristics. At the end of Phase 3, students were assigned to various demonstration patrols[8] across Metropolitan Sydney. Observation was carried out in a total of 13 patrols, which again represented a good range of locations and workload and socioeconomic characteristics. The number of shifts spent at each patrol depended on the number of probationers from the cohort who were stationed there. Because of the wider geographical spread of training patrols, the selection of patrols for observation involved a slightly different process, though again we took steps to ensure wide geographical coverage and a mix of busy and less busy stations. We tried to include female recruits in the observation wherever possible. In the fourth round of observation, we observed four shifts at each of ten patrols, which we selected using similar criteria as before.

We did not target any particular recruits. The usual practice was for the observer to make arrangements with the contact person nominated for the patrol once permission had been granted. Typically, the contact person consulted the roster to see when a member of the cohort was working. Having established a time and date convenient to the patrol and the researcher, the contact person advised the subject, and any other significant people (such as shift supervisor), of the arrangements. If the subject refused, the same contact person made alternative arrangements with another probationer in the cohort.

The NSWPS was protected from legal liability in relation to the field workers by an indemnity signed by the University of New South Wales. Observers were instructed to follow the advice of the police they were attached to in terms of safety issues and exclusion from particular situations. Many patrol commanders, shift supervisors, and contact personnel instructed the officers to treat observers as student police officers in terms of safety and procedure: they were to be dropped off if there was a high-speed chase or if room had to be made for an offender to be transported in the car. Observers were advised to always have sufficient taxi money for such situations. As it turned out, this happened only once: the fieldworker offered to walk back to the station after a beat sergeant who had made an arrest and requested transport of the offender was 'extremely displeased to see [the researcher]' (6mo).

In general, observers adopted a neutral role. However, they asked questions when necessary to clarify what was happening at particular times. Often opportunities for informal interviews presented themselves, and these were taken up more or less at the fieldworker's discretion.

By the end of the project, 115 shifts of observations had been conducted. There were only two explicit refusals to participate. At the same time as refusing the round 2 interviews, one person asked not to be involved in any observations. A second refusal occurred in the observations conducted after Phase 5: after a short time, the subject expressed his own and his colleagues' discomfort with the research, and the observation was terminated (6mo Obs37). An officer who reported in sick on the day of a scheduled observation was taken as a potential refusal, since that person had also refused further involvement in the interviews during round 3. Instead of placing this person in an awkward position, the fieldworker simply arranged with the contact person to be allocated to someone else (without revealing that it might be a refusal). In total, we observed eighty different members of the cohort working over fifty-eight day shifts, forty-two evening shifts, and fourteen night shifts[9] in forty different local areas. Female recruits were observed in forty-five shifts (39 per cent); male recruits were observed in seventy shifts (61 per cent).

We also observed the Phase 2 debriefing sessions conducted at the academy in the first week of Phase 3. Five classes were randomly selected for observation. However, despite meeting with all the tutors on the day of the scheduled debrief, and explaining the purpose of the observation, two classes had completed their debrief sessions prior to the agreed time. We therefore only captured three debriefing sessions.

Additional Data

Documents such as reports, course materials, and official documents were also collected for analysis.

The Research Process

Considering the magnitude and time frame of the study, some problems were bound to be encountered in conducting it. The following highlights some of those problems.

Making Contact

The procedure followed for arranging observation and interviews in the field was for the chief collaborator (Chris Devery) to make the necessary arrangements through the patrol/local area commander. Often the commander nominated a contact person within the patrol (e.g., a tactician, PEDO, or roster officer). Once permission for entry was established, the research assistant was left to make more specific arrangements with the contact person.

This process was not always straightforward. There were times when the contact officer was absent or did not return calls as promised. Sometimes the contact officer suggested a different person to liaise with, and it could take several phone calls to reach the new contact. On several occasions the contact person told us he or she had not received any information about the project, and the research assistant had to get back to the chief collaborator and ask for another contact to be made. These difficulties were both frustrating and time-consuming for the research assistant, and contributed to the delay in completing the field-work. The problem was exacerbated in the later stages of the project, when patrol commanders were changed as a result of organizational restructuring.

As a result of these difficulties, or interviewees being unavailable at the appointed time, three interviews were not conducted in round 3. One of these interviewees cited this 'muck around' as a reason for refusing the interview in round 4. Other examples of communication failure abound: A fieldworker arrived for a shift only to find that the subject had swapped to an earlier shift (Ph2 Obs7). A fieldworker who rang the patrol before leaving home was told that the subject had been sent to the city for special duties (DP Obs19). The subject had called in sick on the day of the observation (6mo Obs8, TP Obs19). No one had the courtesy to inform the fieldworkers about any these changes to the prearranged appointments.

Gaining Entry

In the majority of field visits, no major problems with gaining entry were encountered on the scheduled shift (e.g., DP Obs22; DP Obs1, DP Obs15), even if information about the research had not been dissemi-nated. One supervising sergeant commented that he had only received a handwritten note that day, but no supporting paperwork. Neverthe-less, he dismissed the fieldworker's suggestion that he ring the collabo-rator or chief investigator for confirmation and further information. 'If it's been approved and I've been told to do it,' he said, 'then it's not my worry' (Ph2).

Some shift supervisors and officers were more cautious. However, their caution was alleviated somewhat when the fieldworker provided further explanations of the research, assurances that the research was confidential and anonymous, and promises that they would follow the officers' instructions (e.g., 6mo Obs18, DP Obs26). Other supervisors insisted on confirming that the necessary paperwork, approval, or indemnity was in place before allowing access (e.g., 6mo Obs25). Sometimes the fieldworker was unable to continue with the observation until this had all been sorted out, which could take an hour or more (e.g., DP Obs17, TP Obs11). These problems arose despite the best efforts of the fieldworker.

The fieldwork overlapped with the term of the Royal Commission. This also created problems for researchers. On one shift the chief investigator (Janet Chan) was asked by a senior partner of the recruit whether she was working undercover for the Royal Commission:

> I offered to show him my IDs to prove my identity but he didn't seem to want to see them. He asked me if I was working for the Royal Commission; I told him I was not. He said that because of the Royal Commission, they became suspicious about strange people coming in. I said I was not an investigator but a university academic and I was doing a research project which the Police Service had approved. He asked what I would be doing, I said I'd just be observing the probationary officers and their experiences. He then seemed to relax a bit, and I could not help being a bit 'cheeky' by saying that police officers often told people they dealt with that if they had nothing to hide, they had nothing to worry about. He relaxed a bit more and joked that they don't say that but just tell people they have committed the crime. (DP)

Working a Shift

Fieldworkers' experiences with officers on the shift were mixed. In some cases, observers commented on the lack of interest or curiosity regarding their presence (e.g., Ph2 Obs1, DP Obs23). Sometimes we came across individual officers who were keen to volunteer their views on topics such as training and the organization for the research (e.g., DP Obs11, TP Obs25, TP Obs17). Some officers (either subjects or other officers) went out of their way to do what they thought would accommodate the research or interest the researcher, such as asking the fieldworkers what they would like to do or see (Ph2 Obs2, Ph2 Obs17), rearranging duties so that the subject was out on patrol (DP Obs25, DP Obs11, TP Obs19), showing the researcher the local 'shooting gallery' (DP Obs14) or prostitute strip (DP Obs10), suggesting shift times that were generally more 'eventful' (6mo Obs13), or expressing the hope that the fieldworker will get to see something exciting (Ph2 Obs5) or be in the car with the siren on (Ph2 Obs5). On three occasions the fieldworkers were invited to speak to the muster about the study (DP Obs23, TP Obs15, 6mo Obs25). On another shift the fieldworker was introduced to the muster at the end of the shift (DP Obs4).

Not unexpectedly, fieldworkers were not always welcomed or supported. The two issues that stood out as creating the greatest anxiety for the officers involved were (a) whether the fieldworker was in some way connected with the Royal Commission or some other anticorruption body such as the Independent Commission Against Corruption (ICAC) or Internal Affairs (IA); and (b) the fieldworker's practice of note taking. The Royal Commission was in progress during the course of the research, and perhaps this escalated these anxieties. Similarly, the fact that the letters sent out by the collaborator regarding the project were on the letterhead of the Office of Professional Responsibility (where IA was located) would have raised some eyebrows. These concerns were sometimes raised in a subtle way, such as by asking if the fieldworker was 'spying' (Ph2 Obs2) or carrying a microphone or camera (e.g., Ph2 Obs8, TP Obs13), or by references to corruption (e.g., Ph2 Obs18, Ph2 Obs13, TP Obs2). On other occasions the comments and assumptions were more explicit (e.g., Ph2 Obs19, DP Obs27, TP Obs13). One fieldworker, sensitized from past experience to the possibility of being seen as associated with an investigative or disciplinary body, addressed the issue directly: 'Once in the truck C4 asked me what I was there for. I explained that I was not with IA or with ICAC, and that I was there as part of a study that was following class [x]' (DP).

Sometimes the research was assumed to be a performance assessment or evaluation of the subject or even other officers (e.g, Ph2 Obs17; Ph2 Obs2; Ph2 Obs1; DP Obs25, DP Obs26, DP Obs6, 6mo Obs3). Researchers also fielded questions about whether the study was in any way similar to the 1992 documentary *Cop It Sweet*, which caused great embarrassment to the police service because of the overt racism displayed by officers (see Chan 1997).

Other misunderstandings about the research were sometimes articulated. One fieldworker reported that subjects at various times assumed she was a 'shrink' (Ph2 Obs9), a time management consultant

(Ph2 Obs19), or an ethics researcher (Ph2 Obs19). Another fieldworker was thought to be a reporter (6mo Obs19). One researcher commented on the multiple interpretations of her identity:

> Reflecting on the evening there were two things which stood out. The first was the conclusion drawn by C10 [the senior partner] as to the reason for my presence. On my first observation shift the Constable with the [probationer] had assumed I was with the Royal Commission, on another observation the Constable had assumed that I was there to check up on the Probationary Constable, on this shift the Constable had treated me as though I was there on work experience. (DP)

The fieldworker's practice of taking notes was subject to comment, sometimes by way of jokes (e.g., DP Obs22, DP Obs27, 6mo Obs2, TP Obs2). Other times, concern about what was being recorded was expressed more explicitly (e.g., Ph2 Obs10, DP Obs9, DP Obs26, 6mo Obs3, 6mo Obs26, 6mo Obs29, 6mo Obs33, TP Obs9). Sometimes fieldworkers themselves reported feeling conspicuous when taking notes (e.g., DP Obs25). On one shift the fieldworker was explicitly barred from taking notes during interviews 'as it might get [the police] in trouble' (6mo).

By the final stage of the project, fieldworkers were experiencing fewer problems of entry and acceptance. This could be because at this stage, observers were spending four shifts in the same patrol, and often the same subject was being observed for a second or third time. Researchers often commented that officers recognized them from previous shifts and that subjects were taking them 'on board' without any need for explanation after they had spent one or more shifts together. Some fieldworkers reported that even in the training patrol observations, subjects were familiar with the process, having been involved in interviews and completed the surveys, or they had been observed in earlier stages or knew someone who had been. Sometimes other police remembered the project from those earlier stages. This ease of entry may also have been related to the fact that the Royal Commission proper was no longer an issue; thus, anxiety about the study's connection with the Royal Commission was more easily allayed by the fieldworker's reassurances, or questions were asked less often.

In sum, though researchers were never denied access by patrol commanders, the reactions of individual officers on any one shift ran the gamut from indifference, simple curiosity, and genuine interest and support, through to suspicion, abrasiveness, and rudeness.

Methodological Issues

A number of methodological issues are connected with studies of this type, in which researchers enter a close-knit organization to examine its culture and work practices. Some of the most prominent issues[10] are discussed here.

Longitudinal Tracking

We had intended to track individual changes captured in the survey and interview data through the use of unique identification numbers. This system was successful for the interviews but broke down for the surveys. Each respondent was issued with an ID number when the first survey was administered. To demonstrate good faith (i.e., to show that the researchers had no way of connecting the respondents to the numbers), these ID numbers, printed on wallet-sized cards, were handed out randomly to recruits, who were asked to keep the cards for future surveys. Unfortunately, through either carelessness or fear of being identified, many respondents did not keep their ID numbers for later surveys. There was also evidence that where the same ID numbers were used for later surveys, respondents had provided inconsistent demographic details (e.g., a respondent who was age twenty-four in Survey 1 was twenty-one in Survey 2). As a consequence of this failure in the ID system, we lost the capacity to track changes in individual respondents between surveys. So our analysis of the survey data was restricted to comparing changes in the cohort as a whole, or changes among subgroups.

The identification system for interviews was somewhat different. Since it was important to keep a list of names to enable future contact in the field, the team allocated and maintained a record of interview numbers (not the same as the survey ID numbers). As a result, we were able to track individual changes for interviewees.

Inter-Observer Reliability

The field observation component of this research was the most vulnerable to problems of reliability. Obviously, a fieldworker's sex, age, ethnicity, and life experience can affect his or her ability to establish rapport with the subjects being observed. This in turn can determine the amount and nature of the data he or she is able to collect. For instance, it is unlikely that a female observer in this study would have been privy to the following situation, reported by a male fieldworker:

> It was plain to see that Officer Two [a female] was well liked and re-spected for her ability as a police officer. Her male peers treated her as a work equal but in a social setting her male colleagues watched what they said around her. When the boys were on their own it would be common for the talk to be about sex with the f word being used freely but when Officer Two was present the language used by the male uniformed officers was very much toned down. (6mo)

Fieldworkers vary in their skills and research experience. Although all our observers held degrees in the social sciences, they ranged from new graduates to mature and highly experienced field researchers. Experienced researchers may have an advantage in their ability to 'see' what inexperienced researchers do not; at the same time, their age and maturity can act as barriers in dealing with younger subjects. Similarly, familiarity with the concepts, jargon, and procedures of the group being studied can be an asset in field observation. Our fieldworkers sometimes reported difficulties deciphering radio messages or under-standing the legal or technical side of police work. Yet familiarity can also be a handicap when researchers fail to notice, let alone explore, the meanings and complexities of taken-for-granted assumptions and concepts.

Construct Validity

How can one study an occupational culture when secretiveness is one of its key features? This is a vexing question. We have already described some of the problems we encountered in gaining access to fieldwork – problems that raise questions about whether we were indeed observing and measuring what we had set out to study. For example, to what extent were these logistical difficulties created by (or confounded with) the paranoia, secrecy, siege mentality, and cynicism often associated with police culture? How much of what we observed or were told was purely a 'performance' staged for our benefit? One important consideration is the impact of the fieldworker's presence on officers' speech and action, as the following observers pointed out:

> I think that my presence altered the normal course of events in two ways. First, I think that because S1 put PC1 on general duties, there may have been an extra police car on the road that night. This meant that the two other vehicles absorbed any work that was called on the radio. Secondly I was also sure that my presence inhibited the interactions between PC1 and C2 in the vehicle. Finally, I found that my physical placement in the vehicle inhibited my ability to communicate much with the Officers in the front of the car. (DP)

> The Inspector came into the Statement Room and joked with me that maybe I should come to the patrol more often as Constable A [the subject] had never worked this hard. (6mo)

The use of multiple sources of data (questionnaires, interviews, observations, and documents) is one way to increase confidence in research findings, especially when the findings from those different sources point in the same direction. This is the approach we took. When data from different sources point to different conclusions, this points to ways we can enrich our understanding through further research and theory development.

Internal Validity

The question of causality does not have a simple answer: the analysis of socialization processes is always going to be complicated by the usual factors such as history, maturation, mortality, and testing. For example, in the course of the research the NSWPS was being closely scrutinized by the Wood Royal Commission. The service was also undergoing a major reorganization following the appointment of a new police commissioner. We cannot be certain how much these historical factors affected the changes found in the data. Similarly, the recruits aged three years over the period of study, and this may have resulted in changes that were not necessarily associated with their experiences as police officers. It can also be argued that the changes we observed in the cohort could have been the result of the departure of those who did not 'fit in' to the occupation. Finally, over the course of the study several sets of questions and attitude items were repeated, sometimes more than once, in both the surveys and the interviews. This practice, and the general focus on the one class, introduces the possibility of 'panel conditioning,' 'whereby respondents become gradually interested in the research study, learn more about it and can, in this way, cause distortions in the research findings' (Sarantakos 1993: 136). These issues were partly dealt with by the research design (i.e., the use of multiple sources of data); they are also addressed by a more sophisticated theoretical understanding of culture and practice (see chapter 1).

Ethical Issues

Consent

All surveys, interviews, and observations were undertaken with the consent of the participants; however, we don't know how 'free' their participation actually was. Aside from the explicit refusals already noted, we don't know whether those who failed to attend interviews were in fact refusals. Similarly, we have no information on whether some subjects felt obliged to consent because they had been told by their superiors to do so, given that the police service was a partner in the research project. One fieldworker reported:

> I ask him [the contact person] to allocate me a different recruit if anyone doesn't want to be observed. He says, 'They'll do as they're bloody well told.' I got the impression he was saying this as a friendly gesture to me. I reiterate that I want him to make a new allocation if anyone refuses. (DP)

Sometimes details of fieldwork arrangements were never filtered down to the subjects. There were occasions when the recruit claimed to be unaware that the fieldworker had been assigned (e.g., Ph2 Obs7, DP Obs14, DP Obs15, DP Obs11). Participants were free to refuse to be observed, but we don't know how much they felt obliged to cooperate. The following observation suggests that either the subject agreed reluctantly, or she felt the need to distance herself from the research when questioned by a colleague:

> I was received well and there was no problem with C1 (subject) for me to observe her. An older Sergeant in the beat office did pull C1 aside during lunch to ask about me and C1 did say it was not her choice to be observed. (6mo)

Officers legitimately felt uncomfortable about the study. Being 'shadowed' by a complete stranger for a full eight hours (sometimes longer) could not have been easy, although one recruit tried to joke about the experience:

> In the meantime, a corrective services officer (CSO) entered the room ... She asked me if I was a reporter. I said, 'No,' and briefly explained the study saying it was part of a two-year study of the Academy Class [x]. 'Do you have to follow her around for two years,' she asked. Before I could answer, PR responded by saying, 'Yes ... we are getting married soon.' We chuckled at PR's sense of humour. (DP)

Nevertheless, as the following excerpts from field notes show, recruits' reactions to participation in the study ranged from pride to uncertainty. Most recruits were positive – or at least compliant – about their inclusion in the study:

> I had thought that being in the station would make my job as fieldworker more difficult, but [the subject] seemed determined to make his shift into a good learning experience for me. He explained everything he did. He showed me in detail how to enter a job into the COPS. He was very open when he didn't know what to do (this happened with quite a number of jobs). He asked me on a couple of occasions whether I wanted to ask him any questions. He always asked me whether I wanted to accompany him outside for a smoke. (As I always did, these proved good occasions for a chat.) He showed me round the station – a place that he was clearly proud to work in ... I found him a warm, open and friendly person, though pretty serious about what he was doing. He seemed utterly unthreatened by my presence. (DP)

> PR [the probationer] and his partner entered the station. I introduced myself and briefed PR about the study and what he could expect during the research, ie., observing, note taking and discussion. He quickly began interrogating me about the research, its focus, its due date and exactly what I would be writing in my notebook. PR appeared paranoid and anxious and suspicious about the research. His attitude and behaviour were in stark contrast to nearly all other recruits with whom I had spent time. (TP)

Given some of the unease about the research among rank-and-file police, access to the field may have been granted reluctantly. It may be that the 'problems' we encountered in setting up the fieldwork could have been a subtle form of refusal through avoidance.

Confidentiality

Throughout this project we took seriously our undertaking to protect our subjects' confidentiality and anonymity. All interviewers, field-workers, and transcribers were asked to sign this undertaking before commencing work on the project. In addition, all references to names of police officers and police stations were replaced by codes in field notes and transcripts. Also, we ensured that our research materials were not used for any other purposes than research. We were bound by the confidentiality undertaking even if we came upon incidents of improper or illegal behaviour. This issue became salient quite early on in the project. Because of the collaborative nature of the research, a number of police service employees were involved in assisting with the data collection. However, after the first round of interviews, we decided that serving police officers should not be involved in data collection from recruits, as conflicts could potentially arise between a police officer's legal obligation to report misconduct and the goals of the research.

Our commitment to this undertaking has also led to decisions about how to quote interviewees and observation shifts. Direct quotes will not cite the interviewee or observation number. Rather, we will simply record either the observation stage (e.g., 'DP' for demonstration patrol, '6mo' for the observations conducted six months after the completion of PREP), or round number of the interviews and the age and sex of the interviewee (e.g., 1 / 23-year-old male). Since only a handful of cohort members were over thirty, indigenous, or from a non-English-speaking background, we have made the following decisions: interviewees over thirty will be cited simply as, for example, 'survey 1, female, >30.' When we specifically identify the interviewee as Aboriginal, Torres Strait Islander, or of non-English-speaking background, we will not record the age or sex details. It is also worth noting that some of the transcriptions have been edited for clarity.

In the next chapter, we describe the subjects of the cohort, their reasons for joining the police, and their initial expectations.

3

Joining the Organization

Organizational socialization does not begin at the recruit's entry to the police force. The processes of 'anticipatory socialization' (Merton 1957; Van Maanen 1976) occur much earlier. From childhood to adulthood, citizens of modern societies are continually exposed to images and stories about police work through personal experience, conversations with friends and relatives, crime news, and popular culture. These images and stories provide the basis of a mythic vision (Martin 1999) of police work – one that embodies action, bravery, physical strength, emotional control, and, above all, authority. The courageous crime fighter – in the frontlines of the war against crime, upholding society's law and morality, outsmarting the ubiquitous criminals – is the most popular and enduring icon of the police officer. This is not to imply that the public is unaware of the existence of corrupt police or officers who abuse their powers – these are common themes in police films and dramas. Our point is that the 'sacred canopy' that is drawn over police work (Manning 1997: 21) is rarely touched, let alone lifted. This is because the legitimacy of the police role is fundamental to the stability of our political and social order. It follows that, at least in the minds of those with a stake in the dominant order, to join the police is to take up a noble cause on behalf of society.

Anticipatory socialization, the process through which individuals prepare themselves for police work prior to entry into the organization, can involve a variety of preparatory activities: information seeking, academic studies, physical training, or simply gaining life experience. Once they have made the decision to join the police, applicants begin a subtle process of adjusting their physical and attitudinal characteristics to those which will be expected of them. In Bourdieu's terminology,

applicants recognize the 'game' as defined by the admission requirements and by their own perceptions of the job, and adjust their habitus
accordingly. This does not involve any sudden change in values or
belief systems, but rather a 'softening' of attitudes that leads to a more
'malleable' habitus, 'capable of being converted into the required habitus' for the occupation (Bourdieu 2000: 100).

In this chapter we introduce the recruits who participated in this
study – where they came from, why they joined the police, their expectations about police work, the preparatory work they undertook, and
their reactions to being accepted into the police organization. Drawing
from data collected in Survey 1 and the first round of interviews, both
of which took place during the recruits' first week at the police academy, we describe this first stage of organizational socialization as seen
through the eyes of the subjects.

Characteristics of the Cohort

What kinds of men and women become police officers? Are they still
predominantly male, 'local, family-oriented, military-experienced, high-
school educated, and working-class whites,' as Van Maanen (1974: 87)
found in the United States in the late 1960s? There are reasons to expect
the profile of police recruits in the 1990s to be more representative of
the culturally diverse society that Australia has become. Since the mid-
1980s the NSW Police Service has changed its recruitment criteria to
remove some of the physical barriers that may have inhibited minority
groups and women from joining. There has been a commitment to
'ensure that applicants selected reflect the ethnic composition of the
community ... that an increasing proportion of recruits are women,
[and] that applicants with the highest possible academic achievements
are attracted to the Service' (NSWPS 1988: 59). The new recruitment
policy has not been entirely successful. In the years previous to this
study, the proportion of female applicants was steady at around 25
to 35 per cent. Consistently, there were few applicants of indigenous
Australian or non-English-speaking background; these two groups accounted, respectively, for less than 1 to 2 per cent and 10 to 12 per cent
of applications (NSWPS 1994: 18–20).

The cohort in this study consisted of a class of 150 recruits.[1] Table 3.1
provides some of the basic information about this class.[2] The male-to-
female ratio was about two to one, reflecting trends in the recent past
(NSWPS 1994: 25–6). The class was predominantly young, with more

TABLE 3.1
Characteristics of cohort (survey 1, N=147)

Variable	Category	Frequency	Percentage
Sex	Male	94	66
	Female	48	34
		Missing=5	
Age	18–20	51	36
	21–24	56	40
	25–28	23	16
	29–34	8	6
	35+	2	1
		Missing=7	
Country of birth	Australia	139	97
	Other	4	3
		Missing=4	
Location of home	Capital city	44	31
	Major city	58	41
	Country	40	28
		Missing=5	
Marital status	Not married	117	82
	Married/de facto	21	15
	Separated/divorced	4	3
		Missing=5	
Education completed	Secondary or less	39	27
	Postsecondary	61	43
	Some university	27	19
	University degree	12	8
	Postgraduate	1	1
	Other	3	2
		Missing=4	
Religion	Christian	96	68
	No religion	9	27
	Other	2	1
	Not stated/unclear	2	4
		Missing=6	
Voting preference	Labor	63	45
	Liberal	34	24
	National	7	5
	Swinging	24	17
	Minor parties	10	7
	Not enrolled	2	1
		Missing=7	

TABLE 3.1
(*concluded*)

Variable	Category	Frequency	Percentage
Police among relatives	No	99	70
	Yes	43	30
		Missing=5	
Income from previous job	$5,000 or less p.a.	15	11
	$5,001–$20,000 p.a.	37	28
	$20,001–$40,000 p.a.	70	53
	$40,000+ p.a.	11	8
		Missing=14	

than three-quarters of the recruits under twenty-five. The minimum age was eighteen and the maximum forty-eight, with twenty-two being the median. This is again consistent with recent trends (23–4).

All but four recruits were born in Australia. Very few reported a non-Anglo background: among these, four were Aborigines or Torres Strait Islanders and nine were from non-English-speaking backgrounds (NESB). This proportion of NESB recruits[3] was close to the 1988–93 average, which was 7.4 per cent (NSWPS 1994: 41). Most recruits came from urban areas; just over one-quarter came from rural areas. Over 80 per cent of the recruits were not married; over 10 per cent had one or more children. Education levels varied considerably: just over one-quarter had completed secondary school, and 43 per cent had acquired a postsecondary diploma, TAFE[4] certificate, or trade qualifications, while 28 per cent had either attended or completed university.

Recruits came from a variety of socioeconomic backgrounds. About 8 per cent of the recruits reported that their fathers had no formal education or primary school education. Most reported that their fathers had secondary (39 per cent) or postsecondary (37 per cent) education, about 10 per cent reported that their fathers were university educated. The educational background for mothers was similar, except that over two-thirds had secondary education whereas only 17 per cent had postsecondary education. Most recruits came from average to high income families.[5] Parents' incomes (i.e., combined annual before tax) were as follows: $20,000 or less, 5 per cent; $20,001 to $40,000, 23 per cent; $40,001 to $60,000, 35 per cent; and over $60,000, 28 per cent.[6]

Nearly all recruits had worked somewhere else (full-time, part-time, or casual) before joining the police; only eight reported that they had never worked. Here, the main occupations were general sales (25 per cent), trades (11 per cent), general clerical (10 per cent), and manual labour (9 per cent). Three had been police officers, and seven had been in police or security-related jobs. Nine indicated that they had worked in managerial, administrative, or professional positions. Most had been earning between $20,000 and $40,000 a year.

Two out of three recruits said they were Christians of some kind. Just over one-quarter did not identify with any religion. Most said they voted Labor (45 per cent); about one-third voted Liberal or National Party; 17 per cent were 'swinging' voters; 7 per cent voted for minor parties such as the Australian Democrats, the Greens, and the Independents.

Three out of ten recruits had relatives who were police officers – typically these were cousins, brothers, uncles, or fathers. This proportion was much higher than the average of 21 per cent between 1988 and 1993, but note here that the proportions fluctuated between 12 to 38 per cent (NSWPS 1994: 37–8).

This brief profile shows that police recruits in New South Wales in the mid-1990s were still predominantly young, male Anglo-Australians. Women made up one-third of the class. More than one-quarter of the recruits had had some university education, and most came from average to high income families. The higher proportion of female and university-educated recruits was probably the consequence of changes in recruitment policies since the mid 1980s.

Attractions of Policing

Recruits were attracted to police work for both 'selfless' and 'instrumental' reasons (cf. Fielding 1988: 18). In Survey 1, recruits were given a list of factors influencing their decision to join the police, and asked to rate their importance. Table 3.2 shows the mean ratings of the factors listed in the questionnaire in descending order of importance.[7] The six factors that were rated highest were:

- an interest in police work
- to work with people
- to serve the community
- to have a professional career
- the varied and nonroutine nature of police work
- to have job security

TABLE 3.2
Factors affecting decision to join police (Survey 1, N=147)

	Mean Ratings		
	Male (94)	Female (48)	All (147)
An interest in police work	1.129	1.063	1.110
To work with people	1.277	1.146	1.224*
To serve the community	1.277	1.125	1.231
To have a professional career	1.330	1.125	1.259
Varied/non-routine nature of work	1.351	1.229	1.299
To have job security	1.330	1.250	1.299
The excitement of police work	1.468	1.563	1.500
Good workmates	1.447	1.729	1.537*
To help combat organised crime	1.585	1.583	1.571
An interest in law	1.755	1.667	1.714
Good job prospects	1.798	1.583	1.728
To help maintain individual liberties/rights	1.798	1.708	1.748
Working outdoors	1.882	1.938	1.890
Admiration for person(s) in Police Service	2.192	2.104	2.170
To enjoy prestige of being police officer	2.362	2.532	2.411
Good pay	2.734	2.458	2.633
As a step towards another profession	2.521	2.979	2.660*
Early retirement and a pension	2.989	3.146	3.027
Influence of relatives (other than parents)	3.394	3.438	3.415
Parent's wishes	3.575	3.375	3.510
Influence of a close family friend	3.521	3.458	3.510
I needed a job	3.489	3.604	3.524
Influence of a careers adviser	3.670	3.688	3.687
Influence of a teacher at school	3.787	3.646	3.748
Failed to gain admission to another course	3.883	3.750	3.844

Q: Thinking back to when you made your decision to become a police officer, how important was each of the following to you?
   1. Very important
   2. Somewhat important
   3. Not very important
   4. Not at all important
Note: Information on gender was missing in five cases.
*Significant differences between male and female respondents' ratings (Mann Whitney U test, $p<0.05$).

These six factors were rated as 'very important' by more than three-quarters of the respondents. The next group of factors – rated slightly less important – included a variety of items related to working conditions such as the excitement of police work, having good workmates, good job prospects, and working outdoors, as well as those related to 'public interest' concerns such as to help combat organized crime and to help maintain individual liberties. Prestige, pay, and retirement benefits were considered even less important; the influences of parents, relatives, teachers, and friends were considered least important. These results were similar to those found in a survey of police recruits in Queensland; however, the Queensland sample did not rank serving the community and having a professional career as high as our cohort did (Criminal Justice Commission 1993: 106).

Ratings by male and female recruits were very similar, except that on average women rated 'to work with people' higher than men. Also, female recruits rated 'good workmates' and 'as a step towards another profession' somewhat lower than male recruits. These differences were statistically significant.[8]

This topic was explored in more depth in the first round of interviews. The aspect of police work nominated most often (by 70 per cent of the 73 interviewees) was its variety and involvement with people:

> I think probably too that it changes from day to day. Nothing's the same, everything's completely different. I mean you might be working with different people most days. I mean one day you might be doing an accident and the next day you could just be inside. Just the variety. It's not boring or mundane I don't think. (1 / 25-year-old female[9])

> Basically it's the variety of people you get to meet and there's also a variety of challenges that you're called upon to deal with, so it's always constantly a challenge. There's also different things every day you go to work, you never know what's going to happen. So you kind of jump out of bed and you want to go to work 'cause you never know what's going to happen. (1 / 19-year-old male)

Some recruits pointed specifically to the physical or outdoor aspects of police work as part of its varied nature.

Another frequently mentioned attraction of police work related to its job prospects, security, and working conditions, and to its offer of a 'professional career.' Just over half (53 per cent) of the recruits interviewed mentioned some aspect of this general factor, although rarely as the most important or only reason for joining. One female recruit felt that the police service was a 'good employer of women' because of its equal opportunity policy:

I mean, women, I think, nowadays are getting treated more equally. Women can go into highway patrol, they can become detectives, they can go out to bashings. I mean, even though it's still a man's club, I think they're beginning to accept women a bit more ... And also, too, if at one stage I decide to have a family, they're good with maternity leave, with what I've heard, and also the idea of these crèches that they're starting to do, looking after their females just to keep them on. Restricted duties, like if they are pregnant. I think that's a good idea. (1 / 25-year-old female)

About four in ten interviewees offered altruistic reasons for joining the police, including the wish to help people and make a difference to the community:

The opportunity, I think, to be helpful to people. I get a great deal of satisfaction out of doing that, you know, it gives me a buzz ... I hope to be financially stable and to have a happy marriage and a family, really I think is my greatest desire. But really I wouldn't be happy unless I was making some sort of society contribution as well, you know. And the police force certainly is that. You know, I do think it's a very noble career. I do. And I think that it's very much the front seat of life. You get to see everything right up close and you're able to help a lot of people. (1 / 22-year-old male)

Almost all (96 per cent) of the recruits interviewed mentioned at least one of these three features of police work as its main attraction; six out of ten mentioned at least two of the three; 16 per cent mentioned all three.

A number of recruits (13 out of 73) saw police work as challenging both personally and professionally. A few (8) mentioned the excitement of police work as one of its attractions. Most mentioned excitement as a minor factor. However, one recruit admitted that he was an 'adrenalin junkie': 'I also like the idea of kicking in doors and things like that' (1 / 26-year-old male).

A variety of other factors were mentioned by a small number of interviewees. Some related to the recruit's family background. For example, one recruit grew up in a family in which both parents were police officers, and had always admired police work:

I've just always known it ever since I was born, that, you know, that that's what they did and just stories over the years of, you know, things going on at work and things like that. I've just sort of grown up with it ... I just always thought, you know, dad's job was pretty cool [laugh] and I wanted to do it. (1 / 23-year-old female)

Coming from a totally different starting point, a recruit of Aboriginal background joined the police to help rebuild relations between police and Aboriginal people.

Expectations about Police Work

Recruits generally had a very high opinion of policing as an occupation. Table 3.3 shows how they rated a range of occupations in terms of honesty, prestige, and professionalism. In spite of the publicity given to police corruption at the public hearings of the Wood Royal Commission, recruits rated police highest in terms of honesty (average rating 5.21) – they were considered more honest than clergy (4.92), nurses (4.80), doctors (4.70), social workers (4.66), and defence personnel (4.64). The occupations they rated as least honest were car salesman (1.53), newspaper journalist (1.99), and federal parliamentarian (2.17). In terms of prestige, they rated police (average rating 4.57) as somewhat less prestigious than doctors (5.24) and lawyers (4.82), but more prestigious than defence personnel (4.03), business executives (3.95), federal parliamentarians (3.86), and accountants (3.77). Also, police topped the ratings in terms of professionalism (average rating 5.43), followed by defence personnel (5.16), doctors (5.14), nurses (4.95), and lawyers (4.93). Recruits saw defence personnel (average rating 4.17), social worker (3.87), lawyer (3.72), and nurse (3.40) as the occupations most similar to police work.

Where did this highly favourable image of the policing occupation come from? According to their questionnaire responses, recruits most often learned about police from friends who were police officers (see Table 3.4). Nearly three-quarters reported that friends who were police had had the most influence on their perceptions and attitudes about police. Observing police at work (69 per cent) and personal experience with police (54 per cent) also influenced recruits' attitudes toward police. Media images – especially television news, nominated by six out of ten recruits – also played an influential role. Other media sources were less often cited as influential: newspapers (46 per cent), television current affairs programs (36 per cent), television documentaries (33 per cent), other television programs (22 per cent), and radio programs

TABLE 3.3
Rating of police and other occupations (Survey 1, N=147)

Occupation	Mean Ratings			
	Honesty	Prestige	Profession-alism	Similarity to police work
Police	5.207	4.569	5.434	—
Clergy	4.923	3.627	4.601	2.514
Nurses	4.801	3.338	4.952	3.396
Doctors	4.699	5.240	5.137	2.651
Social workers	4.664	3.186	4.308	3.868
Defence personnel	4.637	4.034	5.164	4.167
School teachers	4.616	3.538	4.295	2.657
University lecturers	4.320	3.662	4.151	1.973
Tradesmen	3.781	3.048	3.993	1.868
Accountants	3.671	3.772	4.390	1.563
Bank managers	3.671	3.731	4.377	1.618
Lawyers	3.401	4.828	4.932	3.719
Union leaders	2.993	2.876	3.226	1.750
Business executives	2.803	3.945	4.397	1.979
Advertising consultants	2.753	3.586	4.007	1.417
Federal members of Parliament	2.166	3.855	3.438	1.639
Newspaper journalists	1.993	2.834	3.007	1.734
Car salesmen	1.528	1.734	2.382	1.197

Q: Please give a rating of the following occupations in terms of *honesty, prestige, professionalism* and *similarity to police work*. Relate *each* to a scale of 1 to 6, where 1 is the lowest and 6 is the highest rating. To assist you with rating you may note the following scale:

   1–2 Not at all honest/prestigious/professional/similar to police work
   3–4 Moderately honest/prestigious/professional/similar to police work
   5–6 Very honest/prestigious/professional/similar to police work

(10 per cent). About one-third of the recruits indicated that their family was an important source of knowledge about police.

This topic was explored in more depth in interviews. Consistent with the survey results, most interviewees had knowledge about police before joining the service, either through family members, relatives, or friends who were police officers or through direct personal experience with police officers (i.e., at work or school, or through chance encounters). One recruit had a friend who had joined the police a few years ago:

TABLE 3.4
Sources of knowledge about police (Survey 1, N=147)

	Frequency	Percentage
Friend(s) who are police officers	107	73
Observing police at work	101	69
Television news	90	61
Personal experience with police	79	54
Newspapers	68	46
Television current affairs programs	53	36
Family	50	34
Television documentaries	48	33
Television programs	32	22
Friend(s) who are not police officers	19	13
Other	18	12
Radio programs	14	10

Q: People learn about police from many sources. Which of the following have had the most influence on your perceptions and attitudes about police?
Note: Multiple responses were available

I guess [I knew] a bit [about police] through my mate who's in the job. He's been in for, oh, I guess, over six years now. Yeah. And I think he's given me a fairly balanced view of it – like he hasn't … he tells me the good things, you know, some of the good things that he likes about the job and he tells me there's a bad side of it as well. (1 / 26-year-old male)

Some recruits didn't know anyone in the police but did their own research by speaking to local police officers:

Since I've applied and during my application procedures I've made an effort to go out to a lot of different stations around me and just have a chat with people in the Service and, you know, what their roles were, what they thought were the pros and cons of the job, and that sort of thing. (1 / 24-year-old female)

Although four out of ten interviewees admitted that part of their knowledge of police work came from the media, nearly one-quarter were sceptical of the media's portrayal of the police. They contended that media stories about police were unduly negative, sensationalized, and not to be trusted. About 14 per cent of the interviewees said they had been attracted to policing by the police service's television advertisements. The following is typical of some recruits' feelings about the media:

> The ads on telly for the police are really good, I reckon. The new ones ... you know the ones where they've got 'He's my brother' and all those songs sort of that you see them looking for lost kids and help people out of accidents and that. But the stuff in the newspaper's usually bad about the police ... corruption, and officers swearing at people and that. They should, just, you know, focus more on the good things that police do. Instead of saying, you know, corrupt police, why don't they say police officer, you know, helped save five people from a burning car or, you know, focus on the good things? Give them a better image. (1 / 19-year-old male)

Some recruits mentioned television ads such as 'Lean on me' and those on domestic violence and 'beat policing' as especially appealing. These ads conveyed the message to the public that the police are 'there to help you ... If you have a problem, give them a call ... They'll be right there for you' (1/19-year-old female).

These interviews suggest that while recruits had an idealized image of the policing occupation, their knowledge of policing was not predominantly influenced by the media; it was grounded more solidly than that, in personal interactions or experience with police officers. Recruits were more or less aware that there was 'a bad side' to policing. However, they preferred to concentrate on the noble and courageous images rather than on the negative, sensationalized ones portrayed by the media.

This does not mean that they saw the occupation through rose-coloured glasses – far from it. These recruits were well aware of what type of job they were getting into. When they were asked to rate on a scale of 1 to 4 how often they thought police had to perform a list of twenty-nine tasks, the top (most frequently performed) five tasks were: handling street incidents, obtaining statements from witnesses, completing criminal offence reports, dealing with domestic disputes, and carrying out random breathalizer tests (see Table 3.5). All of these are fairly mundane tasks involving minimal heroism or excitement. Not all of them were considered particularly important: recruits rated examining crime scenes as the most important of the tasks, followed by giving

TABLE 3.5
Policing tasks – importance and frequency (Survey 1, N=147)

Tasks	Importance Mean (rank)	Frequency Mean (rank)
Examining scenes of crime	1.211 (1)	1.857 (12)
Giving evidence in court	1.231 (2)	2.000 (14)
Handling drink driving offenders	1.233 (3)	1.760 (10)
Obtaining statements from witnesses	1.259 (4)	1.449 (2)
Arresting offenders	1.272 (5)	1.639 (7)
Dealing with domestic disputes	1.293 (6)	1.551 (4)
Working with community to make neighbourhood safer	1.293 (6)	1.719 (9)
Responding to sudden death calls	1.333 (8)	2.381 (23)
Talking to community to help identify policing problems	1.361 (9)	2.061 (16)
Carrying out a random breath test	1.367 (10)	1.599 (5)
Dealing with street incidents	1.381 (11)	1.435 (1)
Providing education to young people about road safety	1.456 (12)	2.490 (27)
Completing Criminal Offence reports	1.503 (13)	1.517 (3)
Foot patrol	1.517 (14)	1.605 (6)
Providing crime prevention education	1.524 (15)	2.401 (25)
Cautioning juveniles	1.537 (16)	1.653 (8)
Doing search for drugs	1.537 (16)	2.395 (24)
Handling missing persons reports	1.619 (18)	2.340 (21)
Crowd control	1.707 (19)	2.122 (18)
Stopping and searching suspects	1.762 (20)	2.347 (22)
Conducting raids	1.762 (20)	2.816 (29)
Random vehicle patrol	1.769 (22)	1.952 (13)
Issuing warrants	1.816 (23)	2.299 (20)
Controlling traffic	1.830 (24)	2.245 (19)
Issuing Traffic Offence Notices	1.884 (25)	1.822 (11)
Handling neighbourhood disputes	1.912 (26)	2.014 (15)
Handling exhibits	1.932 (27)	2.422 (26)
Dealing with the sick or elderly	2.000 (28)	2.568 (28)
Dealing with noisy parties	2.224 (29)	2.102 (17)

Q: Listed below are some basic policing tasks of a Constable. For each of the following, rate how _important_ you believe each of these functions to be *and* how _often_ you think that you will be performing these tasks. For each of these, please write the number which corresponds to your choice where:

Importance:
1. Very important
2. Important
3. Not important
4. Not at all important

Frequency of Performance:
1. Very often
2. Often
3. Not very often
4. Never

evidence in court, handling drink driving offenders, obtaining statements from witnesses, and arresting offenders. Recruits were well aware that police often performed tasks that were not necessarily important. For example, responding to sudden death calls, giving evidence in court, and examining the scene of a crime were perceived as important tasks that were not frequently performed; whereas issuing traffic offence notices, dealing with noisy parties, handling neighbourhood disputes, dealing with street incidents, and completing criminal offence reports were perceived as frequently performed but not very important. Obtaining statements from witnesses, dealing with domestic disputes, and arresting offenders were tasks perceived as both relatively important and frequently performed.

When asked to rate a list of goals of policing and police organizations in terms of their importance (see Table 3.6), recruits demonstrated a clear preference for more traditional 'crime fighting' goals such as providing rapid response to emergency calls, enforcing the law fairly, and reducing incidence of crime and violence. Goals more aligned with a 'community policing' approach such as increasing citizens' feelings of safety, and involving the community in crime prevention or in addressing local problems, were rated somewhat secondary in importance. Professional development or 'human resource' management goals were ranked even lower in importance, except for 'ensure equal opportunity in all aspects of employment,' which ranked fourth, just below 'reduce incidence of crime and violence.' Significantly, 'increase public satisfaction with the police service' and 'make police more accountable to the community' were considered among the least important goals.

When asked about their career aspirations, the great majority of recruits (82 per cent) wanted to be working in a specialized area such as criminal investigation five years after completing their training. A sizeable proportion[10] (43 per cent) indicated that they wanted to be working on the streets. A small minority wanted to be teaching at the police academy (9 per cent), or working in administration (4 per cent) or other jobs within the service (8 per cent), while a few were undecided (10 per cent). None of the recruits expected that they would have left the police service in five years' time. When asked if they would be satisfied to stay in uniform for the rest of their career, 42 per cent said yes, 21 per cent said no, and 37 per cent indicated they weren't sure. A large majority of recruits (84 per cent) intended to undertake further studies in the next five years.

TABLE 3.6
Goals of policing and police organizations (Survey 1, N=147)

Goals	Mean rating
Provide rapid response to emergency calls	1.061
Enforce the law fairly	1.075
Reduce incidence of crime and violence	1.075
Ensure equal opportunity in all aspects of employment	1.247
Increase citizens' feelings of safety	1.313
Involve the community in crime prevention	1.320
Involve the community in addressing local problems	1.388
Improve education and training of police personnel	1.418
Improve professional conduct of police personnel	1.429
Improve methods and strategies for catching criminals	1.456
Provide technological support for police work	1.459
Provide professional development opportunities for personnel	1.466
Manage resources efficiently	1.469
Enhance service to victims	1.483
Encourage the use of negotiation and conflict resolution	1.493
Enhance the investigative capacity of the police service	1.538
Increase public satisfaction with the police service	1.585
Improve quality of working conditions	1.685
Increase the number of patrol vehicles	1.685
Make police more accountable to the community	1.966
Increase resource/training of specialist weapons/riot squads	2.061

Q: Listed below are some goals of policing and police organisations. Please rate these goals according to their importance to you.
1. Very important
2. Somewhat important
3. Not very important
4. Not at all important

Preparation for Joining

Most recruits had put some significant effort into preparing for police work, either before or after submitting an application. Forty-five of the 73 interviewees talked about specific ways they had prepared. Two types of preparation were mentioned often: undertaking academic studies such as HSC[11] or TAFE or skills-based training such as keyboard and first aid (21 interviewees), and gathering information about policing by obtaining brochures and publications, speaking to police officers, or visiting police stations (21 interviewees).

Seven interviewees mentioned working out to improve their fitness:

I had to train a lot to get through the physical test and I was very happy when I did make it, yeah, 'cause I'd put a lot of hard work to make it there ... I was training for about four months before I put my application in. So a lot of hard work ... 'cause I knew you had to be fit and I was far from it. (1 / 20-year-old female)

All the acquisition of academic qualifications, skills, and physical fitness was related to the admission requirements of the NSWPS. Some interviewees said they had deliberately delayed applying in order to gain more life experience. This variously involved apprenticeship in a trade, working in another occupation, or travelling. A few interviewees either did 'work experience' with the police or took policing-related jobs to get a 'foot in the door.' One recruit went to university first, in order to broaden her knowledge and give herself time to mature:

The only reason I did go away to uni was when I came straight out of school I didn't feel I was mature enough to handle it. 'Cause I don't think police work is something that an immature person can handle ... like, it's not, it's not an easy occupation. It's something that's very stressful, especially for a female. So, I knew what I was getting myself into and I didn't feel I was ready for that ... I think university ... developed my confidence in myself – confidence to be, like, sort of, not be scared to express who I am, not be scared to, you know, express my own ideals... I think that is very important. (1 / 22-year-old female)

One type of preparation not often mentioned involved an attitudinal shift – a distancing between the recruit and friends who were not on the 'straight and narrow':

People that are into drugs and, and who, who wouldn't have any concern for me going into the Police Service. They wouldn't care and they might be carrying on themselves when they come over and they wouldn't care ... and so I eliminated a lot of friends before that ... I just went bang – changed the number, changed both my phone numbers ... and that was it. (1 / 29-year-old female)

Initial Reaction to Acceptance

Given the amount of preparation and anticipation the recruits went through before joining the police, it is not surprising that almost all of them reported being pleased with the success of their applications. Just over half the interviewees (39 of 72) said they were overjoyed when they received the news they had been accepted into the academy. They used words like 'rapt,' 'ecstatic,' 'over the moon,' 'unreal' to describe their feelings. Others were a bit more restrained. Seven said they were 'very happy,' 'delighted,' 'thrilled,' and similiar, while 12 simply said they were pleased or happy. A few had mixed feelings – they were happy but also anxious or overwhelmed, or simply relieved.

One recruit who wanted to join the police when she was in Year 10 but worked in a job she didn't like described her reaction this way:

> I was so excited I resigned. I ran around the place, 'Yes, yes, yes! Look, I'm sorry I have to leave now.' I said, 'You have made my week, you have made my year!' just because I'd been trying so long. (1 / 25-year-old female)

Another recruit was also extremely pleased by the news of his acceptance: 'You'd have to have it on videotape. I was jumping around ... I was stoked ... I was walking around with a smile on my face all day ... I felt unreal' (1 / 19-year-old male). Another recruit was both ecstatic and deeply relieved:

> [I was] ecstatic. My fiance's mother can vouch for that, 'cause I got the phone call, and once I hung up – because it's taken me seventeen months to wait for that phone call, was twelve months' study, five months for the application to go through, and it was just built up for that much – when I hung up I just cried. It was just thorough relief. I was just so, yeah, so relieved. (1 / 26-year-old male)

A handful of recruits felt anxious about living away from home for the first time, or being away from their family for six months.

Anticipating the Job

Recruits in the cohort were drawn to policing for both altruistic and instrumental reasons. They were interested in helping people and serving the community; they were also attracted to a secure job with good promotion prospects. Most were keen on what they saw as the varied, nonroutine, and exciting nature of the work. They regarded policing as a highly prestigious occupation, and police officers as top-rate in both honesty and professionalism. This idealized vision of policing was not primarily the result of media influence; it was also grounded in recruits' interactions with police they already knew personally (as relatives, neighbours, or friends) or had met in the course of seeking information about the job. They knew about the negative side of policing – the existence of dishonest or corrupt officers, unpleasant aspects of the job, and so on – but they were more comfortable sustaining the mythic vision of policing, the one that emphasizes its noble and courageous elements and focuses on crime fighting and law enforcement. Most recruits had gone through periods of schooling, physical training, and job experience to prepare for admission to the service. In no small way, they had reoriented their habitus (shaped by many years of socialization in the family, the school, and the workplace) to maximize its anticipated 'fit' with their chosen occupation. Acceptance to the police service marked a joyous and triumphant end to many months (even years, in some cases) of anxiety and anticipation.

Ironically, even in this phase of anticipatory socialization, in New South Wales the mythic vision of policing was being eroded, although many of the recruits were unaware of it. For example, the move toward community policing since the mid-1980s, and the policy changes designed to encourage the recruitment of women and ethnic minorities, had meant that even in the images promoted by the police organization, police work was no longer portrayed in terms of physicality and crime fighting; rather, the emphasis was on service, support, and empathy ('Lean on me'). This new vision was not lost on the female recruit who felt that the NSWPS was a 'good employer of women.' Other reforms, such as the complete overhaul of the academy curriculum toward a 'full professional model' of policing, were even more subversive of the 'crime fighting' model that most recruits tacitly embraced. Again, most recruits would be totally unaware of this shift in vision as they entered the academy. In the next chapter we describe their initial excitement and subsequent disappointment with the academy.

4

Learning at the Academy

CHRIS DEVERY

Recruits' first sustained encounters with the police organization occur at the police academy. After months and, for some, years of anticipation, entry to the police academy represents a highly significant event for them. It involves the crossing of a boundary[1] – from being an outsider to being an insider in an organization they have longed to join. It matters little at this initial stage that they occupy the outermost fringe of the organization or that their continued membership depends on the successful completion of training. This is the stage of organizational socialization when recruits are likely to experience a 'reality shock' (Hughes 1958), depending on whether their expectations about the organization are accurate. If their expectations differ considerably from their initial experience of the organization, this period of 'breaking in' may require a 'destructive phase' or 'unfreezing,' during which individuals adjust their expectations or face disillusionment (Van Maanen 1976).

As discussed in the last chapter, recruits in the cohort went through a period of anticipatory socialization before entering the organization. Their idealized view of the policing occupation demonstrated their interest and investment (Bourdieu's *illusio*) in the 'game' of policing – and there was no doubt in their minds that 'the game is worth playing' (Bourdieu and Wacquant 1992: 98). Many of them embraced the mythic vision of police as heroic crime fighters, and were totally unaware of the transformation of policing philosophy in New South Wales that saw a 'new' model of professional policing built into the recruit training curriculum. In this chapter we describe the experiences of the recruits as they underwent the first three phases of recruit training: eight weeks at the academy (Phase 1), followed by four weeks observing in the operational field (Phase 2) and a further fourteen weeks at the academy (Phase 3). As will be clear from the interviewees' accounts, recruits' experiences during these phases can only be understood in the context of the changes in the field of policing in New South Wales – in particular, the challenge to the crime-fighting vision of policing, a challenge embedded in the new training curriculum. We therefore begin with a brief history of the development of PREP in New South Wales, before describing the cohort's experiences in the first three phases and analysing their reflections on this experience.

History of the Police Recruit Education Programme (PREP)

Unlike traditional academies discussed in classic studies of police socialization (Van Maanen 1973), the academy in New South Wales was the focus of a conscious attempt to reform the nature of policing in the state. The explicit role of police education in NSW was not to reproduce police culture, but rather to effect change. As mentioned in chapter 2, this history of reform commenced with the Lusher Inquiry, which was appointed by the NSW government in 1979 to investigate the structure, organization, and management of the police force. Justice Lusher presented a wide-ranging report to the NSW Parliament in 1981. The report criticized police training as a narrowly focused lecture program conducted in an atmosphere of strict discipline:

> The highly authoritarian approach to the Academy Administration as indicated in the preface to the training handbook and by the classroom discipline, is no doubt aimed at inducting civilians into the ways of what is essentially a disciplined service. Such an approach however is very foreign to the modern high school graduate and cannot be expected to encourage individual initiative. Nor will it produce police who adopt a thinking, analytical approach to police problems. (1981: 363)

At the time of the Lusher Inquiry, recruits were being trained in a twelve-week course at the old academy at Redfern, an inner suburb of Sydney. Lusher's recommendations were radical: they included opening police education to a wider range of outside influences, employing civilian lecturers, selecting police staff at the academy according to their skills and qualifications as educators, establishing links to an existing tertiary institution, and extending the training program to a minimum of twenty-four weeks. Lusher also made a series of recommendations regarding the management of police education; these were aimed at reducing or moderating the police force's influence on education. For example, the academy was to be placed under the control of a police board, and an advisory council consisting of police and academics was to be established, with responsibility for formulating and implementing training policies.

As Chan (1997: 120) has argued, the appointment of John Avery as police commissioner in 1984 'was a turning point in the policing history of NSW.' Avery was seen as an 'academic' – which in the police vernacular meant that he had 'been off wandering around universities and not doing some real police work' and therefore was not 'really a cop' (senior police, in Chan 1997: 120). Avery was a visionary who brought about fundamental change in the NSWPS, and who was driven by the conception of community policing he had outlined in his book *Police: Force or Service?* (1981). Education was one of the key components in Avery's package of reforms. In 1985 the Police Board established an Interim Police Education and Training Advisory Council (IPETAC) on which academics from universities and colleges were represented. The purpose of this council was 'to advise on policy formulation, course development and evaluation of educational programs for police' (NSW Police Board 1992).[2] The essential structure and philosophy of the PREP program was established in a series of reports prepared by IPETAC between 1986 and 1987.

IPETAC's vision of police education still exerts an influence on post-PREP police recruit training in NSW. Fundamental to this vision was that education should support the emerging concept of community policing. Community policing would require police to interact with the community in ways that were new to them. Consequently, IPETAC argued that the 'limited expert' model of police education, with its narrow technical focus, should be replaced with 'an integrated model that takes account of the variety of conceptual frameworks needed to produce effective operational decision making' (IPETAC 1986: 17). The second IPETAC report distinguished three vectors of police education: foundational knowledge, skills attainment, and attitudinal development:

> Foundational knowledge involves an understanding of the social context and fundamental concepts of police service; and recognition that policing takes place within a criminal justice system, and in association with emergency and welfare services.

Skills attainment involves the development of high levels of technical and professional competence, and includes process and interpersonal and communication skills.

Attitudinal development involves an evaluation of personal dispositions and values (including one's own) and an understanding of the relationship between these and those of the various components of multi-cultural Australia: it involves also commitment to professional service, and the adoption of personal responsibility and personal ethical standards consistent with service to all citizens. (1986: 14)

In arguing that police education should embrace these three components, IPETAC was defining a model that it hoped would support the operational and organizational reforms that Avery was implementing. The Police Board commented in 1992:

The PREP program introduces recruits to 'knowing why' as well as 'knowing how and what.' It is competency based and rests on community based strategies of policing. It recognizes that Australian society is diverse. Ethical issues are acknowledged and dealt with. The use of discretionary powers and complexity of issues is taken into account. (NSW Police Board 1992: 2)

IPETAC also recommended appropriate methods of teaching, and wrote a draft curriculum for the new program. Teaching and learning strategies were to be based on the following notions:

1. That the knowledge, skills and attitudes to be learned by, and developed in, police recruits require a *vocational and professional* preparatory education;
2. That the knowledge, skills and attitudes involved relate to an *inter-disciplinary* (or trans-disciplinary) base in the liberal arts/social sciences traditions;
3. That the notion of 'training' is far too narrow a concept for learning the concepts and competencies associated with complex police practice – nothing less than *'police education'* is required, incorporating as this implies high levels of skills attainment; and
4. That police vocational education is best achieved through *alternative experiences in-residence and in-service* providing as this does the opportunity of reflecting upon experience, debriefing and conceptual and personal development. (IPETAC 1986: 26)

When PREP was established in July 1988, it was an eighteen-month program embodying many of the educational principles and structures proposed by the IPETAC report. As outlined in chapter 2, it involved eight weeks' residential education (Phase 1), four weeks' field observation (Phase 2), and a further fourteen weeks' residential (Phase 3). At the end of Phase 3, students were attested as probationary constables. They then embarked on forty-nine weeks of on-the-job training attached to a local area. Probationers returned to the academy for two weeks (Phase 5) for final assessment, graduation, and confirmation.

PREP was in a sense intended to subvert traditional policing models and values. It was instituted explicitly as part of an agenda to sweep away traditional 'crime fighting' models of policing – models associated with the 'limited expert' model of training – and to establish community-based policing predicated on a 'full professional' model of the 'reflective practitioner.' It is not surprising, then, that PREP was controversial. The degree to which it was seen as the lynchpin of organizational and even professional reforms is demonstrated by sections of the 1990–1 version of PREP Course Documentation (NSWPS 1992). The document speaks of the 'late 20th century policing revolution' as the context for PREP and suggests that policing was a discipline stuck in 'Plato's Cave' – police officers were 'Platonic troglodytes [who were] expert at living lives chained in the dark, watching shadows' (NSWPS 1992: 24). According to this extraordinary document, PREP was part of 'Avery's Perestroika,' and amounted to 'a professional survival kit outside the Cave [for] the young, tender bright and largely idealistic new members of the NSW Police Service, [who] were tarred or signified with a new brush and paint – the Police Recruit Education Program' (29). While this rhetoric disappeared from later editions of the course documentation, it suggests the degree to which the PREP program was identified with radical organizational reforms.

An independent evaluation of PREP was carried out in 1990 by the Centre for Applied Research in Education (CARE) at the University of East Anglia. This evaluation was generally positive. In contrast to the highly authoritarian training criticized by Lusher, the CARE report noted:

The decline in authoritarianism and the introduction of a more relaxed atmosphere offers students a much greater variety of role models of police officers and of images of policing and of society than were available before ... PREP also, at the very least, raises consciousness of the discretionary nature of policing and of the complexity in which that discretion is located. There is evidence to suggest that, with respect to issues of sexism and racism, for instance, which are often associated with police behaviour, students are made aware of their own prejudices, which is a first step to their control and possible diminution. (CARE 1990: iii)

The CARE report further praised the NSW Police Academy as 'not the kind of authoritarian, punitive environment that, prior to the reforms, we found to be characteristic of British police training, environments in which there seemed to be a systematic attempt to deconstruct recruits as persons and rebuild them as instruments of policy' (128). Indeed, the report remarked: 'Given the promising start that PREP has made, due attention to its present limitations, and renewed commitment to its values and ideals, we believe that PREP will be the best recruit education programme in the world within five years' (1990: v).

All very nice, but CARE also found that in some respects PREP had failed to live up to the high ambitions of IPETAC. CARE argued that the combined effect of increasing numbers of students, diversification of demands on the academy, and the tendency to 'raid' the human and space/material resources of PREP to meet new needs elsewhere, was to overwhelm a management system that was still based on the traditional command–control hierarchical model. What was needed at the academy was educational management (154). In a much-quoted passage, CARE asserted: 'It is not going too far to say that PREP is badly in need of protection against the organization that created it' (157).

CARE also identified problems with integrating the theoretical and the practical in PREP. Interviews with students and staff revealed that both were sceptical of the value of foundational courses, especially those delivered by what was then the School of Applied Social Science (CARE 1990: ch. 4). The CARE report interpreted criticisms of the theoretical/contextual content of the course as having less to do with resistance to new policing values and more to do with a failure to ensure that theoretical and contextual issues were plainly relevant to operational practice (112–13). This is why CARE recommended that the core of the curriculum should involve studying real operational situations and that reflection about cases should form the core of the learning process. The report also made recommendations about staff development, the management of field phases, the involvement of teachers in curriculum development, and the structure and management of the academy.

In 1994 the Police Board undertook another review of the academy.

This one came about as a result of a submission to the deputy commissioner in June 1994, which raised issues of morale at the academy. In response, the board appointed a review committee to inquire into the academy's organization. This committee reported back to the board in September 1994 – a remarkably short time, considering the sweeping nature of its recommendations. Its report (PARC 1994) focused mainly on the clash between the operational and educational cultures at the academy. The review identified a number of reasons for this clash, including the development of a series of 'independent kingdoms' within the academy, each of them responsible for different programs. As a result there was a failure to maintain strong educational coordination across the academy. The committee recommended restructuring the academy as a series of schools that would service all the programs, supported by various directorates. The committee made twenty-three recommendations in all, on issues such as the ratio of unsworn to sworn teaching staff, the opening of positions to civilian applicants, and the development of a common set of conditions of service for all teaching staff, whether they were sworn or not. The PARC recommendations, once implemented, resulted in a profound restructuring of the academy (see chapter 2). However, the cohort that forms the subject of this research underwent their training under the old program, and so was not influenced by these events.

Teaching at the Academy: Views of Instructors

The academy instructors[3] we interviewed were highly supportive of the PREP agenda, and saw themselves as having an important role to play in providing professional role models for students:

> I think [students] class their tutor as a model. And you can see the difference in class, in students, by what tutors teach them ... So the first thing is being professional as a tutor. You are to be professional in every aspect. And if they see that, then they'll use that as a role model. Or they may. Some you can't change. 'Cause they're going to be unprofessional whatever, that's, *you can't* change that. (Inst6)

A general theme running through the interviews with instructors was that one of the main roles of an instructor is to mould the attitudes of students. Many of the tutors we interviewed saw changing students' attitudes as the personal business of the teacher. Tutors often declared that encouraging certain attitudes and behaviours was their primary task. In particular, they addressed racism and sexism, either by changing attitudes or by weeding out students who had unsuitable attitudes:

Or even if they're just walking around and they're, you know, saying, especially in class, saying comments, you know, racist, homophobic or sexist comments ... Well, in my class I pull them up straightaway. And I pull them aside and talk to them at the end of the class. And I think, if they're going to be professional they can't really have those sort of opinions. (InstC)

We don't only teach them practical policing skills like the OS [Officer Survival] stuff and academic type things, but we need to try and direct their attitudes, I guess, and to show them that ... by virtue of our job, we are really not entitled to enforce the law selectively in any way. (InstB)

One tutor we interviewed had a relatively sophisticated, if somewhat resigned, view of police education:

Oh, we definitely do cover ethics in, in policing, personal lives and so forth. The big problem I have is that, whilst we do cover ethics, we've got a lot of other important professional police initiatives [to cover]. I don't believe we have sufficient time here to change the baggage that they come into the academy with. Their vices, their unethical conduct, their socialization processes prior to coming to the academy. I believe that, their parents, peers, and teachers have had a large influence on what their ethical values are and they come here to play the game, they sit through the sessions, they say what we expect them to hear and they proceed out of here. (InstA)

In other words, this tutor assumed that recruits came to the academy with a habitus already formed, and that any appearance of change was no more than a strategic compliance to fulfil training requirements. This tutor regarded the Phase 4 field training as 'the most important aspect of the entire PREP program,' and also as more hazardous and dangerous, and potentially destructive of good practice:

There's a wide gap between the field and the academic learning. The field basically presumes academy staff teaches irrelevant material to what a police officer requires and they do everything in their power to continually undermine what we are trying to achieve. I guess they don't see the need to develop a problem-solving police officer that turns out to be professional ... They're trying to promote the reactionary model of police officer as opposed to the progressive police officer. (InstA)

A number of instructors we interviewed contended that the operational field was the largest obstacle to the job of producing professional police officers: 'I feel here we're teaching them by the book, but once they get out there they can pick up some very bad habits' (Inst5).

According to one instructor, the process of indoctrination started at the academy, when students started to mix with police who were attending the academy for senior courses and other activities:

There is a police culture. And although not promoted here, I think it starts here. Because they're mixing with other police here at the academy doing courses and things. They see what they do, they see how they behave, and they go out into Phase 2 where they're observing police and see what police are doing in the station and I think that starts their culture. They get this 'you look after yourself, you look after your mates, you look after the police' – you know, the culture's [ingrained] into them then. (InstD)

A number of instructors touched on the lack of common purpose between the academy and the operational field:

I think the other primary thing is when you're talking about linkage between training here and the field is a big gap, a yawning gap between the academy and the police force. Those perceptions and also credibility ... They believe we come here to hide and we have no policing experience. (Inst4)

For another instructor, the problem was that the operational field expected the academy to produce fully formed police officers, and failed to understand that learning continues in the field:

I think the people in the field don't take into account that students haven't finished their training when they leave here in Phase 3. When they go out to Phase 4 I think they expect them to come out a bundle of knowledge. I don't know any policeman that's ever left the NSW Police Academy with all the knowledge, and can walk into a station and do things. And to train these people properly you're looking at eighteen months here. Minimum.

Just to teach them basics ... But the blokes in the field expect them to walk into the station and be fully operational and that they can walk out and just let them go. They forget that they're still continuing their training while they're in Phase 4. And you also get the old 'bullshit castle' and all the rest of the things thrown at us, and I think that's something that I don't know how it would ever be addressed but it's something that needs to be addressed. (InstD)

It seems that by and large, the academy instructors supported the reformist intentions of the PREP architects. Within the (sub)field of the police academy, cultural capital was associated with the reformist ideals of PREP as set by IPETAC. Instructors saw their role as changing students' attitudes and teaching them the correct way to do things, and were aware that in this there was a conflict with the interests of operational policing. In one respect at least, the reform of police education had been relatively successful: academy staff seemed to support the notion of contextual, skills, and attitudinal development through education, and took their role in preparing students quite seriously.

Experience of Phase 1

As mentioned earlier, Phase 1 of PREP consisted of eight weeks of residential training at the police academy. The aim of Phase 1 was to introduce recruits – designated as 'student police officers' at this stage – to the 'foundational studies underpinning professional police work and to an appreciation of the generic competencies of policing' (NSWPS 1993: 42). The emphasis was on providing students with an understanding of the social, legal, and organizational context of police work as well as its ethical and moral demands. The phase 1 curriculum was divided into eight blocks, with an introductory segment on the context of policing. 'Strands' 1 and 2 dealt with society, law, and policing, while strand 3 focused on negotiation and communication skills in police/citizen encounters. Strand 4 introduced students to the legal system, the importance of human and civil rights in a democratic society, and the role of police within the system of government. Strand 5 explored issues of police powers and police discretion and introduced problem-solving skills. In strands 6 and 7, students were exposed to social perspectives of criminality and to ethical issues in policing. Finally, strand 8 was concerned with basic police processes such as investigation, questioning and arrest of suspects, care and processing of an arrested person, and various court and trial procedures (NSWPS 1993: 43).

Overall, the curriculum reflected the liberal reform agenda set out by the Lusher Inquiry and continued by IPETAC. IPETAC's three main concerns – 'foundational knowledge,' 'skills attainment,' and 'attitudinal development' – were the cornerstones of PREP. In broad terms, Phase 1 concentrated on foundational knowledge and attitudinal development, and Phases 2, 3, and 4 on the development of practical skills, in the context of the foundational material in Phase 1. The interview and questionnaire material discussed later in this chapter will suggest that the distinction between contextual, foundational knowledge and practical knowledge was readily apparent to students. Moreover, members of the cohort, as they gained experience, often became highly critical of the program's foundational content.

The Physical Setting

The NSW Police Academy is in the town of Goulburn, around 200 km southwest of Sydney in the Southern Tablelands. The campus was built in the 1970s as a teacher's college, and before it became the police academy in 1984 had been a college of advanced education. The campus comprises a number of yellow brick buildings arranged around a quadrangle (to the north) and a parade ground (to the south). Facilities for students are sparse. There is a large dining hall but no café; there is a gymnasium but little recreational space. There is a bar on campus, but most after-hours activity takes place in the pubs and restaurants in town.

Goulburn is a pleasant town of around 20,000, in a valley. The winter climate is cold by Australian standards, and especially by the standards of most recruits, who come from Sydney. Given that the cohort of this study arrived at Goulburn in May, which is late autumn in Australia, a number of students commented on the climate. One recruit summed up her first experience of the academy this way: 'Cold. [Laugh] The first thing I thought of "I'm going to die of frostbite" [laugh]' (1/24-year-old female). The physical distance from Sydney also represents a social and psychological distance for recruits, many of whom were away from family and friends for the first time. As one of the recruits put it, the academy was a 'new environment and all the strange faces and [it was] sad to say goodbye to family and friends' (1/25-year-old male).

First Day at the Academy

The first significant transformation in the lives of people who are becoming police officers is from civilian to recruit. This transformation begins when applicants are informed that they have have been accepted, and lasts until they present themselves to the police academy. As we saw in chapter 3, recruits had a high opinion of their chosen occupation. This is consistent with Van Maanen's (1973: 410) observation that recruits join the police 'with a high degree of normative identification with what they perceive to be the goals and values of the organization.' In chapter 3 we also described how recruits often undertook a significant amount of preparation during the recruitment process. Many said they were elated – or at least very happy – when they received the news that they had been accepted into the academy. A minority had mixed feelings – both happy and anxious – or they were simply relieved that they had been successful.

When asked in interviews to describe their first day at the academy, students expressed a similarly wide range of emotions. Facing an eight-week residential program away from family and friends, they were generally nervous and apprehensive. These feelings were sometimes relatively positive – 'Really nervous. Anxious too. Eager to learn' (1/24-year-old male) – and sometimes negative – 'Shit scared.' [Q: Yeah. What were you scared of?] 'Just, like, the whole new environment' (1/22-year-old male). Not surprisingly, some students expressed feeling lonely, isolated, and homesick in their first days at the academy:

> We have one girl that, she was really bad. Her parents brought her down here and she's really, really homesick. We've taken her to the priest and said, 'Talk to him,' and she was a mess and actually she ... went out the last two nights, tonight and last night, she's actually coming to terms with it. Life away from home. (1/22-year-old female)

While most students expressed apprehension, a number were very positive: 'It's finally here. I'm here ... I basically wore a grin most of the night – I wanted to be here and I wanted to get down here' (1/24-year-old male).

Induction and the Beginning of Group Identification

It is clear from the interviews that students' expectations about policing and police training influenced their feelings about their first days at the academy. Students reported a wide range of reactions to, and opinions on, their experiences over the first few days. Aspects regarding which there was considerable variation of opinion included the organization of the academy, discipline, expectations about course materials, and professionalism. Thus, although the academy experience was relatively generic, recruits interpreted and understood their experiences in diverse ways. Some of this variation may have been due to differences in individual histories and in the habitus they brought to training.

A common impression in the first days was of chaos, disorganization, and busyness. There was a lot of administration and form filling. Recruits were given information about the routines of academy life, the nature of the course, and expected standards of behaviour:

> Well, we started at two o'clock and we finished at six, and the next day, the Monday, felt like it was half as long as that. And, there's so many things sitting there, and you're filling out forms, you're getting constantly, 'Take this, do this, do that, go here, go there,' and you're going, 'I don't ... have any idea where I'm going or what I'm doing.' But everyone was in the same boat. Everyone was feeling the same way. (1/22-year-old female)

Many recruits were overwhelmed by the experience, and much of the information they were given seemed not to have stuck: 'There were lots of rules and things but I was too nervous to worry about them, I didn't really hear all that stuff' (1/21-year-old male). These responses were very similar to those reported in the CARE report (1990: 19), which characterized recruits' first impressions as 'overwhelming.'

Recruits resorted to a number of strategies to cope with the difficulties of the first few days of training. Some relied on past experience and a determination to get through: 'I came down with no expectations of the academy, only expectations on me' (1/29-year-old female). More often, however, recruits reported that fellow students, the senior class, or staff helped them a great deal to cope with the first days. Some students reported that having a friend on the course helped them get through the first week; more commonly, recruits told us that a sense of belonging and mutual support helped them adjust to academy life. Staff seemed to encourage this approach:

> But with still everyone on the floor [in the residential tower], we're very good friends. The camaraderie's just already starting to really be good. And there's not unhealthy competition here. There's no one sort of want-

ing to closely guard their like notes saying, 'Oh, no, he'll probably get the upper hand in the exam' or something. Everyone's going, 'Yeah, look at this,' and everyone's bending over backwards to help each other. Which is really good. They promote that team sort of environment, which is essential for being out on the streets, 'cause you need that. You don't work alone in this job. I'm pretty confident I made the right choice [of career]. (1/23-year-old male)

This sense of teamwork was also reflected in the learning exercises. In 'case management sessions,' students worked intensively in teams before presenting in class. One student thought it was 'a better way to learn' compared with high school:

I thought it was going to be, we sit down, they give us the work – you know, like a teacher at school. But it's actually group session, really. We get into group talks, and they've been giving us the work, we go and study it up and he [the tutor] puts us on the right track. [Q: Do you like that better than the way they did it at school?] Oh, yeah. Oh, it's a better way to learn. 'Cause everyone is on the right track that way ... Back at school everyone's competing against each other. You get stragglers and you've got people going, but everyone helps each other. [Q: They tell you, you know, that you've got to help each other and get each other through?] They do. They tell you. (1/19-year-old male)

Other interviewees commented that the staff promoted solidarity and mutual support: 'Senior officers tell you pretty much, "Stay off alcohol, stick up for your friends, but don't stick up for them when it's going to jeopardize something"' (1/24-year-old male). Sometimes this message focused on the public's lack of understanding of police:

Our tutor said that you'll find that you'll lose friends – not close friends, but people ... don't understand, and then you'll sort of be frowned upon. And it's not that you're ashamed of your job, but sometimes ... other people don't appreciate you as much. They feel that you're ... I mean, I suppose you are a police officer twenty-four hours a day and I guess that's what they think too. (1/20-year-old female)

Some recruits had very specific views about on-the-job friendships and relationships. A number of them made the analogy between the police service and a family:

Yeah. Definitely make life-long friends. I think probably to definitely achieve, you know, [be] part of that family. 'Cause it is a, like, a virtual subculture, you know, the police service. I mean, it's like you've got to fit in to that subculture. (1/22-year-old female)

You've got a lot of pride in being a police officer, 'cause you've achieved something. But also in wearing the uniform ... Like, as it was explained to us, like a part of a family. (1/22-year-old male)

These responses indicate that very early on in training, students were becoming aware of the pressures that policing can place on old friendships and relationships. As we saw in chapter 3, these pressures can start even before recruits enter the academy. Many students reported that when their friends found out they were joining the police, they responded by cracking jokes. Even light-hearted responses highlight the impact that joining the police can have on friendships and relationships. For example, in a society in which recreational drug use is not uncommon, some recruits will undoubtedly have friends who are recreational drug users. In such circumstances, a change in status from civilian to student police officer and eventually to probationary constable is certain to place heavy strain on relationships or present significant moral and ethical challenges to recruits.[4]

When asked whether it was possible to develop close-knit relationships so early on in training (this would have been no later than the fourth day), one recruit made particular mention of the senior class and the staff:

Oh, definitely. Yeah ... I mean, the ... senior class here, you know, [class number], they're brilliant ... you couldn't hope for more. But right up to the officers, you know, they're all so friendly and they know that in six months' time we're going to be colleagues and they're doing their best to make us fit in, and I think that's really helpful. (1/22-year-old female)

Certainly, many of the students were initially very impressed by the staff at the academy:

A lot of the tutors are good and ... want everyone to pass. [Laugh] They don't want anyone to fail, you know. And they'll do everything, and the class is doing everything to help everyone else. (1/male, age >30)

In terms of help and support, students were most enthusiastic about the assistance of the senior class:

> I was really nervous. If the older students hadn't looked after us I would probably have left. It was very difficult, especially when you arrive and that and you don't know anyone. The others just kind of came up and said who they were and asked you if you were a new student and that and made us feel welcome. (1/21-year-old male)

At the time of this research, classes were organized into subclasses of eighteen to twenty-two students. The senior subclasses organized themselves to take the respective junior subclasses out on their first Thursday night at the academy. This night out introduced the newcomers to a tradition at the academy, Thursday being the traditional 'night out' since most people attending courses at the academy went home on Friday afternoon. It would be tempting to consider this bonding between the senior and junior classes as an important mode of informal occupational socialization. However, there is evidence that the relationship between successive classes was not always so friendly:

> Yeah. We've all fitted in well. I've met the senior class. They said to us, well, the senior class before them treated them like dirt ... didn't bother even like mingling with them. So they said they weren't going to do that to us. (1/23-year-old male)

The interviews revealed that generally, the first few days were disconcerting and very busy. Supportive interpersonal relationships, individual friendships, and support networks within subclasses and on residential floors became essential mechanisms for coping. The students characterized these relationships as essential to operational policing. Staff at the academy as well as the senior class actively reinforced and encouraged these values. The recruits reacted positively to their initial experiences in part because they had expected a relatively harsh, unfriendly academy. They did not find one. Their lives disrupted, away from home and loved ones, they turned to one another for support and were pleased to find that the academy's culture provided it generously. In this environment, gaining the social capital of friendship and mutual support was absolutely vital.

Discipline at the Academy

Discipline is a much debated issue in police education. Some practitioners feel that the discipline in the academy reflects an outmoded command–control management model that prevails in policing organizations. Others argue that the police service is a command–control organization and that students must be equipped with the skills to survive and operate in that context. Commentators (Sykes 1989: 292–3) have emphasized the connection between militarism in policing and attempts to control the power of police through hierarchical accountability and rule-bound behaviour. Fielding considers discipline 'the essential thing many recruits emphasize about the police': 'Discipline may be directed inward or outward. The police are disciplined by an administrative and behavioural code as an hierarchical organization, and they apply discipline as a check on disorder and infraction' (1988: 46). Fielding is suggesting here that discipline is a theme that structures relationships between police, especially in the context of the rank structure. However, he is also suggesting that discipline is a tool that police use to control the behaviour of the public. Conceived in this way, the disciplinary training at the academy has an internal and an external role, and it is perhaps in the context of discipline that students are first exposed to models of interaction with the public.

Among the students during the first week of training, however, there was considerable consensus that the standards of discipline were not what they had expected. Some students were very positive about the disciplinary expectations of the academy staff, but many more were surprised to find that the discipline was less than they had expected, and that police staff were friendlier and more approachable. The students we interviewed expressed views on the academy environment that were by and large consistent with the observations of the CARE review. A number of students expressed excitement about the discipline, or at least indicated that they considered it a necessary and expected part of police education:

> As soon as we got here they [put you] into the lecture room, they [told you] everything ... 'You can do this, you can't do that, you can't do this, if you do this you'll cop this.' It was like, *whoa*. It's pretty intense. But I understand why, though ... The discipline will be good. You need it, in the police force especially. You know, people driving round in V8s and they

got guns and batons and what not ... If you haven't got responsible people, you know, you can do a lot of damage, not only to themselves and to people, but also to the reputation of the police force. (1/19-year-old male)

Some students suggested that discipline would be a positive personal experience:

When we first walked down to the parade ground ... and we saw on the Monday morning the senior class lined up ... and they sort of snapped into attention, like, your spine sort of tingled and went, well, all this discipline! And I mean, that's great. I'm going to be a better person after all this. So I'm going to do it and stick through it. (1/23-year-old male)

Discipline is an important part of training. If you can't cope with it here, how can you cope outside? It's character building. (1/29-year-old female)

Other interviewees expressed a more or less resigned attitude toward discipline:

But I mean, when you're going into a job like this, you sort of have to have self-discipline, like they say. You have to be able to know what's right and wrong. So I don't think anything they said was over the line. (1/19-year-old female)

A number of students, however, expressed considerable surprise at what they perceived as lack of discipline at the academy. In some interviews, this was considered positive:

The friendliness of the sergeants and the senior sergeants ... I thought they'd be very strict. Which ... is good. I expected a bit more like military discipline. Like, I expected to salute every time I passed a sergeant or an acting police officer. But that's not the case. You can say 'G'day' to them. (1/23-year-old male)

Other students were unsure whether the perceived lack of discipline was really such a good thing:

And it was totally different to what I thought. I didn't think everyone would be so friendly ... I probably would've liked it more if it had been,

'Right, name, you're in here and this is your room and I want that bed made' ... because I like the discipline. I feed off it and I thrive off it and that'll keep me in, you know, in line and keep me going. Whereas it was, it seemed too casual, and I thought, 'The police department isn't like this, you know' ... Yeah, I wanted it stricter. You know, I wanted ten push-ups and stuff like that. So, but, you know, it was pleasant. Everyone was friendly and that's what surprised me. They were smiling, welcoming. (1/29-year-old female)

I think that's a joke. I was expecting military-style discipline when I got down here. And I was disappointed in a way because I thought it'd, you know, toughen me up a little bit, you know ... I think the parade is very essential to, you know, it gets you into the formality type of thing. And even the way you address your seniors, the sergeants and stuff ... There's got to be respect for rank. (1/19-year-old male)

These students were disappointed that discipline was less than they had expected. Others were quite reflective about the variance between their initial expectations of discipline and the philosophy of PREP program. These students thought that a system of strict military discipline might not meet the needs of Phase 1 of PREP, with its focus on learning about the community and open classroom participation:

I sort of expected the discipline to be something like the army, and I didn't realize that ... the way that the academy is run, the PREP program, it's more to serve people's needs, to get to know them psychologically and socially, sort of thing. To really get to the base root of a problem, rather than to cure it later on. They want to sort of, bring up the preventative measures now. So I didn't realize that. (1/25-year-old female)

Overall, the students' thoughts on discipline during their first week at the academy indicate that they brought diverse expectations to the academy, and demonstrated a range of reactions to initial experiences. Many students thought they would be subject to strict militaristic discipline while at the academy. Some were relieved to find that discipline was less strict than expected, some felt that discipline was less than expected and were disappointed, and some found that the discipline was about what they had expected and were either pleased or resigned to it. A few reflected on the role of military discipline in the context of the intentions of Phase 1. These findings were consistent with results of

TABLE 4.1
Severity and fairness of discipline at the academy (Survey 2, N=127)

Severity	Frequency	Percentage
Extremely harsh	4	3
Harsh	14	11
Not very harsh	82	65
Not at all harsh	27	21
TOTAL	127	100

Fairness		
Extremely fair	5	4
Fair	93	74
Not very fair	23	18
Not at all fair	5	4
TOTAL	126	100

TABLE 4.2
Personal experience of discipline at the academy (Survey 2, N=43)

Severity	Frequency	Percentage
Extremely fair	2	5
Fair	32	74
Not very fair	7	16
Not at all fair	2	5
TOTAL	43	100

Q: If you were ever disciplined for any rule infringements at the Academy, how fairly were you treated?

the questionnaire survey. Students were asked about academy discipline at the end of Phase 3, in Survey 2. There was a diversity of opinion (see Table 4.1), with most students (86 per cent) expressing the view that discipline was not harsh. The rest (14 per cent) thought that discipline was harsh or extremely harsh. Most students (78 per cent) also thought that academy discipline was extremely fair or fair, but roughly one in five viewed it as not very fair or not at all fair. Table 4.2 indicates that 79 per cent of the 43 students who reported having been subject to disciplinary action considered that they had been treated fairly or extremely fairly. About one in five who had been subject to disciplinary action thought they had been treated unfairly. This is simi-

TABLE 4.3
Discipline at the academy (Survey 2, N=124)

Statement regarding discipline	Agree / Strongly agree (per cent)
Academy rules for proper conduct were made clear to me	93
Academy takes a very tough line on infringements by students	57
Academy concentrates on what we do wrong rather than what we do right	73
The Academy rewards proper behaviour by students	7
A student who reports misconduct is likely to be given the 'cold shoulder'	51
A student who reports another student's misconduct shouldn't expect much support from the Academy hierarchy	9
There is little incidence of rule infringements at the Academy	30
Sometimes you have to break the rules if you want to get on with other students	15

Q: Listed below are some statements regarding discipline at the Academy. Please indicate your level of agreement or disagreement with each by circling the appropriate number where:
1 Strongly agree
2 Agree
3 Neutral
4 Disagree
5 Strongly disagree

lar to the proportion of students who thought that in general discipline at the academy was unfair. These results suggest that being subject to disciplinary action did not increase perceptions of unfairness. Aspects of academy discipline are further explored in Table 4.3. Students were overwhelmingly of the view that academy rules had been made clear. All female students agreed with this statement, as did the great majority of male students (89 per cent). Just over half the respondents agreed that the academy took a tough line on infringements by students – a result that is consistent with the diversity of opinion expressed in the interviews. Almost three-quarters of respondents thought that the academy concentrated more on what they did wrong than on what they did right, and a very small number agreed that the academy rewarded proper behaviour. Half the respondents indicated that students who reported misconduct would be likely to be given the cold shoulder from other students, but very few agreed that students reporting misconduct would not be supported by the academy. Almost one in three agreed with the statement that there was little incidence of rule breaking at the academy, and less than 15 per cent agreed that rule breaking was sometimes necessary to get on with other students.

The overall impression of discipline that arises from the interviews and questionnaire results is that the academy was far from a military-style organization with 'harsh and often arbitrary discipline,' as described in the early literature on police culture (Van Maanen 1973: 410). The situation in New South Wales at the time of our research was more complex than it would have been prior to PREP, when police training was very similar to the militaristic systems that inform many discussions of the socialization of police. There were indeed vestiges of military-style discipline, such as the parade, the practice of requiring students to write reports in response to minor disciplinary infractions, and a general insistence on neatness of dress and grooming. But in the main, the style of interaction between instructors and students reported in interviews was far from what is characteristic of military training establishments, or traditional police academies, and is consistent with the observations of the CARE Report (1990). At the time this research was undertaken, the academy was in transition between the old style of police training and the current, university-based system that dispenses with parades, uniforms, and overt evidence of traditional disciplinary structures. The interview material also belies common assumptions that all students react the same way to influences such as the rank structure and discipline, and that they are unreflective of various forces that may affect themselves or other students and of the potential effects of these forces. The dissatisfaction many students expressed about disciplinary standards at the academy can be interpreted as disappointment over the differences between the discipline they expected of police life and the relaxed circumstances they actually encountered at the academy. As we argue in the next section, this is more than a disappointment in relation to expectations – it has its origins in shared social definitions relating to the nature of a uniformed, disciplined service that exercises symbolic power. This symbolic power is constituted ultimately in the objective power relations of the field of policing. The recruits were disappointed that the symbolic power of police was not more clearly imposed on them at the academy through the exercise of discipline.

The Uniform: Image and the Embodiment of Culture

The obvious outer symbolism of police power is the uniform and its associated paraphernalia – the belts, insignia, batons, handcuffs, oleoresin capsicum (pepper spray), and firearm. Wearing the uniform is a key event in the socialization of student police officers. Students were issued with a uniform during the first week of PREP and started wearing it on the Monday of their second week. In PREP, student police wore uniforms that were identical to those of other police, except that their epaulettes had the word 'student' on them and they wore a plain blue hat band that covered the familiar police blue-and-white checks. Phase 3 students (the senior class) were distinguished from the junior class by their bulky outer belts and holsters, which were issued so that they could undertake officer safety and appointment training (shooting, baton, handcuffs). Typically, student police had a strong desire to be accepted or 'fit in,' initially with the senior class, but ultimately with the operational police they would work with in Phases 2 and 4. In the first round of interviews, they expressed this most clearly in their reactions to getting their uniform. A number of students became emotional and misty-eyed when asked how they felt when they saw themselves in uniform for the first time:

> Yeah. And I like the uniform, that's the truth. I do like the uniform. I like the image associated with it and I like, yeah, I'm impressed by the whole thing. I'm just totally impressed and I don't want to leave here. I want to stay here. [Laugh] I'm happy here. (1/29-year-old female)

A number of students commented that the uniform transformed them:

> I don't know. It just gives you, like it's not as if, you know, you put on the uniform and you feel really powerful or something. You just feel, I don't know, a funny kind of buzz. Like even when I was ... getting fitted, it was really good. 'Cause, probably knowing that you've realized, like, part of your dream. Seeing yourself in the mirror and not really realizing at first that that's you. You've made it. [Q: Did it look really different?] Yeah, you looked totally different. [Laugh] You don't quite recognize yourself. (1/20-year-old female)

Clearly, part of the uniform's mystique lies in its symbolic expression of the objective power relations that are characteristic of the field of policing. Students already understood the power of police as potential objects of its exercise; now they appreciated in a corporeal way ('a funny kind of buzz') their transformation as social actors by the act of wearing the uniform. In some cases this transformation reminded students of images of police from the media:

Like one of the girls [laugh] who stays next to me in my tower, she tried on her uniform last night and she said, 'Oh, my god. I look like something out of *Blue Heelers*.' And she did. [Laugh] And I thought, 'Yeah, that's the first thing that came to my mind.' (1/24-year-old female)

Many students held the view that getting the uniform would make them feel more comfortable at the academy and give them a sense of being accepted as part of the team:

Yeah. I think, oh, the consensus in our class is that once everyone's sort of in uniform, we'll feel more part of the academy, I guess. If it has any psychological effect on us or not, I don't know. (1/male, age >30)

This student was not sure whether the uniform would have any psychological effects. Others thought the uniform affected them significantly. Many suggested besides helping them fit in at the academy, the uniform increased their confidence:

I don't know. I feel like I'm really confident in myself. It gives you a sense of, confidence ... I feel like I'm actually a student police officer ... And can't wait till Family [Day] so me parents can see me in the uniform. (1/19-year-old male)

This student was proud, and wanted his parents to see him, but this act would no doubt also be about seeing how his own social transformation was appreciated by people he knew well. Other students emphasized how the uniform increased their self-esteem and cemented their membership in the group.

I don't know why, but as soon as you put it on, you feel like your self-esteem just skyrockets. You seem to carry yourself a lot better. Pride and things like that. Not necessarily authority. But more pride and, I don't know, it's a feeling of self-worth and things like that. And again, feeling that you're part of a team. (1/20-year-old female)

Many interviewees made the connection between the uniform and the power and authority of the police, and professionalism:

With all uniform jobs there is the prestige with it. And with the police, because they've got the authority, there is prestige in that sense. Because everyone's taught from a younger age, if you've got a query or you've got a question or you're not sure or if you're in danger and things like that, you go to a person in uniform. Or you go to the police. So in that sense you've got the prestige in the image. (1/male, age >30)

One student reflected that the uniform empowers the police to do things that are difficult for civilians:

And you're just a normal person but you're trying to do things that you're not allowed to do. You haven't got the power to do it. If you ask someone to leave, you haven't really got any power to do it. You know what I mean? You've got to use a little bit of force, maybe. Whereas police, I think, the uniform and just the power you get with it helps a lot. Makes it easier. (1/25-year-old male)

The students who made a connection between the uniform and the power of police often recognized the potential that the police role had to change them personally. As Bourdieu observed: 'Symbolic power has to be based on the possession of symbolic capital. The power of imposing on other minds a vision, old or new, of social divisions depends on the social authority acquired in previous struggles' (Bourdieu 1990a: 138). This symbolic effectiveness has also to be based on 'the degree to which the vision proposed is based on reality.' Thus, the symbolic power afforded by the uniform is based on the symbolic power of police, which is founded ultimately on the objective power structures constitutive of the field of policing. The power of the uniform, symbolic of the objective power relations of the field of policing, is understood by recruits, who in the past have been subject to it as civilians. For civilians, all interactions with police carry the potential for the exercise of two kinds of violence: *symbolic*, whereby the socially warranted power of the state subjugates the individual, and *actual*, through the exercise of socially warranted coercive force. This constant potential for the exercise of coercive force forms the basis of the symbolic power and capital of the uniform, and is understood inherently by all.

This is illustrated by an incident early in the research when I went to the University of New South Wales with a uniformed female police officer. The purpose of the visit was to try out the interview instrument for the first round of interviews. Walking through the halls of the Arts building, me in a suit and the officer in uniform, caused a minor flurry of surprise and alarm, with people calling out, 'The police are here!' No one thought at first that we were attending the university for an activities that fitted within the normal daily activity of the university. The presence of a uniformed police officer led automatically to the interpretation that police business was being undertaken, the apperception of the exercise of the symbolic (and actual) power of police in an environment that exists normally at some social distance from the field of policing. This episode illustrates an important point about the symbolic power embodied in the uniformed police person: symbolic power exists only as a social phenomenon, and is recognized as meaningful by people within an objective set of power relations characteristic of a field. The uniform is part of the bodily display that forms an important dimension of the policing habitus. As Bourdieu observes: 'Bodily hexis is political mythology realized, *em-bodied*, and turned into a permanent disposition, a durable way of standing, speaking, walking and thereby of feeling and thinking' (Bourdieu 1990b: 69–70).

Hexis is the socially significant and efficacious body – that is, social order and social powers given corporeal identity and expression and meaningful to others. The 'visceral attachment of a socialized body to the social body that has made it and with which it is bound up' (Bourdieu 2000: 145) is an important aspect of the development of recruit's *illusio*, or attachment to the game. This is illustrated by the interviews during which the students said the uniform made them feel 'part of the academy' or 'actually a student police officer,' and that the uniform gave them 'a funny kind of buzz.' Even if they did not understand the process of socialization, or were not conscious of it, they readily understood the power of hexis – especially in regard to the uniform – in establishing group identity and membership, and more importantly in marking them apart and signifying them to others as police. Uniform and paraphernalia are powerfully symbolic of the essential power of police – their potential to impose sanctions, deprive others of liberty, and exercise coercive force with a baton, handcuffs, pepper spray, or even a firearm. This is most obvious in the physically fit bodies, short haircuts, and special uniforms characteristic of special operations groups and other paramilitary squads; here, the physical body partly expresses police's functions and their socially mandated power to coerce others physically. Bittner (1978) contends that the very great social power of police, as manifested in their unique mandate to employ coercive force, constitutes the distinctive character of policing. These objective social relations are given meaning and expression through the uniform. Learning to wear the uniform, and to participate in the rituals and discipline of the twice-daily parade, is a key means whereby recruits learn how to

'be' police – that is, to assume and communicate the socially meaningful and efficacious behaviours that are symbolic of the social relations
of the field of policing.

The acquisition of the uniform, then, is an important step in the
corporeal socialization of recruits as they begin to adopt the physical
presence of a police officer, redolent as it is of the symbolic role and
authority of police. Bourdieu argues that by and large, socialization
and the development of habitus is unconscious: 'The essential part of
the *modus operandi* that defines practical mastery is transmitted through
practice, in the practical state, without rising to the level of discourse'
(1990b: 73–4). Our interviews suggested that students were aware of
the personal changes that were happening within them, or that could
possibly happen. Some students regarded these changes in a positive
light; others were apprehensive about the potential for personal change
as they adopted the police role. Even very early in training, students
well knew they were being presented with a range of potential role
models, and they felt they had the ability to find their own operating
persona:

> But, I mean, I still want to be myself. I don't want to change ... I mean, a lot
> of people have an attitude problem thinking that because they're in uni-
> form, I mean, they're more superior than, say, anyone else. (1/24-year-old
> female)

> I know a few officers that use their uniform as a form of power. It's an ego
> trip for them, basically. And I've always said I'm not going to act like that
> because I don't appreciate being treated like that. And I expect to be
> treated the way I treat people. (1/22-year-old female)

> I've seen a lot of young police sort of that come out ... 'Don't you know
> I've got this blue uniform on now?' and they're walking around and stuff.
> Masters of the universe. I don't want to turn into that stereotypical sort of
> thing, I guess. (1/19-year-old male)

These students were concerned about much more than the impact of
the uniform. To them, the uniform was symbolic of their perceptions of
a whole host of issues facing them in the transformation from civilian
to police officer. The interviews revealed a general concern about the
effects that the status of police officer was going to have on relationships with civilians. The issues are well illustrated in the following, in

which a student was answering a question about the characteristics of a good police officer:

> I've noticed here with the senior class group there's girls on our floor, they walk around with like a mean, firm look on their face. And like one of them who gave us our uniform inspection, the way she goes, like, she spoke in a tone like, 'Turn around, show me your belt,' or whatever she said, 'Are those pants too tight?' And ... that really annoyed me 'cause there's no need to speak like that now. I think when you're out on the street you do have to speak like that, especially a lady, or a man. Like, make sure they don't know you have leniency toward any of their excuses or their behaviour. But it really annoyed me 'cause it's like once you put the uniform on you become a cold, hard person. And there was really no need for it. (1/19-year-old female)

This student recognized that her work might require her to adopt an authoritarian persona in certain circumstances, but she also recognized that this persona need not change her basic nature. Rather, it was a tool to remove, along with the uniform, at the end of the day. The passage is also a good example of Fielding's (1988) suggestion that discipline is a tool that police use internally and externally. In this case the student was experiencing a model of disciplined interaction that she was initially uncomfortable with. It was characteristic of an official interaction between a superior and a subordinate officer, and had the potential to influence how she eventually interacted with the public and with more junior officers. The passage also illustrates that recruits are aware of the forces of socialization – even those that are symbolic, corporeal, and non-discursive – and suggests there is a degree of choice in how the symbolic power afforded by the uniform and by membership in the police is exercised.

Experience of Phase 2[5]

Recruits had their first taste of the field during Phase 2, when they spent four weeks observing operational policing in a local command area. The main purpose of this phase was 'to give Student Police Officers [SPOs] direct, if limited experience of actual police sites, situations and practices, and direct experience of police-related venues and practices such as courts and trials' (NSWPS 1993: 44). Besides all this, this phase provided 'the opportunity [for students] to test the validity of their foundational studies; to test their capacity to observe, record, report, analyse and interpret; to raise questions and to recognize the relationship between knowing "*why*" and the extent of knowing "*how*" still to be learnt' (44). Formal requirements of Phase 2 training included observing police work and analysing and writing up two cases observed during this phase. The two cases were to be selected from six major areas: offences against property, offences against the person, traffic-related matters, service (field and station), keeping the peace and street offences, and coronial matters (45–6).

The results of Survey 2 suggested that students were indeed exposed to a variety of experiences. Table 4.4 shows that almost all students observed general duties and highway patrol duties, and that the great majority had some exposure to detective, beat, and court duties. General duties work was rated most highly in importance 'for a successful Phase 2 experience.' This was followed by beat policing, court duties, highway patrol, and detective work. These experiences and perceptions did not vary by gender or age.

Table 4.5 indicates that respondents rated general duties officers as the most supportive among all the people encountered during Phase 2. Other police, such as probationary constables, junior officers, other students, and beat police, were also rated as highly supportive. Senior officers and special duties police were rated somewhat less highly. Patrol education and development officers, who were the students' official supervisors, were near the bottom of the ranking in terms of being supportive, on the same level as administrative staff, and only slightly more supportive than members of the public. These results suggest that students found their main sources of support among general duties junior officers, with whom they also had the most contact.

The experience of Phase 2 was explored in greater depth during the second round of interviews and, to a lesser extent, during the debriefing sessions at the beginning of Phase 3 at the academy. Most students remembered feeling generally apprehensive on their first day of Phase 2:

> A number of students said they were nervous, although interestingly this nervousness seemed to be focused on fears of 'getting in the way' or being a 'burden' on operational police ... Particular aspects of the job were also mentioned as things that the students were apprehensive about. One student said that she had been worried and apprehensive about going to a

TABLE 4.4
Experience of police work in Phase 2 (Survey 2, N=127)

	Exposed to experience	Mean importance ratings
General duties	99%	8.74
Beat policing	80%	7.57
Courts	75%	7.19
Highway patrol	98%	6.72
Detectives	87%	5.85

Q: Listed below are some experiences student police officers may have been exposed to in Phase 2. For each of the following: please indicate whether you were exposed to this experience during Phase 2, by ticking (√) the appropriate box for each category, AND please rate how important you believe each of these experiences are for a successful Phase 2 experience (regardless of whether you had the experience) by circling the number on the scale that best represents your opinion, where: 0=not at all important, 9= extremely important.
Note: No significant differences in exposure or importance ratings by sex or age.

TABLE 4.5
Support from people in Phase 2 (Survey 2, N=127)

	Mean rating of supportiveness	Per cent never had contact
General duties officers	8.02	0
Probationary constables	7.88	37
Junior officers (S constables / constables)	7.63	0
Other student police officers	7.42	11
Beat police	7.28	17
Senior officers (Sgts and above)	6.98	2
Highway patrol officers	6.96	1
Patrol commander	6.64	9
Detectives	6.58	6
Patrol Education & Development Officer	6.52	3
Administrative staff	6.52	6
Members of the public	5.69	2

Q: Overall, how supportive was each of the following to you as a Student Police Officer at your Phase 2 Patrol? On a scale of 0 to 9, please circle the number that indicates the degree of support, where 0=not at all supportive, 9 = extremely supportive. If you never had contact with any of these groups or individuals, you do not have to rate the degree of support. Simply place a cross (X) in the box provided.

job in the car, particularly if a pursuit or urgent duty was involved. Others expressed concern about 'dead 'uns,' where police had to attend the scene of a death. A number of students were particularly concerned about having to give death messages, a process where police inform relatives about a death. There was a lot of general agreement expressed by the class regarding these fears. (Ph2Debrief 3)

Even so, students were 'thrilled to be out there, doing something' (Ph2Debrief 2). Nearly every SPO interviewed found Phase 2 a positive experience. Many used words like 'exciting,' 'fantastic,' 'unreal,' and 'excellent' to describe their period of field observation. A number of interviewees described Phase 2 as an 'eye opener' for them – they got to see what police work was really like, and they also saw the world through police eyes for the first time. The following account shows how one student experienced for the first time in practice the social realities of the police hexis, or embodied habitus, as manifested in the reactions of the public:

You look at everything in a different light ... It's the first time you go out in your, like, your uniform, and, like, you just see people's reactions when they see the police or cars drive past or whatever. Just totally different. Oh, you get to see things that, like, you wouldn't normally look at, like different number plates or cars and people acting suspicious and little things that, you know, you'd take no notice of, but are going on every day in the town that I lived in for seventeen years. (2/20-year-old male)

Students experienced street-level police work for the first time. Some were surprised at the range of matters that police had to deal with:

Another student commented that he was surprised that police did a lot of work that he thought should be the job of another agency. For example, on one shift he had spent five-and-a-half hours at a hospital to get someone scheduled [admitted involuntarily]. Another agreed, and told a story about waiting two-and-half hours at hospital to get stitches put [in]. This student was surprised that police did not get some precedence in these circumstances. (Ph2Debrief 3)

A few students did not have a very exciting experience because not much happened in their local area. One student said that Phase 2 'bored the shit out of me' because 'there wasn't a great deal to do' and she felt that she was in the way and didn't want to 'get in their face' (2/29-year-old female). The general consensus among students in one debriefing session was that 'the station was not as busy or exciting as they had envisaged ... they did not expect it to be quite so routine and mundane' (Ph2Debrief 2). Another unexpected aspect of police work that students observed was the delay in answering calls:

> I didn't expect it to be as easy as it was. I thought it might – everyone was on the go all the time: you get a call, you go out. But everyone kind of takes their time and, like, ... I thought it'd be full on, like, faster ... and it wasn't ... This lady rang up: 'Oh, I think someone's baited my dog, can you come out and have a look?' And I thought, well, why don't they go now, they're not doing anything? ... I don't know, I thought, I thought it was rude basically, 'cause if you're not doing anything you may as well go straightaway ... No, we'll have a cup of tea ... we'll go now. And I'm just going, well, why don't you do it straightaway instead of wasting time? (2/22-year-old female)

This 'disapproval' of what seemed to be fairly common work practice came out quite strongly at the debriefing session:

> The next student said that they were not as busy as expected, but even so that there were delays in getting to jobs. This comment struck a chord with a number of students, and a number made comments about this. Because these all came out quickly, and to a degree all at once, it was difficult to record all the details accurately. One said that the police came back to the station, did some COPS [computer reports where the details of each job must be entered] entries, had a coffee and chat before going on to the next job. The implication was that the officers did not have a very dedicated attitude to delivering swift response to calls. The next student was much more upfront about his opinion of the work habits in his patrol: 'Police wasted a lot of time ... Another said that she was surprised that there seemed to be some discretion about whether to accept a job that was called over the radio. (Ph2Debrief 3)

Reception and Treatment in the Field

Some students were unsure of themselves and felt vulnerable because they lacked knowledge and experience. Generally, though, they found the station a welcoming and supportive place. One SPO's experience was exceptionally positive:

> Everyone, although I was a student, they looked after me really well. They actually got me involved in a lot of things ... You know, first or second day I was there, the patrol commander invited me up to his office and had morning tea and that was really good. You know, he just talked about things and then there was a note three weeks later just before I came back down [to the academy] and pulled me back in again, same thing, just had a chat about things. All the sergeants were great and, you know, all the people all looked after you ... [I] couldn't ask for more. (2/29-year-old male)

A male SPO in his early twenties contrasted the mateship and intimacy he enjoyed in the field with being treated like a student in the academy:

> I didn't probably think they'd treat you like that ... They really treated us like mates out there, like people ... 'Cause here [in the academy] they sort of promote adult education but on the other hand they sort of don't treat you like adults ... Like if you're, say, two minutes late for a class here, like, then they'll go, 'Oh, we want a report as to why you were late' ... But out there [in the field] it was a lot, I think it's just a lot more sort of a mateship sort of thing out there. Like a lot closer. You could be on, more on your level ... [They] joke with you and stuff like that. (2/21-year-old male)

Thus, recruits were beginning to compare their treatment in the operational field as colleagues with their status as students at the academy. This was the beginning of a process whereby recruits transferred their allegiance to the field of operational policing, as they identified opportunities for building social capital as police officers more with the operational field than with the academy.

Some students did encounter a degree of initial coolness. This was partly a result of rumours floating around at the time that students were being used as 'field associates' by the Royal Commission to spy on operational police, and partly a result of the natural suspicion that police hold against newcomers:

> The only real difficulty you have is breaking in the first couple of days. In the very first week, everybody's sort of got their backs up a bit. They don't know, you know ... students ... taking notes ... and stuff like that, especially

with the [Wood Royal] Commission going on. So I think everybody was a bit standoffish at first ... I did expect it. When I walked in, I thought this is going to be hard to break down all these barriers at first. So I just left it, I didn't try hard ... Yeah, and they got used to me being around, and they were fine. They were really good in the end. (2/21-year-old female)

The only interviewee who had a generally negative experience felt left out by the police at the station, and was upset and disappointed with the way he was assessed:

When I did the night shifts I was with a crew of people and unfortunately I felt like I was being left out when, say, when we came back to the station after doing a patrol, they'd sit down and play cards and they said to me, 'Look, just go upstairs and sit in the room and watch TV.' You know, not, you weren't actually part of the group ... Beyond that I was a bit disappointed in the report that I got, purely because the person who did it spent three hours a night asleep in the back of the truck and then called me too keen. That's basically why I, it was – as far as I was concerned, it was a farce. (2/24-year-old male)

However, even this SPO enjoyed other aspects of Phase 2 and mentioned officers and supervisors who were 'good' and supportive.

Variety of Policing Styles and Role Models

One fairly common observation the interviewees made related to the variety of policing styles they encountered. Sometimes this was positive, in that students got to experience different models of practice:

Basically in Phase 2 you get to see different styles because you work with different people all the time ... And so that was good, you get to see different types of police officers and different ways that they do it. Like some would take harsher action and the other ones wouldn't. The other ones would sort of tend to be a bit lighter on certain people, which was good. You get to sort of see which way you want to be, I think. You get to know who's a bit lazy and who's really good. (2/21-year-old female)

A number of students saw differences between the younger and the older officers in the field with respect to their degree of professionalism. Generally, they suggested that the younger police were more eager and involved. For example, one student found the 'pros' (probationers) 'more enjoyable ... because they were enthusiastic, they were just younger and more fun ... They loved their job, [while] the seniors seemed a bit tired and just laid back type of thing, like, oh-just-another-day type of thing' (2/19-year-old female)

Students were able to articulate different policing styles and express their preferences for certain work practices. This indicates that to some extent they were quite reflective about how police work should be conducted. The observer of one debriefing session was impressed with their willingness to criticize poor practices:[6]

> What I found particularly impressive was that the students were able to both identify and be critical of poor work practices observed during Phase 2. These included the following:
>
> • One student (male, late 20s) explained how he had noted that some officers after receiving a call had not bothered to do a COPS check on the person and as such had put themselves in a potentially dangerous situation. The student explained how on receiving a call regarding a serious domestic violence incident, the constables, had failed to do a COPS check. Luckily on arriving at the incident, the SPO had known this person and his past history (the offender had both guns on the property and a past history of pointing a gun at the head of his wife), and was able to warn the constables to be careful ...
>
> • There was also a general consensus among this subclass that many of the officers they had come into contact with during Phase 2 were 'lazy.' A female SPO (Anglo, early 20s) noted that while on patrol they were not 'interested' and did 'not bother to look for work.' She added that she had played cards for an entire night shift. Another student added that while on patrol she was quite shocked by the fact that certain constables did not attend jobs, while on patrol, simply letting the other car take responsibility. Students generally nodded and agreed that they had similar experiences. The tutor ended this conversation that it was up to the individual student to decide whether 'you want to be lazy or a worker.'
>
> • A further [comment] was the fact that many police are very cynical and hardened. One student commented (male, late 20s) that some officers 'have a sick sense of humour.' He further clarified that they joke about 'everything and anything' except that pertaining to 'babies and children.' (Ph2Debrief 2)

Traumatic Experiences

Most interviewees reported encountering one or more traumatic situations. These incidents reinforced in students' minds the inherent dangers of policing and the role police play in dealing with distasteful and
distressing matters. Many saw a dead body for the first time, although
this was not necessarily distressing (Ph2Debrief 2). A twenty-two-year-
old female SPO's experience was both horrible and tragic, but she
admired the way police handled the situation:

> The one night we had the two deaths was a bit traumatic for me ... This
> poor old woman who just happened to step out at the wrong time as a
> truck was coming around the corner and her son happened to be watch-
> ing at the side of the road, didn't realize she was actually walking across
> to come home ... And then we had to go up to another death where a
> woman got bashed to death by her husband. There were two little kids in
> the house and I had to baby-sit them. And I looked at family photos
> around the room, and I'm thinking, oh my God, was that actually – seeing
> the body at that time, that was that poor woman, that's what she looks
> like, what about these kids, what's going to happen to them? What about
> him, you know, he was sitting near us the whole time, and he just gave me
> a real creepy feeling, it was like an animal sort of thing ... I watched the
> police as well at the scene, how they were acting, you know, just treated
> like another, another job. I mean they weren't harsh or not caring, but they
> weren't crying or letting it really get to them in, you know, in front of
> everyone – doing their job, doing it the best they could, getting the body
> off the road and everything else and dealing with the son ... They were
> great with the husband even though he did kill her ... Didn't bash him
> around even though they knew, you know, he was the murderer. Treated
> him really well. (2/22-year-old female)

A young male SPO felt vulnerable in a stressful situation but took
comfort in the fact that he had other police around him and 'they knew
what they were doing':

> There was one that was a brawl on a Saturday night at a party ... There
> was a lot of youths at a party and three of them got out of control and they
> arrested three of them. And I was pretty much like in the centre of it all. So
> that was a little bit stressful having, like, fifty people around you and

there's only about, say, ten policemen there. And you're in there and, and the worst thing was that you've got your student epaulettes on so you look a lot more vulnerable and you've got no protection like guns or batons or anything. So you're virtually on your own, fending for yourself and that was probably a little bit stressful, but [I] felt OK because I had all the policemen with me and they knew what they were doing. (2/21-year-old male)

Dissatisfaction with the Academy and Identification with Operational Police

A few respondents felt impatient about returning to the academy after Phase 2; they enjoyed the field so much that they wanted to get back there:

> When I finished Phase 2 ... I didn't want to come back here [the academy]. I just wanted to go straight to work. So – I mean that was because the way they sort of let me fit in. So I just want to fit in again, I suppose. (2/23-year-old male)

This desire not to go back to the academy was fuelled partly by rumours and criticisms about the academy that students heard in the course of their field observation:

> I guess you pick up that some people weren't happy with the system ... Police weren't too happy about things that were happening ... Yeah, they reckon they're changing, you know, ... We're changing this course so that it's more sort of academic sort of course. That's not what they want. They want to see ... not someone that knows numbers and the theory of it, [but] someone that can actually do something ... I'm a hands-on person, strictly hands-on person all my life ... So I think the course is long enough, you know ... You're actually sick and tired of it and you want to get out. And what we want to do is get out on the street. (2/28-year-old male)

Some students, as they developed a good rapport with the police they met in Phase 2, took criticisms of the academy in their stride (2/19-year-old female).

Some students thought that Phase 1 did not adequately prepare them for the realities of police work – especially in relation to survival skills – and felt extremely vulnerable when faced with dangerous situations. This is consistent with the results of Survey 2, in which 57 per cent of respondents thought they were well prepared for Phase 2, but

29 per cent did not think so and 13 per cent weren't sure. An interviewee described how she felt:

> I enjoyed Phase 2 but I felt very vulnerable, to offenders and things like that. I didn't think I was prepared ... and I think that was the fault of the curriculum in Phase 1, not the officers out in the field. I mean, just your officer survival skills and things like that ... [There] could have been a lot more emphasis on communication skills and things like that. (2/20-year-old female)

Similar sentiments were expressed at a debriefing session we observed:

> A female SPO (Anglo, approximately mid 20s) commented that there was not enough emphasis on safety in Phase 2. Though she did not elaborate on the specifics of the situation, she explained that she was put into quite dangerous situations where she felt she did not deal with that situation adequately. With reference to this issue, there was a fairly general consensus that it was not realistic for an SPO to be 'dropped off' (let out of the police vehicle) in the event of danger. They felt that it would possibly be a more dangerous situation to be on the street in uniform, without any weapons, especially in 'dangerous suburbs' such as where there is a high proportion of Aboriginals. A further consensus was the implicit assumption that the SPOs would be given weapons and asked to help in the event of an emergency. One female SPO (mid 20s) described a situation in which 'I shit meself' after being given a baton to use in a pub brawl, while guarding the door to the pub. She further commented that she did not think that Phase 1 prepared them for the reality of police work though not elaborating on this point. (Ph2Debrief 2)

Some students were taught 'short cuts' in operational work that they felt were justified:

> Most of them were really good. Because of staff shortages there was a lot of short cuts ... The short cuts they do don't endanger anybody or really go that much against all the guidelines – it's just sort of something you develop that really hasn't been put into a process yet ... So I didn't have any problem. (2/23-year-old male)

The tension between the short cuts encountered in the field and the 'right way' taught at the academy is well illustrated by the experience of an interviewee:

> The only down side to it is, like, during exams you think back to especially
> station procedures. You think back, 'How did it happen in Phase 2?' And
> of course out there ... they do it the easy way, which isn't always ... the
> right way ... They, they take more short cuts. (2/26-year-old male)

During one of the debriefing sessions, some students were openly
critical of their Phase 1 training. They felt that Phase 2 only served to
highlight how much they did *not* know, and started to reject the academy's entire approach:

> [The student] felt that it was best to get hands-on experience and then
> learn the 'best way of doing it for yourself.' He further indicated that he
> believed this was a better method than learning the standard, by-the-book
> approach taught at the academy. Most students seemed to nod agreement
> with this attitude. (Ph2Debrief 2)

Besides adopting a more critical view of training at the academy,
students started to develop a 'street cop' view of the world. Students'
initial nervousness about the operational field and their desire to 'fit in'
and feel accepted perhaps encouraged them to identify with the values
and attitudes held by officers they encountered. One way they tried to
fit in was by adopting the language used by operational police. This is
indicative of 'dictionary' cultural knowledge, which categorizes the
things and persons that police encounter in their work:

> Students had assumed the specialized language of operational police ...
> Student Police Officers are SPOs, pronounced *spos*; housing commission
> residents are 'trogs' (short for troglodytes) or 'housos'; 'dead 'un' for a
> deceased, 'hoodlum' for any younger person considered to be likely to be
> an offender or to come into contact with the police; 'warb' for derelict; and
> 'loser' for any person who they see is a potential trouble-maker and who
> manifests underclass culture. (Ph2Debrief 3)

Students began to appreciate how unrewarding the job of policing
could be. As a result, they tended to identify with the frustration and
alienation felt by the officers they encountered in the operational field.
For example, the idea that the criminal justice system is too lenient
toward criminals – one of the important elements of taken for granted,

axiomatic truths of policing (see Crank 1998: 255–66) – was reinforced by students' experiences during Phase 2:

[A student] was really affected by a day spent in court, and in particular, 'the light sentences handed out.' They told a story about attending a case involving an offender with 'pages of priors' who had been apprehended after a high-speed pursuit in a stolen car. The person had just got out of jail for similar offences and was granted bail. The student said that he could not believe that this offender was granted bail. This struck a chord and a number of similar cases were mentioned. It seems clear that some of this opinion about the 'lack of support' given by the courts to police was received opinion from comments of the police the students had been with. Nevertheless, the experiences of the two or three students who had spent some time in court and who made a comment were, in their minds, consistent with this received view. One commented that 'this makes you more lax because all of your work comes to nothing when the magistrate does not support police.' (Ph2Debrief 3)

Our observation of students in Phase 2 suggests that some students learned early from operational officers a disdain for paperwork:

8.05 a.m. ... This job required following up someone for some reason which was not given. The person no longer lived at this address, which was now occupied by an Asian male student, aged approximately mid-twenties. The civilian was obviously not comfortable with the police standing in his doorway. Constable X was very polite and apologized for interrupting him so early. On leaving the building, Constable X expressed that she was pleased that the person could not be located because the 'paperwork stops here.' SPO10 nodded her agreement in an exaggerated fashion. Clearly, the SPO had already adopted a very negative attitude to paperwork. (Ph2)

Another example from our fieldwork shows that even at this early stage, the SPO had learned to stereotype citizens and rationalize what turned out to be a premature dismissal of a citizen's call about a suspicious situation:

At 8:25 a.m. we went to a unit by the beach. A woman (probably in her late 50s or early 60s) met us at the door ... She was very articulate and calm. She said that she heard strange noises within the building. She thought that people were fighting. Then she saw a man in his 50s leave the building. The woman said that she was alone, her husband had gone to work. She then took us down to the garage area, because she heard noises there and thought that the man must have got out through a gap in the security gate. We followed her and the officers tried opening the garage doors but they were locked ... One of the officers went halfway up the stairs to the second floor, took a quick look and concluded that there was nothing there. The woman apologized for troubling the police. The officers told her to call them if she heard anything else ... We then all went back to the truck. I was quite surprised that the officers didn't make any further checks of the building and they seemed not terribly concerned about the incident. They put it down to the fact that it was not uncommon for 'old ladies' to complain about this sort of thing because they were afraid. I did not think that the woman was in any way paranoid; she seemed intelligent and calm, though troubled by what she thought were strange noises. (Ph2)

The incident turned out to be a serious case of 'home invasion,' during which a man was tied up and locked in a garage and about $9,000 was taken from his unit. When the researcher expressed her surprise that the officers had not done a more thorough check of the building, the SPO defended their actions by saying that police often get complaints from old people who are afraid of crime and that usually nothing comes out of these complaints.

On another shift, an SPO seemed to be taking cues from other officers in laughing at the belligerent behaviour of a prisoner in custody:

On return to the station office, [I] could hear the sound of a woman crying quietly in the fingerprint dock of the charging room directly next to the office. The woman (Anglo female, approximately late 20s) who was obviously quite drugged (probably heroin) later cried out 'You're a fucking bastard.' This was directed at a detective ... who[m] she apparently blamed for her not receiving bail after being arrested for break and entry. He was very amused by this, as were the rest of the officers present ... A civilian receptionist who had been reading a magazine also laughed. SPO13 looked around, and seemed to be taking cues about how to react to this outburst. When the others laughed loudly, he began to laugh also, adding 'Yeah, you should not have even arrested her.' It appeared to me that SPO13 was attempting to fit in, establish himself as part of the group. The woman in the fingerprint dock who had heard the laughing in response to the outburst continued to cry, commenting between sobs something to the effect,

'You're all very funny.' A few minutes later the female probationary constable ... who was obviously experiencing great difficulty attempting to get this woman to co-operate during fingerprinting, stormed through the office commenting 'Fucking bitch.' SPO13 chuckled slightly almost to acknowledge that the comment had been made. I felt that the whole episode had been very unprofessional conduct, particularly given that a civilian ... was at the desk of the office completing an accident report form. (Ph2)

One SPO volunteered to the researcher that her attitudes toward Aborigines had changed considerably since entering the field. She had described the patrol area as having 'a high Aboriginal population in a section of the area':

The SPO stated that my visit was at the beginning of her fourth week and she volunteered the information that she had already changed her attitudes a lot since entering [the academy]. As an example of this, she stated how much her attitudes to Aboriginal people had changed even in that short time. She had written a paper in the academy and had been given a very high mark, basically espousing equal treatment for Aboriginal people and stating they should not be treated differently from other racial groups such as white groups. She stated: 'I know it's terrible but my attitude has changed already since I have been here. But I can see how you just have to treat people differently because they are different. A lot of the trouble is in the areas where the Aboriginal people live.' (Ph2)

Phase 2 was generally a positive experience for students. They initially felt vulnerable in the field because of their lack of knowledge and experience, but the welcoming and supportive treatment most of them received from operational police made them feel at home. Their favourable attitude toward Phase 2 was reflected in Survey 2, which reported that 91 per cent of the respondents felt that this phase had met their expectations. The rest had a variety of complaints – for example, the station was not busy enough so that they missed out on experiences that a busier station might have provided. A large majority (84 per cent) also reported that their experience in Phase 2 had increased their desire for a career in policing. During the four weeks, they had come across a variety of policing styles and formed a deeper understanding of practical police work. Most had received a taste of how traumatic and frustrating police work can be, and many began to identify with the attitudes and values of operational police. They had been exposed to the complexities and contradictions of police work, and in many cases their expectations of a busy, exciting work experience had not been met. However, their disappointment over the mundane nature of much police work, and the attitudes of many officers to work, was tempered by the welcoming and supportive treatment most of them received.

Some students started to see the deficiencies of the training they received at the academy. If one of the purposes of Phase 2 was to provide students with 'the opportunity to test the validity of their foundational studies' (NSW Police Service 1993: 44), then it would appear that many students started to question the validity of Phase 1 as a result of their initial exposure to operational policing. Some students were impatient that they had to return to the academy for further training in Phase 3. As we will see, Phase 3 was academically demanding, but since it provided the knowledge students needed to work as police officers, it was tolerated to some extent. Students were anxious to begin Phase 4, the field training component of PREP.

Experience of Phase 3

Phase 3 focused much more sharply on field practice. Its curriculum was organized into seven blocks: property theft, personal safety, road safety, service (station/field), street offences/alcohol and drug related issues, criminal justice and the courts, and Coroner's Act and safety in custody (NSWPS 1995). There were sixteen distinct assessment items in the fourteen weeks of Phase 3. These ranged from traditional examinations, through presentations, essays, and competency assessments relating to firearms and officer safety, to guided self-assessments.[7] Considering the wide range of issues dealt with in the Phase 3 curriculum and the large number of assessments facing each student, and keeping in mind that Phase 3 was dealt with in fourteen weeks, it is not surprising that many students found Phase 3 much more difficult and demanding than Phase 1 – 'like the sledgehammer' (2/male, age >30). Phase 3 was stressful in part because of the heavy workload. However, worry about assessment was also a major factor:

> [It's] more stressful than the others, especially the last few weeks ... I have the obstacle course, I didn't pass firearms ... I've still got to do that. Then you've got exams and the big emphasis on the exams ... people failing the first couple of exams. Driver training, it's all these little things you've got

to pass and as soon as you get over one hurdle you find another ...
Nothing but stress. (2/25-year-old female)

One student thought that learning to deal with stress was necessary
in operational policing, and that the stress of Phase 3 was therefore
useful:

Well, Phase 3 is of course much more difficult than Phase 1 – a bigger
workload. Really putting the pressure on you, you really have to get
down and do the work, you can't afford to get behind because there is so
much to learn. I think you get to a point where you get really stressed
because everything seems to be due at the same time and you've got
exams, but I guess they're the sort of pressures we have to learn to deal
with, so in a way it's good. But yeah, I seemed to cope with it OK. (2/24-
year-old female)

The idea that stress was a deliberate aspect of the training regime was
echoed by another student:

I think I can see the method to the madness piling it on ... They want to see
how people react under pressure and stuff like that. But, yeah, it was a bit
of a shock actually, the first couple of weeks. But yeah, you get used to it.
(2/19-year-old male)

A number of students reported that the stress and hard work in
Phase 3 had affected relationships in the subclasses:

Yeah, about halfway through Phase 3, they talk about the 'Week 8 Syndrome' and ... Yeah. Even tutors told us about it. They'd say every class
that'll come through here, virtually around week eight or so, they start
their bickering and stuff. But, yeah, that sort of happened with us. We go
'Oh, no, it won't,' but it did, it happened. And that was strange but I think
you virtually sort it out after a few weeks and you get ... back to normal
sort of thing. (2/21-year-old male)

Students' anxiety about assessments was given focus when a number of students failed examinations. These students were offered a
'post' exam. The consequences of failing of the 'post' included relegation (i.e., to repeat Phase 3) and even dismissal. This was obviously
stressful for the people involved, one of whom described it as 'major

pressure' (2/22-year old male). Some students reported a sense of loss when valued team members and friends were removed from the class through relegation or dismissal:

> Oh, very demoralizing ... People are getting relegated and sacked and things. Like, you're sort of thinking, well, you know, this could be us ... And you do sense a loss when people ... get relegated. Like your class-mates become part of your sort of culture and your friendships and they're sort of then flicked. (2/23-year-old male)

Students found that the support and encouragement of classmates was important for helping them cope:

> I was given the choice of either going back to [class #] or staying in this class ... but my confidence was shot. And I wasn't too sure if I was going to pass or not and ... I don't know, all the fellows in my class said, 'Well, you stay and we'll just put our heads down for the next two weeks,' which we did, and come test day I felt really good about the test and I got my marks back last week, 85 per cent, so ... One of my friends in the class, yeah, he stays here every weekend and he said we'll just have the books for the whole weekend for the next two weeks and we did. (2/23-year-old male)

A number of students mentioned that the teaching staff were very supportive of students who were preparing for 'posts.' Some organized remedial classes; others served as advocates for individual students:

> Our personal tutor is great. We get on with him really well. He's always there for us if we need help or if you want to ask questions. He supported ... a few of us who had failed an exam a couple of weeks ago and were given a show cause notice, which meant that we had to show them why we should be allowed to stay. We had the choice of relegation or staying and our tutor wrote some good reports for some of the people, just saying that he would support them if they decided to stay on and they did. They decided to stay on and they passed. (2/22-year-old female)

In the interviews during which students spoke about relegation, one can discern themes of loyalty to the group, and the emergence of a sense of conflict between group interests and organizational interests. Many students commented that one of the positive aspects of Phase 3 was that it bound them more tightly as a group. Students were generally very complimentary about their tutors, who by and large represented the lower levels of the academy hierarchy. The distinction between operating and management cultures is, of course, a recurring theme in the literature on police culture, and in part probably reflects the inevitable conflicts between the interests of colleagues as a social group and those of the organization (see Reuss-Ianni and Ianni 1983).

Students often reported that Phase 3 was stressful and that the work was hard; even so, very few were negative about the experience. To them, the difficulties were worthwhile because Phase 3 was about learning to be a police officer. One student said that Phase 3 was when he really started to feel like an officer: 'You don't start to feel like or think like a cop until, you know, Phase 3 when you see too many briefs and things like that' (2/20-year-old male). Others were simply happy to be learning material that they thought was relevant to the job:

Well, Phase 3 left Phase 1 for dead, and that's when I started coming out of my shell ... The work was more interesting and a lot more hands-on. (2/23-year-old male)

Ah, Phase 3's a lot different to Phase 1. Phase 3, I felt as if it was real police training. There's a lot of role playing, things like that ... I felt as though I was being trained for the job ... The whole lot was satisfying. (2/20-year-old female)

A number of interviewees noted that learning to be a police officer meant learning the things they thought were missing from Phase 1:

Oh, everything [was good], like the real police learning stuff. Like you're driving, you're shooting ... We started our briefs and all that kind of stuff for court ... All the building searches, vehicle stops. All the things that, like, we're going to do every day. COPS system, you know, dealing with people. Like more relevant type stuff with people ... Like the death message type things and things like that that were not fun things to do ... Infringement notices, all our traffic stuff, all our stealing offences. Things that, you know, we could've been doing in Phase 1, I suppose, but ... it's a little bit crammed toward the end. (2/20-year-old male)

It seems that during Phase 3, students were generally happy to be at the academy because the material they now were learning was more relevant to operational policing. As one student put it: 'In Phase 3 it makes you determined to pass everything because you had so much fun in Phase 2 and you got to see what it's really like out there' (2/24-year-old female).

The Passing Out Parade

The highest expression of ritual and symbolism, and a highlight of training for the recruits, was the passing out parade.[8] After the relief of passing exams or post exams, students went through an intensive drill week (known as 'drink and drill week') in preparation for passing out day. Some students had been relegated, and some had been lost as a result of indiscretions, but most looked forward to what was commonly described to them as 'one of the best days of your career.' Staff encouraged students to enjoy themselves, though constantly warning them against throwing their careers away as a result of indiscretions, usually associated with alcohol. On Wednesday of drill week, students had a formal passing out dinner. The parade was held on Friday. Every morning there was a 7:30 parade duing which students were inspected for clothing, grooming, and evidence of hangovers. On the Thursday afternoon there was a full dress rehearsal, and students were informed – as was the custom – that they were 'terrible.' Friday was a long day. Students were issued with identification, firearms, and ammunition, and attended another full rehearsal before the formal parade, which commenced at about 11:30 a.m.

The parade is a major event in the academy calendar. It is attended by the Minister of Police, the commissioner, and deputy commissioners and regional and other senior commanders, as well as by local politician and the families and friends of students. The parade for this cohort was noteworthy for being held in the town of Goulburn rather than on the academy's parade ground. The attestation was held outside the civic centre and involved the students, a colour guard carrying the Australian, NSW state, and the NSW police flags, academy staff, police officers, the police band, mounted police, and a dog squad detachment. After the attestation ceremony, there was a parade through Goulburn to the post office, where the graduates were granted Freedom of the City (see *Goulburn Post*[9]).

Before attestation, a police chaplain asked for blessings for the Minister, the police service commissioner, the staff of the academy, and the students. He then asked God to 'grant that there may never be a shortage of men and women of courage, intelligence, character, and honesty who will volunteer to train and serve you in the course of law and order, justice and the common good.' After the prayer, the recruits were sworn in, taking either the oath or the affirmation of office. The wording of the oath was as follows:

> I, [Name], do swear that I will well and truly serve our Sovereign Lady the Queen as a police officer without favour or affection, malice or ill-will until I am legally discharged, that I will cause Her Majesty's peace to be kept and preserved, and that I will prevent to the best of my power all offences against that peace, and that while I continue to be a police officer I will to the best of my skill and knowledge discharge all my duties faithfully according to law. So help me GOD. (*Police Service Regulation* 1990, Clause 12)

After being sworn in by the commissioner, the students who had taken the oath put their Bibles back in their pockets. After a pause, all the students – now probationary constables – took a half-step back and removed, in unison, their plain-blue hat bands, revealing the familiar checked hat bands and thereby transforming themselves symbolically into police officers. This happened to great applause from their family and friends, who did not expect this to happen so dramatically. The Minister and commissioner then made speeches.

The Minister underlined the 'historic' character of the parade, congratulated the students, and told the recruits they had chosen a 'demanding, yet rewarding profession' at a time when the NSW Police Service was under the greatest scrutiny ever (referring to the Wood Royal Commission). The Minister said that the Royal Commission would lead to far-reaching reforms of the police service and that he had the full support of the commissioner in this. The Minister also underlined the importance of education in lending 'guidance and set standards for you to follow along the many paths of policing that you may choose to pursue.' He emphasized that 'the success and future direction of the police service is directly related to you the individuals who serve the people of the state.' He continued: 'I believe being a police officer is one of the most difficult and challenging jobs in our society, and I commend you all for taking up the challenge.' After thanking the families of the recruits, the Minister concluded: 'Policing is community. Policing is family.'

The commissioner's speech emphasized the pride felt by students, families, and police colleagues on this day. He added that the parade was evidence of the community's pride in the police service, and that holding the parade in the heart of the city was a way of reaching out to the community. The commissioner's speech concentrated on the public's support for police and was clearly meant to militate against the revelations of the Royal Commission. This speech focused on the commitment of police to help others, as police would be expected to 'place the safety and care of others ahead of themselves.'

After the speeches there was a presentation of money raised for charity by recruits. Then six police officers were presented with awards for bravery. These awards were especially symbolic of traditional policing, in that they reflected themes of danger, public service, selflessness, and the crime-fighting nature of police work. They served also to reinforce the sentiments of the commissioner's speech. The incidents included the following:

- The attempted rescue of a diver trapped in a saltwater inlet pump house by an officer who was not trained in underwater diving. The officer recovered the diver, who later died.
- The rescue of a man from a burning vehicle under intense flame and heat.
- The subduing of a man who was disturbed and threatening police with a large lump of concrete.
- The arrest without injury of a man threatening members of the community with a sawed-off shotgun, by two officers.
- The arrest of two offenders with the assistance of an officer who continued to participate in the pursuit even after suffering a knife wound.

In the formal and symbolic atmosphere of the parade, these awards highlighted for the community and for the families of recruits the value of policing and the selfless nature of police service. They also emphasized the *doxa* of policing to recruits and serving officers, and strengthened their bonds to one another and to the service by offering a heroic vision of the profession.

All of this took some time, and staff ran an informal sweepstakes on the number of students who would faint on the parade. Weapons instructors waited at the back of the parade to assist students who fainted; they were referred to as the 'body snatchers.' Before being dismissed, the students gave three cheers to the police service, three cheers to the police academy, and three cheers to themselves. After being dismissed, they threw their hats into the air and were joined by relatives and friends. This ended the academy part of training for the cohort, apart from one week at the end of Phase 4, prior to confirmation.

Bourdieu (2000) has commented that the disciplinary training imposed by totalitarian regimes is the limiting case of the principle of ordinary cohesion. Symbolic dress, rituals, and parades are 'intended to symbolize the (social) body as unity and difference' – that is, to mark some people off from others by establishing their oneness (145). The parade represents the culmination of the 'rites of institution'; the sense of achievement at overcoming the 'initiatory tests of preparation and selection' strongly favours the development of the *illusio*, or investment in the game (165). Recruits' own feelings of identification were reinforced by the Minister, the commissioner, the police who received medals for heroism, and the senior officers who came from all over the state to celebrate the transformation of recruits to police officers and to reinforce the *doxa* of traditional policing.

Reflections on Training at the Academy

At the beginning of this chapter we discussed the high hopes that the designers of the PREP program had for reform through recruit education. PREP was designed to provide foundational/contextual knowledge and skills as well as attitudinal development. It was hoped that this would support the shift away from traditional enforcement toward community-based policing. In this section we draw on the survey and interview data to describe recruits' assessments of their training at the academy.

General Assessment of Phase 1

Recruits expressed a very wide range of opinion about Phase 1. We briefly mentioned their dissatisfaction with this phase in an earlier section. Early criticisms were aired in debriefing sessions held at the end of Phase 2:

> The students as a class felt that they have a great deal to learn and this experience only served to highlight how much they do not know. One male student (Anglo, approximately early 20s) commented that he felt he had learnt more during his first day 'on the job' than the whole 'five weeks' of Phase 1. (Ph2Debrief2)

This mirrors comment reported by Harris more than twenty-five years ago in his study of the police academy at 'Rurban County': 'I learned more on the precinct in a week than I did here' (1978: 286). When asked what he had learned in Phase 2, one student mentioned 'procedures, paperwork, warrants, everything,' as well as the 'short cuts' that operational officers used in their work (Ph2Debrief2). Consistent with this view, which valued practical, operational, and procedural knowledge and skills, a number of students at the debriefing were critical of the foundational content of Phase 1. One student suggested that the theoretical content of Phase 1 was superfluous, since it all boiled down to treating people with respect.

> Another male student (Anglo, approximately early 20s) in response, commented that he could not see the benefit of Phase 1 in terms of sociology, structure of society and Aboriginal issues. Although after some questioning by the tutor, he did concede some relevance, his final comment was that it was not necessary, stating, 'All you need to do is treat everyone with respect, then you don't really need to know any of that stuff.' A lot of the other students seemed to nod agreement with this. (Ph2Debrief 2)

Yet one student observed that prejudice and stereotyping were problems:

> Another SPO (male, early 20s) commented disapprovingly that he had witnessed a lot of prejudice and stereotyping towards certain groups in society. Unfortunately he did not elaborate which groups, but stated that if certain people did not look 'respectable' or looked like they were 'on drugs' or 'scumbags' then the 'beats would harass them.' Surprisingly, when the tutor asked them whether the work done on stereotyping in Phase 1 was important (in response to an earlier argument by an SPO that Phase 1 had been a waste of time), two of the more vocal male SPOs stated firmly, 'No.' (Ph2Debrief 2)

Criticisms of Phase 1 were also common in the second and subsequent rounds of interviews. Not surprisingly, students who were about to be attested as probationary constables (at the end of Phase 3) placed a premium on operationally relevant knowledge:

> [Phase 1] was positive, but like I said, there was a lot of ... I think it was a lot of stuff that we won't even use, you know. Probably won't ever use. I

think they waste eight weeks ... where they could be providing us with a bit more knowledge of the street. [The] warm and fuzzy stuff you could probably take four weeks of Phase 1 to do that and maybe even the next four weeks could go in depth more into the law and stuff. (2/22-year-old female)

Many students, even some who were quite positive about Phase 1, used the term 'warm and fuzzy' in reference to it. In the second round of interviews, eleven students used that term forty-one times to describe the contents of Phase 1. Almost all the students who were critical of Phase 1 thought that the social science content was irrelevant and took up time that could have been applied to more operational issues.

Nevertheless, during the second round of interviews, reviews of Phase 1 were generally positive. A number of students said that Phase 1 had brought about an improvement in their interpersonal skills (2/27-year-old male). Another student said that Phase 1 had changed for the better his approach to thinking about things:

I liked it. I enjoyed it because, as I said before, it laid a good foundation ... It started you thinking along different lines rather than purely black and white, 'This is what I have to do, this is what I have to achieve.' It got you thinking along different lines. Which is important, I mean when you go out there in the field and you're actually a probationary constable or you become a policeman, confirmed as a police officer, you've got the power to take somebody's freedom of movement off them. And that's a basic human right. So you've got to be able to take into consideration all the aspects of the situation before you take any steps so that you're fully informed or, or you've got an idea of what's going on rather than just saying, 'Well, this is what I have to do,' and do that. (2/24-year-old male)

This student represented a success for the Phase 1 curriculum and teaching. It seems that he attributed to Phase 1 the development of a reflective approach to police work, was aware of the tensions between human rights and police powers, and had taken some steps toward developing a flexible, problem-solving approach to policing. Other interviewees expressed similar assessments of the foundational material in Phase 1, suggesting that 'it certainly provided us with a basic background for Phase 2, which was in its way helpful' (2/21-year-old-male), and that it taught about tolerance, which was 'a main weapon in the armour of policing' (2/male, age >30). All of this suggests that at

least for some students, PREP was achieving its stated aims of providing foundational and contextual information and encouraging attitudinal
development. However, not all students in the second round of interviews were as positive about the contextual material. In one thoughtful
interview, a student questioned whether attitudes and prejudices could
be changed:

> [There was] a lot of sociology stuff ... which I love but a lot of people
> hated. ... I think it's important but I have really strong views. I feel that a
> lot of people have already, unfortunately, got their own prejudices and
> *they come* into the job ... and there's not a lot that you can do. You can try
> but I don't know how successful it is. [Q: But do you think it's worth
> trying?] Oh, yeah. But I think there'd have to be some kind of training, I
> don't know what. But something where you could really get people to see.
> (2/29-year-old female)

Another student said he enjoyed the multicultural content of Phase
1. Yet while positive about learning about different people, he did not
think this knowledge would actually help him deal with them:

> [Q: And did what they taught you in Phase 1 actually help you deal with
> these people?] No, not really. See, what you do is you go with the flow of
> the situation and most of the police officers I worked with out in the field,
> they were really good and then again, they've all had experience with it
> before. (2/29-year-old male)

Here we encounter the nub of the problem of trying to bring about
reform through courses at the academy: students will bow to experience and 'go with the flow.' Much depends on the quality of operational role models – an issue discussed in chapter 5. These interviews
also indicate that some students make conscious effort to 'fit in' and
adjust their behaviour to the rules of the game whether they are at the
academy or in the field. This was recognized by a tutor:

> Students are very cunning. They can tell you what they think you want to
> hear. So they will support you while they're here at the academy, and yet
> when they get out to the field they'll be very quick to jump. And I guess in
> their position, very few people would do otherwise. I mean, they are
> coming out [to the] field, they're trying very hard to fit in, and I don't

think challenging what their peers are doing would enable them to fit in. The pressure of the culture of the organization, I think, has a lot to do with that. (InstA)

It was clear in a number of interviews that students tended to value training materials that they thought would be useful for operational policing. Phase 1 contained some elementary material on police powers and officer safety. Students who commented on this aspect of Phase 1 said that this was the part of the phase they enjoyed most and considered most relevant: 'Yeah, officer survival ... the handcuffing and the hand-to-hand combat ... That was, sort of, as soon as we got into that it sort of sprung everyone to life' (2/23-year-old male). This interview again underlines how students are attracted to the immediate, direct, and skills-based aspects of the training – the material that they think is going to be of practical use and that transmits the special craft knowledge of policing. There is the obvious rationalization that this material is essential because of the dangers of policing. But skills training is far more obviously about learning to 'be' a police officer than is learning about the social context of policing. As such, it is much more attractive to students who are intoxicated by the *illusio* of operational policing.

In part, views about Phase 1 in the second round of interviews reflected students' concern about being attested, and having to go out into the field as probationary constables. Students felt that they needed to be prepared, and they wanted to be able to get the job done and be accepted by operational police. This was manifested in their desire to possess directory knowledge; from the students' point of view, acceptance came with being competent and not being a burden to operational police. Overall, the points of dissatisfaction with Phase 1 that can be discerned in some of the interviews need to be balanced against the generally positive responses contained in others.

Recruits' opinions of Phase 1 seemed to become more negative as they gained experience. As mentioned before, more than half the respondents in Survey 2 thought they were well prepared for Phase 2; fewer than one-third felt unprepared, and the rest weren't sure. Surveys 3 and 4 asked respondents about the effectiveness of academy Phases in preparing them for police work. Responses to these surveys (see Table 4.6) indicate that members of the cohort did not regard their Phase 1 training in a very positive light, at least in terms of its contribution to preparing them for police work. In fact, in Survey 3, 92 per cent

TABLE 4.6
Effectiveness of Phase 1 (Survey 3, N=130; Survey 4, N=86)

Effectiveness of Phase 1	Survey 3		Survey 4	
	Frequency	Per cent	Frequency	Per cent
Very effective	2	2	0	—
Effective	9	7	11	13
Not very effective	48	37	31	36
Not at all effective	71	55	44	51
TOTAL	130	100	86	100

Note: There were four missing values for this question in Survey 3 and one in Survey 4.

of respondents thought that Phase 1 was not very effective or not at all effective in preparing them for police work. In Survey 4 some 87 per cent of respondents were of the same view. Although this may suggest that the percentage of respondents who were positive about Phase 1 had increased in Survey 4, the response rate of Survey 4 was low relative to the other three surveys, so this difference may be due to response bias.

By the third interview, interviewees had had the benefit of one year of operational experience and were about to graduate and be confirmed in the rank of constable. Some had difficulty even remembering what had happened in Phase 1: 'Phase 1 – I didn't see, I didn't benefit anything from that. ... I can't even recall many things that we did in Phase 1' (3/26-year-old male).

Like some students at the second round of interviews, probationers thought that Phase 1 was too long and did not dwell sufficiently on practical issues:

Like, I think Phase 1 was a bit long, it dabbles more into the psychology of things, like how people think. Like, that helps, but I think they could have shown us more relevant things ... such as ... the breath analysis machine and ... how to charge somebody on the computer ... More officer survival skills, more physical training, that's dropped right off now ... Actual front-line police work, yeah, I think that a bit more emphasis can be placed on that. (3/23-year-old male)

One probationer seemed to suggest that lack of practical knowledge in Phase 1 made the job of field trainers more difficult. This comment underlines students' fears of being a burden to operational police:

> Maybe just cut out a lot of the stuff we learned in Phase 1 too. Like they could just intensify the whole training into say three months of intensive training ... You'd be such a better copper, you know, and it'd be easier on the trainers out in the field ... Because it does get you down when people say, 'Oh, say, did you learn that down there?' And you go 'No.' And they go, 'Oh, what are they bloody teaching you?' (3/19-year-old female)

By the fourth interview (6 months after confirmation as a police constable), only two interviewees mentioned Phase 1 specifically. One was dismissive of all the content of Phase 1 and had a low opinion of academy training in general:

> I reckon [training at the academy is] crap basically ... They're doing I suppose the best with the things they've got at hand but there definitely should be more discipline and physical work and things like that. Less wasted time studying meaningless subjects that won't affect the way you fulfil your job as a police officer. [Q: Aha ... do you want to give me an example of those?] Oh basically all Phase 1 of the training program. Fundamentals in sociology and psychology and things like that – those sort of things come with common sense and learning that on the job. I do understand what they're trying to do but once again that comes with experience and just having people skills basically. (4/19-year-old male)

The other constable was also unimpressed with Phase 1, but was much more positive about the rest of the academy course:

> I mean they did a lot of simulations and things like that which were good but I don't know. They're just – I suppose it just seems more real and you can learn a lot more from it when it's a real situation. But yeah, the academy – Phase 1 was a bit of a waste of time but the rest of it was good. (4/21-year-old female)

Having tasted operational policing in Phase 2, students were impatient to complete their studies and get out into the police stations. Though Phase 3 was hard work, it was tolerated because the material was perceived as operationally relevant. Students resented Phase 1 as a waste of time. That time could have been spent on operationally relevant material.

TABLE 4.7
Effectiveness of Phase 3 (Survey 3, N=134: Survey 4, N=87)

Effectiveness of Phase 3	Survey 3		Survey 4	
	Frequency	Percentage	Frequency	Percentage
Very effective	9	7	11	13
Effective	97	75	50	59
Not very effective	22	17	20	24
Not at all effective	1	1	4	5
Total	129	100	85	100

Note: There were 5 missing values for this question in Survey 3 and 2 for Survey 4.

General Assessment of Phase 3

In Surveys 3 and 4, respondents were much more positive about Phase 3 than about Phase 1 (see Table 4.7). In Survey 3, less than 20 per cent of respondents thought that Phase 3 was not effective or not at all effective in preparing them for police work; 92 per cent of respondents expressed similar views about Phase 1 (see Table 4.6). In Survey 4 the proportion of respondents who had negative views about the effectiveness of Phase 3 had increased to 29 per cent. The proportion of respondents who thought that Phase 3 was 'very effective' in preparing them for police work increased from 7 per cent in Survey 3 to 13 per cent in Survey 4. However, some caution is necessary in interpreting these results because of possible response bias in Survey 4.

One constable interviewed in round 3 said that Phase 4 brought about a complete reassessment of academy training. For this student, operational realities suggested that it was time to start learning all over again. Yet, for this student, this did not mean that academy training was irrelevant:

Oh the sergeants were good, very helpful, very approachable, some of them reminded me of war stories that I heard from people here, like, you know, you get out there and they turn around and say to you, 'Forget all that shit that you've learned at the academy, you're in the real world now.' [Q: And how did you respond to that?] I just took it in stride basically. I mean, it's up to the individual to make up their own mind what they want to forget and learn, but for me it was sort of maintain most of what I learnt down here [at the academy] and use that to refer to whilst I was working. (3/24-year-old male)

This student went on to discuss the usefulness of academy training, and stated that academy training was essential. For him, the residential nature of academy training was beneficial because his family did not understand the demands of the course:

> I don't think that I would have been able to perform out in the field had I not had the training at the academy ... I don't think I would have done half as well as I did, or concentrated myself as well as I had, if it weren't a residential experience ... It was hard in that respect – being down here and away from [my family] – but it was good that if I weren't down here I don't think I would have done as well as I had done or concentrated my effort as much as I had. (3/24-year-old male)

This interview raises the cultural theme of difference (the theme of 'Outsiders' in Crank 1998), and suggests how police training and the occupation of policing come to be associated with the view that police are outsiders. Van Maanen (1973) argued that police see themselves as a distinct occupational group, apart from society. This interview hints at how training at the academy, and on-the-job training as experienced in Phase 4, can have an impact on intimate relationships, reinforcing powerfully the belief held by both police and the public that police distinguish sharply between themselves and 'others.' This issue is taken up in chapters 5 and 6.

Danger and Its Effects on Perceptions of Training

The interviews and survey data suggest that members of the cohort tended to value what they perceived as operationally relevant material (i.e., as opposed to theoretical). Many articles and books on police occupational culture have discussed the profoundly instrumental nature of police culture. In our material this theme is perhaps most evident in comments about the need for officer safety training. Many interviewees emphasized that police work was essentially dangerous, and criticized the training they received at the academy for paying so little attention to officer safety issues.

Some interviewees saw danger as a special case of a more general conflict between the police and the public and other organizations and interests. The risks involved in policing – whether direct or indirect – make it especially necessary for police to be able to depend on their colleagues. In the fourth round of interviews, one constable regarded solidarity as a key positive aspect of police culture:

> Once again you know that ... if you're in danger or something you can rely on your friends to do their utmost to help you out. Basically it's a job where in today's society you're an easy target and it seems to be that most organizations, being the public, the judicial system, whatever, are geared against you and you're always criticized, as opposed to complimented for the good aspects of the job. And I'm talking there about the police as a whole. Not any individual officers, so it's good to know that you can count on the people that you work with to stand behind you to a certain extent. (4/19-year-old male)

Many students entered the academy convinced that policing is dangerous:

> My father, when I first applied, like, right back at school I was talking about joining the police force and he was like 'no, no, no.' He didn't want me to do that because of the danger, of course. It is not a very safe profession. (3/25-year-old male)

> I've read all my sister's police journals and ... they have investigation section and how they found out criminals did this and they showed you actual photos ... One of them I remember was a bullet hole straight through the back of a head and like people just don't realize ... what it's all about. It's not just out there picking up criminals, there's putting your life in danger to save others. (1/22-year-old female)

> Probably another [fear] is being hurt as well. Which I think goes through everyone's mind whether they admit it or not. But I also know that, probably down the track I'll be getting a good training anyway with the survival thing that ... we'll be doing in a couple of weeks or so ... [Q: But it's just the physical danger that you're concerned about?] Yeah, yeah, pretty much. I mean I think a lot of people who say that they're not are telling lies. [Laugh] (1/21-year-old female)

According to Crank, danger and its anticipation is one of the central themes of police work:

> Danger is a poorly understood phenomenon of police work. Academicians will paint a picture of work that is rarely dangerous, characterized

primarily by monotony. Police will describe a darker picture, danger and violence is an endemic hazard of their environment. Well which is it? Part of the answer lies in how danger is measured, and part of the answer lies in how danger is viewed through the lens of culture. (1998: 105)

Drawing on work by Cullen and colleagues (1983), Crank (107–8) comments that concern over risk and danger, though out of all proportion to the actual risk of injury, is nevertheless an important functional adaptation to the potential risks of police work. At the same time, concerns over danger contributed to work stress and a depressive symptomology.

Many of those we interviewed emphasized the importance of officer safety (OS) training. Some simply stressed the relevance of OS:

> Well, a lot of it was relevant. The OS side of it – the officer survivor skills and things like that in regards to handcuffing, the holds, your own safety holds, holds for prisoners, and things like that. Ah ... skills in regard to approaching houses, all that side of it's very relevant. (3/male, age >30)

Others emphasized that OS training can save lives:

> Oh, [Phase 3]'s been great. The information is so much more relevant ... We do a lot. We do firearms which is good, batons. [Q: Officer survival?] Yeah, OS, yeah. 'Cause those sort of things save your life and those are the sort of things you want to do a lot. (2/19-year-old female)

Some probationers thought that training at the academy was too controlled and not realistic:

> The OS is good, but the problem with it also is down here it's very controlled and, you know, you do handcuffing, and, you know, the bloke's happy to put his hands behind his back. You're just never taught what to do when someone's trying to swing ... at you and you've got to take them down and lock them up, put the handcuffs on. You're just never taught that, or you're never taught to deal with someone who's drunk, or, you know, aggressive and basically doesn't give a shit. (3/20-year-old male)

This begs the question of exactly how the training could be less controlled and still safe. Other interviewees were more thoughtful about the responsibility that comes with police powers to use coercive force:

On the day we're attested, we're issued with firearms. [Q: And how do you feel about that?] Once again, I think it's ... a big responsibility again ... That's a real lot of responsibility sitting on your hip ... It's there, I don't know whether it'll be something that you get used to. It's just the thought of having to use it, I guess, and the thought of having to make that decision in a split second and know that it's the right decision I guess. [Q: Do you have much training about that?] With the firearms and everything you do, yeah. I think there could be a little bit more training on the OS side of things, but yeah, basically the operation of firearms and batons and the procedures you've got to follow and the various, I guess, safeguards that have to be in place before you use any of them – you get trained up really well on those. (2/23-year-old male)

Danger is one of the key themes in the doxic vision of policing. That is, danger is an element of axiomatic knowledge of police culture, self-evident to police practitioners, and as indicated by the presuppositions that recruits brought to the academy, also self-evident to the public. There is no dispute that police work is inherently dangerous. The realities of police work are pretty mundane and boring, but the recruits we interviewed tended to evaluate their training in terms of its relevance to operational policing, and valued above all those aspects of the training that they identified with danger management. In part, this reflects the truth of Bittner's (1978) argument – accepted both by recruits and by police in general – that the use of coercive force is the factor that distinguishes policing from other professions. The socially mandated potential for exercise of force is what everyone knows implicitly about police, and what influences all interactions between the police and the public. In valuing danger management training above all other aspects of training, recruits are expressing at the level of habitus the symbolic power that has its origins in the social relations constitutive of the field of policing.

Table 4.8 indicates the degree to which students at the end of Phase 3 valued different elements of training. This table shows that consistent with the interview material, students tended to rank officer safety items very highly; in fact, officer safety and survival skills, use of firearms and batons, and weaponless control had the highest rankings. Even so, there is also very little variance in the scores for each item. Only the Starpower game[10] and close order drill had average scores greater than 3 (not very relevant); the great majority of items were rated between 1 (very relevant) and 2 (somewhat relevant).

Male and female students tended to rank the elements of academy

TABLE 4.8
Relevance of academy training (Survey 3, N=134)

Aspect of training	Score			Rank	
	Mean score	Male mean score	Female mean score	Male rank	Female rank
Officer safety and survival skills	1.02	1.01	1.05	1.0	2.0
Use of firearms and batons	1.04	1.05	1.02	2.0	1.0
Weaponless control	1.09	1.11	1.05	4.0	3.0
The law	1.10	1.12	1.07	5.0	4.5
Child abuse and sexual assault	1.11	1.10	1.14	3.0	7.5
The legal system	1.16	1.21	1.07	6.5	4.5
Role of police in society	1.24	1.21	1.31	6.5	16.5
The ten fatal errors	1.24	1.29	1.14	10.0	7.5
Crimes of assault	1.24	1.23	1.26	8.0	13.0
Communication and interpersonal skills	1.24	1.26	1.21	9.0	11.0
Police procedures and policy	1.27	1.30	1.19	11.0	9.5
Driving skills	1.28	1.33	1.19	12.0	9.5
Role: Victims, witnesses, suspects	1.30	1.40	1.10	19.5	6.0
Sudden and suspicious deaths	1.31	1.34	1.26	13.5	13.0
Property crime	1.32	1.34	1.27	13.5	15.0
Street safety	1.34	1.38	1.26	16.5	13.0
Written communication skills	1.36	1.38	1.33	16.5	18.5
Policing the roads	1.37	1.40	1.33	8.0	18.5
Physical fitness	1.39	1.37	1.43	15.0	25.0
Problem-solving	1.40	1.40	1.38	19.5	20.5
The causes of crime	1.41	1.41	1.39	21.0	22.0
Loss on survivors, relatives	1.42	1.44	1.38	22.0	20.5
Police health	1.46	1.49	1.40	23.0	23.5
Community-based policing	1.48	1.51	1.40	25.0	23.5
Ethics and professionalism	1.48	1.56	1.31	26.0	16.5
Police 'Mission' & 'Statement of Values'	1.51	1.50	1.52	24.0	27.0
Presentation and dress regulations	1.62	1.68	1.50	28.0	26.0
Police intelligence procedures	1.63	1.63	1.62	27.0	29.0
Policing ethnic communities	1.72	1.80	1.55	30.0	28.0
Policing Aboriginal communities	1.73	1.77	1.64	29.0	30.0
Discipline at the Academy	1.86	1.87	1.86	31.0	31.0
Non-law enforcement policing	1.97	1.98	1.95	32.0	32.0
Starpower Game	2.19	2.24	2.07	33.0	33.0
Close order drill	2.83	2.99	2.52	34.0	34.0

Q: The following areas were addressed in your Academy training. Based on your experiences so far, please rate your opinion of the relevance of these to practical police work where:

1. Very relevant
2. Somewhat relevant
3. Not very relevant
4. Not at all relevant

training in a similar manner. The correlation between the ranks of average scores for males and females was 0.91.[11] Even so, there were some differences in average rankings of areas of training by males and females. For example, males ranked the role of police in society, policing the roads, and physical fitness, higher than females. Females ranked ethics and professionalism and roles of victims, witnesses, and suspects higher than males. We need to be mindful that scores for these items had a very small range, so caution is required in the interpretation of these data.

Anticipating the Field

The data presented in this chapter suggest that recruits in the cohort brought with them a wide range of expectations and assumptions when they joined the police. Their initial experience at the academy was not so much 'reality shock' (Hughes 1958) as a mixture of apprehension, confusion, and some pleasant surprises. Although some were anxious and fearful of the new environment and very conscious of their lowly position in the organization hierarchy, most found comfort in the solidarity of classmates and in the support shown by the senior class and academy staff. The importance of 'social capital' (e.g., friendship and support networks) became obvious early on in recruits' socialization experiences. The overall sense of common purpose and symbolic power was reinforced by the uniform and by the paraphernalia that formed part of the policing hexis.

Recruits often found that their expectations of the academy were not met, but some regarded this as a positive rather than a negative. Some were surprised that the academy was not as harsh and militaristic as they expected. This was a disappointment to those who saw strict discipline as an integral part of policing. For these students, the discrepancy between their expectations of police training and the relaxed postreform academy became a source of dissatisfaction. Recruits' dissatisfaction with the academy increased considerably after Phase 2. The part of the Phase 1 curriculum directed at raising social awareness was dismissed as 'warm and fuzzy' and irrelevant to training. Most students identified strongly with the attitudes and values of operational police, who played some part in discrediting the academy. Recruits endured the stressful and academically demanding Phase 3 only because they were eager to return to the field in Phase 4.

In some accounts of police socialization, the police academy is portrayed as the first and often most influential mode of transmission of police culture. For example, both the Wood Report (1997) and the Fitzgerald Report (1989) mentioned the academy's role in promoting negative police culture among recruits. Typically, such accounts assume a common purpose among field and academy police, and fail to recognize that a police organization is not monolithic and may well harbour varying – and perhaps even conflicting – sets of interests. These accounts may also overemphasize the impact that a short period of training can have in the face of a working lifetime of operational policing. Our interviews with students and staff suggest that in the postreform era of police education in New South Wales, the academy–field divide was one of the more fundamental divisions in police occupational culture. Many police in the field criticized the academy for not producing recruits who were operationally competent. Many recruits soon internalized the same kinds of views, and were critical of the perceived lack of relevance of significant portions of the academy curriculum. At the same time, academy staff sometimes regarded the operational field as the enemy. From the perspective of many academy staff, operational police actively undermined the academy's attempts to mould the student's attitudes and behaviours. They did so by belittling the curriculum, by criticizing the competence of staff, and by establishing in the minds of students the need to cut corners and not do the job right. Recruits who joined the police bearing the mythic vision of police as crime fighters were initially surprised by the social science content of the Phase 1 curriculum, but many appreciated its value. However, operational officers' criticisms encountered in Phase 2 undermined recruits' confidence in the academy teaching and raised doubts about the validity of the community policing model that formed the basis of PREP.

We suggest that, in the case of New South Wales at least, the academy is best viewed as a subfield distinct from the field of operational policing. The academy constituted a relatively idealistic, formal environment, based on conceptions of proper behaviour and liberal hopes for reform through education. Relative to the controlled, restrained, and formal environment of the academy, operational policing presented a more organic, coercive, and powerful socializing environment. This was in part a result of the obvious visceral realities of operational policing, which captured the imagination of so many recruits during Phase 2. Compared to 'real' policing, the academy – which recruits had been so pleased to become part of at the beginning of Phase 1 – became a pale substitute, and increasingly the focus of criticism for its lack of realism and remoteness from operational concerns. Thus, socialization at the academy involved not only learning the rules of the game proper to the subfield of the academy, but also beginning to refine and develop an anticipation of the game of operational policing. In sum, recruits went through a second phase of anticipatory socialization in Phase 3 as they prepared for induction as probationary constables and participation in the 'real' game. In developing a feel for the game of operational policing as probationers, the cohort became more and more critical of the academy experience – in particular, those aspects regarded as not directly concerned with preparation for operational duties. This shift reflects recruits' apperception of the essentially practical nature of policing and their growing awareness of the divide between the academy agenda, driven by reformist aspirations of community policing, and the agenda of the operational field, still dominated by the *doxa* of crime control.

5

Learning in the Field

By the time they began their field training in Phase 4, recruits were glad to discard the lowly status of 'student police officer' and assume the new rank of 'probationary constables.' With this new status, they crossed all three types of boundaries (Schein 1968b): vertical, radial, and circumferential. They had moved higher in rank, closer to the centre of policing, and to a new set of duties. Since first being exposed to operational police work in Phase 2, they had gone through a second wave of anticipatory socialization: all of Phase 3 was in preparation for 'real' police work in Phase 4 and beyond. Criticisms of the academy encountered in Phase 2 pointed ominously to a disjuncture between the 'full professional model' promulgated by the academy curriculum and the 'street cop' view of policing competence. Students sensed that the 'game' played in the operational field was going to be quite different: the theoretical knowledge they were gaining from the academy was going to have little currency on the street. Many recruits were disappointed with the academy's training and did not see what use they would have for the 'warm and fuzzy stuff' – the psychological, sociological, and ethical aspects of the curriculum. In some sense they were still holding on to the mythic vision of policing that they had first projected onto the occupation. Phase 4 was where this vision was going to be realized – operational policing promised to be lively, adventurous, and full of opportunities for probationers to fight crime and make a difference.

In this chapter we describe the experience of probationers in Phase 4 as they learned the practical craft of policing. It shows how recruits adjusted to the demands of a different field – 'real' police work as defined by the complexities and exigencies of operational policing –

using various coping and adaptive strategies. Once again, they found themselves at the bottom of the hierarchy in the new environment in terms of knowledge and power, and had to strive to 'prove themselves' and gain acceptance. In the local area commands they were sent to, they were exposed to a range of practice models, both 'good' and 'bad,' and had to actively negotiate a 'fit' between what they had learned at the academy and what was required by this new field. Their experience suggests that Phase 4 was not so much 'training decay' (CARE 1990) as a period of incremental adjustments of the habitus, during which they acquired a 'feel for the game' of operational policing.

The Requirements of Phase 4

At the time of the research, field training in New South Wales took forty-nine weeks: the first twenty-four, probationary constables worked in designated demonstration patrols[1]; the remainder, in training patrols. Their placements were arranged so as to 'ensure that Probationary Constables are provided with an appropriate range of policing experiences within a supportive training structure' (NSWPS 1993: 72). In formal terms, the probationers worked under the 'mentorship' of field training officers (FTOs). They were required to prepare case write-ups of their actual work; to pass examinations on police practice, law, and procedures; and to complete various assignments.

Probationers went through an eight-week induction period at the demonstration patrols. The induction period was to give probationers 'the opportunity to make themselves familiar with both the geographic and demographic aspects of their Patrol' (NSWPS 1993: 72). During this time they were 'partnered' by two FTOs (known as 'buddies') for four weeks each. Following the induction period, probationers were to work with qualified FTOs for the remainder of their time in the demonstration patrol. The point of using FTOs was to ensure that probationers were 'inducted into policework by officers to whom they can relate and use as a role model' (73). At the training patrols, probationers formed part of the 'authorized strength' of the patrol. The official position for this period of training was that every effort would be made to ensure that probationers 'work only with qualified Field Training Officers,' and where these were not available, 'the Patrol Commander and Patrol Training Officer must ensure the availability of those police officers whose experience makes them suitable for working with Probationary Constables and who are also able to help in the completion of Case Write-ups' (73–4).

For case write-ups, probationers were to choose at least five policing tasks from a list of ten general duties case types. In these cases, they had to have had a 'major involvement as primary response and/or investigative officer' (74). The case write-ups were considered 'central' to the 'learning and assessment methodology of PREP'– a methodology that 'maintains continuity in the cycle by which students learn by watching in Phase Two, learn by watching and doing during simulations in Phase Three, and learn by doing and reflecting upon their experiences during Phase Four' (74).

In these write-ups, probationers were to demonstrate a range of generic skills: 'understanding and analysis of problems, decision-making and case management, and written and oral communications' (77). Besides the case write-ups, probationers also had to complete two pacer examinations on 'need to know' subjects such as firearms and police powers, a major examination, and a field assignment (79–80).

Teaching in the Field: Views of Field Training Officers

Unlike the academy instructors described in chapter 4, the FTOs who participated in interviews[2] for this research had very little understanding of the philosophy of PREP. In fact, most seemed to regard field training as separate from PREP rather than one of its phases. FTOs generally had no direct dealings with the academy. The Field Training Directorate (FTD) was the coordinating body, and the education and development officer (EDO) in each local area command (LAC) was the local coordinator. In some LACs there was little communication between the EDOs and the FTOs. On the whole, there was a lack of understanding between the academy and the FTOs. This breakdown in communication meant that the transition from the academy to the field was not well coordinated. Nor, as one FTO pointed out, was it considered important:

> Number one, they need to look at the transition period from the academy to the street. The people who are teaching the new recruits that are coming out ... they never meet them until they arrive at the patrol. Quite often they're not even introduced to them. They'll just turn up one shift and say, 'I'm your new buddy,' and you haven't even been told that you've got a new buddy. Really poor, because for a start, that destabilizes the person. They start to think that they're not worthwhile. Nobody spent the time to give them a decent integration ... Where really I think as field training officers we should be taken to the academy, allowed the time to go down

there and meet your new buddy, and have a talk to them, see what their fears are, see what their aspirations are, and go from there. (FTOG, 30-year-old male C)

There was no formal procedure for selecting FTOs. A number of interviewees told us they had been asked by their local area commander to become FTOs because there was a shortage of senior police in their LAC. Some officers became FTOs because they found the job rewarding: working with keen probationers could change the trainer's own level of motivation and job satisfaction. Some FTOs genuinely enjoyed teaching – they got 'a real buzz' out of it (FTOH, 34-year-old male SC). Others saw the job as one that could contribute to raising the standards of practice, since 'a lot of the people who are teaching now weren't taught properly in the first place by people who weren't taught properly' (FTOJ, 34-year-old male SC). A number of interviewees were heavily influenced by their own field training experience, where they had 'really good' FTOs who were 'fantastic' teachers and they learned 'the right way' (FTOI, 29-year-old male SC). They believed that probationers often mirrored the attitudes of their FTOs. The selection of FTOs came under some heavy criticism from the interviewees. Often, FTOs were not chosen on the basis of their communication or teaching skills:

There are no ... really good screening processes as to who are the better teachers. In my observations there are a lot of very, very poor FTOs out there and they're not teaching well, so as a result the person goes through their first four weeks with one buddy, their second four weeks with another buddy and they can have real problems and I've seen that happen time and again. (FTOG, 30-year-old male C)

Because of the lack of proper selection and screening, a probationer's field training experience could be badly affected by a poor FTO:

I don't know what the culling procedure is but there are some FTOs who fall into that category [of those] who have not been shown properly. So they're teaching poor practices themselves ... I see FTOs that sit on their arse, the poor probationary constable sitting on their arse inside and they wait ... for the radio to call ... and they go out and do the job; they do the job, come back down and they sit down on their arses ... that's not right. (FTOJ, 34-year-old male SC)

Most FTOs were not aware of the existence of any guidelines for field training. The only guidance they received was 'the actual rules concerning procedures such as when reports have got to be handed in, what reports are to consist of, that kind of information – more administrative stuff than actual educational stuff' (FTOC, 28-year-old male C). FTOs saw their job as introducing probationers to the nature of police work and showing them practical skills such as use of correct procedures, how to speak to the public, and how to work with other officers. As one interviewee summarized it, the goal was to ease the probationer into the role of police officer, to 'get them up to a certain level of knowledge where they're comfortable performing as a constable' (FTOA, 29-year-old male SC). Though training emphasis varied, it was clear from the following FTO that probationers were not expected to become 'a copy of someone else,' but to choose from a variety of role models the 'best bits' to integrate into their own practice:

I'd like to think that when I'm finished with a prob that they're keen to go out and like I always tell them I'm not perfect, don't copy me but pick some good things that I do, pick some good things that your next buddy does, pick the best bits out of everyone and put them all together, and try and make yourself that because you want to be yourself, you don't want to be anyone else and I like to think that I've helped them become them, not a copy of someone else. (FTOZ, 25-year-old male C)

Some FTOs spent time getting to know the probationer personally to 'break the ice' (FTOC, 28-year-old male C). Others insisted on maintaining a more formal teacher–student relationship, at least initially:

One thing I say to them is ... don't try and be my mate and my friend and the rest of it. I'm here to teach you and if you learn in the right way, naturally we will just become friends, whereas you'll get some people that'll come out and their FTO on the first shift, they'll go, 'Let's go down the pub for a drink' and they'll sit down and they'll talk to them just matey-matey, blokey-blokey things and you get that blokey-blokey attitude and then you think, 'Oh well, I can just kind of not really do this because you know he's my mate,' and all that sort of stuff. And that's not the attitude that you should have. It should be straight cut and dry, 'I'm here to teach you things, and it's up to you to learn as much as you can.' (FTOI, 29-year-old male SC)

Although field training was largely ad hoc and unstructured, we were impressed that some FTOs independently developed their own teaching plans, role-play techniques, and even handouts:

> I always make sure I show them how to do their notebooks, the exact same way every single time ... I give them a handout of how to write it up properly and then I expect them to write it that way every single time. And it's a bit like doing a shopping list because you know what's going to go after everything ... The first shift I'd give them the photocopy of the notebook, they have to go through it all and I say, 'That's how you're going to do your notebook ... while you're working with me.' And all the time they always adopt that same method because it's so simple. (FTOI, 29-year-old male SC)

> I have a handout which I give them, which is a laminated card to put in their notebook which is the legal way, the correct way to do it ... 'cause I'm sick and tired of them not doing it right. (FTOJ, 34-year-old male SC)

Most FTOs agreed that it was important to provide probationers with positive feedback and reinforcement to boost their confidence. One interviewee described how he consciously adopted this approach because of his own probationary experience, which was 'very ordinary.' He was trained by unskilled and disinterested FTOs, and as a result he 'made some monumental stuff-ups, just out of nervousness':

> Generally if there's enough of the 'Yes, you did that well' ... Yeah, they become more confident. They feel happier about the job ... They're more keen to get in and do the job themselves ... I feel good when I give someone positive feedback. (FTOC, 28-year-old male C)

The FTO was required to fill out a progress report at the end of the four-week training period with the probationer. This report consisted of a self-assessment by the probationer and an assessment by the FTO. Utilizing a checklist of skills, knowledge, and attitude items, it indicated whether the probationer's progress was satisfactory or unsatisfactory. This report was administered by the EDO in each local area. Some FTOs didn't like the self-assessment dimension, seeing it as unrealistic and as ineffective for identifying problems: 'We're not taught to be open about our weaknesses. So nobody is going to be putting their jaw out to get their head knocked off. They're going to be all lying, saying they're capable and they're doing well' (FTOG, 30-year-old male C). FTOs were often unwilling to give honest feedback about a probationer's performance:

A lot of it I think is the FTOs are not a hundred per cent honest. They never want to write any nasty things about people or say that the person needs help, and then when it comes to the crunch, you know, the EDO's just reading it and that's all they've got to go by, and they're saying, 'Oh, the person's doing OK, you know, no major problems, a few minor problems' ... And then down the track sort of just before they're supposed to go back for Phase 5, someone says, 'They shouldn't be going back for Phase 5, they've got all these problems,' you know, and the EDO says, 'Well, no one conveyed their problems to me. I don't know anything about it. It's too late to do anything.' And they then become a confirmed constable and they're senior person on the truck and all the problems snowball and that's happened. (FTOF, 30-year-old female C)

Some FTOs told us that when performance is unsatisfactory, there ought to be a meeting mediated by the EDO so that the problem can be handled fairly. According to most interviewees, probationers rarely got the sack during Phase 4, probably because the organization had already invested so much on the training.

FTOs were surprisingly critical of the field training program. Many felt that insufficient time and inadequate resources were devoted to it. Several suggested ways of making the initial buddy period more conducive to proper training – for example, the use of a separate training car (FTOB, 38-year-old male SC), or setting aside one day for clearing the backlogs and explaining things to the probationer (FTOE, 41-year-old male C). Probationers were not always partnered with a buddy during their first eight weeks. Some FTOs saw this as evidence that training was not seen as a high priority when duties were rostered:

The continuity is very, very poor because the actual rostering and things like that don't see being with your buddy as a high priority. Quite often you're not rostered with your buddy and your buddy is just thrown into the pool of constables, which is a really bad way because they're insecure when they come out of the academy, they're looking for someone to latch on to and they're hoping they're going to get some good teaching when they come out of the academy, and they rarely get any of that. OK? So it's a sink-or-swim approach ... the realities are that quite often your buddy might have court, your buddy may have rest days, may have days in lieu, may have a holiday ... so therefore you're just thrown into the general pool of constables and you may not even be with an FTO, a trained FTO – just another guy more senior to you. And you're swinging in the breeze. That's how it operates. (FTOG, 30-year-old male C)

The practice of rostering two probationary constables together was 'supposed to never happen,' but according to one FTO it happened 'quite often.' Even though in these situations one of the probationers was 'generally nearing the end of their training period,' it was still unsatisfactory as 'it takes you at least three years to be really ... competent' (FTOG, 30-year-old male C).

FTOs usually carried a heavier workload. In busy patrols, some took in one buddy after another until they burned out. Their work was not always recognized:

There's people here that are FTOs that are prepared to have a bit of a break from it ... At one stage we were getting like ten probationary constables every three months and they were virtually doing buddy periods non-stop ... but basically [they] have burnt out and they're prepared to have a break from it. So I think ... there could be a bit more support for the FTOs ... a bit more awareness from the rest of the station about who are and who aren't the FTOs. A bit of recognition. (FTOF, 30-year-old female C)

In general, the field training program was seen as haphazard and poorly organized, with no time for debriefing when buddies changed over. According to some, this showed that field training had 'a very, very low priority' in the organization (FTOG, 30-year-old male C).

Even though they did not identify themselves as part of PREP, most of the FTOs we interviewed seemed motivated by a desire to pass on a version of professionalism – they wanted probationers to learn how to do things properly, but also efficiently and in a way that satisfied legal and bureaucratic requirements. They also shaped probationers' attitudes (though not always consciously) by encouraging them to 'listen,' to be enthusiastic about the job, and to use their common sense. Some FTOs were careful not to criticize the academy; even so, the impression we got from the interviewees was that few FTOs were aware of what was taught at the academy, unless they themselves had been through PREP recently. The old saying, 'Forget everything you learned at the academy,' was more a caricature than part of reality. FTOs themselves distinguished between the positive and negative aspects of police culture, and they were not apologists for bad practice:

> I definitely saw the negative or the ugly aspects of a police culture when I first joined, I suppose ... People knew they could get away with it and took advantage of it, and that was certainly a part of police culture that was very negative and of absolutely no benefit to anyone at all. (FTOK, 29-year-old male SC)

FTOs in some ways saw themselves as protecting the probationers from the external environment. They taught probationers strategies for survival in an occupation that brings practitioners face to face with the worst of society's problems on a daily basis, that does not offer a great deal of reward except from fellow officers, and that is a minefield where one wrong step can bring on complaints, disciplinary actions, or prosecutions.

First Week at the Demonstration Patrol

Probationers described[3] their first week at the demonstration patrols as 'nerve wrecking,' 'daunting,' and 'scary.' However, this nervousness was often accompanied by a sense of excitement, as well as relief that they were finally out in the operational field. Many interviewees said they were nervous because they lacked confidence. Even the confident ones soon found out how little they knew and how unprepared they were for the job:

> When I left the academy after Phase 3, I thought that I knew pretty much everything, because I had scored ... really good marks ... And the first week I was there, my buddy who was extremely good said to me, he said, 'Look, for the first couple of days sit back, watch what goes on, don't do too much' ... And it was about the second day that I realized that I actually knew bugger all, and it was time to start learning all over again. (3/24-year-old male)

The idea of actually doing police work was both overwhelming and exciting:

Oh, it was pretty full-on, really ... It's exciting I suppose for the first week, first couple of weeks. Then you realize how much you've got to learn. (3/19-year-old male)

A great deal of probationers' fear and nervousness was related to how operational police would perceive them. Some sensed a degree of suspicion towards them at first – a suspicion they themselves felt subsequently toward new probationers:

People [at the demonstration patrol] were very sceptical ... I think it's with people coming out of the academy as a whole, because of the things that are happening at the moment with the Royal Commission ... I suppose we all become cynical like they were ... But you probably don't realize it until such time as you're at the other end, you know, when you're looking at these new people coming in and you think, 'Oh, maybe I shouldn't say things,' and then you realize that the day you walked in the door that's exactly how you were perceived as well. (3/27-year-old male)

Most probationers found that they were eventually well accepted by people in the patrols. Some fitted in very quickly and were treated as 'part of the family':

Even though you're a new probationer, they tend to see you as being operational police straightaway ... It was like a family sort of thing. Like, everyone said, you know, you're part of the family. It really was, yeah ... I mean, like, the police service is a culture and it's good to sort of feel that you can fit into that. (3/22-year-old male)

Clearly, probationers were quite aware of their initial 'outsider' status and consciously decided to try to fit in:

I think I fitted in pretty well, yeah ... Like, everyone seemed to have the same interests, I mean, like, fitted in like as one of the boys, I suppose, for want of a better term ... There's a certain police culture and if you don't fit in with that police culture, you're not in, basically ... I try very hard to fit in, and I did. (3/23-year-old male)

Probationers were relieved to find out that they were not expected to know a great deal. Because they were an extra resource, they were generally valued by officers in the demonstration patrols. One interviewee, however, felt that the reception he received was 'indifferent' rather than friendly. He rationalized this in terms of the difficulties created by the high turnover of probationers in that patrol: 'They would have been getting people through every, you know, thirteen weeks and that, so I suppose they're not going to try and really get to know too many people in that time' (3/21-year-old male). This view was shared by another probationer, who worked in a demonstration patrol where seven probationers came in and seven left every three months: 'You turn around like fourteen people every three months ... It's pretty hard, I suppose, for people actually at the station' (3/20-year-old male).

These accounts show that probationers were acutely aware of their lack of practical knowledge and their status as outsiders. Their perceived deficits in technical and social capital motivated them to do their best to fit in, to prove themselves, and to gain the confidence of operational police.

Leaving the Academy Behind

As probationers entered the operational field, they left the academy behind both physically and mentally. The knowledge and skills they had acquired at the academy soon lost their currency. Interviewees repeatedly referred to the operational field as 'reality,' 'the real world,' or 'real life,' compared with the academy, which was about 'theory,' 'scenario,' 'play acting,' or 'made up' reality. The difference was said to be 'total' (3/24-year-old male), '100 per cent' (3/24-year-old female), or like 'chalk and cheese' (3/29-year-old male). Many differences related to the greater pressure in the field, and the higher number of constraints. These made learning 'faster':

[At the academy] you've got ... time to do things, you don't have five or six jobs on your plate. You know, your hair is not on fire. You're trying to get to the next job ... Yeah, the different pressures of working in the field make it faster, a faster learning experience. (3/24-year-old male)

Once out in the operational field, probationers began to see the gap between the knowledge they had acquired at the academy and the skills they needed to survive in the field. This gap was sometimes

presented as evidence of deficiencies in academy training, which was
seen as not sufficiently practical:

> If you ask me, the academy is a heap of bullshit, the stuff they teach you
> down there. The streets are totally different. You get to the patrol and you
> are thrown in at the deep end. (3/20-year-old male)

> Everything at the academy is really clinical and sort of staged, whereas
> you're at the demo patrol and you know basically you're in the real world
> and it's nothing like what you learn at the academy. (3/23-year-old male)

One probationer contrasted the uncooperative attitudes of people
'out in the street' with the simulations at the academy, where people
were deferential to police (3/26-year-old male). Because people were
much more difficult to deal with than they had imagined, all the role
play at the academy about trying to be fair was seen as irrelevant
(probationer observed in DP Obs28). Similarly, the 'warm and fuzzy'
academy training about understanding different types of mental ill-
nesses 'counted for very little when you got out there':

> If someone's ... crazy and they're going off the handle, you know, you
> schedule them, take them to hospital and you don't, you know, you don't
> sit there, you don't have time and you don't really want to get that
> involved to analyse what's actually wrong with them and things like that.
> (3/21-year-old male)

While this devaluation of academy training was based partly on the
harsher realities of their field experience, some probationers acknowledged that the view that 'everything you learnt at the academy is
bullshit' was fostered at least in part by operational police. Our field
observation during Phase 4 and our interviews with FTOs confirm that
probationers regularly encountered criticisms that their training at the
academy had been inadequate and that PREP was ill conceived. These
criticisms were directed mainly at what operational police regarded as
irrelevant aspects of the curriculum, such as cross-cultural, social, and
ethical training:

> [A senior constable at the station] argued that the training they had now
> [at the academy] wasn't any good because they have taken all the physical
> training out of it. [He] argued that every year the wall got lower and the

runs got shorter ... and that new police officers weren't ready for the job when they came out. [He] argued that there was too much emphasis on Affirmative Action. (DP)

[A senior constable at the station] said, 'They don't know anything down there [at the academy]. They fill all the young ones' heads up with all this stuff about Abos and who knows what, and they don't really teach them anything. You can't teach people what they need at the academy.' (TP)

Similarly, there was a great deal of criticism from FTOs about the amount of time the academy spent on social and ethical issues instead of practical skills:

Well, I think [laugh] personally, I think more emphasis on the practical side of things and more realistic scenarios and a lot less emphasis on multiculturalism, ethics, and all the things that we spent eight weeks on that have made no difference to the way I would have approached anyone ... You know, you either are or you aren't racist, as far as I can see, and it doesn't matter how many times they tell you not to be, you know if you spent the last twenty-five years being racist, it's not going to make a great deal of difference. It might make you stop and think, but you'll only need to be told once and you'll stop and think. (FTOF, 30-year-old female C)

PREP –Phase 1 in particular – was also criticized for trying to indoctrinate some kind of political correctness among recruits. Some people resented this deeply. One FTO saw the process as 'brainwashing' and spoke with great resentment about a class where an Aboriginal woman allegedly advised recruits not to charge Aboriginal children because they deserved a chance (FTOZ, 25-year-old male C). Even classes in the history of policing came in for some ridicule, as this topic was seen as irrelevant to practice (FTOJ, 34-year-old male SC). The impression from the operational field was that the academy was exaggerating the risk of corruption and trying to produce a 'new breed of supercops' taught not to trust officers in the field. Field training officers in turn developed strategies to restrain probationers within their sphere of influence to avoid things being 'blown out of proportions' (FTOA, 29-year-old male SC).

Probationers generally did not contradict these views held by their superiors, even though their own assessment of academy training might have been different. A few probationers told us that the academy provided basic knowledge, on which they could draw later in the operational field. They felt there was a place for theoretical knowledge and that academy training was not meant to replace field training:

> You learn all your law and procedure [at the academy] ... When you're out in the field there are things that come up, you may not know how to do these practically out there. You've got a lot of theory in your head, knowledge sort of thing, and you do apply what you learn here at the academy out there as well. But one of the most important things I learned [at the academy] was officer survival. (3/25-year-old female)

> Well, after going through it all, I'd disagree [that academy training was 'bullshit']. Like, certain things you know aren't realistic, but when you do something that's real, it's just, it's sort of like an instinct, it's there, you've learnt it here, and it's up the back of your mind somewhere and it comes out. (3/25-year-old male)

> Like, a lot of people knock the academy but I think it does a pretty good job for, you know, for what they can do. They can only prepare you for so much. But it's just trying to put all that theory into practice which is ... hard. (3/20-year-old female)

> The academy was good. It taught you the basics of everything, but ... actually putting into practice, you can't actually learn it until you go out there ... The academy sort of can't give you that because it's just experience I think. Just getting out there and doing it. (3/22-year-old female)

One probationer noted, however, that this attitude of treating academy knowledge as 'bullshit' was not what he found in his demonstration patrol:

> I was under the impression ... that they would think of us as dummies and that we wouldn't know anything, you know, and don't worry about that academy stuff, you know, because ... that's not how it's done in the street. But I found that totally opposite, actually. I found that a lot of the comments was, you know, you just got out of the academy, you should know. So it was good, and a lot of the times we did know. (3/28-year-old male)

We also found that not all FTOs were critical of the training at the academy. A few did concede that theoretical knowledge is necessary, though its relevance may take years to become apparent. One FTO was critical of PREP, yet acknowledged that it made for more well-rounded police officers:

> I would have loved to have gone through the PREP system myself, because ... the way I was taught was only for eleven weeks ... I think at the end of all the training they've definitely come out ... a more rounded police officer ... It'd be helpful, you know ... to do the university degree or whatever else, you know ... That's a luxury I never had. And I think, you know, ... in the end ... I suppose you could say ... a better police officer ... In principle, it's a top idea. (FTOH, 34-year-old male SC)

Some FTOs saw the gap between academy training and field experience as a natural consequence of applying theory to practice (FTOK, 29-year-old male SC).

After spending time in the field, some probationers regarded the academy as 'not a nice place' because students were there 'under duress' and it was 'really isolating' (3/29-year-old female). Others felt that they were treated more equally, and less like students, in the field, whereas the academy 'didn't take into account that a lot of the students had been working for five, ten, sometimes fifteen years, and treated them as straight out of school' (3/23-year-old male).

Coping Strategies

The demands of operational police work accentuated probationers' feelings of inadequacy regarding their knowledge and competence. To cope with the challenge of doing 'real' police work and to fit in among their new colleagues, probationers developed a number of coping strategies: listen, observe, ask questions, 'not say too much' (3/20-year-old male), and – most important – not challenge anyone's practice openly. The aim was to come across 'as someone who was prepared to listen and learn,' and not someone who questioned senior officers' actions 'in front of the public.' They knew that a 'know-it-all' would have a hard time being accepted by operational police (3/24-year-old male). The best strategy was to 'keep your mouth shut' (3/20-year-old male) and 'be seen and not heard' (3/29-year-old female). Some probationers learned quickly that respect for higher ranks was recognized as the hallmark of a good police officer:

I'm the sort of person that I won't say anything with a senior person around, like whatever he tells me to do I'll do and that's what I think this organization needs ... more respect for higher ranks and stuff like that, which a lot of people just don't have at the moment ... I find that the best police officers I know have all got that. (3/19-year-old male)

Our interviews with FTOs confirmed that these were precisely the qualities regarded as desirable in a probationary constable. FTOs liked probationers to be keen, interested, thorough, and willing to listen and follow instructions:

Someone who's motivated, asks a lot of questions, is shown how to do a task and who tries to do that task and then eventually gets through that task and where you know that they're switched on and they're listening. Someone that's ... sort of not too gung-ho ... Someone that knows their place ... And what I make a point of saying to them is, 'Look, hey,' you know, 'we're going to a dangerous job so you stay with me all the time, and I don't want you running off' ... I like them to be ... keen and moti-vated and interested. (FTOB, 38-year-old male SC)

For a start he's keen ... doesn't mind getting in and having a go, not afraid to work, confident although not afraid to ask questions ... doesn't pre-sume they know it all ... willing to learn. (FTOZ, 25-year-old male C)

Somebody who's keen, motivated, enthusiastic, at the same time knows when to talk and when not to talk. (FTO13, 28-year-old male SC)

Our observation in Phase 4 also shows that operational officers ex-pected probationers to listen and not to question – let alone challenge – established practices. Some police officers were especially critical of the academy for teaching probationers to question senior officers' judgment:

[SC said she] had experienced some 'hopeless' probationers ... An exam-ple of a 'hopeless' probationer is one where the individual thinks they know the job, fails to listen, and has little respect for senior officers. She observed this trend in recent years and blamed the academy. She under-stood that police training had undergone considerable reform in recent years. In her opinion the shift of emphasis from physical fitness, officer survival and crime fighting skills to other community based policing techniques had produced less able police recruits. (TP)

[The senior constable said that] these days, 'some recruits talk too much,' and they are encouraged by the academy to talk and question what they are shown in the field ... He said that as a result of recent reforms with training, the academy explicitly told recruits to think that they were 'superior—a new breed of "supercops,"' in comparison with earlier batches of recruits. Further, they were encouraged to think independently and question cultural conventions. The above comments about attempts to create a superior breed of 'supercops' designed to question and ultimately undermine cultural conventions echo comments from other officers in other patrols I had visited. (TP)

The encouragement of recruits to question conventions was seen as part of the police service's strategy to foster a 'new breed' of police to act as 'white knights' in the bureaucracy's fight against police corruption. Operational police saw it as a source of tension and division between them and the probationers:

[The probationer] said lecturers/teachers at the academy explicitly encouraged recruits not to be intimidated by senior police and to report any signs of unprofessional or corrupt police practice. They were told that the organization would support them and actively recognise their noble efforts. SC [the senior constable] was aware of this academy policy shift and ... said that officers are sceptical and suspicious of recruits when they arrive at their patrol until they feel they can be trusted. This creates tension and division between recruits and other officers, not dissimilar to a 'generation gap,' SC said. (TP)

As one senior constable told us, the price of not respecting senior officers might be all-round rejection by officers in the field:

SC [a senior constable who graduated from the academy eight years ago] said she had noticed changes in the attitudes and views of Student Police Officers (SPO) at her patrol from the academy. Most demonstrate good police characteristics, but some show less respect for authority and question the judgment and discretion of senior officers. For example, there is a senior and long-serving officer within her patrol who occasionally purchases a six-pack of beer before the local bottle shop closes and returns with them to the station so he has them to take home after his shift finishes. One particular SPO observed the officer walking into the station with the beer and said to the officer, 'I hope you don't intend to drink those while on duty.' In SC's opinion, this comment was a sign of disrespect. News of the SPO's comments soon circulated throughout the station's officers. As a result, not only did the senior officer snub the SPO, so did many of his colleagues. Although most recruits respect authority, understand their place in the police hierarchy, and therefore are potentially good police, the academy appears to be encouraging free and critical thought in recruits. SC implied that this is potentially problematic. (TP)

Probationers recognized that in order to fit in they would have to 'prove' themselves among their co-workers so as to gain trust (3/21-year-old male; 3/19-year-old male) as well as respect.

There's probably a difference between being accepted and, you know, being respected ... Respect is something that comes about through your deeds, whereas acceptance is 'OK, you're here, we'll take you on, you know, we've got a responsibility to train you up' (3/27-year-old male)

Probationers also saw the importance of socializing as a way of developing bonds:

[The probationer said that] one of the things that she loved was that she had made some of her best friends while at the academy. [She] said that 'you have to socialise in this job, go to barbecues, and go out together, so that you get to know who you are working with and who will back you up.' (DP)

Thus, by their own accounts, probationers coped with the new environment by doing what was expected of them: keeping a low profile, knowing their place in the hierarchy, showing respect for rank and experience, and proving their trustworthiness by their actions. In this way, they accumulated much-needed technical expertise also increased their social and symbolic capital among their new workmates.

Mentors and Role Models

In Survey 3, probationers were asked to rate the contributions of various people they came into contact with during field training to their development as police officers. Table 5.1 summarizes the results. Probationers tended to identify general duties officers as the main contributors to their development during field training (average rating

TABLE 5.1
Contributors to probationary officers' development (Survey 3, N=134)

Officers/staff	Mean rating
General duties officers	7.99
Junior officers (S constables & constables)	7.48
Field training 'buddies' in weeks 1–8	7.39
FTOs throughout Phase 4	6.32
Senior officers (sergeants and above)	6.12
Other probationary constables	5.71
Education and Development Officers (EDOs)	5.68
Detectives	5.57
Beat police	4.64
Highway patrol officers	4.35
Members of the public	3.95
Patrol Commanders	3.48
Administrative staff	2.89
Student police officers	1.18

Q: How much have each of the following contributed to your development as a police officer during Phase 4? (Scale from 0=none to 9=very large contribution)

7.99). Specialist police such as detectives, beat police, and highway patrol police played less significant roles in their training (4.35 to 5.57). Among the general duties police, junior officers (i.e., constables and senior constables) were rated more highly (7.48) than senior officers (i.e., sergeant and above – 6.12) in terms of contribution. Patrol commanders were rated extremely low (3.48) – even lower than members of the public (3.95). Clearly, there were rank-based differences in the perceived contributions of other police to the probationer's development. This partly reflected the hierarchical nature of police organization; mostly however, it was a consequence of the field training arrangement, whereby probationers spent a great deal of time with their shift partners, most of whom were of junior rank. For example, our observation found that probationers worked as part of a car crew on 88 per cent of the shifts, and on these shifts their partners were usually constables or senior constables.[4] Among junior officers, the field training 'buddies' to whom the probationers were attached during the first eight weeks on demonstration patrol were seen as by far the most significant contributors to the probationer's development (average rating 7.39), followed by the FTOs (6.32). The local Education and Development Officers (EDOs) were perceived as far less important to their development (5.68).

As some of the FTOs acknowledged in interviews, the field training experience our cohort received was not entirely in keeping with official policy. For example, although probationers were supposed to be 'partnered by two qualified Field Training Officers, each one accompanying them for four weeks,' (NSWPS 1993: 73), only 19 per cent of the respondents in Survey 3 indicated that they had never worked with an officer other than their 'buddy' during the first eight weeks of field training. The rest had worked from one to ten times (60 per cent) or from 11 to more than 40 times (12 per cent) with officers who were not designated 'buddies.' A small percentage of respondents stated that they had worked with such officers 'plenty,' 'lots,' or 'several' times without giving an estimate of the actual number. One probationer who didn't have a buddy assigned to him during field training found his experience 'unsettling' and 'a bit annoying,' since he was 'working with a different person every shift' (3/23-year-old male). Similarly, although probationers were supposed to work with qualified FTOs for the remainder of their time at the demonstration patrols, only 13 per cent of the respondents had never gone on patrol with an officer who was not a designated FTO. The rest worked from 1 to 10 times (38 per cent) or from 11 to over 40 times (28 per cent) with non-FTOs. About 16 per cent indicated that they had worked with non-FTOs 'many' times or 'lots' of times. More disturbingly, about half the respondents indicated that during their field training, they had gone on patrol with another probationary constable without a senior officer, although for most respondents this happened only once or twice.

Most probationers held highly favourable opinions of their FTOs. In Survey 3 we asked probationers to indicate their level of agreement or disagreement with a series of statements about their FTOs. The percentage of agreement to positive items ranged from 66 to 84 (Table 5.2). There was a strong consensus that FTOs were willing to help with probationers' problems, and willing to answer questions, and had a sound knowledge of laws and procedures. The only items that attracted more than 10 per cent unfavourable ratings involved the extent to which FTOs

- had too high expectations of probationers' knowledge (38 per cent),
- praised good performance (17 per cent),
- were unfairly critical of probationers (13 per cent), and
- displayed a strong commitment to integrity in their own practice (11 per cent).

TABLE 5.2
Probationers' opinions of field training officers (Survey 3, N=134)

Statements about field training officers	Per cent agree (A/SA)	Per cent disagree (D/SD)	Mean rating
My FTOs were willing to help me when I had problems.	84	4	1.88
My FTOs were always willing to answer my questions.	81	6	2.00
My FTOs had a sound knowledge of the laws and procedures that guide police work.	80	5	2.09
My FTOs took time to teach me the skills necessary for policing.	75	10	2.17
My FTOs had the skills and experience to teach me how to become a good police officer.	74	8	2.17
On the whole, my FTOs motivated me to learn and develop as a police officer	70	10	2.22
I consider my FTOs to have been good models of professional police work.	74	10	2.23
My FTOs gave me enough information for me to perform my tasks.	72	9	2.25
My FTOs displayed a strong commitment to integrity in their own practice.	68	11	2.29
My FTOs praised me when I performed well.	66	17	2.37
My FTOs expected me to have more knowledge of law and procedure than what I had. (N)	38	29	2.78
My FTOs were unfairly critical of my performance. (N)	13	66	3.76

Q: Below are a list of statements about your Phase 4 training. Please indicate your level of agreement with each of them by circling the appropriate number where: 1=strongly agree, 2=agree, 3=neutral, 4=disagree, and 5=strongly disagree.
N = negative items

Although most probationers held a high opinion of their FTOs, Table 5.2 indicates that depending on the statement, from 4 to 38 per cent of respondents gave unfavourable answers. This suggests that a minority of probationers did not have FTOs they found helpful. These findings are consistent with what probationers told us in interviews. Around 80 per cent (43 interviewees in round 3) spoke highly of their buddies,[5] whereas eight probationers had at least one buddy who was not very good, and three did not have buddies at all.

According to the interviewees, good buddies were approachable, helpful, and interested in the probationers. They were experienced or knowledgeable, confident, and professional in their work. They always had time for the probationers, answered their questions, and did not assume that the probationers knew a great deal. One probationer thought his buddy was excellent, even though he was only a young constable with three years' experience:

> He was prepared to talk to you as a person. I mean, I've spoken to some people in my class and they said their first or second buddies who were of a higher rank didn't talk to them that much. They didn't get that much feedback from them, and they basically didn't know where they were doing the wrong thing or where there were doing the right thing. Whereas the buddy that I had, he said to me, ... while we were away from the public, 'You made a blue there,' 'You should have done this,' or 'You could have done this, you could have done that,' 'You did good here, you did good there, but you made a blunder here' ... I got the general impression that he was interested in what I did and interested in my development as a probationer, rather than saying, 'Oh well, he's here for a month, I've got to deal with it, you know, just get through the month and then get rid of it' sort of thing. (3/24-year-old male)

There were only seven female first buddies mentioned by the interviewees. Most of them were considered 'excellent' or 'very good':

> She knew ... what the requirements [were] we needed for the academy and [was] very approachable ... She basically knew from the start how much I'd know and how much I wouldn't. She didn't take for granted, 'Oh yeah, you can do that,' but on the same token she'd let you, like, do something first and then wait to ask for help, so [she] didn't sort of stand over your shoulder and say do this and do this and do this. So you didn't feel like a complete idiot. (3/26-year-old male)

> Excellent – a senior constable, and really knew her stuff ... You could be driving around or doing something and no matter what I'd ask her, whether it was something really minor, or something really complex ... she always knew the answer, and ... if you'd ask why, she would always be able to give you a why ... and if you didn't like that, she'd give you, like, an alternative. Like she was just really good. Like, you don't find many FTOs like that. (3/22-year-old female)

The minority of interviewees who did not have very good buddies complained about the buddy's laziness or lack of interest. One probationer told us his first buddy had the 'Senior Constable syndrome':

> It's where they get, you know, probably a bit over six years' service and decide that they've had a gutful of what they're doing and, like, they're at the stage where they've been senior constable or they've been doing the job for ... quite a few years and the next step is obviously progress, but they know that, oh, you know, to go to a sergeant ... that's going to be a number of years off, so they're, you know, in 'nowhere land' as such ... He wasn't interested in what he was doing. He never wanted to go out. ... He kept swapping shifts so that he could stay in the station ... I had to stay with him, so if he didn't want to go out, well, I had to just tag along. (3/ male, age >30)

Another probationer encountered a similar style of buddy in his second month, but he explained it in terms of people's disillusionment with the 'system,' the pressure from outside to make police accountable, and the lack of support from 'the bosses' (3/27-year-old male).

The importance of a good buddy, however, went far beyond the field training experience. One perceptive probationer reflected on the influence of his first buddy:

> I've no doubt that the way that [my buddy] dealt with things basically set up my views on the police service itself ... Well, they say first impressions are the most important. Like, we spent a month with our first buddies. In that month, especially with someone who's impressionable and who's just come out of the academy, and as I said doesn't really know the way to do things, if you get a bad buddy, it's going to take you that much more time to get over the bad habits that they've taught you. (3/24-year-old male)

The important role played by the buddies in the probationer's development was acknowledged by the FTOs themselves:

> I think you do play a major role, [a] role model for them ... If you're slack, I think that after a couple of weeks with you, they would probably have the same negative, unmotivated influences. (FTOB, 38-year-old male, SC)

One officer we interviewed said he wanted to become an FTO because he had been so impressed with the way his buddies taught him (FTO13, 28-year-old male, SC).

TABLE 5.3
Perceived importance of learning methods (Survey 3, N=134)

Method of learning	% 'very important' or 'somewhat important'	Mean rating
Hands-on experience in the field	99	1.15
Advice from supervisors	97	1.33
Observing other police officers on the job	97	1.37
Feedback on performance	94	1.38
'Buddy' training in first 8 weeks	96	1.41
Advice from other police	93	1.43
Specialist attachment	86	1.72
Commissioners' Instructions	89	1.83
Examinations	87	1.86
Progress reports	84	1.92
Self assessment	72	2.08
Formal debriefing with EDOs	75	2.09
Formal debriefing with FTOs	74	2.10
Interview with patrol commander	73	2.11
Stories told by police about their experiences	68	2.16
Pacer evaluations	72	2.19
PREP incident reports	64	2.31
Performance enhancement programs	65	2.36
Case write-ups and assignments	31	2.88

Q: During Phase 4, Probationers learn about policing in a number of different ways. Please rate the importance to you of the following methods of learning about policing in Phase 4, where 1=very important, 2=somewhat important, 3=not very important, and 4=not at all important.

Methods of Learning

Probationers were asked to rate the importance of various methods of learning during their field training. Table 5.3 indicates that for the large majority of probationers (over 90 per cent), the most important methods were *doing* (hands-on experience), *observing* other police officers on the job, and *listening* to advice and feedback from supervisors and other police. Formal examinations and various formal assessments, feedbacks, and remedial programs were rated as important by most probationers (65 to 87 per cent). In contrast, case write-ups and assignments were rated as important by only 31 per cent. To some probationers, case write-ups and assignments were 'a waste of time' (3/22-year-old female); to others, they represented unwelcomed additional paperwork:

But the amount of paperwork and stuff – it's just ridiculous, that gets you down, really gets you down. I mean, you've got all your stuff from the academy to do, plus your normal workload ... especially in the first ... couple of weeks when you don't know how to do your COPS entries. You've got case write-ups, you've got files which they send out ... You just seem to lose sight of it. (3/29-year-old male)

In our field observation, we came across references to the practice of plagiarism to fulfil these requirements:

[The probationer said that] research-based learning was ineffective as a way of teaching, or measuring whether learning had taken place in the student. The assignments were not scrutinized or evaluated adequately to give students feedback on whether they were on the right track of knowledge. For example, [the probationer] witnessed students' research on a particular topic that produced incorrect information outcomes in terms of correct policing procedures. These errors remained unnoticed by the lecturers/markers. As a result of this, students blatantly copied each other's assignments. This practice was rampant according to [the probationer], and defeated the whole objective of teaching and learning. (TP)

Given that the case write-up was considered 'a central part of the learning and assessment methodology of PREP' (NSWPS 1993: 74) and a key tool for encouraging self-reflection, probationers' lack of appreciation of this method of learning suggested strongly that they rejected the 'reflective practitioner' model.

To describe how probationers learned in the field, we draw on what they told us in interviews and what we noted during our observation. One probationer described his Phase 4 training as a process of initially doing what you were told, being shown how by your buddy, then finding your way through trial and error, asking for help, gaining confidence, and finally accumulating experience (3/19-year-old male). For example, one probationer described how he basically followed his buddy's instructions during the first couple of months:

I'd go out with him, and if we were doing a break and enter or something like that, I'd get my notebook out and I'd go start writing some details down myself. [He'd be] telling me what I need to ask and that sort of thing. Just sort of guiding me through what was needed to be asked and, you know, [telling] me who to call up as far as fingerprints and that sort of thing. (3/28-year-old male)

Another probationer found his second buddy's instructions and tips extremely useful for learning how to work smoothly and efficiently:

He was really organized. He was really good ... He taught me how to do my notebook so you could do it straight onto COPS. He gave me a little checklist of what to do so I never missed anything. And when I went ... to a job I knew what I was doing ... He gave me a little stick-it note with about ten points on it ... things like time, the date, the place – so that everything just went smoothly. Look for witnesses. Take witness statements. So I could just check things off and get them done in time ... It's good because you're not ringing back the victim all the time, and it's embarrassing when you ring back a victim the second time. (3/20-year-old male)

One of the most direct ways probationers learned the job involved being shown how to do various things by their buddy or FTO. One probationer spoke of how her buddy would demonstrate and then invite her to try doing the work:

How did he teach me? I guess [by] keeping me busy, showing me lots of things ... He was very good. He was keen, he was keen to teach me ... He would show me work first, he would show me as an example. He would do a job first, and then he'd ask me if I felt confident enough to have a go, because that's the best way to learn. (3/24-year-old female)

Some probationers spoke of their initial field training experience as like being 'thrown in the deep end' to 'sink or swim' (3/19-year-old female). However, most were guided by their buddies. One probationer who did not have any buddies to guide him through the first eight weeks told us how he managed to learn by watching and through trial and error:

And the way I found out, I've made a couple of mistakes, but I'm not scared to make mistakes, because ... once I've done it once, I'll never do it again. I think that's part of the learning curve – you've got to make a mistake ... On a COPS entry, for instance, you might fill in an unnecessary field or a wrong field, and you get a resubmit on that, and just the sergeant would explain to you, 'Well, in this circumstance it's not appropriate and you don't need to fill it in, or you need more detail in here to say that' ... But it's like everything, you've got to fall off a bike to learn how to ride it, and it's just one of those things. (3/20-year-old male)

One FTO told us that 'the police service and its culture do not tolerate mistakes, so learning through one's mistakes is virtually out of the question' (TP Obs 12; see also TP Obs 17). Yet probationers found that most police officers in the patrols were understanding and that one did learn from one's mistakes, at least in relation to minor technical matters:

Some people were [tolerant of mistakes], some cranky old sergeants weren't, but most people knew – they'd been through it, you know, you learn by your own mistakes. There was no major sort of mistakes, just little things and you just didn't do them again. (3/25-year-old male)

At the second patrol, they're a lot stricter on processes and up-to-date notebooks and how you fill out certain forms. They've got to be filled out correctly, and, like, you get bungs [notes] in your pigeonhole to say, you know, this is done incorrectly, fix it ... They're good because they're something that you'll never – like, you know ... that that time you've done wrong, and you'll never forget it again, and you always fill that part in or fill the right part in next time. (3/20-year-old male)

Probationers told us they were able to ask for help from their FTOs, partners, or other officers in the station. This was supported by what we observed in the field. For example, during one shift in a training patrol, we observed how one probationer repeatedly sought help from whoever was around to get through her 'paperwork' on an Apprehended Violence Order. This included asking the supervising sergeant for help and advice, asking several officers working in the station to assist with various details of computer entry, and asking her shift partner (a constable) about how to set AVO conditions. We observed that help was always forthcoming from the other officers (TP). Other instances of seeking help included asking a senior partner to verify a piece of legal advice regarding a traffic accident (DP) and getting detailed advice from a detective on how to check the serial number of a stolen car engine (DP).

Some probationers lacked confidence at first, and appreciated having buddies who were prepared to let them watch before actually doing the job:

> [My buddy] always offered, said, 'Do you want to do this?' and I, a couple
> of times, I said no because I didn't feel confident and I wanted to watch
> him do it first. But he always offered. (3/19-year-old female)

Throughout Phase 4, probationers gained experience and confidence through doing different things, seeing more people, and working with different people:

> Well, sort of the more things you do, the more people you see ... I sort of
> think you've got a bit more experience and a bit more learning at the end
> of the day. You're always learning something ... And, also, like, every
> person you work with as well, like, I think you're also learning something,
> just different ways of doing a job. (3/20-year-old male)

Although most probationers felt more confident by the time they completed their training at the demonstration patrols, some found that their confidence went down as they entered a new workplace or encountered an unfamiliar situation:

> I think I feel less confident in the second patrol. I don't feel as 'streetwise'
> as I did in the first patrol because it's a much more metropolitan area and
> I'm not from Sydney ... I certainly feel like the people on the street know a
> heck of a lot more than I do about being on the street ... I think I was more
> confident in my first patrol because I wasn't as afraid to make a mistake
> and, yeah, I felt like I understood the people better that I was working with.
> (3/22-year-old male; also 3/male, age >30 and 3/22-year-old female)

For some probationers, gaining confidence was a step-by-step process. There would always be situations they were not familiar with, so at the end of the probationary period they could not honestly say they 'knew the job':

> I don't think I'll ever know the job ... Some of the time I do know what I'm
> doing, yeah, so, I mean, that makes you feel good ... I mean, there's so
> many parts of the job you never know how to do all of the job. There's
> always something. Every situation is different. (3/24-year-old female)

When asked whether there was a point at which they started to feel like a police officer, probationers offered a variety of answers. Some felt this from the time they were attested and given a gun and a badge, although their confidence came much later:

> I suppose the day that you're attested you feel like a police officer ... I mean, you got the gun and, you know, your badge that I suppose is the symbol of it ... But then ... after a little while, like the first month or so, you don't feel like you're fully operational yet because, you know, you don't feel confident of doing jobs all by yourself ... After a few months, I think, you feel a bit more [confident] because, you know, you're able to do a job, you know what you're doing ... and you're not sort of asking your partner, 'Oh, is this right? Is this right?' the whole time. (3/20-year-old male)

One probationer felt like a police officer when she was out on the streets and saw that her actions had consequences on people:

> Probably the first few months at the demonstration patrol ... The way the people react to you and the way people see you ... You see the people, and you see the influence that you have on other people's [behaviour] and on other people's lives. Like, you might arrest somebody and it's, you know, they lose their job, and they lose everything, so one thing that you do could, like, have a huge impact on somebody else's life that you might be unaware of. (3/20-year-old female)

Others pointed to specific stages during Phase 4 when they felt they could do the job. Examples: their first arrest, working 'job for job' with their partners, starting at the training patrol, giving someone advice, being commended by a supervisor, finding that their work was no longer being returned for 'resubmit':

> The first arrest, I think. You actually say, oh yeah, look, I can actually do this ... When you get out there you're wondering whether you can do it, whether you can wheel someone over and ask for their licence ... I think the first arrest is the turning point. (3/23-year-old male)

> [During the fifth or sixth month at the demonstration patrol] when you're working job for job ... like, two out in a car, your partner does the first job, and then you do the second. And then you do that no matter what the job is, that's when you feel like a police officer. (3/19-year-old female)

> Probably when I got to my training patrol after the first six months, because you start knowing what you have to do. You start knowing

everything sort of systematically and you can carry out, you know, just about everything by yourself from start to end, you don't need hardly any help at all. That's when you start to know that you're doing everything right. (3/21-year-old female)

Well, that probably came three months into it [demonstration patrol] ... I did probably about four deceased with my first buddy, and so I sort of logged the procedure down fairly well with that, and I was working with someone who had just become a constable, and at their demo patrol they ... hadn't even had a deceased or anything, so I was working with them, and I could give them some advice. So I thought, well, I would go and give them a hand sort of thing. (3/29-year-old male)

I think I was halfway through Phase 4 and I had some sort of idea that I could go out and actually do a job and not have to be told how to do it this way, and the supervisor saying things like, ... 'You did this job good.' (3/23-year-old male)

Probably after about three months, two to three months of doing it. ... Things start to fall in place a little bit. You know, go and do this COPS entry, and you – *poom, poom* – done, and not get it resubmitted, which is a major ... thing ... You start to sort of, you get into the swing. (3/28-year-old male)

Models of Practice

Inevitably, probationers came across positive as well as negative role models in the course of their field training. Forty-three per cent of the respondents in Survey 3 reported having had at least one experience during field training that had a significant positive impact on them. These involved observing examples of good police work, working with other officers as a team, getting support from other police, helping the public, and learning how to handle situations. Thirty per cent reported having had at least one experience that had a significant negative impact on them. These involved working with 'shonks' (officers who were lazy or who 'flicked' jobs), negative attitudes of some officers, poor treatment by supervisors or other officers, poor treatment by the public, and aspects of the police organization. Working with positive role models can have a significant positive impact on probationers; working with negative role models can have the opposite effect. To explore what positive and negative models of policing practice consist of, we draw on what probationers told us in interviews and what we observed in the field.

'Good' Police Work

Recruits in the interview component of the study were asked at the second and third interviews whether they had seen any examples of 'good' police work.[6] At the time of the second interview, the only experience subjects had of operational police work was during the four-week field observation. Nevertheless, most were able to articulate the qualities they saw as 'good' policing. By the third interview, the subjects had had almost a year of on-the-job policing experience. The examples they provided at this stage painted a fairly consistent picture of what 'good policing' is all about. The following is a composite picture based on the interviewers' comments:

> Good policing is about being able to handle difficult situations effectively. This requires excellent communication skills and 'people skills,' being able to deal with people with compassion, sensitivity, and confidence. It also demands dedication to the job and a genuine concern for people. Good policing means being calm, treating people with respect, and being able to control difficult situations by talking. While technical knowledge and skills are important, good policing also requires a caring and non-judgmental attitude. Teamwork is also part of good policing.

Interviewees cited many examples of 'good' police work. One probationer described how his partner took over a potentially explosive situation – made more difficult by the inappropriate action of a less experienced officer – and 'calmed everything down':

> In my first patrol I went [into] a pub and there was probably thirty or forty Aboriginals there and they'd had an argument with the bouncer, and one of them had been thrown out and they're out on the footpath and they were a bit peeved and it was across the road from the station. And a couple of people went across and, well, I was in the car with my partner and we were doing a job and we've come down to this thing and they were already out there talking to the people and then ... One of the girls has sworn at one of the guys from the station, and he's gone 'Right,' you know, he's grabbed her and he's going to, you know, lock her up for

offensive language or whatever ... Everyone just *started*, set everybody *off*, you know. And my partner's ... just gone, 'Look, just let me handle this,' and then he calmed everything down, and I was really impressed the way he handled it. (3/26-year-old male)

Another interviewee was impressed with officers who 'listen to what people are saying' and 'work something out.' These officers didn't 'just brush people off' when dealing with difficult situations:

Like you go to a domestic sometimes and people don't listen – they just brush people off. But I've seen good police work where people will listen, where the police I'm with will listen to what people are saying and work something out instead of just brushing them off and not listening to what people say. I've seen people go into a situation and they just make it worse – they just escalate the situation. (3/24-year-old male)

An example of the sensitive handling of a potentially dangerous 'domestic' dispute was given by another probationer:

We went to a domestic. The constable I was working with, he's been out for about three years, and the male person was just 'troppo,' he's just going off the handle. And, instead of ... making a big deal out of it, he just calmly talked ... this person down and after a period of about ten minutes this bloke's sitting in a chair sort of nearly crying, where before he's, you know, telling us he's going to kill us and all this. And just by ... using your mouth and just taking time to think about what you're saying in a situation, it can just resolve so much. (3/20-year-old male)

A female probationer recalled a dangerous situation during which her buddy acted with courage and restraint, showing good judgment and tactical skills in overcoming an armed man with mental health problems:

We went to a job over in a [department store] and a man was walking around with a large carving knife ... He was in the manchester [linens] section and he was schizophrenic and he was walking around with his shirt half undone as well and he was holding it like this and there was me and my second buddy, another car off there and another off-duty police officer there, and I had the radio and the other female in the other car crew had the radio and we called for backup and so some more cars were coming on their way ... My buddy spoke with, conversed with the offender, tried to calm him down and had his baton out should anything happen. He was standing in a full-on defensive position ... The other constable had climbed up onto the bed behind this gentleman ... and positioned himself standing on the edge of the bed waiting for an opportunity to pounce on him and disarm him, which was very ... courageous. But the opportunity arose and he jumped on him and grabbed him around [his neck] ... and managed to hold the arm that had the knife. The guy was ... rather small but he was schizophrenic and he was really strong ... And then my buddy stepped in and tackled and they both fell to the ground and then they stumbled around a bit and then they got the handcuffs and handcuffed him and the knife came flying toward me and I picked up the knife and called, 'No further cars.' (20-year-old female)

Another probationer described how much she admired her buddy who handled the use of force in a way that was consistent with the recommended approach taught by the academy. She had made his approach part of her own practice:

At the academy you learn about your different coercive levels. ... I know with some police officers they may start at the middle of the coercive level and work up, whereas [my first buddy] had this ... very relaxed approach with offenders, with victims, you know ... at a speaking level, from the bottom. And if he needed to use more force, or whatever, he'd work up [to it], but he was always ... very approachable. He's always spoken to me of how to handle situations, how to be cool if someone's ... swearing at you or if they want to hit you or anything like that. How to avoid those situations, and basically if someone's going off their nut at you, just to keep talking to them nicely and just settle them down, because you don't want to escalate the situation at all. And that's one good thing that I've actually learned from him, which I practise now. [Examples of dealing with potentially violent situations involving crowds or mentally ill people] Instead of going in with your batons and trying to control a person that way, I've always gone in and taken them aside, talked to them, calmed them down. I find that they become very cooperative in that way, and that's all because I've learned it all from my first buddy. (3/25-year-old female)

During our field observation we also came across instances of what we regarded as 'good' practice models for the probationers, although it is not clear to what extent some of these practices were displayed for our benefit. Many officers were courteous and empathetic in their dealings with the public. For example, a senior partner on one shift displayed a great deal of patience with a woman who was not fluent in English:

> As we were approaching the job, [the senior partner] SC remarked on the low socioeconomic status of the area (Housing Commission), 'This is a rough area' ... We stopped kerbside and entered a three-storey block of brown brick units that typically dominated the landscape. The inside of the stairwell was dimly lit and graffiti peppered the walls ... We knocked on a second-floor unit door and a woman in her thirties of Asian descent welcomed [us in]. Inside, the unit was untidy. SC sat down with the woman. He first asked how she was feeling and then proceeded to record her statement of the traffic accident involving her. The woman was not fluent in English. SC was very patient and thorough with the process of ascertaining the accident's details. (DP)

We also observed the decisive and effective way in which a senior partner took control of a potentially dangerous situation:

> An urgent radio call indicated a sighting of the fugitive in a block of units nearby. We sped to the location. We were the first to arrive; [the senior constable] assumed command in a decisive manner. He instructed other arriving units what to do in terms of setting up roadblocks. This was apparently the standard operating procedure for the first unit at a crime scene. I perceived team effort response; there were no heroes. (DP)

In another incident encountered during field observation, a senior partner (a female officer) handled a homeless assault victim in a way that impressed the observer as 'incorporating rigorous police investigation and compassionate welfare work':

> We arrived at the hospital to find the victim sitting alone waiting to be seen by a doctor. [The senior partner] SC sat beside her and began asking questions, first about her condition and injuries and then the attackers and their motive. SC demonstrated genuine interest in the woman's circumstances and concern and compassion for her predicament ... The interview ended with SC giving general advice to the woman about getting off the streets and finding suitable work. More particularly, SC gave the woman specific advice on how to solve her immediate problem of finding some-

where to stay while she recuperates from her injuries ... SC was knowledgeable about emergency accommodation and services for homeless
people. SC gave the woman a card with her telephone number and said,
'Call me if you need to talk or need help with refuge accommodation.'
(TP)

Later in the same shift, this senior partner took charge of another
difficult situation in a patient and restrained way. In that incident
police were called to the scene of 'a woman going crazy in a hotel
lobby.' The woman turned out to be a seventeen-year-old who had
checked into the hotel with her boyfriend the night before. The manager tried to evict her in the morning, but she refused to leave. She told
the officers that just before leaving the hotel that morning, her boyfriend had physically assaulted her and held a gun to her head. She
said she could not return home because her father abused her. While
showing compassion, the senior officer told the woman she was techni-
cally causing a disturbance and had to leave. The woman became more
hysterical and screamed that she was being victimized. The officer
maintained her composure and offered to take the woman to a nearby
women's refuge. The woman refused and stormed out of the hotel
lobby, crying and shouting abuse at the police. When she mumbled,
'Life is not worth living, I want to die,' the officers grabbed her by the
arms and tried to put her in the back of the truck. The woman shouted
in disbelief, 'I have not done anything wrong and you are arresting
me – I don't believe this!' What happened next is best described in the
words of the observer:

As we drove off, SC voiced her thoughts to the probationer, 'What are we
going to do with her? We can't take her back to the station – should we
have her scheduled ... or take her to a woman's refuge?' The probationer
said little; he just drove. SC suggested that her irrational behaviour could
be the result of drugs, e.g. speed or LSD. She then instructed the probationer to drive to a nearby woman's refuge. Meanwhile, [the woman]
continued to shout her innocence and thump the sides of the cabin. Her
cries signalled our arrival to the refuge workers, who emerged with questioning facial expressions. One of the staff began to wave her hands and
shake her head, signalling that [the woman] was unwanted, 'Take her
somewhere else, we can't deal with her.' The officers were not prepared to
take no for an answer, at least for the moment. They went to the rear of the
truck and opened the door. Then a couple of refuge staff decided to at

least take a closer look at [the woman]. Perhaps because she was quite young, the refuge workers reconsidered and attempted to calm her with an invitation to go inside, have a cup of tea and talk about her concerns. Despite the genuine and compassionate efforts of the police and refuge staff, [the woman] continued her fixated verbal abuse of the police for not believing her account of events back at the hotel. Finally, the refuge workers convinced her to go inside. Once she was seated on the refuge's verandah we left the location. There was a noticeable silence in the truck as we drove back to the station. SC and the probationer were obviously disturbed by the incident. SC in particular expressed her concern for [the woman]'s well-being and immediate future. This was a very difficult and emotional situation for all of us. The officers demonstrated extreme patience with [the woman]. They maintained focus and followed the job through to its completion. (TP)

This incident illustrates how much of police work is ambiguous as well as unrewarding. The senior partner seemed to combine a sensitivity to the suffering of the woman being evicted with a capacity to endure the antagonism aroused by the paradoxical use of coercion (cf Muir 1977).

'Bad' Police Work

Interviewees were also asked if they had come across examples of 'bad' police work. Most officers provided some examples but were quick to point out that 'bad' policing was not something they saw a great deal of, whereas they saw 'good' police work 'every day' or 'all the time.' The important point to bear in mind in interpreting these data is that, contrary to the popular notion that the 'police culture' supports corruption and malpractice, these officers were willing to distance themselves from what they regarded as 'bad' practices. Far from being moulded uniformly and passively by the 'street cop' culture, our subjects were actively trying to make sense of their occupation, and sorting out the 'good' from the 'bad' among the models they encountered. The following composite picture of 'bad' policing is constructed from the interviews:

'Bad' policing is epitomized by the 'shonks,' officers who are lazy, who try to find ways to avoid picking up jobs, or who don't do their work properly. It is also about poor communication skills and an uncaring attitude –

about not being willing to listen to people. Sometimes it involves being overly aggressive or escalating conflicts.

One probationer explained how 'shonking' worked in the demonstration patrol he was in:

At the demonstration patrol there was usually two vehicles running when a job would come across, and you could tell that both vehicles would sort of sit off the job waiting for the other one to pick it up, rather than just getting in there and doing it ... I guess on the odd occasion you see people run off and do their own errands. Really, when you think, it's probably not the right thing to do – it's not the thing that I would do. (3/23-year-old male)

Most interviewees observed that shonks tended to be more experienced officers. Their attitude created a negative work environment for new probationers:

[Bad police work is] basically being a shonk, and I've seen quite a few examples of it ... You find that people who are a junior in the job, like under four years' experience, have a tendency not to do it. Like, the further you get on, the more it appears to me, ... the more prone you are to shonking jobs ... People just generally don't care ... and are just there to whinge and bitch to their workmates about how bad the job is. ... I can't stand those people, you know – the job's bad because *they're* bad, basically. (3/24-year-old male)

One probationer witnessed an officer beating up a drunken man who was not under arrest but was being transported home. Both he and his partner found the action disturbing enough to report it to the shift supervisor:

There was a fight in a car park at a pub, and there was police come from everywhere. And, like, things were fairly heated – there was about thirty, forty people in the car park. Everything was sort of settled down, we were actually putting one guy in the back of our truck – he wasn't under arrest, we were just taking him home, he was really intoxicated. And I guess he didn't fully understand why he was going in the back of the truck. This police officer came in, I didn't know who he was or where he was, and just hooked into him. This particular officer came in like, kicked him a couple of times and then hit him and then the dog was there and that was it. So once we got into the truck I said to my partner, I said, 'Look.' Well, he said too, you know, 'That's just not on.' That's why we mentioned it to the shift supervisor. (3/26-year-old male)

One probationer found that even in a non-confrontational situation, insensitive policing could undo the good relations built up through community policing:

I was working night shift – pulled up at an intersection and there was a man in his pyjamas just waiting on the side of the road. He was an Asian man, he was waiting for his girlfriend to drive home, and he was just out there to greet her. And ... I knew this man because he had reported an accident to me before, and it was just a coincidence that I knew him. Anyway, my partner called him over to the car and said, 'What are you doing out here?' which was fair enough, he was out in his pyjamas at two in the morning. And he said, 'Oh, just waiting for my girlfriend,' and then he went to walk away, and this officer said, 'Oh, you stay here while I'm speaking to you.' And then I could see it in this man's face that, you know, he was degraded and it was ... just disrespectful how this officer acted. And then as he walked away I went to say 'bye and he didn't even say 'bye. And he came up to me when we first saw him as happy as Larry, you know, I knew him. I said, 'How are you going?' And then he walked away and just hated me, gave me a look like he hated me. (3/19-year-old female)

An example of a negative role model comes from the observation data at a demonstration patrol, in which the probationer and her partner for the shift, a constable first class, were called to attend a robbery. The reckless driving behaviour of the partner endangered lives. It was also totally inefficient and unproductive in terms of crime control:

[The constable C decided to drive the vehicle]. C was driving and he reversed the vehicle at high speed down the driveway that ran beside the police station. He reversed the vehicle straight across the pedestrian footpath without even slowing or checking for anybody who may have been walking along the footpath. He then proceeded to drive (with lights and sirens activated) at high speed up a main road toward the small shopping centre where the alleged robbery had taken place. During this time he frequently went onto the wrong side of the road and directly into the path of oncoming vehicles. The traffic was quite heavy and it was obvious that other road users were confused or unaware of where the police car was coming from. He was driving in a frenzied state and seemed to be oblivious to the danger he was posing to other road users. C drove through two red lights with only a cursory attempt to slow down. If at any stage another vehicle had been approaching or moving through these intersections C would have certainly caused a major accident.

When we reached the small shopping centre C started yelling out to [the probationer] PC that he didn't know where the take-away shop was located. It appeared that in his frenzied departure from the police station he had neglected to get the address of the shop. We drove past all the shops but we couldn't see a sign of any disturbance. By this stage C was hunched over the wheel, with no seat belt on, and was obviously completely obsessed with capturing the armed robbers. It was obvious to me[7] that anybody who had robbed the shop would have been long gone as such an offence is usually committed within a matter of minutes. This fact seemed to have completely escaped C who was in a state of extreme agitation.

At this point C must have decided that he was looking for the shop in the wrong shopping centre. As it happened there was another small shopping centre about one km down the road from where we were currently looking. C did a U-turn and then proceeded to head in the direction of this other shopping centre. The road that led to these shops was a main two-lane roadway. There was about a 1/2 km steep downhill run before the road went up and over a crest (with traffic lights on top of this crest). The shops we were heading towards were on the other side of the crest. C drove down this road at extremely high speed and as we were heading down a steep hill the vehicle gathered an excessive amount of speed.

As C was hunched directly over the steering wheel I could not see the speedometer but I could see that he was pushing the vehicle to its maximum speed. I estimate from the shuddering of the vehicle that we were going 120–140 km per hour. As the vehicle was a caged Hi Lux truck it was therefore not a stable vehicle at extremely high speeds. At this point in time C had exceeded the point of acting in a rational manner in the execution of his duties. He was driving in a highly dangerous manner which put at risk the lives of those in the police vehicle and the lives of other road users. He was driving at such an excessive speed that he was not in proper control of the vehicle. At such a speed loss of control of the vehicle would most certainly have resulted in fatalities. At the crest of the hill the traffic lights were red. C was going so fast that his cursory touch on the brakes would have been insufficient to stop the vehicle in time had any other vehicle been at those lights. Upon reaching the shops at the end of the road all was quiet. C again turned the vehicle around and drove in exactly the same dangerous manner back to the original shops from where we had come. As we reached these shops we saw [another police car] parked outside a take-away shop and the police manning that vehicle were inside the shop taking details from the victim of the robbery. (DP)

The observer, whose life was endangered by this officer's reckless driving, made the following comments:

In summary, C had driven in such a manner as to exceed all his powers as a police officer. Urgent duty runs are undertaken only by the consent and courtesy of other road users and the police have no legal dispensation to exceed the speed limit or disobey traffic lights. C acted irrationally and illegally. He had no right to endanger other people's lives for his own personal gratification in seeking to come face to face with alleged armed robbers. It appeared that he was unable to rationalise his actions and weigh up risk versus outcome. Apart from this, his actions clearly indicated his total unsuitability for a role in training new police. (DP)

It should be noted that our observers encountered high-speed driving by police on a number of occasions.[8] It was not at all clear to us that the risk taken on those occasions was justified.

Our field observation also revealed a variety of police practices that would normally be considered unprofessional, although they were not criminal offences. For example, one probationer spoke to an observer about 'being junior with a female officer who told him just to drive around and she went to sleep in the car' (DP). On another occasion, the senior partner of a car crew in the demonstration patrol 'verbalized his intent to avoid involvement in any large or complex jobs during the shift' so he could watch a police football match (DP). We also observed a senior officer who did not have much regard for 'customer service':

Apparently a member of the public was waiting at the counter to see constable X with whom he had an appointment at this time. The constable on counter duty had looked up the roster only to find that constable X was not on duty that day. What should he tell the man waiting at the counter? The Station Officer told him to tell the man that constable X had been called out on urgent duty and that he would be unable to see him that day. The man should go home. (DP)

One of the senior partners dealt with non-English speakers in a way that showed a lack of both communication skills and cultural sensitivity. Ironically, the probationer who was being trained by this senior officer was more proficient:

I found [the senior partner's] manner with the public ... rather brusque and unfriendly. He seemed to find it difficult to be pleasant with the public, rather as though he didn't really like or trust people ... He seemed to save his worst behaviour for Asians and other people who couldn't speak English very well. He simply did not believe that they were not understanding him. When they did not understand him, he got very angry and frustrated and repeated what he had said, only louder. He never attempted to reformulate what he was saying in easier language because he thought it was already very simple. But actually it wasn't. For example, he asked one non-English-speaking person, 'What is the reason you are here?' The man didn't understand him. He repeated it several times. Finally, [the probationer] said very slowly and deliberately, 'Why are you here?' The man instantly understood and replied appropriately. (DP)

In another situation, the senior partner responded to a traffic infringement in a reckless manner. His actions were also contrary to the shift sergeant's instruction not to use the police truck for high-speed pursuits:

A vehicle [was] at a set of traffic lights 100 m in front of us heading in the opposite direction. It accelerated, spinning the back wheels and creating a cloud of burnt rubber smoke. The vehicle, a four-door 1970 Ford Falcon with a loud performance engine, roared past us in the opposite direction. 'Let's book him,' [the probationer] said. In that instant, [the senior constable] SC negotiated a U-turn in front of the oncoming traffic. Not only was our safety threatened by the bulk of traffic, a vehicle travelling in the outside lane and shielded from view by an approaching truck skidded and nearly hit the passenger side of our vehicle. 'God, that was close,' I said in a calm tone trying to conceal my safety concerns. We pursued the traffic offender with lights and siren activated for a short distance until the driver exited into a shopping centre car park ... SC eventually issued the driver with a ticket for negligent driving. (DP)

During their field training, probationers often came across negative or cynical attitudes about policing as a profession and about the police service as an organization. For example, 97 per cent of the respondents reported that they had heard officers expressing negative or cynical opinions about the policing profession during their field training: 33 per cent heard this occasionally (one to five times); 64 per cent heard this often (more than five times). Similarly, 99 per cent of the respondents heard officers expressing negative or cynical opinions about the NSW Police Service: 20 per cent occasionally, and 70 per cent often. However, officers who were cynical were not necessarily unprofessional in practice. For example, on one of the shifts we observed, the shift partner of the probationer – a constable who had graduated only six months earlier – showed a great deal of professionalism in his work, even though he was very critical of the organization:

[The senior] spoke a lot about work conditions, the lack of resources, and expressed some cynicism about the purchase of new guns which has recently been reported in the press. He seemed to me to become more cynical in his views the more he spoke. Yet observing him in practice, this cynicism did not come through: at the arrest, he treated the man with respect throughout any interaction that I was able to observe; when he pulled over the car, and the baby cried, he asked if the baby was all right; during [the probationer's] personal phone call, he interrupted, asked if it was a personal phone call, and when that was established, said what he wanted to say to [the probationer]; he spent time supervising probationers with their COPS entries, appearing to me from a distance to be teaching them ... ; and he gave [the probationer] a booklet of traffic offences to help him make out his traffic ticket. In fact, I guess I was struck by the professionalism of [the senior's] performance against the cynicism of his views, which emerged more as the shift progressed. (DP)

Another observer similarly noted the contrast between the liberal use of profane and sexist language among detectives and their apparently professional practice:

Despite the presence of a female and myself within earshot, [the detective D] liberally used profane and sexist language while attending to the sexual assault case. The other detectives appeared to feel comfortable with using this type of language, i.e. fuck, bitch, dickhead, shit, etc. On the basis of this kind of language, I expected to see a lack of professionalism to policing practice. However, in terms of protocol, procedures and the law, D and the other detectives exhibited precise and strict adherence to policing practice in an objective manner, using appropriate labels, terms and language. (DP)

Differentiation of Experience

As expected, field training was highly regarded by the recruits in this study. When asked at the end of their eighteen-month training (Survey 3) to rate the relative importance of the two components of their training, they rated field training (including the four weeks of field observation) as more than twice as important as academy training: mean ratings 72 versus 28 per cent, with identical standard deviations of 12.8 for both components. This roughly corresponds to the ratio of time spent between the two training components: 69 per cent (fifty-three weeks) in the field and 31 per cent (twenty-four weeks) at the academy. It also reflects the reality that for general duties policing, many of the required skills can only be acquired through hands-on experience and practice in a wide range of situations.

Probationers took in both positive and negative experiences during Phase 4. When asked to describe the best aspects of their field training in Survey 3, respondents (only 118 responded) referred to the knowledge and experience gained (31 per cent), the fact that they were actually working or being 'operational' (33 per cent), the teamwork and camaraderie involved in working with other police (14 per cent), and other aspects such as doing 'real' police work, the variety of that work, and being treated fairly by the police and receiving good feedback from the public (2 to 3 per cent each). Regarding the worst aspects of their field training, 28 per cent of the 95 respondents mentioned a host of problems relating to police work – excessive paperwork, treatment by the public or offenders, workload, lack of resources, office politics, and so on. Others mentioned having to complete PREP requirements such as case write-ups and examinations (20 per cent), treatment by other police or the police service (19 per cent), feelings of insecurity or lack of confidence (16 per cent), working with 'shonks' (11 per cent)-and other miscellaneous problems. In addition, 30 per cent of the survey respondents reported having personally experienced some form of verbal or physical harassment during their field training (almost half of such incidents involved harassment by the public, and about one-quarter involved harassment by other police). Also, 22 per cent reported having observed other police being physically or verbally harassed (about half of these incidents involved harassment by the public, and about one-third involved harassment by other police). In sum, during Phase 4 probationers were exposed to the best and the worst aspects of policing.

Probationers' experiences during Phase 4 varied substantially with the patrol (local area) they were sent to, the patrol commander, the shift supervisor, and their shift partners. Three-quarters of the respondents to Survey 3 thought that their learning experience at the demonstration patrol was 'very different' (33 per cent) or 'somewhat different' from that at the training patrol. A similar proportion of probationers (74 per cent) felt that the personality or working style of the patrol commander made some difference (53 per cent) or a great deal of difference (20 per cent) to the way they carried out their duties during Phase 4. Similarly, 87 per cent thought the shift supervisor made a difference (59 some, 28 a great deal). Finally, 91 per cent indicated that their shift partner made a difference (37 some, 54 a great deal). Clearly, probationers' practices were most affected by the personality and working style of their shift partners, their shift supervisors, and their patrol commanders, in that order. This is consistent with earlier results showing that probationers felt junior police made the greatest contribution to their development.

Shift Partners

Shift partners had a direct and significant impact on probationers' daily experience. The importance of buddies and FTOs was discussed earlier. One probationer contrasted the advice she got from her buddy with the advice she got from other police: her buddy wanted her to 'learn the right way' and would 'sit down and explain things,' whereas other police in the station gave her contradictory or 'shonky' advice, or could not be bothered with her (3/19-year-old female).

Having as shift partners officers who were not keen to go out could make a difference to how work was conducted on that shift:

> With people that have been in the job, you know, anywhere above seven years, I think, ... five, seven years – they start, you know, to want to sit in the station a little bit more, and they're not keen to go out and drive around. Whereas the younger people, you know, they go – keener to go out and look for work ... I've heard some senior constables say, 'You know,

mate, you're only hurting yourself locking people up,' because, see, in the end of the day you get paid the same to do as much, ten arrests or no arrests, and the more arrests you do, the more paperwork you get. (3/20-year-old male)

Yet it was possible for a probationer to maintain enthusiasm in spite of his partner's lack of interest. On one occasion, we observed a senior constable showing 'little zeal or enthusiasm for the job ... going through the motions.' In contrast, his junior partner, the probationer, 'appeared keen, conscientious and prepared to think laterally when investigating a case' (DP).

Supervisors

A number of interviewees noted a difference in supervisory styles between the demonstration patrols and the training patrols. Some supervisors were stricter than others in terms of general discipline:

Some of [the shift supervisors] are easy [and] some of them are really strict, you can't do anything. You can't joke around with anyone or sort of muck around a bit. It's more fun when you can sort of have a joke about a few things, and some of them will ... come out and start talking to you. Some of them will just sit in their office all night and won't come out and speak to you at all. (3/19-year-old female)

There were also differences in terms of how closely paperwork was checked and how often it was returned for 'resubmit':

Some supervisors will watch your work more closely than others or with the computer work, your COPS entries. They'd jump on you harder at one patrol, like to put more information in, and the other one they wouldn't worry so much. (3/23-year-old male)

At the first station [all my COPS entries] got accepted and verified straight-away. When I got to my training patrol everything got resubmitted. I'm probably doing better COPS entries ... but they're still getting resubmitted. (3/21-year-old male)

This probationer felt there was no consistency in standards between sergeants, or even with the same sergeant. He had heard stories that 'people just put it straight back in exactly how they were, they leave it for a couple of days to the same sergeant, and then he verifies it' (3/21-year-old male). Some probationers seemed to dislike close supervision and put it down to supervisors not kept busy enough with other work:

> Where I am now it's over-supervised. I think there's a lot of supervisors and they've got less to do and so they're onto your back quite a bit ... checking up on you and checking what you're doing. You know, they've got more time on their hands, so they spend more time looking at your entries on the computer and sending them back to you to redo, whereas you barely got any at the first station because it was a busy station, the supervisors were kept busy, so they didn't have the time. (3/27-year-old male)

Others preferred their supervisors to be more thorough and knowledgeable:

> You'll sort of get to know who is a decent supervisor and who is not. You'll have ... simple things like checking your notebook. You'll have people that just flick through and sort of just check anything and say, 'Oh, it's all right,' but then you'll have the proper, like, decent sergeants who'll actually look through and make sure that you've done all your work ... And just general knowledge things. Like, sometimes you can't know everything in this job, there are so many things get changed and updated, you're never going to know anything. But some of the sergeants are really up-to-date and ... they've got so much knowledge that if you ask them, they just know everything. (3/20-year-old male)

According to another probationer, if the supervisor was competent and approachable, it took some of the pressure off the learners and made them less fearful of asking for help. This probationer gave an example of an incompetent supervisor on whom he felt he could not rely:

> I went as a guard to the hospital with a domestic violence offender with a supervising sergeant, and we went up to the hospital, and the supervising sergeant there let him make a phone call. And certainly I'm no person to say he can't make a phone call ... and he's called his wife who's just got an AVO [Apprehended Violence Order] out against him, just, you know, just hours before, saying you can't call this person. And [the supervisor] just wasn't competent, like, he just didn't seem to have a clue, you know, and

it just made you edgy to be with him because you think he's going to get into trouble. (3/22-year-old male)

Another factor was the extent to which supervisors were out on the road. In some patrols, supervisors stayed in the office and would only come out on the road when they were needed. In others, there were mobile supervisors who were 'always right next to you when you need them' (3/19-year-old male). In small stations that did not have backup cars, the supervisor often acted as a backup (3/24-year-old female).

Patrol and Patrol Commanders

A large proportion of interviewees said that their experience in the training patrol was quite different from the demonstration patrol. In this, workload was an often cited factor. One probationer commented on the contrast between a busy demonstration patrol and a less busy training patrol when it came to getting advice:

[The demonstration patrol] was probably a little bit too busy ... It was hard to get time out of some people to give you advice and that, but good in some ways and bad in others. Like, good in the way that you got a lot of experience 'cause they were so busy, but bad in [that] sometimes you tend to be a bit ignored and do a lot of things on your own ... My training patrol is a lot quieter ... Everyone's got a lot of time where you can ask things and it's been good for me to slow things down and go right through the process and, you know, ask all the questions now. (3/25-year-old male)

Workload could also affect the culture of the patrol – that is, whether people formed 'cliques' and became more conscious of seniority:

[At the demonstration patrol] no one has got time to sit around and bitch about ... each other, and you don't really care what the other ... people are doing, but at the training patrol, though, because it's a bit more relaxed, people have got time to sit back and they start organizing in their little clique groups ... and, like, you can see how people congregate and senior-ity starts to creep in where people will say, 'Oh, I'm senior to you.' (3/20-year-old male)

The two patrols also differed in the degree of enthusiasm officers showed. Work culture affected this. One probationer noted that people were much 'more keen' and positive in the training patrol he went to: they were prepared to 'go out there and ... just straight onto the job' and more ready to back up other patrols (3/23-year-old male).

Other probationers commented on the difference in the number of experienced officers in the two patrols, and how this affected learning:

> The demonstration patrol was not very experienced. Sometimes I would be out on the truck with someone only a year or so above me. Some of them had only been out for twelve months. It was hard because I was in a new situation, and I had to learn what to do and how to do things. It's different at the training patrol. I'm one of the most junior people here. Mainly I work with senior constables and constables and that. And you can notice the difference. They just know what to do better. They know what you can do under the law, and they know how to go about things. Senior blokes will explain to you how to do things. They will say, 'Don't do it that way, you will get into trouble if you do it that way.' (3/20-year-old male)

The personality or working style of the patrol commander also made a difference. One probationer said that a commander who could 'get the troops on side' while being clear about expectations was more likely to have his instructions heeded than a disciplinarian who ignored his staff:

> The commander at the demo patrol ... couldn't get his message across and everything with him was, like, discipline ... I've got nothing against discipline, but you've got to get the troops on side and he's another guy you'd walk past in the corridor, and, you know, 'Good morning, Sir,' and he'd ignore you or say, you know, 'Straighten your name tag up,' and no acknowledgment of your existence ... Just hopeless. But at the training patrol ... it's, oh, excellent boss ... Friendliest guy in the world. Doesn't beat around the bush, if he's got a problem he will bloody tell you and make sure you know it ... But, yeah, from day one, day dot from getting there, took you aside and told you what's expected, what the go is, and laid down the law. He's great, though, you know, he'll come up and just have a chat, you know, in the meal room having lunch, he'll come and sit down and have a chat in the afternoon about the footy or whatever ... He jokes and pays out on you. He's a great bloke, and because he gets along with everyone he can put his message across without going berserk and ... getting on his high horse sort of thing. And you know, he only has to say

something and he can say it half-jokingly, but ... you listen to it and you do what he bloody says ... And he's got a great method of communication like that. (3/21-year-old male)

Another interviewee said that at the demonstration patrol, the commander was 'hardly ever seen'; in contrast, the commander of the training patrol actually came down and congratulated him on his work: 'I felt about twelve foot tall ... 'cause you don't often get praise from anybody' (3/22-year-old male).

Individual Adaptations

In its evaluation of PREP, the CARE report (1990) pointed out the tension between formal learning at the academy and experiential learning in the field. The report suggested that:

> the ideal is that both ways of learning should be used critically in relation to the other ... Thus, while it is essential that academic and formal learning should be open to the criticisms that practice will, inevitably, produce, it is also essential, in any reflective practitioner based course, that practice should be open to theoretical and moral critique. (66)

The CARE report found a 'fundamental imbalance in the learning mechanism,' where 'theory is criticized by practice, [but] the reverse process rarely happens' (66). This imbalance still existed at the time of our study. But at the same time, we found that given the opportunity (e.g., at interviews), some probationers were quite willing to criticize certain practices, and distance themselves from them. While it is true that training at the academy came under a great deal of criticism (see the section 'Leaving the Academy Behind'), probationers did not simply agree with everything they saw and heard in the field. Our data suggest that individual probationers formed judgments about police work and the police organization based on their own experiences, and were able to distinguish between 'good' and 'bad' police work (see the section 'Models of Practice'). As one interviewee pointed out, probationers came across different models and worked out which ones were 'good' and which were 'bad':

> And also [with] every person you work with, I think you're also learning something. Just ... different ways of doing a job ... good and bad. Like, you

know, at the end of working a shift with one bloke you might think, 'Oh, I wouldn't do it that way,' and now I've seen the results of doing the job that way. And then you see some blokes and you think, 'Yeah, that's not a bad way of doing that, I've never seen it done like that. I might start doing it that way.' (3/20-year-old male)

Similarly, a mature-age probationer told us that his own life experience and working with more experienced officers later on helped him see the strengths and weaknesses of his first buddy's practice. He thought his buddy was quite young and 'a little immature.' He would often quietly disagree with the way the buddy handled some situations, but in other situations, he thought, 'Oh geez, you handled that well, there's no way I could have done that' (3/28-year-old male). As one of the interviewees said, the experience of Phase 4 was about sorting out for oneself what type of officer to become:

Well, I think that's what your Phase 4 is there to do. See, you work with all different people and they're there. See, I'm only just developing my way of doing it now and I've been out for twelve months, seeing all these different ways of, like, because there's no one way to tackle any situation. You just have to weigh it up and just work it out yourself. That's the thing. There's right ways of doing it and wrong ways, and you have to work out which way you're going to do it. (3/22-year-old female)

Another probationer thought that the academy taught them the 'right way' of doing things, but that there were other – different but not necessarily wrong – ways to accomplish the same tasks. The learning process involved comparing different practices encountered during training in order to develop a personal style (3/20-year-old male). Probationers did not automatically follow the advice of operational officers who told them to 'forget that shit you learnt at the academy':

It's up to the individual to make up their own mind what they want to forget and learn, but for me it was sort of maintain most of what I learned [at the academy] and use that to refer to while I was working. (3/24-year-old male)

During our field observation, we also saw evidence that probationers did not simply accept everything they were told by more experienced officers. For example, one probationer told the observer that he did not entirely share his senior partner's pessimism about promotion opportunities within the police service:

> While returning to the patrol area, [the senior partner] SC commented on changes to career structure, promotion pathways and specialization opportunities in the Police Service. In his opinion, the past ten years or so have seen career opportunities within the Service become limited ... The organisation has also seen changes to promotion procedures. Now, promotion is based on merit rather than seniority. As a result, officers must engage in further study to enhance their promotion prospects. SC said he acknowledged the merit of the changes but questioned ... what officers who are not academically inclined [could do]. We arrived back at the station. SC announced it was time to stop for a lunch break. While walking from the truck, [the probationer] commented on SC's comments about limits to police careers. [He] suggested that SC's views and attitudes towards the Service [were] 'bitter.' He said, although what SC says may be accurate, it is one's attitude that makes the difference between a positive or negative experience of circumstances. (TP)

Another probationer told our observer that her age made her 'wiser' than some of her seniors and that she was able to distinguish between good and bad role models:

> As it happens, at 27 [the probationer] was considerably older than my two other subjects and she commented on this. She said that in her view people should not be recruited into the police until they were at least 21 or 22 because they were far too immature and inexperienced to do such a difficult and responsible job until they were at least that age. [She] told me that she was sometimes embarrassed to be so much older and wiser in the ways of the world than her senior. On the other hand, her age gave her the advantage of being able to discriminate between the good and the bad policemen – those you could and those you couldn't learn from. (DP)

Similarly, another mature-age probationer felt that her age was an advantage in that she was less likely to compromise her moral and ethical values:

> [The probationer] said that her 'mature age' status was an advantage when working with less proficient officers. Her maturity ensured that her moral and ethical values were shielded from taint ... [She] demonstrates

that she has a mind of her own and has the ability and motivation to think for herself on issues of culture, morals and ethics ... I asked if ethics was studied at the academy. 'Yes,' she said, 'but it is a personal thing you pick up as a kid.' (DP)

In spite of these individual expressions of autonomy, we found that probationers almost never openly questioned their seniors' actions or judgments, most likely for the sake of 'fitting in' (see the earlier section 'Coping Strategies'). Our observers described many occasions when probationers simply kept quiet while their seniors expressed strong opinions about a variety of issues:

On the way, [the senior partner] SC issued a monologue about the limitations of proactive policing these days. The essence of his story was thus: in the old days if we had strong enough evidence of criminal activity we would just go and apply a little pressure or knock them around a little to either get a confession or at least deter them from further criminal activity. The tone of his speech was not malicious but rather nostalgic for the 'good old days.' [The probationer] did not engage SC in further discussion on this topic; she simply listened and kept driving. (DP)

Sometimes probationers tried to defend their seniors' actions and their own tolerance of certain practices. For example, a female probationer was tolerant of her senior partner's use of profane language throughout the shift:

[The senior partner] SC punctuated his monologue liberally with denigrating and profane language e.g., fuck, bastards, little shits, etc. ... I did not observe any response from PC on this issue; she appeared unperturbed ... [Later in the shift] She said that although she does not endorse that kind of language, she is tolerant. She explained thus: it is the intent behind coarse language that determines whether she accepts or rejects it. If the language is malice driven or is derogatory, she has no hesitation in making her protest known irrespective of the officer's rank. She championed her rights to her own interpretation of a situation where coarse language is used and defended the use of this kind of language by SC. (DP)

Another example of a probationer's willingness to defend his senior partner's actions was observed on one shift after the breath analysis machine had failed to work and the senior partner (a senior constable) recorded this as a 'fail alco test' on the fact sheet:

> I was struck by a sentence on the fact sheet which said that [the accused] had 'failed alco test' and then refused to take the breath test. I asked [the probationer] to explain that since a layperson's interpretation of 'failing' a breath test would normally be that the accused had gone over the limit, not that the equipment had failed. [The probationer] immediately explained that [the accused] had probably put in his tongue to stop the air from flowing and that was why the equipment didn't work. My question must have bothered [him] somewhat because later he asked [the senior partner] about the sentence in the fact sheet. [The senior partner] said that the test didn't work, so it 'failed.' He also repeated [the probationer's] speculation that [the accused] had put his tongue in to make the machine not work. (DP)

On one occasion, the senior partner, who had just been cross-examined in court for two hours and said 'her head was spinning,' told the probationer that that was why they should make contemporaneous notes. When the probationer challenged her senior partner's instructions, she was told that 'that's the way it's always done':

> [The senior partner] SC said 'That is what we should do now about that bloke that we just took to the hospital. We should sit down and make contemporaneous notes.' [The probationer] said 'At the academy they told us that you shouldn't do that, and that you should make individual statements. They said that we don't do that any more...that the courts don't like it. I remember that they said that even where you are standing makes a difference to what you see happening.' SC said 'No, that's the way you do it. That's the way it's always been done, that's what you do.' SC said that a lot of the stuff that they teach at the academy, 'you just don't do it that way.' [The probationer] said 'A lot of things I've been taught at the academy, you don't think that you remember it, then when something happens I remember something that they taught at the academy.' (TP)

On another shift, the probationer's questioning of the legality of an arrest turned out to be well founded. The situation was one in which a male suspect was breathalyzed, but he was not driving at the time – it was late at night and his car was parked on the side of the road. He told the police he was out of petrol and was waiting till the morning. He was over the limit and placed under arrest and brought back to the station. At the time of the arrest, the probationer whispered to his senior partner, a constable who was six months past his graduation. Later, out of hearing of the arrestee, the probationer told the researcher that his whispered asides to his partner were about his uncertainty about the arrest, as the man was not driving the car. He explained to the researcher that there was a difference between DUI and PCA charges. Back at the station, while the man was being interviewed by the probationer in an interview room, the researcher remained outside and observed 'almost everyone in the station at that time having some input' into deciding whether there was an offence and what offence it might be. In addition to discussion among officers (including the shift supervisor), there were also phone calls seeking advice. The ultimate decision was that the man should not have been arrested. He was returned to his car by the police (DP).

Another probationer told our observer that he felt quite relaxed about openly disagreeing with a shift partner who was only one class above him, even though he was 'counselled' for 'going over her head':

> [The probationer] PC said that at the time he arrested the girl he had been working with a female constable who was only one class above him. He said that he felt that he had much more experience than the female constable because he had been working at a busy station during his demonstration Patrol and had made several arrests already. He said that when he arrested the girl, he asked her to make a recorded interview (ERISP). The girl had said that she didn't want to. PC had wanted to make a recording of her declining the ERISP. The female constable had said that he didn't need to do that. PC said that he then went and asked the detectives at the station who told him that he should. PC went back to the female constable and said that the detectives said that he should pursue making the recording of the girl declining the interview. The girl refused again. What happened then was that the female constable complained to the 'boss,' and PC was 'counselled' for 'going over her head.' I asked him how he felt about that, and he replied that 'It didn't worry me. They had to do it. She shouldn't have made such a big thing out of it.' He said that he knew that he was right, and that she didn't have enough experience. (TP)

Learning a Feel for the Game

Operational policing presented new constraints and new resources for probationers. While they felt handicapped by their lack of practical knowledge, they were also excited by the learning opportunities and by the willingness of experienced officers to teach them. Compared with the academy, operational policing was 'real,' exciting, and where they wished to belong. Feeling inadequately prepared for operational work, probationers – desperate to be accepted by this new 'family' – learned to keep their mouths shut, to listen, and to defer to more experienced officers. They concentrated on acquiring practical knowledge and expertise, and on bonding with fellow police officers.

During field training, probationers came face to face with the clash between the academy's and operational officers' visions of policing. Operational police were suspicious of the academy's efforts to liberalize police education and to inject recruits with social, cultural, and ethical awareness. They saw the 'new breed' of probationers as undermining police solidarity and the traditional respect for rank and experience. Most operational police were not aware of what was actually being taught at the academy, but that did not deter them from criticizing its curriculum. To the probationers, shell-shocked by the realities of operational policing, many of the criticisms seemed valid (e.g., that there was insufficient preparation for practical work, and too much emphasis on social and cultural issues). Given how much they wanted to be accepted by their new workmates, probationers found it simple to distance themselves from the academy training, even though some were consciously aware of its value and others were unconsciously affected by it.

Yet remnants of the 'professional model' of policing still lived in the psyches of the probationers. This was evident in their articulation of 'good' and 'bad' policing. When given a chance to voice their opinions, probationers were discerning – they distinguished between practices that were 'shonky' and counterproductive and those that were competent and productive. Their vision of competence and productivity embraced technical expertise as well as interpersonal skills. There was abundant evidence from our observation that some probationers exercized independent judgments and were conscious that they had a choice in what kind of police officer they would become. In short, some of them had become the 'reflective practitioners' that the academy had intended. But learning a 'feel of the game' also meant that one did not openly challenge or criticize one's seniors, even when one disagreed with them. Survival in the workplace depended on knowing one's place and on building credibility, as opposed to being a 'loud mouth' or a 'know-it-all.' In this sense, compliance to the conventional wisdom may simply be a mask that novices learned to wear in order to survive in the organization (cf Fielding 1988). Like police work itself, recruits' socialization experience was packed with contradictions and uncertainties, paradoxes and dilemmas. Perhaps, in the end, the only way for them to cope was to compartmentalize these contradictions and live with the uncertainties.

In this chapter we have described the learning experiences that probationers went through during Phase 4, their mentors and role models, their coping strategies and adaptive responses. For most of the cohort, the transition from recruit to constable was successful: less than 10 per cent of the cohort left the police service through resignation or termination (see chapter 2). Consciously and unconsciously, probationers had adjusted their habitus to the field of policing in which they found themselves. In the next chapter we analyse the changes in habitus they had undergone by the end of their field training.

6

Taking On the Culture

Van Maanen (1976) describes the final stage of organizational socialization as one requiring some form of metamorphosis on the part of the recruit in order to meet the demands of continued membership in the organization. His research shows that recruits generally followed 'the line of least resistance' (1973: 415): to survive in the organization, they adopted many of the values, assumptions, and strategies found to have 'worked' for operational police. In other words, 'successful socialization' implies that recruits have internalized the norms of the organizational culture. Yet as Manning and Van Maanen (1978: 271–2) have argued, we cannot assume that the socialization process is uniform or linear: there can be many 'twists and turns' in a police career as individuals adapt to new circumstances and environments. Neither can we assume that within a police organization there always exists a single, dominant, stable culture to which recruits eventually become acculturated (Chan 1997). As we have seen in chapters 4 and 5, recruits were not exposed to a uniform set of values, attitudes, and practices during their training. They had to come to terms with various models of practice and decide for themselves what type of police officers they would become. This is not to deny that the transition from recruit to constable demands a great deal of personal adjustment. It is therefore reasonable to ask this question: By the end of their training, to what extent had the recruits adjusted their dispositions (habitus) to the new position (field) they occupied? How uniform was this 'metamorphosis'? How complete was the transformation?

In this chapter we draw on the survey and interview data to examine the changes that we were able to measure and that our subjects themselves were aware of over the eighteen months of their recruit training.

The statistical trends are generally consistent with Van Maanen's (1973) finding of growing disenchantment with the job and increased cynicism about the public and the police bureaucracy. But these trends hide the subtle and contingent nature of the change. As we saw in chapter 5, recruits were discerning and reflective in making judgments about practices they encountered during their training. Like the recruits described by Fielding (1988), they did not always accept the conventional wisdom of the occupational culture. Some of them, instead of simply 'taking on' (i.e., acquiring) the values and assumptions of the culture, were quietly 'taking on' (i.e., opposing) aspects of cultural conventions. We will argue that the socialization process is not a straightforward matter of adjusting one's habitus to 'fit in'; rather, it involves a conscious adoption of survival tactics, during which process some private sense of independence is retained.

Changes in Habitus

We asked probationers at the end of their field training[1] whether they thought they had changed since joining the police. Almost three-quarters of the respondents thought they had: 49 per cent noticed positive changes, and 8 per cent noticed negative changes, while 17 per cent noticed both positive and negative changes. Those under twenty-six were more likely to have noted a positive change in themselves. Many thought they had become 'more mature' (3/20-year-old male); others thought they had gained confidence but at the same time lost some of their idealism, tolerance, and naivety (3/23-year-old male; 3/25-year-old female; 3/21-year-old male). Part of the transformation that recruits experienced was perceptual. One interviewee explained how she had become more aware, more observant, and more alert to what went on around her:

> I think my eyes have been opened up to ... a lot of things ... When you're driving around you can pick up ... you take more notice of things. [Q: More observant?] Yeah, more observant. You take more notice of people, the way they're dressed, what they may be doing ... at that location, you know. Yes, I think you're much more observant and your senses are more alert. (3/24-year-old female)

Another dimension of the change was physical. A few interviewees mentioned that they had taken on the physical and verbal mannerisms of a police officer, including the voice, the walk, the way of knocking on doors, and the way of looking at people:

In a way, I feel that people know that I'm a police officer ... You really do stick out. Even when you're off duty, people say, you know, 'You walk like a cop' ... Or you sit there and you'll look around at people and they'll say you're staring at people like a police officer would, and that's how they pick you ... Yeah, me fiancée sort of commented a couple of times that, you know, I tend to, in a way I'm a bit more standoffish when I meet people than what I used to be ... I'll stand back now and I'll maintain a two-foot distance from them like I would out in the street. It just becomes this triangle safety thing, and you're sort of back from them ... she said, like, 'You'll stand back from people, you'll look at them ... up and down. If they've got their hands in their pocket, you'll look at their hands and watch where their hands are going.' Like, I used to not be as strongly spoken ... Now I've learned. I suppose it just comes with talking to people, too, like in your capacity, you direct your voice more. [Q: So it's a stronger voice ...?] A lot stronger, a lot more authoritarian ... My family, they all reckon ... like nowadays if I'm yelling at someone, especially at home, if I yell something ... they said, you know, they don't want to be in me way if I'm in the job, because, you know, it's a scary sort of voice. (3/22-year-old male)

Yeah, I think I'm a lot more confident and probably a bit more cocky. That's what my mum says ... I went to my brother's house and I knocked on his door, and I knocked on it really loud and he said, 'Oh, you've got your copper knock down pat' ... Or sometimes I'll be driving along in the car and I'll say to my brother, 'Oh, you're up to $150 worth of tickets already.' He'll say, 'Shush.' (3/19-year-old female)

These changes in physical deportment (hexis) and ways of seeing the world may eventually have led to changes in attitudes and personality (3/20-year-old male). Some interviewees told us that their relatives noticed they had become harder, less patient with people (3/27-year-old male), and less compassionate (3/24-year-old male). Many admitted that they had become more cynical and more suspicious of people, although they did not necessarily see this as a negative change (3/22-year-old female, 3/26-year-old male, 3/21-year-old male, 3/20-year-old female). In contrast, a few interviewees thought that they had become more understanding of the problems faced by people from different cultures, as well as more tolerant (3/26-year-old male, 3/20-year-old female). One recruit felt that he had become a better person – more appreciative of what he had, and less selfish as a result of seeing deaths and other human tragedies:

> I've become a better person, I believe. Perspectives are broadened. I appreciate things a lot better. I appreciate what I've got and what I've worked for. Also, I've probably changed in other areas for the worse as well. I'm sort of a pretty easy-going sort of person, but I'm getting harder and harder as times go on ... I'm not as selfish as I used to be: especially with the death sort of experiences and things like that, it probably brings a lot back to me and you think, oh, you know, 'We're on this earth for a short time, so' ... My wife thinks it's a lot better. I'm a happier person for it. (3/29-year-old male)

Nearly one-quarter of interviewees felt that they had not changed over the eighteen months. For one interviewee, this was the result of a conscious effort not to change:

> [Q: Do you feel you've changed as a result of the job?] Personally, no. Like, I've always told myself, once I joined the job, I was ... going to try and stay much the same as I am, and I think I've done that ... I've got two brothers, and one's a police officer and the other one, he's of the opinion that as soon as he joined the job ... he changed into a, pardon the language, an 'arsehole,' and I've always told myself that I was going to try and keep as straight as I could. And even ... my friends, they even said, 'Well, once you join the police, you're going to be, turn into a different person.' And I said, 'Righteo, I'm a hundred per cent sure that I wouldn't change a bit.' So, I still have the same friends, I still do the same things. (3/23-year-old male)

These accounts suggest that most recruits were aware of changes in their habitus – of the physical, cognitive, and attitudinal changes that reflected the requirements of the job of a police constable: to convey the appearance of confidence and authority, to be vigilant about dangers and disorders, and to protect oneself by becoming harder and more suspicious of people. To examine these changes in habitus schematically, we analyse recruits' metamorphosis in terms of the dimensions of cultural knowledge as outlined in Sackmann (1991) and elaborated in Chan (1997) and in chapter 1.

TABLE 6.1
Police functions most appreciated by the public (Surveys 1, 2 and 3)

Percent of respondents who nominated	Survey 1 (n=147)	Survey 2 (n=127)	Survey 3 (n=127)	Significant difference*
Crime prevention	71	59	52	1-2, 1-3
Maintaining order/keeping peace	64	65	61	
Arresting criminals	63	70	58	2-3
Emergency service/public safety	54	53	35	2-3, 1-3
Crime investigation	20	18	20	
Crime detection	10	20	17	1-2

Q: Below is a list of police functions. Which of the following do you think the public appreciates the most? Circle only three options.
*Chi-square tests, p<0.05

Axiomatic Knowledge: Disillusionment with Policing

Axiomatic knowledge refers to fundamental assumptions and beliefs about why things are done the way they are in the organization. Recruits came to policing with the ideal that they would serve the community and make a difference (see chapter 3). They saw the primary goals of policing as providing rapid response to emergencies, enforcing the law fairly, and reducing the incidence of crime and violence (see Table 3.6). In Survey 1, they rated crime prevention, maintaining order, and arresting criminals as the three police functions that the public appreciated the most. These three functions remained at the top of the list for the two subsequent surveys, although the order was slightly different each time (see Table 6.1). In Surveys 2 and 3, however, respondents were significantly less likely than in Survey 1 to think that the public appreciated crime prevention as a police function. Similarly, between Survey 2 and Survey 3, there was a significant drop in the percentage of respondents who rated emergency/public safety and arresting criminals as police functions appreciated by the public. These changes are consistent with other indicators discussed in this chapter, which show a growing disenchantment with aspects of police work and general cynicism about the public as a whole.

In the third round of interviews we asked probationers whether they thought their opinions about police work had changed since they completed their field training. Just under one-fifth (17 per cent) of the respondents reported no change. Most felt that their views of 'the job' had changed – 60 per cent had more negative views of the job, and

15 per cent had both more positive and more negative views, while only 6 per cent had more positive views. This tendency toward a more negative view of policing arose regardless of gender, age, ethnicity, education, or having police as family members.

Recruits had expected to be arresting criminals and giving out speeding tickets, and were disillusioned about the job's heavy bureaucratic and accountability requirements. The most common complaint was the amount of paperwork:

> Well, a lot more work than I thought it would be – paperwork, that is. What I was going for I thought, you know, police work and arrest people. You know, speeding tickets and that. I didn't realize it would be this involved with court and paperwork, computers, yeah ... Everything now, you've got to just more or less cover your arse and do ... the paperwork with every charge and that, and make sure the job's done properly. (3/23-year-old male)

Some interviewees felt that the need to be 'accountable' generated extra workload and pressure – 'it's making us less effective' (3/21-year-old male). Their frustration was directed at managers, Internal Affairs, and external agencies such as the Ombudsman, all of whom demanded this high level of accountability:

> I had a different perception of what we'd be doing. It's just a lot of ... paperwork and a lot of processes that if you don't do, you can be, you know, you're held accountable. If you forget to do something, well, you're the one that's going to be in trouble ... You feel like someone's sort of on your back all the time saying, 'Well, if you don't do this, this is what's going to happen to you' ... I don't think it's so much the boss and that, I just think it's all the external agencies and also internal, like you've got IA and the Ombudsman. (3/20-year-old male)

Another major source of disappointment was the public's lack of appreciation for the work police did:

> It made me think ... is it all worth it? Is it really worth it being a police officer? Like, you get abused, and the money that you get, you think, is it really worth it? But then I think, you know, I love it. I don't want to do anything else, but just that you want to be appreciated for what you do. But no one appreciates you. Sometimes the force suffers and ... morale is

low everywhere and I just think, if you get appreciated for what you do. But no one wants to know, the public don't. I mean the public, some of the public, they hate the police and that, but when they need help they call us [Laugh]. (3/24-year-old female)

Some interviewees had abandoned their ideals of wanting to help people because people 'don't want to be helped':

When I first came into the job, and I did this interview I think in Phase 3 ... I said that I wanted to help people and make a difference. Now I'm just happy to get through my policing without a complaint against me. I still would like to help people, but the question is, 'Do they want to be helped?' Nine times out of ten you try and help people, and they don't want to be helped. (3/24-year-old male)

When I first started I wanted to get into domestic, like the domestic violence side of things, but ... they really annoy me now. I don't enjoy going to domestics at all, because I don't think I've been to a domestic where they haven't phoned me up the next day and say they want to not have an order taken out or they want charges to be dropped ... You don't like going to them because they're a victim then but the next day they turn into these people that don't want anything done, and then a couple of months later, they'll call you again and expect you to do something about it. And you just go there with such a negative attitude ... I get really annoyed going to domestics now. (3/25-year-old female)

Others were disappointed by the limits to what police could do for victims:

It's hard explaining to the public that you have only got a certain amount of, like, power I suppose you would say, to follow up or investigate something they've reported to you ... It's really hard ringing up the victim and saying, 'Look, there is nothing further I can do about it.' That's really hard to do. But there's nothing, and I found that was a really disappointing aspect of the job. (3/22-year-old female)

Even the anticipated excitement of arresting 'criminals' did not live up to expectations. As this probationer discovered when making his first arrest, there was nothing heroic or noble about locking up somebody in the circumstances:

He was a young guy. [We'd found him] in the really early hours of the morning and we'd been for a 'possess prohibited drug' and this particular individual had cerebral palsy and I suppose I had visions of the first person I locked up being some big burly criminal. But this bloke was only – he was only young, suffered from cerebral palsy and I'm thinking, no, this is not, it didn't seem quite right to me to be locking him up ... I felt sorry for him because here's this poor guy, he slurred his speech, he walked with a limp, and, you know, typical of someone that does suffer from those disorders. And I thought, you poor bugger, and I felt guilty because I was about to lock him up and arrest him ... We arrested him, he'd broken the law, he had something on him that he shouldn't have a had ... That was my first arrest. (3/27-year-old male)

As pointed out in chapter 3, most recruits were attracted to policing because of the varied nature of police work. But even here they were disappointed – the job turned out to be more routine and less diverse than expected:

Things are more routine ... now than I thought they would be. I had this expectation of going to work and having a different job every day. Jobs may be different and you go to different locations, but the format and the procedure for every job is nearly the same. So, yeah, it's really not as diverse as I thought it would be. And I think the only way that's going to change is if I diversify and branch into something else later on. (3/27-year-old male)

At the same time, some found the range of duties police are expected to carry out too all-encompassing:

I think police ... are required to attend to too many things, too many duties ... too many portfolios in the one job. You're expected to be a marriage counsellor, and then a grief counsellor, and then the world's best fighter to try and get yourself out of a situation, and then a psychologist ... I knew it was going to be hard and I knew that thanks were very sparse, but I didn't sort of realize it was expected of me to sort of like solve everyone's problems for them. Every job you go to they expect ... well, it's my feeling that they expect you to solve their problems. That's where it gets a bit monotonous. (3/20-year-old female)

Some felt that the job was harder than they had expected because the public showed little respect for the police:

> [When I started] I thought people would show a bit of respect for police and stuff, but that soon changed. Like, people aren't scared to have a go at you or tell you where to go ... Before I joined the police, I would never say, 'Get fucked,' but now, like every day you hear it. I just never thought I would say anything like that. And there's nothing you can do about it. What can you do? (3/20-year-old male)

The disappointment these recruits felt was palpable. Many of the assumptions and beliefs they held about police work were turning out to be false. Police work was routine and monotonous rather than diverse and exciting. Police spent most of their time doing paperwork and 'covering their arses' rather than catching criminals. It was frustrating trying to help people because people did not want to be helped and did not appreciate the help they got. Police could make very little difference, yet they were expected to solve everyone's problems. Far from being treated as members of a noble occupation, police did not get the respect they expected from the public. Often there was more pathos than heroism in their war against crime. In general terms, the *illusio* – the commitment that recruits had initially invested in the 'game' – was being undermined. The started to question 'Is the game worth playing?' and also, given the competing ideals of policing they were exposed to, 'What *is* the game?'

Dictionary Knowledge: Sorting and Labelling

Dictionary knowledge refers to the descriptive definitions, categories, and labels that people in organizations develop to make sense of their world. As they acquired experience in policing, probationers began to slot the events and people they encountered in their work into categories. Very early on, they learned to distinguish between the theoretical knowledge they had been taught at the academy and the 'real' knowledge they were gaining through experience. In their view, real life was too ambiguous and complex, and people were too uncooperative and dishonest, for theory to be relevant to practice:

> [At the academy] they teach you about different groups in the community, and how you should treat them and this and that, but once you get out there and you're dealing with these people, it's completely different in

theory to what it is in reality ... They talk about ... how people are trapped in a cycle of poverty, and it goes from generation to generation. Yet when you're out there, and you see these people in Housing Commission estates, and you come to deal with them all the time, you just can't. ... You just look upon everyone and ... you become very cynical because you sort of see these people and you think, well, 'They're not helping themselves and all they're doing is getting themselves into trouble and waiting for government handouts and so forth.' And then you end up locking them up, and you just think, well, what was the point of learning about how to treat them, when they just don't want to do anything for themselves? (3/27-year-old male)

Some probationers developed the view that the public generally does not like police and so it is important to have good workmates. This 'us versus them' mentality arose from the contrast between the support provided by other police and the unfriendly attitudes displayed by the public:

It makes a big difference working in a station [with] a good crew, good atmosphere, because you go out on the road and you're dealing with a lot of depressing things. A lot of people don't generally ... like the police and you don't want to have to come back to your work environment in the station and be uncomfortable there and out on the street as well. When you've got a close-knit type station ... it's good when you can rely on your buddies, rely on your comrades to be there to help you. It's good. (3/25-year-old female)

This negative shift in attitudes toward the public is evident when we compare responses to an identical set of questions in Surveys 1, 2, and 3. Table 6.2 shows the items used in the survey (rated on a five-point Likert scale). An index was constructed by adding up the ratings of fourteen items[2] after appropriate reverse coding, so that a higher score indicated a more positive attitude toward the community or the public in general, Aboriginal and ethnic groups, the poor, journalists, and people who make complaints against the police. The results show that the mean score dropped from 41.99 in Survey 1 to 39.83 in Survey 2 and 32.89 in Survey 3. These differences were statistically significant, indicating that recruits' attitudes toward the community became progressively and significantly more negative over the eighteen months. This negative shift also involves a homogenization of attitudes between

TABLE 6.2
Change in perception of the community (Survey 1 vs Surveys 2 & 3)

Index items

Q: Listed below are some statements regarding the community and the police. Please indicate your level of agreement or disagreement with each by circling the appropriate number where:

    1=Strongly agree
    2= Agree
    3=Neutral
    4=Disagree
    5=Strongly disagree

Item	Code
The community shows a lot of respect for police.	R
The community tends to obstruct rather than cooperate with police.	
The community appreciates the difficulty of police work.	R
Journalists often assist police by raising public awareness about crime.	R
Aboriginal communities are difficult to police because of their lifestyle.	
People who make complaints about the police usually have a 'chip on their shoulder.'	
Public support for the police seems to be growing.	R
The public is ignorant about the nature of police work.	
Police should disband groups of kids who hang around public places.	
Ethnic people have no respect for Australian laws.	
Poor areas should be patrolled more frequently because they have more troubles.	
Police operations must be decided by the police, not the public.	
Aboriginal communities tend to be supportive of police.	R
Housing Commission areas breed crime.	

(Note: R=reverse coded)

Results

Mean score	Survey 1 (n=146)	Survey 2 (n=127)	Survey 3 (n=131)	Significant difference*
(14 items)	41.99	39.83	32.89	1-2 2-3 1-3

*t-tests, $p<0.05$

male and female and between older and younger recruits. In Survey 1, female recruits held significantly more positive attitudes toward the community (mean scores of 44.52 for females vs 41.18 for males); by Survey 3, this difference had disappeared. Similarly, older recruits were marginally more positive about the community in Survey 1 (44.57 for those over twenty-five, vs 41.95 for those twenty-five or younger), but age no longer made a significant difference by Survey 3.

These results were consistent with what probationers told us in the third round of interviews when they were asked whether they saw the world or people outside of the police differently by the end of their field training. The great majority (84 per cent) thought they had become more aware of negative aspects of social life (55 per cent), more likely to stereotype people (19 per cent), and more suspicious or cynical (10 per cent). Only 2 out of 42 thought they had become more tolerant or open in their view of the world. There was no variation of attitudes by gender, age, education, or ethnicity.

Interviewees felt that they became more aware of the presence of 'bad people' in the community:

> Yeah, I'm a bit more a cynic now. ... I drive along the street and I look at people and I think, oh, you know, he's ... probably a druggie or something ... Before I came on the job I didn't realize that there were so many criminals out there, or just so many bad people. Now I know. (3/23-year-old male)

One probationer went so far as to label 'people out there' as 'animals' because of the types of behaviour they engaged in:

> I realize [now] people out there aren't human beings. They're like animals, really. I know it's sad to say but you realize ... You just can't believe how people are like, you just can't imagine the things that people do, like especially being in a holding station. The things they do in the cells and the way they talk to you and things like that ... You just can't believe what people can be like ... It's something that I haven't seen before and probably became a shock just to see that people can be really like that. I won't go into details because it will probably make you sick. (3/24-year-old female)

As a result of this awareness of 'bad people,' probationers became more suspicious of people. One interviewee admitted that he started to 'hate' criminal offenders and drug dealers:

> I suppose your views on people change a bit, and you become more suspicious ... of some people. Basically I think you get too used to seeing sort of, you know, the dregs of society time and time again ... I think I get a bit dinkum, like. Before I joined, I didn't care about the drug problem to

start with, but now I just start realizing how much I hate these drug dealers, the bastards. They're the problem for about 80 per cent of the crime that takes place ... I get a bit shitty with them because that's what causes all the busts and the assaults, and that's why people nick money and that's why they thieve. (3/20-year-old male)

Interviewees also reported that they no longer felt as sorry for victims, because 'a lot of people bring a lot of things upon themselves':

Now I sort of don't feel as sorry for people, because ... from what I've seen a lot of people bring a lot of things upon themselves with different situations. I mean, they might be the victim, but they're sort of to blame as well. A lot of people ... try and get police help, but they've tried fifty other times and you'll take action for them, and they don't turn up to court, and different things, so you just do your job and if it works, it works, and if it doesn't, you can only help to a certain extent. I don't care as much, I guess. (3/20-year-old female)

As noted earlier, probationers felt more cynical about the public, who generally showed no appreciation for what police did for them. Besides classifying the public as 'them' as opposed to 'us,' probationers readily admitted resorting to racial and other stereotypes for targeting people. A number of interviewees were aware that they were not supposed to stereotype people. They justified it in terms of their experience:

You tend to come across the worst people in society ... You tend to lose a bit of faith in humans after a little while ... just dealing with the same sort of crimes over and over again. You ... do tend to see the stereotype and believe it. These sort of people, they're just rubbish. They're out hanging around so they must be doing something wrong – that sort of thing. You tend to after a while ... see the worst in people. (3/21-year-old female)

I wouldn't say I am racist, but I would say that I tend to ... personally stereotype ... We can't necessarily predict what situation we are going to go to, but to be blunt, if I was to say go to an incident involving a group of Lebanese, I would definitely expect trouble. I would definitely expect to be hit, spat on, told you were scum ... and if I was to be involved with Vietnamese, I would think drugs, do you know what I mean? ... Well, you're aware that you're not supposed to do it, but it is so hard not to, because you only see the bad things. (3/20-year-old female)

Adopting an 'us versus them' mentality did not mean that probationers saw all police as the same. Many distinguished between officers
who were keen and interested in their work and those who were not.
They learned who would be helpful and who could be trusted to
provide good advice when needed.

> There's some people who've been in the job for a long time, and they ...
> avoid work and that sort of stuff, and they'll try and shonk as many jobs
> as they can, and there's some people who're really interested in the job,
> they know a lot, they've kept up with the times, and ... they're willing to
> help you ... I found once you got out of your buddy period, you knew
> basically how to do things, but you still didn't know quite a lot, and you
> sort of knew who you could go and ask, and who you couldn't, or who
> would be more helpful. (3/22-year-old female)

We saw in chapter 5 that recruits felt quite comfortable articulating
examples of 'good' and 'bad' police work that they encountered during
their training. To analyse whether their conceptions of 'good' and 'bad'
police work changed over time, we compared their responses in the
three rounds of interviews. Tables 6.4 and 6.5 summarize the descriptions of 'good' and 'bad' police work provided by the forty-six respondents who attended all three interviews. The coding categories we
used, and some examples, are provided in Table 6.3.
   Table 6.4 shows that at the second interview, after the recruits had
spent six months at the academy – including four weeks of field observation – the most frequently mentioned aspect of 'good' police work
related to 'people or communication skills.' This was mentioned by 63
per cent of respondents. The second most frequently mentioned aspect
was 'technical knowledge or skills,' mentioned by 56 per cent of the
respondents. Other attributes nominated by more than 10 per cent of
the respondents included attitude to work, ability to assert authority or
take control of situations, and acting in a fair and impartial manner. At
the third interview – after a year of field training – 'people/communi-
cation skills' and 'technical knowledge/skills' remained at the top of
the list, nominated by 63 and 50 per cent of the interviewees respectively; also, 'effort' and 'law enforcement outcomes' were mentioned
more often than before (35 and 33 per cent respectively). By the fourth
interview – after six months working as a constable – 'technical knowl-
edge/skills' (61 per cent) and 'law enforcement outcomes' (43 per cent)
had become more prominent than 'people/communication skills' (37
per cent) and 'effort' (33 per cent).

TABLE 6.3
Coding categories and examples of good/bad police work

Category	Good Police Work	Bad Police Work
People/communication skills	• Come in and calm the situation down	• Treat people like kids, degrading them in front of family • Inflamed situation by behaving aggressively toward people
Technical knowledge/skills	• Doing good briefs • Know what they're doing, know the ins and outs of the law and what they can and can't do	• Inadequate preparation for trial • Poor officer survival skills
Attitude to work	• Do jobs whatever they are, not just pick easy jobs	• Stuck in a rut, disillusioned, just come to work
Effort	• Take extra time to do investigation	• Slack, sitting in a station and waiting for a job instead of being out on the road patrolling • Do anything they can to get out of doing a job • Shonking • Taking short cuts • Abuse of authority
Authority/control	• Able to keep authority and treat 'hoodlums' and 'ratbags' like human beings and with respect	
Impartiality	• Unbiased • Fair	• (none cited)
Law enforcement outcomes	• Getting good convictions	• Avoiding arrest when he should have • Strip search kids out of boredom

TABLE 6.3 (concluded)
Coding categories and examples of good/bad police work

Category	Good Police Work	Bad Police Work
Autonomy/discretion	• Use caution instead of charge	• (none cited)
Image/presentation	• Good personal presentation	• 'Don't care' attitude in the way he speaks to people and the way he dresses
	• Speak well to public	
Teamwork	• Good teacher	• (none cited)
	• Backup in dangerous situations	
Customer service	• Victim satisfaction	• Rudeness to people at counter
Improper/illegal/corrupt behaviour	• (N/A)	• Avoid paperwork by not charging an offender
Other	• Professional, confident	• Overconfident or underconfident
	• Always on the lookout for suspicious things	
	• Local knowledge	

Table 6.4
Change in nominated categories of good police work (N=46)

Dimension	Interview 2		Interview 3		Interview 4	
	Frequency	Per cent	Frequency	Per cent	Frequency	Per cent
People/communi- cation skills	29	63	29	63	17	37
Technical knowl- edge/skills	26	56	23	50	28	61
Attitude to work	10	22	8	17	5	11
Effort	9	20	16	35	15	33
Authority/control	9	20	5	11	2	4
Impartiality	7	15	4	9	1	2
Law enforcement outcomes	3	7	15	33	20	43
Autonomy/ discretion	3	7	3	7	–	–
Image/presentation	3	7	–	–	–	–
Teamwork	2	4	5	11	4	9
Customer service	1	2	–	–	2	4
Other	23	50	11	24	7	15

Note: Multiple responses coded, percentages do not necessarily add up to 100 per cent

Table 6.5
Change in nominated categories of bad police work (N=46)

Dimension	Interview 2		Interview 3		Interview 4	
	Frequency	Per cent	Frequency	Per cent	Frequency	Per cent
Effort	19	41	27	59	24	52
Attitude to work	15	33	13	28	16	35
People/communi- cation skills	11	24	17	37	13	28
Improper/illegal/ corrupt behaviour	4	9	6	13	6	13
Technical knowledge/skills	3	7	8	17	12	26
Image/presentation	3	7	–	–	–	–
Customer service	2	4	2	4	–	–
Authority/control	1	2	1	2	2	4
Failure to arrest/ enforce law	–	–	2	4	6	13
Other	–	–	6	13	2	4
(Did not encounter any)	15	33	5	11	8	17

Note: Multiple responses coded, percentages do not necessarily add up to 100 per cent

In summary, it seems that as recruits progressed from being a novice to a constable, they were more likely to cite 'law enforcement outcomes' as examples of 'good' police work; the proportion who nominated this increased from 7 per cent to 43 per cent. At the same time, they became less likely to define good police work in terms of 'people/communication skills'; here, the proportion *decreased* from 63 to 37 per cent. 'Technical knowledge/skills' was consistently considered central to good police work (nominated by 50 to 61 per cent). When the interviews were analysed individually, we noticed that for around four out of ten interviewees, conceptions of good police work had changed so as to place greater emphasis on law enforcement and technical knowledge or skills.

Table 6.5 indicates that at the second interview, one-third of respondents said they had not encountered any examples of bad police work. This was partly due to the fact that the respondents had had limited contact with operational police during their first six months of training. Nevertheless, two-thirds of the interviewees provided examples of what they considered bad police work. The examples were most likely to relate to 'effort' (mentioned by 41 per cent), 'attitude to work' (33 per cent), and 'people/communication skills' (24 per cent). These three aspects remained the most frequently mentioned ones at the third and fourth interviews, during which far fewer respondents said they had not come across any examples of bad police work (a drop from 33 to 11, then a rise to 17 per cent). In the last two rounds of interviews, respondents were also more likely to cite instances of poor 'technical knowledge/skills' as examples of bad policing – an increase from 7 to 17, then 26 per cent. In rounds 3 and 4, a few respondents mentioned incidents relating to failure to arrest or enforce the law. There was also a small increase in the number of respondents who mentioned 'improper, illegal, or corrupt behaviours' as examples of bad police work.

These results show that there was not a great deal of change in interviewees' definitions of bad police work: effort, attitude to work, and people/communications skills remained important yardsticks in all three rounds of interviews. When the interviews were analysed individually, however, we found again that for around four in ten respondents, conceptions of bad police work had changed. Some now denied that they had ever seen bad police work, while others became more concerned with technical skills than with people skills.

The evidence presented in this section illustrates the cognitive changes that recruits experienced as they gained experience in operational policing. Less than two years earlier, they themselves had been members of the public; now they viewed the public with suspicion and cynicism. They had been taught at the academy not to stereotype people on the basis of their appearance; now they saw such stereotyping as inevitable. At the core of their world view was the division between theory and practice, between the liberal theoretical teachings of the academy and the hard practical realities of operational policing. Yet in spite of their growing disenchantment with the job and cynicism about the public, they remained discerning in their conceptions of 'good' and 'bad' police work. As they gained experience as constables, however, they tended to value 'law enforcement outcomes' such as getting good arrests or convictions and technical knowledge and skills more highly than communication skills, which they had considered the hallmark of 'good' police work throughout their training.

Directory Knowledge: Experience and Discretion

Directory knowledge informs police how operational work is routinely carried out. Novices acquire the other dimensions of cultural knowledge without actively seeking to do so; in contrast, the gaining of directory knowledge is a conscious, active process. General duties policing requires police officers to perform a variety of functions. In the course of their training, recruits pick up a range of practical skills and tried-and-true methods for helping them get their work done, take charge of different situations, and deal with various types of people. Our intention in this section is not to provide a complete catalogue of the skills and methods learned; rather, it is to highlight the more important aspects of directory knowledge.

As discussed in chapter 5, learning how to get the job done was a matter of great urgency for probationers 'thrown into the deep end' of operational policing in Phase 4. At first, probationers hungered for basic technical knowledge – what the rules are, how to make notebook entries, how to fill out forms, how to handle situations, whom to speak to, and where to look for help. Typically, they spent their first weeks at the demonstration patrols getting to know the simple, routine procedures the job demands. According to one probationer, one of the first tasks he learned was how to fill out the Vehicle Diary:

Just in the first week, that's what he had me doing ... At the end of every shift you have to fill out the Vehicle Diary, which involves all the equipment that's in the vehicle, who you were with, the number of the last ticket and how many tickets you used. And then you have to write down times and everywhere the car's been and the amount of petrol you've put in it, and the amount of kilometres that were used, and you have to sign it all off ... I mean, that's kind of ... your sacred duty when you get there is you have to do the Vehicle Diary. Junior man driver does the Vehicle Diary. (3/22-year-old male)

Later, probationers learned that with some supervisors their paper-work had to be 'spot on.' This meant following the correct procedures and satisfying the bureaucratic requirements:

There's a lot of people who check your work and everything's got to be right [or] you just got to do it again or you've got to do it right. You'll have the sergeant come and tell you this is how it's done, or the brief handling manager will come and say this is not good enough, do it again, or do it this way ... yeah, your briefs of evidence, or your COPS entries if they're not up to date. Like, for example, victim follow-up. We have, where I'm at the moment, we have a three-day victim follow-up, so if you go to a break and enter, three days later you call them and say, you know, is there anything else we can do for you, have you found any of your stuff, no we haven't found any ... The supervising sergeant, he's on your back until you do those follow ups, right, and so it's all got to be done. (3/22-year-old male)

Part of directory knowledge flows naturally from dictionary knowl-edge in the sense that how officers see their world often determines how they carry out their work. Thus, officers who see the public as generally uncooperative and hostile tend to believe they should ap-proach people with constant suspicion. Similarly, having developed indicators of normality and respectability, police generally target the out-of-place and the disreputable. One interviewee justified such prac-tices in terms of applying accepted 'professional' knowledge of who were likely suspects. He admitted that when questioning people, he tended to target young people, especially young males of minority ethnic groups, people with untidy appearance, or people who were intoxicated or under the influence of drugs:

To be professional you've got to sort of view everyone as the same [but] well, on the other hand, in a professional sense, I think we tend to – well, I know I tend to look out more for younger blokes, especially young males of ethnic or Asian origin or people that sort of appear from a lower-class background, 'cause you sort of tend to know that a lot of the people that dress like, you know, they've slept in their clothes for six weeks, and you know you can see they're drunk or they're stoned or whatever at ten o'clock in the morning, they're the ones that are going to be doing the break and enters ... You'd probably notice them a lot more I think than I would if I saw a bloke walking down the street in a suit. Even though that bloke might have just gone and broken into a house, I probably wouldn't take any notice of him unless I was looking for someone like that ... I think in a way it's not really racist, but it's more being a professional police officer and you know what you're looking for. I mean, I don't go out of me way to pick on Vietnamese, or I don't go out of me way to pick on anyone else for that matter – but it's just a fact of the job. If you don't stop people and talk to them, ... you're not going to find anything out. (3/22-year-old male)

Because police routinely find themselves in unpredictable situations, directory knowledge is ultimately developed through practical experience. Experience is therefore an extremely valuable commodity in policing. Knowing how to 'take control' of difficult situations is one of the most important skills novices need to master. Although taking control may involve the use of coercion or physical force, probationers were also taught how to use certain demeanours and tactics to maintain authority and defuse potential conflicts. The following excerpt from field observation is illustrative:

While driving to the next job, [the senior constable] SC explained to [the probationer] the rationale for his actions in the previous event and ways of dealing with offenders who were less cooperative or elected to challenge police authority. SC said it is important to 'take control' of the situation. If the offender senses weakness in an officer, they may attempt intimidation tactics that can undermine the officer's authority to issue the infringement notice. It was important to remain, at all times, calm, because losing one's temper was not productive. It is far better to negotiate through a situation to defuse it rather than use bully or aggressive tactics. If a driver challenges an officer's authority or refuses to acknowledge the officer's intention to issue an infringement, then the officer can simply continue to note defects on the vehicle. It is surprising how offenders conform when the potential fine begins to escalate in dollar terms, SC said. (DP)

As pointed out in chapter 5, probationers were impressed by how their buddies could use 'people skills' to calm people down:

> He just basically showed me that you can get out of everything if you use your mouth the right way. It can get you into trouble and it can get you out of trouble, and it can calm a lot of people down who are very aggressive. He could calm them right down just through him talking to them ... He always showed everybody, no matter what kind of person they were, he would always show a lot of respect toward them, so that way ... he sort of won everybody over with his charm sort of thing, so to speak. But he could calm a very aggressive situation down to a very friendly level just through his mouth. It was unbelievable. I've never seen anything like it. (3/21-year-old female)

Part of the 'people skills' involved knowing how to act in different situations:

> [My buddy] just knew how to talk to people and ... relating with them, and when to stand back, and when to step in, and when to use the heavy-handed tactics, and when not to. Excellent. Just watching him work ... you learn a lot. (3/male, age >30)

Another aspect of control was learning how to cope with the stress of the job:

> In my second station I started to get a lot of work and it was all starting to build up and it was just learning how to cope with it all. How to not worry about certain things ... and how to organize your time and your stuff a little bit better and perhaps being a little bit more assertive instead of just taking everything and letting it build up and thinking that you have to do it all on your own. Just start perhaps asking for a bit more help. (3/21-year-old male)

To deal with the varied and unpredictable nature of the job, probationers learned they had to use 'common sense' to exercise discretion appropriately:

> Everyone that I've worked with ever since I came out has impressed [on] me ... that to use your discretion you've got to have common sense and

sometimes what's written [in] black and white you've got to work around that to suit the situation. And, I mean, it works ... I think to me common sense is knowing the difference between right and wrong to start, but ... if you're going to ... have the power of discretion ... you've got to use that discretion so you can't sort of deal with every situation the same. You've got to use what you know and your life experiences, and ... you've got to judge every situation on its own merits and away you go. (3/22-year-old male)

Probationers learned from experienced officers not only how to do things, but also how not to get into trouble:

I work with senior constables and constables ... They just know what to do better. They know what you can do under the laws, and they know how to go about things. Senior blokes will explain to you how to do things. They will say, don't do it that way, you will get into trouble if you do it that way. (3/20-year-old male)

By observing experienced officers at work, probationers also got to know various short cuts and ways to 'dodge the system':

A lot of the senior blokes, they all make it from point A to point B, so to speak, but certainly achieved the same result. But you know, after you've been in the job a bit longer, I suppose, you start working out a few short cuts ... a bit of efficiency, and a bit of knowing how to dodge the system a bit ... Just in how you take a phone, what sort of questions you ask. True, it's a bit of efficiency, and a bit of taking the easy way a few times, because they've been there and learned from their mistakes. (3/20-year-old male)

From the discussion in chapter 5 and in this section, it should be clear that the probationers in this study were exposed to a variety of policing styles and more than one model of practice. As far as we can tell, accepted practice often varied with local culture, management, and supervisory preferences and even with individual styles. In short, there was no single, monolithic style of institutionalized practice that one could label as 'the police culture.' Recruits seemed to learn both positive, 'problem-solving' strategies, such as using communication skills to take control of volatile situations, and negative; 'anxiety avoidance' mechanisms, such as 'how not to get into trouble' (see Recipe Knowledge).

Recipe Knowledge: Cynicism and Self-Protection

Recipe knowledge refers to the normative dimension of cultural knowledge – what should or should not be done in specific situations. Two
dominant themes in the literature on policing relate to recruits' taking
on the cynical attitudes that 'street cops' have developed toward 'management cops' (Reuss-Ianni and Ianni 1983), and the 'code of silence'
among officers that operates to protect them from outside scrutiny.
Both themes are variations of the same concern: how to survive individually and collectively in the job.

Very early on in field training, for example, a probationer was told by
his first buddy to 'cover your butt' (3/19-year-old male). The same
advice was given to another probationer during one of the shifts we
observed, where the officers were following up a 'fail to pay' complaint
from a petrol station:

> It appeared the driver of the vehicle (male) was related to the woman
> [answering the door] by blood or marriage. She asked the officers what
> she would need to do to resolve the issue. In her second breath she offered
> to pay the officers for the petrol. [The Senior Constable] SC told the
> woman that she or the offender must return to the petrol station and pay
> for the petrol, otherwise the police would need to take further action. She
> understood and we left. Back in the car, SC warned [the probationer] for
> his future reference that police are not debt collectors. Moreover, accept-
> ing any form of money or kind from the public for whatever reason must
> be avoided because that kind of activity can implicate officers in the eyes
> of Internal Affairs. 'You have to cover your arse at all times,' he warned
> [the probationer]. (DP)

In response to a probationer's stated preference for doing things
'properly,' his senior partner (a constable who had graduated six months
previous to the observation) offered similar advice about protecting
himself:

> [The probationer] says he likes to do things slower and do them properly,
> his perception is that there's a bit of 'shortcutting.' [The senior partner]
> says 'Yes, and then you get the person who complains because you're
> taking longer than you should to do something.' Then [the senior partner]
> said something like 'Yeah, well, what you've got to make sure you do is
> cover your bum.' (DP)

This kind of thinking was, according to a senior partner of the probationer we observed, the direct result of 'poor or weak management' in the police service:

[The senior partner] SC said that officer morale was low at the present time. He proposed that the style and approach of management significantly influenced officer morale. His analysis focused more on current bureaucratic policy of rotating patrol commanders ... This is not conducive to a patrol commander developing a sense of ownership for the Patrol, its staff or future, he said. The problem of poor or weak management is complicated by a culture in which managers are afraid of making mistakes. As a result, SC said, managers avoid making hard decisions for fear that if the decision is wrong they would be subjected to disciplinary action. This produces a 'cover your arse' approach to work. This means that at every decision point one has to ensure that there is no room for any problems or recourse to occur. (TP)

This comment is consistent with the growing disenchantment with police management that we found in our interviews with probationers. When asked in the third interview whether their opinion about the NSW Police Service had changed since they joined, 65 per cent indicated that their opinion had become more negative, and only two out of 52 felt more positive, while 15 per cent gave noncommittal or vague answers (possibly because they felt uncomfortable criticizing the organization in front of researchers). About 12 per cent told us that their opinion about the organization had not changed, while one respondent spoke about both positive and negative changes. This dissatisfaction with the organization did not vary by gender, age, ethnicity, or educational level.

Most interviewees picked out 'management' as representing the 'organization.' A distinction was made between operational police and 'desk workers.' Many of the latter were seen as 'bludgers':

Some management can be really shot. Like they put those people in big positions and they don't seem to do anything. They sit behind a desk all day. All those desk workers. Like, I know some people have to be there and that's their choice, and some people do a good job while they're there, but there's a lot of people just bludge. (3/22-year-old female)

The most frequently raised complaint was that management did not support police at the 'front line' when they got hurt on the job:

> To some degree I still have this some sort of faith in the top management
> [that] they're going to look after you and that if something happens, but
> it's becoming obvious that that doesn't exist, that doesn't happen. You
> know, like you get injured or you get hurt or you do something wrong in
> your job, act in good faith and that, and the first thing, from what I've
> seen so far, the first thing they want to do is jump on you. (3/21-year-old
> male)

Interviewees complained that when allegations were made against
police, police were dealt with more harshly than criminal offenders.
There was a perception that police were vulnerable to unfair disciplinary action or criminal charges, even for unintended errors:

> That's the premise that it works on ... not you're innocent until proven
> guilty, you're guilty until proven innocent and that's it, full-stop. And if
> they can't find something to prove you innocent, then you're guilty, you
> did it ... It pisses me off really badly because ... you make decisions in a
> split second and they've got months to pore over, analysing you've done
> this or you haven't done that, or – and they always seem to try to ambush
> you, like they show it with these mountains, mountains of information
> that they have at their control, and they turn around and expect you to
> explain it on the basis of your memory ... Like, you know you can't go
> away and get your notebooks or anything like that, no, I'm sorry ... and
> everybody knows about it, too ... and you're basically judged, you know,
> it's like the trial by media ... the result's assumed before any sort of official
> things come through. (3/24-year-old male)

> I feel like if a police officer does something wrong, they get treated worse
> than a civilian, than what a crook does. You get dragged through the coals
> ... They want to get rid of police corruption, so an officer only has to put
> one foot wrong ... in one direction, forget to do something and it can
> automatically become criminal charges, if not departmental charges ...
> Yeah, so you can't afford to do the wrong thing because police officers,
> when you do do something wrong, you are treated worse than a normal
> crim ... I just feel that we don't get the support that we need from our ...
> commanders ... They're all so scared because of the Royal Commission
> and they're always there to cover their own butts, and they don't really
> care about the other staff that work for them. (3/25-year-old female)

Probationers resented the fact that they were constantly under surveillance and called to account. They spent a great deal of time recording and entering information, which was then checked and audited by others:

Police are becoming more accountable ... They're always under the microscope, so to speak. You know if you make an honest mistake, you'll be dragged, you could quite honestly be dragged before ... an inquiry, and have to explain why and all that sort of stuff ... The fact that all a crim's got to do is make a complaint about you, make up some bull crap story. I mean, I know that I've already been up for three ... investigations against me already ... I didn't realize that there was going to be so much hassle as far as that goes. I didn't realize that whatever you do ... I mean, we've got people checking in the computers for your entries, you've got people that, as soon as you log on, people know that you're logging on. You've got auditors doing that sort of thing. You know you can't even ... do a quick inquiry, you've got to write it down in your book ... time, date, place, why you're doing it ... You know, it's absolute garbage ... That ticks you off real bad because you know it's just ... time wasting. (3/28-year-old male)

As one interviewee observed, this concern with accountability was distorting police priorities and wasting police time:

Our station controller ... heard a rumour that the auditors were coming through the station, so he was going through ... absolutely every single book making sure that everything from, oh, 1980s had been signed pretty much ... Anyway, he'd gone through these [gun register cards] and found out that someone in 1991 hadn't signed it when they got back from leave, so we had to get the card ... The car crew, we've only got the one on for our whole patrol, we had to take this card over to district office and find this person that hadn't signed the card ... He was letting work stack up on his desk for, you know, weeks ... because he thought the other thing was more important because he might get in trouble over it. But I mean, he could've easily come undone the other way because there were reports there that [had] deadlines, but, you know, don't worry about them. (3/21-year-old female)

The burden of accountability was also made worse by constant changes in policies and procedures – changes seen as 'ridiculous' or 'impractical' by operational police:

Things changing from week to week or people trying to drum something down your throat just because it'll bring favour with someone higher up ... you know, some higher rank and all that sort of thing ... Some of the things they suggest or bring out are just so ridiculous ... Well, they probably could be doing things that are a bit more realistic. I mean there's just so much work out there to do and so much paperwork. I think they should be doing everything they could to alleviate that rather than create more policies and more procedures so you're doing more doubling up of work and that sort of thing. And just because they've got auditors, you know, the threat of auditors coming through the station every minute and all that. They, you know, bring in all these new forms that you have to sign to double-check and triple-check that this has been done. (3/21-year-old female)

Management was perceived as out of touch with 'how things are done in the street,' self-serving 'to get their extra bit of rank,' and unwilling to back rank-and-file police (3/20-year-old male). There was a great deal of criticism about the organization's leadership, which was seen as 'extremely ineffective ... run by academics now that have no idea' (3/19-year-old male), and its lack of direction – 'It's a shambles ... Nobody knows which way they're headed' (3/21 year-old female). The inadequacy of resources was also a bone of contention: most police stations did not have enough computers for police to do their work (3/23-year-old male, 3/22-year-old female). Some probationers described a deep sense of disillusionment and uncertainty at the street level about the future of the organization:

Currently now ... everyone's disillusioned ... Rumours go around on what's going to happen and what's going to change, but you don't know exactly what's going to happen, and that just sort of makes you wonder ... who's actually running it. 'Cause you hear a source, this is going to happen, and then you hear it from another source that something else's going to happen. And you don't know which one to believe so you don't know where you stand. (3/23-year-old male)

Two interviewees thought that the organization had changed in that corruption was no longer tolerated:

When you speak to people who have been in the job for a while ... they'll tell you stories and stuff. You go, you're kidding, like did you really do that or did that happen? You just can't get away with anything now.

Like, you can't do anything that's like, borderline corrupt or anything like that. Anything that's frowned upon you can't get away with it now – you can't do it, basically. It's probably a lot more straight down the line now. (3/22-year-old female).

Cynicism among probationers was directed not only at police management but also at the criminal justice system. When we compared recruits' attitudes toward the criminal justice system in Survey 1 with those in Survey 3, we found that the mean total score[3] dropped from 35.35 to 28.80, indicating that they had developed a significantly more negative attitude toward the criminal justice system over the eighteen months (see Table 6.6). Similarly, they expressed negative views about the Wood Royal Commission.[4] Almost half the probationers (48 per cent) commented that the commission had negatively affected policing; 14 per cent thought it had no effects, 14 per cent spoke of positive effects, and 18 per cent listed both positive and negative effects.[5] Again, sex, age, education, and ethnicity did not seem to make any significant difference to interviewees' perceptions of the Royal Commission's impact. Some probationers blamed the commission for the loss of public respect for police and for low morale among officers:

Well, there's just too much emphasis on corruption and the likes of police doing bad things, whereas they should try and tell us, instead of decreasing our morale more than what it is ... [Morale] was obviously low when I went out there, you know, with every allegation of a police officer doing that, this, and everything else. It just gets ridiculous ... Respect within the community has virtually disintegrated – there's just *nothing*. (3/20-year-old female)

I think [the Royal Commission] pisses a lot of people off at, you know, sort of my level, at general duties level, because it's like day-to-day, you know, we're the ones, you know. We went to a job once and found 80,000 dollars cash, and the two of us didn't even think of, you know, whacking a $50 in the pocket, and so I just don't know what they get off on everyone corrupt on the news and stuff. They're not corrupt, and I've never seen anything corrupt, *ever*. So I think it's a bit of shit. The Ombudsman or whatever her name was yesterday said something, you know, 'One in ten are corrupt.' Well, I've never seen anyone corrupt. I don't know anyone corrupt ... I think the general public sees that uniform and goes 'Yeah, corrupt,' the whole lot of us. They wouldn't put it past us, I think. (3/20-year-old male)

TABLE 6.6
Change in perception of the criminal justice system

Index items

Q: Listed below are statements regarding the criminal justice system. Please indicate your level of agreement or disagreement with each by circling the appropriate number where:

1= Strongly agree
2 = Agree
3 = Neutral
4 = Disagree
5 = Strongly disagree

Item	Code
The courts are too lenient on criminals.	
Prisons are 'schools of crime.'	
Prisoners should not get parole too easily.	
The police get all the blame for the failings of the criminal justice system.	
The powers of police should be increased.	
The courts treat everybody equally.	R
The courts often undermine the work of the police.	
Victims should have more say in criminal justice decisions.	
Defence lawyers often waste court time.	
Prisoners are let out too early before they have served their full sentence.	
Professional criminals know how to manipulate the system to their advantage.	
The criminal justice system is loaded in favour of the defendant.	
Defence lawyers are more interested in money than justice.	
Crime victims are doubly victimised by the criminal justice system.	
Too many guilty people avoid conviction because of technicalities	
The legal rules often prevent the true story being told in court.	

(Note: R=reverse coded)

Results

Mean Score	Survey 1 (n=143)	Survey 3 (n=130)	Significant difference*
(16 items)	35.35	28.80	1–3

*t-test, $p < 0.05$

Complaints of excessive paperwork and accountability as a result of the Royal Commission have already been mentioned. Some interviewees also thought that police had become 'too scared to do their job' for fear of complaints being made against them. Furthermore, management had become afraid to make decisions or 'back the workers up' (3/ 24-year-old male). A number of interviewees repeated the complaint that police named by the Royal Commission had not been given the same legal protections as criminal offenders (3/23-year-old male). Some probationers were very critical of the bad media coverage generated by the Royal Commission. One objected to the naming of an officer who was videotaped (3/22-year-old female); another thought the media had blown the extent of corruption out of proportion (3/20-year-old female); a third dismissed the Royal Commission as 'just a kneejerk reaction' (3/24-year-old male). One interviewee was critical of police who 'rolled over' and turned informant for the commission: 'You realize how there's a lot of people out there that are willing to turn you over for their own good' (3/19-year-old male). A few interviewees had some good things to say about the Royal Commission, but it was a topic they were happy to avoid.

Our overwhelming conclusion from the qualitative and quantitative evidence is that by the end of their training, recruits had become very cynical about both management and the criminal justice system. They were especially hostile to the amount of accountability required in their work, and they felt vulnerable to unfair disciplinary actions. Because of this sense of vulnerability, they had learned to protect themselves at all times. Among probationers, there was a sense that rank-and-file officers were in all the same boat, having to live with uncaring and self-serving managers as well as a hostile political environment. Yet it is not at all clear that this in-the-same-boat feeling was readily translated into a 'code of silence' that allowed police to cover up wrongdoing or escape external scrutiny. We consider these issues in the next section.

Change in Ethical Values

To explore whether recruits' ethical values changed over the course of their training, we analyse the attitudinal data and responses to hypothetical scenarios collected through the surveys and during the fourth round of interviews.

General Attitudes

Table 6.7 shows a set of items included in Surveys 1, 2 and 3 to measure respondents' attitudes toward the rule of law, due process, the use of physical force, work practice, and concealing misconduct. The results[6] show that there was no change in the respondents' mean scores between Survey 1 and Survey 2 (both scores were 45.47); however, there

TABLE 6.7
Change in ethical vlaues

Index items

Q: Listed below are some statements about policing. Please indicate your level of agreement or disagreement with each by circling the appropriate number where:
- 1 = Strongly agree
- 2 = Agree
- 3 = Neutral
- 4 = Disagree
- 5 = Strongly disagree

Item	Code
Code	
Police should uphold the rule of law at all times.	R
Police need to support each other when under attack.	
Police should always conceal their conduct when it may result in disciplinary action.	
Police should expose all forms of corruption within the force.	R
There are times when a police officer must act 'above the law' to achieve justice.	
Force is the only language that law-breakers understand.	
Police who get caught doing something wrong or illegal should not implicate others involved.	
Police should never use illegal means to obtain evidence.	R
I have no confidence that whistleblowers will be protected by the police service.	
Police officers should not work too hard as supervisors will come to expect this level of work all the time.	
The nature of police work makes an officer vulnerable to corruption.	
The use of physical force is rarely justified in arrest situations.	R
Police officers should not expect their bosses to support them.	

(Note: R=reverse coded)

Results

Mean Score	Survey 1 (n=146)	Survey2 (n=127)	Survey 3 (n=130)	Significant difference*
(13 items)	45.47	45.47	42.25	1–3 2–3

*t-tests, p<0.05

was a significant drop between Survey 2 and Survey 3. This suggests that recruits' ethical values did not change during their training at the academy, but there was a significantly negative change following their field training (cf. Wortley 1992). Analysing these variables by gender, age, and education, we found only one significant result: in Survey 1 female respondents were more 'ethical' than males (means score of 46.48 compared to 44.99), but this difference had disappeared by Survey 3. This finding suggests that by the end of their field training, female recruits had become more similar to their male colleagues in ethical values (as measured by the items shown in Table 6.7).

Attitudes toward Specific Conduct Scenarios

To further investigate changes in ethical values, we compared recruits' attitudes toward specific scenarios of questionable police conduct in Survey 1 with their attitudes toward the same scenarios in Survey 3. Using an instrument adapted from similar surveys conducted by the Criminal Justice Commission (1995) and the National Police Research Unit (Huon et al. 1995; see also McConkey et al. 1996), we constructed eleven scenarios involving police behaving inappropriately or illegally. Table 6.8 lists the scenarios as they were presented to the respondents, who were asked to rate on a scale from 1 to 10 how serious, justified, or corrupt they thought each conduct was. The scenarios embrace a range of questionable behaviours. Table 6.9 summarizes the changes in the 'serious,' 'justified,' and 'corrupt' ratings of these scenarios between Survey 1 and Survey 3.

Figure 6.1 shows the scenarios sorted by their seriousness ratings in Survey 1. For example, the scenario 'Accept beer' was seen as the least serious (mean rating 4.02 in Survey 1), whereas 'Racist language' was seen as the most serious (mean rating 9.20 in Survey 1). In Survey 3, some of these scenarios were rated as significantly more serious ('Accept beer,' 'Take cigarettes,' and 'Lie in court 1'), and others were rated as significantly less serious ('Private business,' 'Hit youth,' 'Avoid RBT,' and 'Racist language'), while the seriousness ratings of the rest were not significantly changed ('Fabricate report,' 'Threaten violence,' 'Lie in court 2,' and 'Steal and lie').

Figure 6.2 shows the same scenarios sorted by their 'justified' ratings in Survey 1. For example, the 'Racist language' scenario was considered the least justified (mean rating 1.91), while 'Accept beer' was considered the most justified (mean rating 5.16). For most of the scenarios, the 'justified' ratings went up in Survey 3 (in six scenarios the difference was statistically significant). Only two scenarios were rated as less justified in Survey 3: 'Lie in court 1' and 'Threaten violence'; however, the change in 'Threaten violence' was not statistically significant.

Figure 6.3 shows the scenarios sorted by their 'corrupt' ratings in Sur-

TABLE 6.8
Ethical scenarios presented in Surveys 1 and 3

No.	Scenario description	Abbreviation
1.	An off duty police officer who has drunk a little too much is stopped for an RBT by police officers he doesn't know. The off duty officer is obviously a bit under the weather. He identifies himself as a fellow police officer in an effort to avoid blowing in the bag.	Avoid RBT
2.	The local bottle shop has been broken into for the third time in so many weeks. The responding patrol officers enter the premises to wait for the owner to arrive and sort out the mess of cigarettes and liquor lying all over the floor. One of the officers bent down, picks up a torn pack of cigarettes from the shattered window display, and puts the pack in his pocket.	Take cigarettes
3.	In a pub brawl a young female First Year Constable, responding with her partner to a 'disturbance' call, receives a nasty black eye from a tattooed youth wielding a billiard cue. As the arrested youth is led into the cells, the male team member gives him a savage kidney-punch saying, 'Hurts, doesn't it'.	Hit youth
4.	During a quiet period on patrol, two officers decided to test how the rear of the police vehicle would slide on the deserted, wet car park. Their attempts resulted in a minor collision with a shopping trolley. Rather than go into full details about the scrape when reporting the damage, the driver stated the car was 'sideswiped' by an unidentified vehicle while they were attending to an inquiry.	Fabricate report
5.	On a quiet Sunday afternoon an officer decides to travel well outside his area to get some equipment for *his* Sunday building job. In radio contact all the time he picks up the gear and returns to his patrol area.	Private business
6.	Two patrol officers pick up a drunk who is creating a disturbance in a pub. While frisking him, they find he has $500 on him. On the way back to the station, Officer A drives, and Officer B sits in the back of the car with the drunk who is difficult to control. Back at the station, the drunk cannot find his money. Officer A suspects of having taken the money, but says nothing. Later the drunk presses charges against the two policemen. At trial Officer B denies ever having seen any money. There are no other witnesses and no further evidence. In his evidence, Officer A also denies knowledge of any money.	A: Lie in court 1 B: Steal and lie

TABLE 6.8
(*concluded*)

No.	Scenario description	Abbreviation
7.	The publican of a local tavern requests some extra police patrols as he is experiencing some problems with troublesome patrons. The officers at the station accept a couple of cartons of beer sent by the publican to the stations' Christmas party in appreciation of the officers' service during the year.	Accept beer
8.	A police officer, who particularly dislikes Aboriginals, is stationed in a rural community with a large Aboriginal population. When interacting with Aboriginals, he continually uses racist and offensive language. He treats all non-Aboriginal members of the community with respect.	Racist language
9.	Two officers are called to investigate an assault at a party. The alleged offender denies involvement. The two officers take the man aside and Officer A threatens physical violence if he does not confess. The alleged offender eventually confesses to the assault.	Threaten violence
10.	At the trial of the alleged offender in the above scenario, his lawyer raises the issue of intimidation in an attempt to have the confession excluded from the trial. Officer B (the only witness to Officer A's threat), under oath, denies that any intimidation or threat of violence occurred.	Lie in court 2

TABLE 6.9
Change in ratings of scenarios (Survey 1 vs 3)

Scenario†	Serious mean scores		Justified mean scores		Corrupt mean scores	
	Survey 1 (N=147)	Survey 3 (N=134)	Survey 1 (N=147)	Survey 3 (N=134)	Survey 1 (N=147)	Survey 3 (N=134)
Avoid RBT	8.10	6.77*	3.39	4.19*	7.10	6.44*
Take cigarettes	7.14	8.09*	2.43	2.70	6.77	8.26*
Hit youth	6.83	6.02*	4.48	5.27*	5.07	5.02
Fabricate report	7.31	6.81	2.74	3.50*	5.80	6.35
Private business	5.67	4.63*	3.54	4.62*	4.06	4.43
Lie in court 1	8.22	8.63*	3.11	2.81*	7.37	8.31*
Steal and lie	8.92	9.02	2.37	2.63	8.51	8.82
Accept beer	4.02	4.76*	4.89	5.16	3.77	4.95*
Racist language	9.20	7.90*	1.91	2.65*	6.41	6.18
Threaten violence	7.88	8.17	2.90	2.74	6.06	7.46*
Lie in court 2	8.65	8.48	2.62	2.90	7.53	7.86

Q: This section presents 11 brief scenarios that represent the sort of situations police may find themselves in. Please read the situations and rate each on a scale of 1 to 10 in terms of how serious, corrupt, and justifiable you believe the police officer's actions to be in each case. Please note that there are no right and wrong answers, just your opinion. (1=not serious, 10=extremely serious; 1=not justified, 10=extremely justified; 1=not corrupt, 10=extremely corrupt).

*Difference statistically significant, p<0.05, Mann-Whitney U test.
†Scenarios are described in Table 6.8.

Figure 6.1. Seriousness ratings of scenarios (Surveys 1 vs 3)

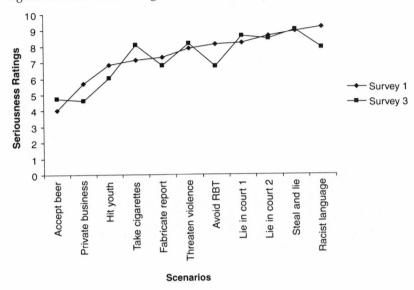

Figure 6.2. Justified ratings of scenarios (Surveys 1 vs 3)

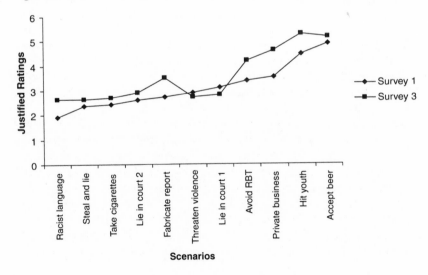

Figure 6.3. Corrupt ratings of scenarios (Surveys 1 vs 3)

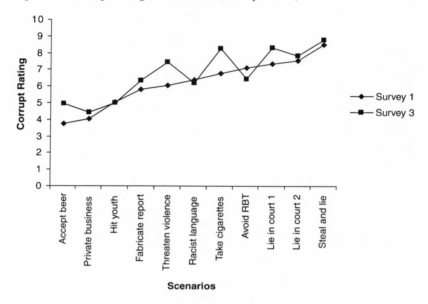

vey 1. 'Accept beer' was considered the least corrupt (mean rating 3.77); 'Steal and lie' was considered the most corrupt (mean rating 8.51). The ordering of the scenarios is very similar to that in the 'serious' ratings, except that 'Racist language' (which was seen as the most serious) was considered slightly more corrupt than 'Threaten violence,' but less corrupt than 'Take cigarettes.' In Survey 3, the 'corrupt' ratings of most of the scenarios went up (in four scenarios the difference was statistically significant). The ones that went down in 'corrupt' ratings were 'Avoid RBT,' 'Hit youth,' and 'Racist language.' However, only in 'Avoid RBT' was the difference statistically significant.

To investigate whether there were any significant differences between male recruits and female recruits with respect to these attitudes, we compared their ratings within and between surveys. Within Survey 1, we found only three measures where male and female respondents' ratings were significantly[7] different. The first measure related to the scenario 'Hit youth': female respondents rated the male officer's action as significantly *less justified* than did male respondents.[8] The second and third measures concerned the scenario 'Racist language': female respondents felt the officer's action was *less justified* and *more corrupt* than did male respondents.[9] These trends suggest that when recruits first joined the police, they shared similar attitudes about police ethics, except that female officers were less likely to condone violence and racist behaviours. However, by Survey 3 these differences had disappeared. Male and female respondents' ratings did not show any statistically significant difference in any of the three measures in relation to the eleven scenarios.

Similarly, we examined whether younger recruits responded differently from older ones and whether their attitudes had changed in a similar way.[10] We found that in Survey 1, older respondents regarded 'Fabricate report' as *less serious* and *less corrupt*,[11] 'Private business' and 'Racist language' as *less corrupt*,[12] and 'Lie in court 1' as *more serious*[13] than young respondents did. By Survey 3, however, these differences were not statistically significant. In the six instances where there were significant differences in Survey 3, recruits in the older age group rated the behaviours described in the scenarios as *more serious*, *less justified*, and *more corrupt* than the younger group did.

Finally, we compared the ratings by respondents who had no university education with the ratings by those who had some university education. The only significant differences were as follows: in Survey 1, those with some university education rated 'Take cigarettes' as *less serious* as well as *less corrupt*, 'Fabricate report' as *less serious* (6.68 vs 7.62), and 'Steal/lie' as *less justified*[14]; however, all these differences became statistically insignificant in Survey 3.

To sum up, recruits' responses to the hypothetical scenarios suggest that their attitudes had changed significantly over the eighteen months. Perhaps as a result of the Royal Commission's publicity about police corruption, recruits had rated virtually every scenario as *more corrupt* than they did when they first joined the police. The only significant departure from that trend was that in Survey 3, 'Avoid RBT' was rated as *less corrupt* than in Survey 1. 'Hit youth' and 'Racist language' were also considered *less corrupt*, but the differences were not statistically significant. At the same time, recruits' perceptions of whether the actions taken in the scenarios were justified changed significantly between the two surveys: except for 'Lie in court 1' and 'Threaten violence,' recruits rated all the other actions as *more justified* in Survey 3 than they did in Survey 1. In other words, even though recruits regarded these actions as more corrupt than they originally thought, they also felt that they were more justified or justifiable. In turn, their perceptions of the seriousness of these actions also changed, though not in a single direction: officially defined 'corrupt' behaviours such as accepting free beers for service, taking cigarettes from a crime scene, and lying in court to conceal a fellow officer's theft from an offender were rated as more serious in Survey 3; yet less visible behaviours such as running private errands while on duty, hitting an offender in response to his assault of a female officer, avoiding random breath tests, and using racist or offensive language against Aborigines were considered less serious. As with earlier findings on general ethical attitudes, all gender and educational differences in ratings found in Survey 1 completely disappeared in Survey 3. However, age did seem to make a difference in that recruits who joined the police after turning twenty-one were more likely to rate some of the conduct as more serious, less justified, and more corrupt in Survey 3 than their younger colleagues did.

Expected Actions in Response to Specific Scenarios

In another part of the survey, respondents were asked to indicate what action they would take if they were to hear about the incident described in each scenario from a very reliable source. Respondents could tick as many options as they wished. The options were categorized as follows: no action, take formal action within the NSW Police Service, report to the Ombudsman, take informal action with a trusted officer, raise directly with the officer, and other.[15]

Figure 6.4 shows the scenarios sorted by the percentage of respondents who selected 'no action' in Survey 1. The ordering is roughly the reverse of that found earlier in the seriousness rating (Figure 6.1) – for example, the likelihood of taking 'no action' was lowest for the scenario rated as the most serious ('Racist language'), and highest for the scenario rated as the least serious ('Accept beer'). For most of the scenarios, the option most frequently selected was 'taking informal action with a trusted officer.' This was followed by 'raising the matter directly with the officer involved,' then 'formal reporting within the Police Service' and taking 'no action.' 'Reporting to the Ombudsman' was not a popular option, chosen by less than 10 per cent of the respondents for most of the scenarios except 'Lie in court 2' (13 per cent) and 'Racist language' (10 per cent). The pattern of responses to the same scenarios in Survey 3 is shown in Figure 6.5. In almost every scenario, there was a statistically significant difference between the responses in Survey 1 and those in Survey 3 (see Table 6.10). These changes are discussed in more detail below.

Figure 6.4. Responses to scenarios – Survey 1

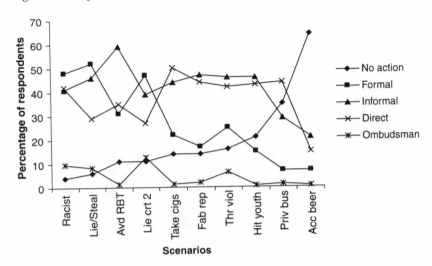

Figure 6.5. Responses to scenarios – Survey 3

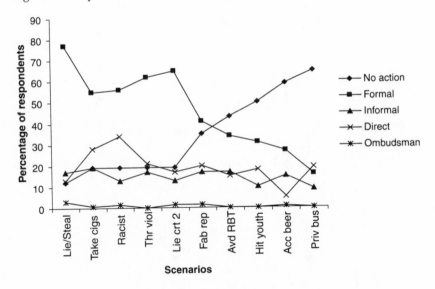

TABLE 6.10
Change in expected action re scenarios (Survey 1 vs 3)

Percentage† who nominated	No action		Formal Report within NSWPS		Informal action with trusted officer		Raise directly with the officer	
Scenario	Survey 1 (N=147)	Survey 3 (N=134)	Survey 1 (N=147)	Survey 3 (N=134)	Survey 1 (N=147)	Survey 3 (N=134)	Survey 1 (N=147)	Survey 3 (N=134)
Avoid RBT	11	43*	31	34	59	17*	35	15*
Take cigarettes	14	19	22	55*	44	19*	50	28*
Hit youth	21	50*	15	31*	46	10*	43	18*
Fabricate report	14	35*	17	41*	47	17*	44	20*
Private business	35	65*	7	16*	29	9*	44	19*
Lie 1/Steal	6	12	52	77*	46	17*	29	13*
Accept beer	64	59	7	27*	21	15	15	5*
Racist language	4	19*	48	56	41	13*	42	34
Threaten violence	16	19	25	62*	46	17*	42	21*
Lie in court 2	11	19	47	65*	39	13*	27	17*

Q: This section presents 11 brief scenarios that represent the sort of situations police may find themselves in…As a serving police officer, what action would you take if you were to hear about the incident from a very reliable source? Circle as many options as appropriate.
†Percentages do not add up to 100 as multiple responses were available.
*Difference statistically significant, p<0.05, Chi-square test

Figure 6.6. Response – No action (Surveys 1 vs 3)

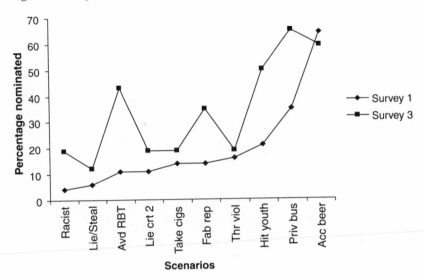

Figure 6.6 shows the scenarios again sorted by percentage of re-spondents who selected 'no action' in Survey 1. For all the scenarios except 'Accept beer,' the likelihood of taking no action increased in Survey 3. The increase was statistically significant in about half the items ('Avoid RBT' from 11 to 43 per cent, 'Hit youth' from 21 to 50 per cent, 'Fabricate report' from 14 to 35 per cent, 'Private business' from 35 to 65 per cent, and 'Racist language' from 4 to 19 per cent). These results suggest that probationers were much more willing to 'turn a blind eye' on misconduct by the end of their field training.

Although there was an increase in likelihood of recruits taking 'no action' against misconduct in Survey 3, paradoxically, there was also an increase in the proportion of respondents who said they would take formal action within the police service against the same sets of conduct. Figure 6.7 shows that the percentages of respondents who would take formal action increased significantly in Survey 3 for every scenario except 'Avoid RBT' and 'Racist language.' Some of the increases were quite dramatic – for example, 'Threaten violence' went up from 25 to 62 per cent, 'Take cigarettes' from 22 to 55 per cent, and 'Fabricate report' from 17 to 41 per cent.

In contrast, respondents in Survey 3 were much *less* likely to select

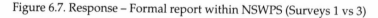

Figure 6.7. Response – Formal report within NSWPS (Surveys 1 vs 3)

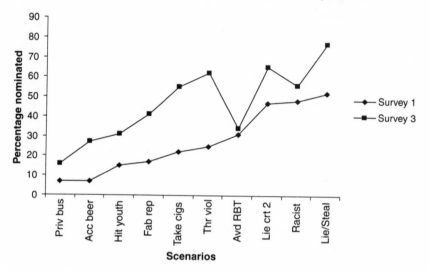

'informal action with a trusted officer' as a way of responding to misconduct. Figure 6.8 shows that the percentages dropped significantly in every scenario except 'Accept beer,' for which the drop was very slight. These data suggest that recruits were more likely to make use of the formal system of reporting than to take informal action. This is a complete reversal of the situation in Survey 1, where informal actions were favoured over formal ones in most of the scenarios.

Raising the matter directly with the officer involved in the misconduct also became a less popular choice in Survey 3 (Figure 6.9). The difference was statistically significant for every scenario except 'Racist language.' As mentioned before, reporting the matter to an external body like the Ombudsman was not at all popular in Survey 1. By Survey 3, this option was even less popular, being chosen by less than 2 per cent of respondents for most of the scenarios and by *none* of the respondents for four scenarios ('Avoid RBT,' 'Hit youth,' 'Private business,' and 'Threaten violence').

Expected actions in response to the given scenarios did not show a great deal of difference between male and female respondents,[16] between older and younger respondents,[17] or between those with some university education and those without.[18] In summary, by the end of

Figure 6.8. Response – Informal action with trusted officer (Surveys 1 vs 3)

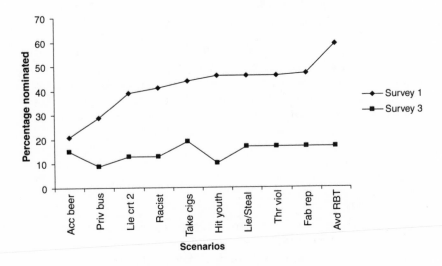

Figure 6.9. Response – Raise directly with the officer (Surveys 1 vs 3)

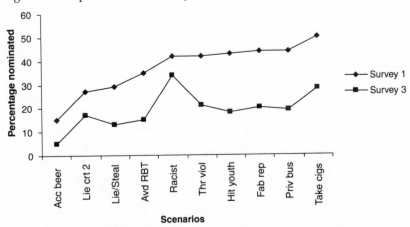

their field training, probationers were more willing than before to 'turn a blind eye' on virtually all the misconduct described in the scenarios. The change was statistically significant for 'Avoid RBT,' 'Hit youth,' 'Fabricate report,' 'Private business,' and 'Racist language' – the same group of conduct that probationers regarded as more justifiable in

Survey 3 (Table 6.9). At the same time, probationers also indicated more readiness to report these forms of conduct formally to the police service. Formal reporting was the most frequently nominated action for all scenarios except 'Avoid RBT,' 'Hit youth,' 'Private business,' and 'Accept beer,' where 'no action' was preferred. These results suggest that probationers were generally not willing to cover up unethical conduct or to protect unethical police officers. How much of this attitude was translated into action is difficult to tell, but we were told of a number of occasions where recruits had formally reported unethical conduct to the police service (see chapter 7). We have no reason to suspect that these interviewees were deliberately feeding us misleading or socially desirable responses.

Metamorphosis or Camouflage?

We set out in this chapter to examine the extent to which recruits had adjusted their habitus to the new position they occupied. There is no doubt that by the end of their training they had taken on many of the cognitive and attitudinal attributes commonly referred to as the 'street cop' culture. Most probationers were aware of changes in themselves; some had become more mature and more confident but had lost some of their idealism and tolerance. Physically, they looked, sounded, and moved like police officers. They had also started to see the world through the eyes of a police officer: they were more alert, more cynical, less trusting, and more suspicious. Having joined the police to help people and to make a difference, they were becoming frustrated by many perceived barriers in their job: the excessive accountability requirements, the lack of support from management, the legal and practical limits of what police could do, the ineffectiveness of the criminal justice system, and the lack of respect or gratitude from members of the public. Their attitudes toward the public and the criminal justice system became significantly more negative over the eighteen months of their training. They were starting to view segments of the public more cynically and were not averse to stereotyping people on the basis of their ethnicity or appearance. Though genuinely appreciative of the camaraderie of their fellow officers, they recognized the need to protect themselves at all times, not only against internal discipline by management, but also against external watchdogs such as the Ombudsman and public inquiries such as the Royal Commission.

Our data suggest, however, that the cohort's adoption of the 'street cop culture' was by no means automatic or unconscious. Recruits demonstrated repeatedly that they were reflective and discerning. Because of the highly publicized hearings and findings of the Royal Commission, they were much more sensitized to the changing political climate. They had to resolve the conceptions of 'good police work' as taught at the academy with those as taught in the field. Throughout their training, recruits had been able to articulate for the researchers what they regarded as 'good' or 'bad' police work. Initially, people skills or communication skills were cited most frequently as characteristic of 'good' police work, followed closely by technical knowledge and skills. As recruits progressed from novices to constables, however, they tended to value communication skills and people skills less, and to place more emphasis on good arrests and convictions. Technical knowledge and skills remained central to their definitions of 'good' police work. Recruits' conceptions of 'bad' police work did not change a great deal over time – effort, attitude to work, and people/communication skills remained important considerations.

Recruits' responses to the hypothetical 'ethical' scenarios showed that they had become increasingly sensitized to a new organizational emphasis on integrity. They tended to view certain actions as more serious than when they first joined the police, especially where the actions were visible or detectable. They also showed a greater willingness to report certain unethical behaviours formally. These findings suggest that generally, the recruits did not simply follow 'the line of least resistance' (Van Maanen 1973) and adopt the values of the 'street cop culture.' The changes they underwent over the eighteen months were not completely a process metamorphosis; perhaps they also involved a strategic use of camouflage so as to give the appearance of 'fitting in.' To a certain extent, recruits were engaging in 'reflective practice' both in checking theory against practice and in evaluating practice against theory (CARE 1990: 66). Perhaps the academy's lessons against social and racial stereotyping had been abandoned in the face of repeated negative experience, but those on professional and ethical practice did not fall entirely on deaf ears. This is because changing political and organizational conditions made ethical practice no longer simply a matter of personal morality, but a real necessity for survival. In the next chapter we discuss how changes in the field of policing may have modified the 'rules of the game' and inadvertently allowed the academy's model of professionalism to resurface among recruits.

7

Negotiating the Field

In chapter 6 we concluded that by the end of their training, recruits had taken on many attributes of what the literature refers to as the 'street cop' culture: a more cynical view of police work and police management; a greater tendency to stereotype people on the basis of appearance; and a more suspicious, less trusting mentality that justified the need for them to protect themselves at all times. We also noted that these changes were not automatic or unconscious – recruits were not simply following 'the line of least resistance.' They remained reflective about what constitutes 'good' and 'bad' police work. In response to hypothetical scenarios of unethical conduct, they showed a growing tendency to ignore less visible behaviours but also a greater willingness to report more serious misconduct formally to the police service. These findings illustrate the limits of conceptualizing organizational socialization in terms of gaining a 'final' perspective. As discussed in chapter 1, we cannot assume the existence of a homogeneous and stable culture within an organization, nor that recruits were passive recipients of cultural knowledge during their period of socialization. More important, we cannot understand socialization as a process independent of the social and political conditions (i.e., the field) of policing.

In this chapter we resort to recruits' own accounts to describe the 'police culture' as they experienced it. These accounts are unusual in that researchers have traditionally derived notions of police culture from their observation of police officers in action (e.g., Skolnick 1966; Ericson 1981, 1982). Some of these were insiders' accounts, in that the researchers were themselves former police officers (e.g., Holdaway 1983; Young 1991). It has been rare, however, for researchers to actually ask serving police to define and describe police culture. Since recruits had been quite willing to share their experiences with us over the two years, it seemed natural to tackle the topic directly with them. Given the frequent mention of 'police culture' in the Fitzgerald and Wood inquiries, the term would have been familiar to every Australian police officer. We were confident that recruits would want to have a say about this topic. As it turned out, our questions generated some extremely thoughtful responses and important insights.

Recruits' accounts suggest that far from being homogeneous and stable, police culture in New South Wales was in a state of flux at the time of the research. This was due to successive waves of reforms in the police service following government inquiries. This instability of organizational culture had implications for the socialization process: instead of adopting unthinkingly a dominant set of cultural beliefs, recruits were constantly revising and adjusting their habitus in the light of new experiences and new constraints. Their 'breaking in' period involved not only learning a 'feel' for *the game*, but also continually finding out for themselves *what the game was*.

Reflections on Police Culture

We chose the fourth and last interview for broaching the topic of police culture. By this time, recruits (now police constables) had completed six months of academy training, nearly one year of field training, and six months working as constables. They had been in the organization long enough to have got to know 'the culture' but not so long as to have taken it totally for granted. Interviewees[1] were asked whether they thought there was 'such a thing as police culture,' and if so, to describe what they thought it was and to identify its positive and negative features. They were also asked to indicate whether they themselves felt 'accepted' by the culture, and to describe what happened to people who were 'out of step' with the culture. As it turned out, the constables in the cohort were as reflective about police culture as they had been about 'good' and 'bad' police work. Only a handful of interviewees denied that a police culture existed. Two told us there was no such thing as a police culture because they had never seen it (4/male, age >30, 4/27-year-old male); two others (4/20-year-old female, 4/25-year-old female) thought there had been a police culture in the 'old days' or 'pre-Royal Commission days but did not think there was one now. One of them, however, conceded that 'I might be part of the culture ... and just not aware of it' (4/25-year-old female). Most interviewees did think there was a police culture and were able to describe it, mostly in positive terms though – for at least half the interviewees – also in negative terms.

Positive Features

The positive features mentioned include the sense of friendship, mutual support, and shared understanding that helped officers cope with and survive in an occupation that is dangerous, unpredictable, and unpleasant. A common response was that police culture was about camaraderie, mateship, and support in the job. Some compared it to 'being in a family,' with all the support and social interactions one gets from a family:

> It's hard to define in words. I'd just say sort of camaraderie, friendship, ... looking after your mates – yeah, just looking out for one another and stuff like that, really ... It's like being in a family. On weekends we'll have a barbecue, like we're all working, we'll have a barbecue ... out the back [of the station] and everyone will pitch in ... Even the bosses will come out and have some ... Just like we often meet after work for drinks and stuff like that and you know play touch footy together and all that sort of stuff. (4/19-year-old female)

Several interviewees pointed out that in some ways, this bond is stronger than the bond officers have with their families, because only other police understand what you go through at work:

> It's like a big family ... You speak to people at work about anything. I mean, it's like everyone's there to help each other. Everyone works together, we go out and socialize together, so ... we can talk about different things because we understand each other. We understand what each other is going through ... If your mum [or] friends say, 'Oh, how is work?' my comment [would be] 'Oh, good.' You don't say, 'Well, today I did this and that.' They ... want to know the big, gory details but that's not the side you want to tell ... but they don't understand. Like, the only person who really understands exactly what you're feeling about that particular thing would be another police officer. (4/20-year-old female)

This common understanding among police comes about because as a distinct occupational group, they encounter situations that most other people would never come across (4/male, age >30). One remarkable consequence of this is that even if a person is a total stranger, he or she is accepted automatically in police circles because 'you're in the job':

> I think that the police culture being the common denominator overcomes a lot of other social barriers. It really does ... It doesn't matter whether the people out there are richer or poorer or what, because once you're in the uniform you're one of us, you get a say, so yeah, that's great. (4/22-year-old male)

Because of this common understanding that police share, you have '14,000 mates' and if 'you're in trouble on the road ... everyone's going to do what they can to help you' (4/25-year-old male). The culture is therefore a support mechanism, at both a professional and a personal level. As one interviewee pointed out, police work is peculiar in that 'the person next to you could be the one that saves your life and you could save their life' (4/26-year-old male) – a feature not usually found in other occupations except the armed forces. So it would be 'pretty scary' if police did not trust that their partners would back them up:

> I see [police culture] as a good thing. I don't see it as a bad thing at all. I see it as a support mechanism for the police ... When [name of police officer who was a workmate] got murdered, there was people here [who] would help me out, like do anything for me, if you know what I mean. ... I see that as a police culture. I see it sometimes as an 'us and them' thing too, if you know what I mean – them being the crooks out there ... In this job you've got to depend on other people. You've got to have the belief in other people that you're working with, to believe they're going to be there for you ... So I definitely think that there is a culture and I think it's a necessary trait ... it's something that binds people together and you feel common aims ... It'd be pretty scary if you didn't trust that your partner [would] be over there to back you up. (4/24-year-old male)

Socializing with other police is a form of debriefing that helps officers cope with the stress of the job:

> Like we've got a little group here at the station that go and play golf ... We love golf. We don't talk about work. Occasionally we might talk about things that happen at work or situations we've been in at work ... If you really want to call it something, it's counselling. And it's debriefing and

it's destressing, I suppose you could say, 'cause you're talking about it ...
That's probably our way, I suppose, of ... getting it ... off our chest and
telling someone about it, someone that actually can realize and understand what you're talking about and can help you with things. (4/19-year-
old male)

The trust that comes from sharing a common understanding was
seen as essential for teamwork (4/21-year-old male). One officer summed
up the positive side of police culture in a way that is reminiscent of its
textbook definition (see Schein 1985 in chapter 1):

It's a group of people, they're police in this case, who are exposed to
similar situations for a lot of the time and sort of work together with each
other to work out what the best solutions are or how just to deal with it
themselves ... And just the, yeah, the need for acceptance and belonging ...
I've seen more positive aspects of it than negative aspects ... It's just an
outlet ... just the fact that you're not in things alone. (4/24-year-old male)

Negative Features

Nearly one in four interviewees told us they had never experienced
any negative aspects of police culture. However, many others had no
difficulty recognizing the negatives: the readiness to stereotype, the
paranoia and cynicism, and the cover-up of misconduct. One negative
aspect of police culture – related to its insularity and in some ways the
flip side of sharing a common understanding – is that police tend to
reinforce one another's perspectives, with little input from outsiders:
'If you always associate with police, well, you're not going to get any
input or any other perspectives of what's going on and things like that.
That's probably the main negative' (4/male, age >30). This can lead to
ethnic stereotyping, which this officer regarded as necessary ('that's
probably half the reason why we do good police work'), even if it was
not always justified.

Another negative feature is the need that officers feel to protect one
another against the organization. This grew out of a fear of getting into
trouble for making mistakes, as well as a cynical attitude toward management, who are perceived as 'persecuting' workers:

Unfortunately, we often feel that we have to protect each other from the
organization ... We have to protect each other ... because we have this
perception, you know, 'There but for the grace of God.' When someone

does stuff up, we often feel like we've got to protect them from that because, you know, what if I stuff up one day, how will I feel? And I think it's because of the fear and paranoia of the culture that that is the case ... I think the negative [aspects of police culture] are evidenced in the ... cynicism ... where they perceive the organization has persecuted them ... Often when a policeman goes in and becomes a commissioned officer, they say, 'Well, he's had the injection,' you know – he's become the organization as opposed to the police. (4/22-year-old male)

This need to protect one another can lead to lying for one another and covering up illegal or unethical practices. One constable saw this as 'the bad side' of police culture:

Backing up another copper can be a good thing if it's in the right perspective, but if it's for an unlawful or unethical practice, I mean, that's when you're getting into the bad side of your culture. ... When you start going out of your ethical and your moral grounds ... that's probably where it gets its bad image from, I suppose, like a Royal Commission and corruption and stuff like that. (4/19-year-old male)

Most interviewees who spoke about mutual protection did so in the abstract. A few, however, gave specific instances of such behaviour that they themselves had encountered: One interviewee told us she had been complicit in a cover-up in relation to a relatively minor incident:

I have been in a position where I've had to write a report in relation to something that happened at work where ... I won't get into the details, really, but more or less everyone knew that someone had done something wrong [played a practical joke on another officer], but, like, no one sort of ... We all had to write reports and no one said anything. You know, we all tried to write ourselves out of it ... We just didn't want to become involved, so we just wrote ourselves out of it. (4/19-year-old female)

Another interviewee was quite blunt in describing police culture as part of the 'lurks and perks' of the industry:

I'll just give you one example. You know, you can get pulled over if ... you've been speeding a little bit and all you've got to do is show your badge and that – you know, have a bit of a chat, talk about a few things – and that's it and off you go. That's what I define as police culture ... I think it's like any industry – you have your lurks and your perks ... The positive thing about it is that you don't have to pay the government any money, and the bad thing about it is that you are mostly just as bad as anybody else but you've just been let off. (4/28-year-old male)

A third interviewee mentioned a situation where an officer was reported for a misconduct that was widely known in the station. Only two officers gave details; others (about five officers) denied any knowledge. He thought this was 'where police culture goes wrong':

> I think it is important for police to stick together and back each other ... through whatever the circumstances. Where it gets to the point where they're lying for each other, that's ... probably where police culture goes wrong ... It's good to have it but it's hard to have it there where it's not going to ... become a dangerous thing. (4/26-year-old male)

Formation of Culture

A number of interviewees pointed out that culture exists in every workplace, not just with police (4/25-year-old male, 4/22-year-old female). A culture forms wherever people who work together have 'things in common' that they can't discuss with those outside the workplace or occupation:

> I think general members of the public don't understand what a police officer goes through, you know, in ... the time frame of even a day, let alone a week. If you have a big day, you may have seen someone that's shot himself with a shotgun, you may have seen a fatal accident, you may have seen, you know, all gruesome sort of things like that. And I think it's easier to talk to a police officer about that sort of thing because they understand and they may themselves have seen it ... Even all the paperwork you go to. You know, the things you see, the things that people actually say to you, the abuse you cop, all the complaints you get. (4/24-year-old female)

Police culture forms as a 'defence mechanism' in response to the hostile circumstances in which police were placed. One constable compared policing to fighting battles on several fronts:

> I think you get a culture when you place a group of people in circumstances that make them unique ... and I think that the kind of circum-

stances that you place them in will determine what the culture itself is like ... Police are placed in circumstances where often the people you have to deal with don't like you. And so we tend to ... like each other, you know, simply as a defence mechanism. And we have social interactions with each other for that reason. That's where we get our acceptance ... I think we do perceive it as a battlefront, if you like, that we do have a battlefront in public, and we have a battlefront of public image, we have the battlefront of the media, we have the battlefront of the organization, and we have the battlefront of the crims. (4/22-year-old male)

This view was endorsed by another interviewee, who saw the culture as a 'shell' or a 'front' that officers put up in order to cope with the pain and abuse of the job. For her, police culture was manifested in 'what you don't talk about':

There's things you talk about and things you don't talk about. I think the culture is, you know ... a front that you put up ... It's a coping mechanism. If you expose yourself totally and wholly, you obviously, you know, you open yourself straightaway to ... become too sensitive, to feel too much emotions ... If you go and have a row with someone, every time you pull someone over for a traffic matter, if you take it to heart then you're going to end up a basket case ... You sort of shed up a bit of a shell around you and ... that's what I think the culture is ... I think it's a natural defence. You don't want to open yourself to being hurt, being a target of particular individual abuse. (4/20-year-old female)

Another interviewee explained the culture as a natural consequence of the work hours and the nature of the work:

All the police socialize together mainly because it's the work hours. Like, you're on shift work and when you're off, everybody's working ... and vice versa. Like you're out, you're working every Saturday night when everybody else is out, going out, which makes it hard to maintain your friends outside ... Yeah, and I think probably because of the nature of the work ... I suppose you do a hard job and sometimes it's a thankless job, and you kind of build very strong relationships with the people you work with, you know, if you're out in the car together and you're out there for twelve hours. (4/20-year-old female)

According to one constable, the insularity of police culture is in part the result of how non-police relate to police officers in social settings:

> I don't think I've met one person since I've been in Sydney that's not a
> police officer ... You just find it is a lot harder to meet people once they
> know what you do – they either don't want to know you or ... they just
> don't know how to treat you, don't know how to take you. (4/21-year-old
> female)

In sum, though not unaware of the negative side of the culture –
given the 'bad press' police had during the Royal Commission, it could
hardly have escaped their notice – constables spoke favourably of its
positive features. Their accounts point out features of police culture
similar to those noted in the literature on policing (see chapter 1): the
bonds of solidarity, the sense of common purpose and mutual understanding, the feelings of alienation from the public and from management, and the need to develop a 'shell' of cynicism and self-protection.
They also explain the formation of culture in terms of the police's lack
of power to control the nature of the job, the gruesome, horrible situations they have to confront, the abuse they receive from the public, and
their sense of being alienated from the organization.

Acceptance and Non-acceptance

Nearly every interviewee felt that he or she had been accepted by the
culture. As one respondent put it, you knew you were accepted 'when
you start to feel comfortable with them, they feel comfortable with you'
(4/20-year-old female). One indicator of acceptance was being invited
to social events (4/21-year-old male). A more important one was 'if
they're willing to trust you with ... feelings, emotions' (4/21-year-old
female).

Most of these accounts seemed to indicate the existence of a unitary,
dominant culture; however, not everyone saw 'the culture' as a single
entity. One interviewee did not think it made sense to talk about being
accepted or not accepted, because there were different groups and
people just got along with one another:

> It's what you make it, I suppose. I mean, it's like going to school. It's the
> same thing as school. Like you've got your little groups at school. You've
> got your popular groups and you've got your nerdy groups and you've
> got your people-that-want-to-study groups and you've got your mixed

groups. I suppose you could say that we're just one big mixed group and we all accept everyone. I mean ... everyone is accepted ... It's not a matter of being accepted or anything. It's just, it's more of a friend-type thing and a workmate type thing and youse all get along with each other, you know, 'cause you've all got to work together and live together. (4/19-year-old male)

Another respondent felt she had been accepted by the positive culture, but she didn't rule out the existence of a negative culture – only that if there was one, she was not trusted enough to be told anything about it:

I think people tend to be able to read people from the start anyway, and if they know what you're like and what you'll accept, they'll keep that sort of stuff away from you, or, you know, if it's not going on, then it's not going on ... I think if you're taking culture as a bad thing ... then I don't [feel accepted] because I don't hear of anything or see anything that goes on. So they obviously don't feel like they could trust me in that way. The culture that I'm involved in, getting along with everyone and the good aspects I see of it, yeah, I think it's a good thing and ... I fit in. (4/21-year-old female)

When talking about the consequences of being out of step with 'the culture,' constables seemed to be implying that there was a dominant culture at each station. A young female interviewee pointed out that if someone was different or acted in a different way, he or she would not be accepted:

When you come to a new station everyone sort of susses you out to see what you're like ... If you're different or you do something a different way, like, if you dob people in for stuff like ... 'Oh, he hasn't got shiny boots' or whatever, you know, no one likes you ... You don't get asked to drinks and stuff like that ... That's what it's like ... If you're a bit of a loser, a bit of a nerd, and people find out, you don't get included. Or ... when you go out ... if you don't drink or whatever, 'Oh, they don't drink or they don't smoke,' so [laughter] yeah, it's kind of like that a bit, so it's a bit sad, isn't it? (4/19-year-old female)

According to another constable, a new officer is always watched closely. Those deemed not trustworthy are excluded in a subtle way:

Police are very wary. When there's new police officers around, especially when you're first out of the academy, they sort of sit back and watch you for a while and work out ... Like, they're careful of what they say ... And there's occasionally people that aren't [accepted] ... There's usually one or two of them at a station that perhaps rock the boat ... Through their actions, through their own thoughts perhaps they are not trusted by the others and as a result of that they're excluded to a degree ... Oh, it is very subtle ... very rarely it's blatant. They're the people that are talked about ... when they're not in the room ... They're very careful in what they tell those people. (4/21-year-old male)

One of the interviewees got into trouble when he called a sergeant 'mate':

Like, I got pulled up when I was a probationary constable, you know, ... when I said, 'Sergeant mate' or something like that. They've pulled me up and put me on paper and I've been counselled about it. (4/28-year-old male)

Some constables saw themselves as relatively independent of the culture. One interviewee said he was not concerned about being accepted or not accepted; he felt he had a more mature attitude because of his age. He did not worry about fitting in as long as 'they respect the job I do':

Well, I don't really care in respect to that whether I am accepted or whether I'm not accepted. It doesn't worry me whether I get out to the RSL across the road and have a drink after work. I can do that one day or not do it for the next three months and it doesn't offend ... any of the others that I do go or I don't go ... So it doesn't worry me. I'm too old to worry about whether I fit in, so that's [laugh] ... You know a nineteen, twenty-year-old or what not, they worry ... about, well, 'Am I fitting in, am I getting on with everyone, does everyone like me?' It doesn't worry me as long as they respect the job I do – that's all that matters per se in respect to that. I've got my own circle of friends, some are police ... and some are not police ... [Younger recruits] will do things to be accepted that I suppose if they were older they'd sit back and think, well, 'Should I go out tonight and drink twenty beers?' I'm just going to end up spewing up. Who am I impressing? (4/male, age >30)

Another interviewee said he chose not to accept the culture completely. He deliberately kept a distance:

> I don't choose to accept [the culture] completely because I'd rather not ... make this job my whole life ... There's a lot of things I could probably do that I miss out that kind of alienate me from the culture a little bit ... But I'd rather keep the friends I've already got. (4/24-year-old male)

In sum, constables' accounts point to the existence of a single, dominant culture into which newcomers may or may not be accepted, but also to the existence of loose groupings of individuals (or even isolated individuals) who did not necessarily belong to the culture or care about belonging.

Breaking the Code

Without using the term directly, a number of constables spoke of 'a code of silence' within the culture. One interviewee explained how it worked: an officer who complained against another police was regarded as 'dangerous' because he or she could get others into trouble. The initial fear had more to do with not wanting to be punished for 'stuffing up' (making mistakes), but it evolved into a form of solidarity and a strategy of ostracism against those who made complaints. This interviewee described an incident during his field training where a constable hit a 'kid' on the head in the interview room and told him to give a statement. The probationer was about to intervene but his buddy told him to 'back off,' and let him out of the room while he 'called the bloke over and ... had words with him.' In retrospect, he was glad his buddy handled it that way, and he explained why: the consequences of 'dobbing in your mate' were such that the complainant, even if not ostracized outright, would always carry the stigma, and fellow officers would not 'stick their neck out for you':

> Because there is this atmosphere of fear, ... you really do not want the other police to have the impression that you are ... the kind of guy who might get them in trouble, otherwise they don't want to work with you and they do make life unpleasant ... because they perceive you as dangerous, as someone who could get them into trouble. Because we all stuff up, we know we all stuff up ... and a lot of the time it's only the fact that

people don't know or don't complain that ... we don't get in trouble ...
There's this police culture of not dobbing in your mate and in my opinion
that's the reason for it. Because if you do, you make life hard for yourself.
And Internal Affairs and that will say stuff like, 'Well, we guarantee it,
you will not be discriminated against if you do.' How the hell do you
guarantee somebody else's opinion of you? You can't. You can't do that.
There is no such thing as Thought Police and while a police might be
outwardly very pleasant to you, they also will not stick their neck out for
you, and they won't be around you any more than they have to be,
because they consider you as dangerous to ... their jobs and, or, you know,
could land them in real trouble, in jail, or something. (4/22-year-old male)

Another interviewee gave an example of an officer who was kept at a
distance because he had made formal complaints against other police:

Well, there's a police officer here that goes over the top a bit ... He's very
serious and he's put a lot of police on paper from the various patrols
around the area and that hasn't gone down too well with the other police.
So, like, he's seen to be distanced from everybody else because he's always putting people on paper. (4/23-year-old male)

In spite of this danger of being kept at a distance, when asked
whether they thought that 'officers should stand by each other, no
matter what they have done,' a number of interviewees were quick to
point out that to put one's job on the line to cover up for someone else
was not worth it:

There's not enough privacy and protection for someone who will come
forward and say so-and-so did this or whatever. But then, also, if you
don't, you're jeopardizing your career too, because if somehow they do
find out ... what someone else has done and you're with them, then you're
going to go as well. I think from experience, and seeing things happen,
you've got to protect yourself, and ... if you're put in that situation, you
don't have a choice. You've got to dob them in. (4/22-year-old female)

If a person's a criminal, they're a criminal – I suppose it doesn't just
involve criminal matters, but I mean if they're doing something that
shouldn't be done, I mean, you're only putting your own job at risk, you
know, and there's no way I'd put my own job on the line for someone
[who's] rorting the system, just an out and out criminal ... (4/21-year-old
female)

If it's something substantial or there's illegal acts involved, there's no way you should stand by. By covering it up, you're effectively participating in what's ... taken place, and you shouldn't. The person actually doing it shouldn't expect you to stick up for them and cover up his misdoings ... I would feel very, very bad about [dobbing a fellow officer in] but that's the way it would have to be, because by not telling you're putting your own reputation and your own job on the line. (4/20-year-old male)

Many interviewees wanted to distinguish between honest mistakes and misconduct:

I mean it really depends. I'll stand by somebody as long as they haven't killed somebody for no particular reason and what I think that they've done is wrong. I think it really depends on the situation ... If they haven't done something when they should have, I mean, I don't mind helping out and doing it for them, but ... I wouldn't cover up for them if they've shonked it off and they have no intention of doing it whatsoever. I mean, I'm not going to take the rap for them. I'm not going to get in trouble because of them. (4/25-year-old female)

I mean, you've got to stand by your mates, as long as you're in the right, or even if you've made a mistake honestly – yeah, stand by, that's what I say ... I mean, you can make honest mistakes and you expect people to stand by you, 'cause nobody joins this job to be corrupt or to do the wrong thing. People have got to realize that. You know, you're out there ... to do good ... Mistakes and misconduct are two different things. I mean, if one of us makes a mistake, we try and cover it up ... to try and remedy the situation, make sure it's all right ... But misconduct and that ... I wouldn't feel comfortable covering it up. (4/21-year-old male)

Yet not all respondents thought that mistakes should be covered up. One felt that people should accept responsibility for their mistakes:

My personal view is if you stuff up ... you accept responsibility for it, cop it on the chin. And then if you've done the wrong thing knowingly, well, then you deserve everything you get. If it's an honest mistake, then I think it should be treated as an honest mistake or maybe handled through a managerial sort of thing ... Maybe some remedial training or something ... Honesty's always the best policy ... If someone's asked me or said, 'Oh, look I've stuffed up, blah, blah, blah, what do you think I should do?' I've said, 'Sit down at the computer and write a report out now or ... tell the supervisor. Go and tell him. You know, if you cover up and you get away with it, somewhere down the track you're only going to get found out and it's going to be worse.' (4/29-year-old male)

One interviewee who had been counselled for an honest mistake felt that he benefited from the experience by learning what the proper procedure was:

Yeah, well, I benefited from it ... I don't see it as being dobber or an informer or anything like that. I think you're bettering the police service for it. You're only providing a better environment for other police. (4/26-year-old male)

Some respondents wanted to make a further distinction between more serious misconduct, such as corruption, and less serious actions, such as bending the rules:

[Q: Do you think that officers should stand by each other no matter what they have done?] That's a good question. Yes and no. Out and out corruption, no. But bending the rules, so to speak, by clipping someone over the ear or whatever, you know, yes ... Like, people say it's black and white – it's not black and white, there's a bit of grey ... If it was going to bring, if it was safety-related, [or] blatant corruption or where criminal charges would be laid to a person ... if a member of the public did the same thing that the police officer did, yeah, it wouldn't worry me [to dob in another officer] ... If I saw someone taking money for whatever, well, that's out and out corruption. But [not] little, how shall I put it, misdemeanours, so to speak ... (4/male, age >30)

I'm not going to dob someone in for ... maybe ... shonking off a job, or not doing the job by the book, 'cause I know the job gets done the best way. Not all the time it is by the book, but it is the best way. But ... I would dob someone in for corruption, and I think everyone here would. (4/20-year-old male)

One respondent said he would stand by another officer in public but air his disagreement in private if another officer made an inappropriate decision:

[Q: Do you think that officers should stand by each other no matter what they have done?] You're getting into a difficult area. [laugh] To a degree, to save face in front of people ... It depends. If it comes down to one of those ethical things and if there's a grey area where an officer makes a decision, instead of standing there arguing in front of ... people, the two of you, you stand there and you either don't say anything or you back the person up ... You both stand together, you are one team, you are a unit. But then you go back and you say, 'Well, I don't agree with that sort of thing but I'll back you up there.' It's all acting professionally, I think. If you can't act professionally, if you've got two coppers arguing about the points of view in front of people ... (4/20-year-old male)

A few interviewees told us they would never report police misconduct to anyone external to their unit:

I'd be reporting it to somebody else who I felt was on my team. There's not a hope in hell that I'd call the Royal Commission or the Ombudsman or the Internal Affairs. No way. Right, I just wouldn't. But what I would do is go and tell the supervisor, go and tell the sergeant, because I know the guy, right, and I know that he has to take action and I know he will, right, because of the relationship I have with him. He will know that my concern's a valid thing ... I do have problems going to Internal Affairs or something like that because I don't think it's as effective. I think it creates our cynical senior constables who say, 'Well, the organization's got me,' you know, or something. (4/22-year-old male)

The stress of informing on another police could be enormous, as an interviewee who had done it out of a sense of justice for the victim, another police officer, described:

It puts a lot of stress on you. I mean, when you really think of it, if you get there and get up in court and speak against another officer, you know, then your identity's known and it's not a very nice thing to sort of think about. That was probably the most pressure that I've ever felt in this job ... I don't know, if I had my time over, sometimes I wish I never did it. Sometimes I sort of say to myself, you know, 'Well, we did the right thing,' and that's it. (4/28-year-old male)

Some said they would report misconduct only if they had to, but they would have to be prepared for a difficult time ahead, because 'dobbers' were hated by everyone:

I'd do it if I had to, but I wouldn't feel good about it ... mainly because I'd be worried about what other people ... If other people found out, I'd be worried about what they'd think ... You know people find out you've been, you know, you can't be trusted, then they find it very hard to get on with people they don't want to work with, things like that ... It'd always be in the back of their mind that you'd done it once. Like even if you had to do it, or you acted in the right manner ... No one wants to work with them. Everyone hates them, and ... you get a hard time. (4/19-year-old female)

It depends on the conduct ... and I don't want to be in a position where I have to do it. If something is majorly wrong ... something drastically wrong, yeah, well, I'll just have to. If it puts me in that position, I'd have to say something. But ... if it's minor things, you know, people not pulling their weight and what not, if it doesn't affect me as much, I'd try not to worry about it. ... Eventually the person will get caught by the right people, it's just a matter of time. And it doesn't need a dibber-dobber turning around and going, 'Uh, so-and-so's done this, blah-blah-blah,' because before long you'll be finding yourself an outcast. It's unfortunate that's the way it is. (4/20-year-old male)

Another interviewee said he would be very angry if someone put him in that position, but he would still report:

No, I wouldn't feel all right about [dobbing in a fellow officer's misconduct]. I'd feel very angry that that officer put me in the position of having to do that to them. You know, because, number one, I suppose, if he does it, then he deserves to get dobbed in, and it would make me so angry that I'd have to do something like that, you know. Oh, it wouldn't stop you. You'd have to do it, I mean. You don't need police like that that do things unethical. (4/19-year-old male)

One respondent also felt uncomfortable about dobbing in other police, but thought that most people would respect the person who had the courage to do so:

Wouldn't say you could feel all right about it, but you'd have to do it and certainly I value my job too much to not do it, and I'm sure everyone else would understand because they'd put themselves in the position and know the right thing to do ... There'd certainly be whispers behind your back sort of thing and that you're one of those super grasses or whatever they want to call them and stuff, but ... I think the majority of the people there would actually respect what you did ... When people get arrested for that a few of them will say, 'Oh, what a scumbag,' but the majority of them say, 'Good on him. He's got a lot of courage for doing that,' and they actually get a lot of praise for it and people thank them and say, 'Well, you know, you've done something that a lot of people find very difficult to do. And you've set the precedent.' So, yeah, it's a very positive thing. (4/23-year-old male)

A recruit who had reported some officers for being 'very drunk' on duty said she had 'worn it ever since,' but she never regretted it and felt that other police agreed with her action:

Like people know me here that I wouldn't dob someone in for nothing. I'm not one of these people who'd run and tell the boss, oh such and such burnt the carpet, or, you know, little things. But when it comes to, you know, something that's serious and could affect your work, well, you know, I would. [Q: Was that a difficult thing to do?] Yeah it was ... When I came here I knew that everyone knew about it, but I didn't care. Like, if I heard someone, or if I knew someone knew, I just said, 'Look, you know what happened. I don't regret what I did. I don't care what you think because what they done was wrong and they're stupid to have put me in that position.' And everyone, you know, seems to agree, and I've had no problem since, because they know me for me and they know ... I'm not the sort of person to rat on someone for something pathetic. But in circumstances where it ... is serious, you've got to say something. I mean, ... you don't want to get in trouble later and dragged into it because you haven't said anything at the very least. (4/20-year-old female)

It is clear from these accounts that the 'code of silence' was not absolute: where police had committed illegal acts, interviewees thought they did not have a choice but to report – otherwise they would be putting their own careers on the line. But 'dobbing in' a fellow officer was not something that constables would do lightly. They wanted to distinguish between serious corruption and simply 'bending the rules,' between misconduct and honest mistakes, because the consequences for the 'dobbers' could be very unpleasant and stressful. Nevertheless, reporting misconduct was not simply a sign of courage because not reporting could be taken as evidence of complicity. These accounts are consistent with the responses to the hypothetical scenarios in chapter 6: respondents were likely to take 'no action' if the conduct was seen as less serious or less detectable, and to report formally to the police service if the conduct was serious. The NSW Ombudsman (2002) found that in 2001 almost two-thirds of the officers criminally charged as a result of complaints had been reported by other police officers. This adds weight to the suggestion that more and more rank-and-file officers are reporting police misconduct.

Changing Culture

Nearly half the interviewees told us that police culture was changing. As one respondent observed, the pre–Royal Commission culture of heavy drinking and criminal cover-up was no longer as prevalent. He attributed this change to the fact that police could be criminally charged as well as dismissed from the police service:

> I think [police culture] did exist say back in the eighties, or certainly prior to the Royal Commission ... but I don't think [heavy drinking] happens, or certainly not to the degree ... it used to happen. Like people don't knock off work and go to the pub with all their workmates and, you know, get on the grog and then drive home obviously well over the limit. No doubt it does happen ... but, you know, I don't think that the culture is sort of as prevalent as what it used to be ... You know, it can be police thinking that ... they're above the law and that type of thing. I mean, that doesn't happen. I guess from my point of view now from the police we get a double whammy and probably even more than that if we do something wrong. Certainly, something that is criminally wrong we can be charged through the court system like an ordinary member of the public can. And you can also get charged internally ... and departmentally. I mean, ... you can lose your job over it ... The culture, generally this mateship, this covering up for your mates, you know, putting false evidence before court and all that sort of thing, I certainly haven't seen too much of it since I've been in the job. (4/male, age >30)

Another interviewee said that people were accepting that it was all right for 'coppers to lock up coppers,' and saw this change in attitude as a good thing:

> I think a lot of people are accepting it now, that it's a good thing. And it

doesn't put the pressure on us any more because people learn that coppers will lock up coppers and sort of attitudes are changing, so I think it's a good thing. I've certainly actually seen examples of that where the old copper might be drunk, and [he's] been arrested and they've said, 'Right, off we go to the station, you're under arrest,' and [he's] said, 'Oh, I'm in the job,' and they've said, 'Well, so am I. I'm doing my job.' (4/23-year-old male)

One interviewee described an incident where an officer who used excessive force on a suspect was confronted by another officer and his action was reported to a supervisor:

I don't think the police service protects its members at any cost now. And members of the police service don't at any cost ... Not too long ago there was people from another station came to a job and this very large Islander, he was a juvenile still, but he was big, oh, he was huge, and we had to restrain him against this wall, right, just till we could calm him down. And I had one hand on his chest ... and there was a guy on each arm, and this other one guy had put his had around his throat. Right ... and he'd calm down but ... I mean, it was so blatantly wrong, you know, the guy had gotten over the time when he'd gotten aggressive, right? And one of the constables I was with like, we went back to their station because it was in their patrol. And the constable I was with, immediately after we put him on the back of the truck, he took that bloke aside and he said, 'What the hell did you think you were doing? That was way out of line. That was wrong.' Right, and he's confronted the bloke right there, which is much more acceptable in the police force because that doesn't get in trouble but it still pitches them ... And we got back to the patrol, and he went and told the supervisor he's done this, it's way out of line and it could come into a complaint. All right. And so I think the police service isn't just accepting anything any more. I certainly don't, you know, and there's not a copper here in this station who'd see someone take a bribe and not say, 'Mate, you've lost it completely. You've lost the plot' ... So I think that the culture has changed from that old school of all stand over and you protect your mates at any cost. (4/22-year-old male)

This view was supported by another interviewee who had personally complained to a senior officer against an officer who turned up for work drunk on a number of occasions. He compared this changing culture to changing community attitudes to drink driving:

I think more and more these days it's becoming accepted that if ... you see something, you've got to report it. Yeah, that's becoming accepted. You're not sort of, as in days gone by, ... ostracized or black labelled ... I guess it's probably like the changing community attitude to drink driving. Like years ago, if you got caught, it'd be, oh, you know, bloody coppers at it again. But now people are just saying, 'Well, if you're caught, you're an idiot. If you drink and drive, you're an idiot.' And ... the same sort of attitudes are creeping its way in that if you do something that's unethical, well, you're an idiot ... Basically, everyone's well aware of the consequences. Basically, it means your job and if you do anything unethical, well then you're an idiot. (4/26-year-old male)

As one interviewer said, the corruption that occurred in the 'old days ... can't happen today' because of closer surveillance and tighter supervision:

Well, in the old days ... working with the same people you get to know them, what you can get away with with the other person – I'll scratch [your] back, you scratch mine. But things that happened in the past can't happen today, or if they do, they're quickly found out and handled ... I don't think going around knocking off someone, things like that, bribes, happen much any more. I think ... people know that they're being supervised so they don't do it. (4/26-year-old male)

Another reason given for the changing culture is that there is a greater diversity of people joining the police. People with more life experience are joining the service, and they are less easily moulded by others:

I think there's a sort of ... diversity in the police that are coming into the job now ... There's not that uniformity before, you know, where they've gone out and drank. You know some people here don't drink at all. Some people go out and just drink Coke and stuff like that, and I think it's breaking up this thing that people have to ... conform ... Yeah, people tend to think for themselves a bit more. Also, I think too ... you know, before when people came straight out of school ... they're more easily moulded into a way of thinking, whereas someone comes out and they've been out in the workforce for a while, they've got their own views and they're not so easily swayed. (4/26-year-old male)

The rising number of female officers was also seen as a reason for the cultural change:

> There's a lot more females in the job like today ... [Q: Why does that make a difference?] Oh, just, I don't know, family-oriented ... I wasn't around back then, but here just seems to be a lot more younger people in the job that are female and, you know, their ideals and things are different ... [So] the blokes don't stand around in a group and swear and carry on, I guess, like they would've and stuff like that. (4/20-year-old male)

These anecdotal comments cannot, of course, be taken as evidence that police culture in New South Wales had in fact changed. What the interviewees were describing was their perception that there were major upheavals in policing – that new constraints were being felt and new strategies were having to be pursued. It is to these changes in the field of policing that we will now turn.

Changing Field of Policing

As we discussed in chapter 1, the social and political environment of policing has been changing, not only in New South Wales but also in other Western democracies. In his summary of the changes in the sociopolitical context of policing since the 1970s, Manning notes that in Britain there have been changes in the position of ethnic minorities, changes in the gender and ethnic composition of police force, judicial inquiries and national commissions that have led to a new emphasis on efficiency and productivity, and an increase in the use of weapons and violence (1997: 321–4). In the United States, police are becoming more 'military,' and private security is growing in importance (324). In both countries, as well as in Australia and Canada, there has been an increasing dominance of managerialist discourse and the use of 'new accountability' or risk management technologies to govern police practice (Chan 1999; Leishman et al. 1996; Manning 1997; Ericson and Haggerty 1997). The globalization of markets, culture, and criminal justice policy (Tomlinson 1999; Chan 2000a), the transnationalization of crime and policing (Sheptycki 1998), and the proliferation of communications technologies in policing (Ericson and Haggerty 1997; Chan et al. 2001) are all changing the field of policing.

Policing in New South Wales has undergone a major transformation.

Among the most significant changes in recent decades, two waves of reforms stand out as having profoundly affected policing in the state. First, there were the reforms implemented in the mid to late 1980s following the Lusher Inquiry – the formation of the Police Board, the appointment of John Avery as commissioner, the crackdown on corruption, the introduction of community policing, the liberalization of recruitment policies to improve the ethnic and gender balance of police officers, the design of a new recruit training program (PREP), and various changes to organizational structures and the criteria for promotion. Chan's (1997: 214) study in the early 1990s concluded that 'a certain degree of cultural change did occur among relatively senior officers'; however, the organization was divided in its support for a new vision of community policing, with the middle ranks (constables first class and senior constables) being most resistant to change. Also, the findings of the Wood Royal Commission suggest that the culture of corruption had not been broken. Nevertheless, as we showed in chapters 4 to 6, reforms during and after the Avery years – especially the introduction of PREP, with its greater emphasis on professionalism and integrity – succeeded in destabilizing the old culture to a considerable extent. Our observation shows that operational police commonly believed that there was a deliberate strategy on the part of the NSW Police Service to produce a new breed of 'supercops,' who were to become the 'white knights' in the bureaucracy's fight against corruption. They believed that academy instructors were encouraging recruits to think independently and to question cultural conventions. Recruits were explicitly told not to be intimidated by senior officers, and to report unprofessional or corrupt police practices, and that their integrity would be supported and rewarded by the organization. We have seen how the lessons of the academy remained a source of guidance for recruits as they gradually learned the craft of policing. In the longer term, the increased recruitment of women and visible minorities has the potential to transform the predominantly white, masculine police culture (see chapter 8).

Of more immediate significance to our cohort, however, was the second wave of reforms implemented as a result of the Wood Royal Commission. These included the establishment of a permanent Police Integrity Commission to investigate serious corruption and monitor the reform process; the appointment of a new police commissioner; further tightening of accountability and corruption prevention procedures, including the introduction of 'Commissioner's Confidence' provisions that gave the commissioner the power to sack police judged incompetent or corrupt; the authorization of targeted integrity testing and random alcohol testing of police; and the introduction of a performance-based accountability system for local area commanders. Obviously, the impact of measures such as these can be uneven or even non-existent. For example, Moss (1998: 6) has expressed concern at the 'significant and undesirable delays' in the management of the 'Commissioner's Confidence' process and at the growing backlog of cases that has resulted. Dixon (1999) was justifiably sceptical of the hyperbole of the reform rhetoric, and of imported strategies such as the NYPD's Compstat process and zero-tolerance policing. Nevertheless, given the way the police rumour mill works, it is difficult to imagine that operational officers would not take some notice of the fact that, as of the end of January 1998, 380 police officers had been listed for consideration for dismissal under the Commissioner's Confidence provisions (Moss 1998: 7); that by mid-December 1997 nearly 4,000 random alcohol tests had been carried out at 256 locations (Ryan 1998: 3); or that thirty-three targeted integrity tests had resulted in the termination of ten police officers (3).

The present study was conducted at the height of the Wood Royal Commission. There were rumours that student police officers (recruits at Phase 2 of their training) were being used by the Royal Commission as 'field associates' to spy on operational officers. Possibly as a result of this, probationers were not uniformly warmly welcomed in the field. Some of the subjects reported brief periods of coolness during which they were 'sussed out.' Others, however, felt that police were naturally suspicious toward outsiders and that newcomers were always going to have to prove themselves.

It is possible to discern from recruits' accounts that a number of the changes noted above were indeed responsible for what they saw as 'cultural change' in the police service. As we discussed in chapter 6, the impact of the Royal Commission on the police organization and policing in New South Wales was picked up in interviews. The perceived effects included loss of public respect for police, a drop in police morale, excessive accountability, that police had become too scared of complaints to do their job, and that management had become afraid to make decisions or 'back the workers up.' Some of the new accountability initiatives were clearly unpopular; even so, they were prominent in the consciousness of interviewees as the main causes of cultural change. As discussed earlier, a number of interviewees mentioned the perceived increase in risk of being charged or losing one's job as a deterrent. Similarly, when asked whether they thought 'officers should stand by each other, no matter what they have done,' many interviewees were quick to point out that to put one's job on the line to cover up for someone else was not worth it. One aspect of change in accountability mentioned was tighter supervision and monitoring of police work. A less dramatic change in the field mentioned by the subjects was the apparent change in the composition of recruits in the police service, both in terms of age and in terms of gender. One suggestion was that people who have more life experience are less easily moulded by others. We also noted examples of non-conformist recruits who were not concerned about being accepted by the culture.

The picture painted by some of the constables suggests that in the wake of the Royal Commission, police had become more conscious of the constraints and risks their job entailed. By the end of their training they had learned how to negotiate in their daily work what looked like a minefield: the risk that a wrong move might lead to a complaint from the public, being 'put on paper' by a colleague or supervisor, being tested for integrity, being investigated by some internal or external agency, or even the loss of one's job because of association with corrupt officers. But was there actually a cultural change? The answer to this question will have to await more comprehensive and systematic evidence. Our claim is a more modest one – that changes in the field have made the socialization of police recruits a less predictable, more diverse and open process than before.

Negotiating the Field

We have argued that the complexity and contingency of the socialization process in New South Wales was due to changes in the field of policing. In effect, reforms since the Royal Commission have sought to redefine the nature of the 'game' – the axiomatic dimension of cultural knowledge (see chapter 1), or what policing 'is about.' When they first entered the police academy, recruits occupied a position of low status. To use Bourdieu's terminology, their most important capital was the social capital they acquired from the relationships they formed among their peers. Then, during field training, they were at the bottom of the hierarchy among operational police. Once again they saw fitting in, socializing, and generally establishing camaraderie with operational officers as ways of increasing their social capital. At the same time, they valued the accumulation of cultural capital by learning practical skills and operational competence.

Changes in the field (mainly as a result of reform) have led to some major shifts in the weights of different types of capital. Police – both newcomers and old-timers – soon realized they could lose their job (economic capital) or legitimacy (symbolic capital) if, in trying to accumulate social capital by supporting their mates, they covered up or became complicit in the misconduct of other officers. The tightening of supervision and surveillance had increased the likelihood of detection. Also, a number of police had been dismissed under the Commissioner's Confidence provisions. In effect, the social field on which police operated was now structured against reliance on social capital in favour of the accumulation of symbolic capital.

Bourdieu's framework suggests that these shifts in the field would lead to adjustments of the habitus. In the New South Wales case, this happened as police gained experience in the reconstituted field – they consciously and unconsciously learned that certain strategies worked and others didn't. It was through the *interaction* between the field and the habitus that practice was produced. Thus, changes in rules (such as the 'Commissioner's Confidence' provisions) did not in themselves lead to changes in practice. It was only through practice that constraints were struck, which in turn caused the habitus to adjust. If rules were not enforced strictly or consistently, then no adjustment would be made. For example, the PREP curriculum attempted to change the attitudes of recruits by emphasizing integrity, procedural correctness, and the social and political context of policing. These attempts to change the habitus did not make a great deal of difference because recruits' main concern was to maximize their social capital by making connections among their peers. The effect of the Royal Commission and subsequent reforms was to increase the value of the symbolic capital attached to integrity and the courage to uphold it. Nevertheless, officers were not unaware that there was still room for negotiation and contestation: the malleability of rules was bound to be tested, and some were prepared to turn a blind eye on less visible or less serious misconduct, or to overlook 'honest mistakes.'

Given that some of these changes to the field have taken shape only since 1997, and that implementation is quite uneven, we cannot expect the organizational habitus to have changed radically. The commissioner's message to rank-and-file police officers – 'Leave the system of reforms to me and my management team to take the lead and let's get on and catch the criminals who are making life such a misery for large sections of the community' (Ryan 1998: 5) – can easily be interpreted as advocating a shift back to the crime-fighting ethos that dominated prior to the reforms of the 1980s. In fact, a recently published report of the 'Qualitative and Strategic Audit of the Reform Process' (QSARP) concludes that 'culture change' has not even been a reform priority in the NSW Police Service: 'The long term nature of the reform process envisaged by the Royal Commission has largely been ignored and has given way to the Commissioner's focus on "ethical, cost-effective crime reduction"' (HayGroup 2000: ix). The complexity and diversity of the socialization process observed in this study is probably a reflection of the presence of these contradictory forces and the instability of the organizational habitus as it adjusts to the changing field.

In conclusion, changing conditions in the field have created a need for new coping strategies. Members with habitus shaped by the 'old' field have been obliged to either leave the organization or adjust their habitus; their efforts to discredit the changes have been only partially successful. New recruits soon realized that the nature of the 'game' was changing. They felt the need to rely on the social capital of camaraderie in order to survive in the organization, but they also encountered a contradictory and unstable organizational habitus. These changing conditions made the socialization process more diverse and contingent. They also required recruits to be more reflective and more discerning in their adoption or rejection of cultural values. In other words, organizational socialization became less a process of 'fitting in' with the dominant habitus than one of negotiating a changing and uncharted field.

Our discussion of the changing field in this chapter has concentrated on the tighter accountability mechanisms introduced following the Royal Commission. Another aspect of the changing field – the increased recruitment of women and visible minorities into the police service – is in principle an equally significant development that has the potential to transform the culture of policing in the long run. Unfortunately, because of the small number of recruits from indigenous (four) or non-English-speaking (nine) background in the cohort, it has not been possible to carry out any meaningful analysis of ethnic differences. Women, however, made up one-third of the cohort, and some interviewees had commented that the increased numbers of female officers were making a difference to police culture. The attitudinal data in chapter 6 nevertheless suggest that any differences between male and female recruits at the beginning of their training had disappeared by the end of Phase 4. Does this mean that female recruits eventually succumbed to the dominant male cop culture as a result of organizational socialization? In the next chapter, based on the accounts of female recruits who were interviewed, we describe the process of negotiation these women went through to overcome constraints and develop strategies to survive in a male-dominated occupation that had only opened its doors to women since the mid-1960s. We will also explain why the increased recruitment of women is much less likely than anticipated to affect police culture.

8

Doing Gender

SALLY DORAN AND JANET CHAN

Female recruits made up one-third of the cohort in this study. Their experience requires special attention and analysis because the active recruitment of women in recent decades was intended to produce a radical change in the field of policing. The policy of equal employment opportunity encourages women to become police officers, but women who join the police are highly conscious of the fact that they are entering an occupation that is traditionally dominated by men. The literature on women in policing has long recognized the significance of gender to the occupational culture of policing. As Martin observes:

> Gender is deeply embedded in the police culture ... Despite changes in the past two decades, the idealized image of the representative of the forces of 'law and order' and protector who maintains the 'thin blue line' between 'them' and 'us' remains white and male. (1994: 397)

As we argued in chapter 1, the gendered nature of the policing habitus is embedded in the various dimensions of cultural knowledge. In particular, the *doxa* of traditional policing that takes for granted the crime-fighting and coercive nature of police work has meant that policing is equated with physicality. This in turn implies that policing is naturally a man's job, so that police culture is predominantly masculine (Heidensohn 1992: 244; Crank 1998: 179). Being female therefore carries negative symbolic capital in the field of policing. Studies of women's experience in policing have shown that despite legislative and policy advances that aim to make women equal, female police have faced resistance and barriers to their integration (Jones 1986; Brown 1998; Heidensohn 1992; Martin 1980, 1990; Brown and Heidensohn 2000).

This resistance and these barriers have operated at the organizational and interpersonal level; they have also changed over time in both form and strength. Women have had to cope with both police *men* and the masculine ethos of policing, even though women as a group are able to perform the job of policing as competently as their male counterparts.

Various explanations for why men resist women in policing have been suggested. First of all, men explain their opposition to women in policing in terms of women's weaker physical ability which may disadvantage them in confrontational situations (S.E. Martin 1996). Another theory is that men resist women as a means of dealing with the dilemma of sexual identity that women in policing present (Martin 1980, 1990). For men, police work is intrinsically 'men's work.' To maintain consistency with his sex-role socialization, and thus to preserve his manliness, a policeman, as a man, needs a woman to be in need of his protection; as a policeman, he needs a partner who will back him up. If she acts like a policewoman, 'she becomes a threat to his ego; he wants to be able to depend on a partner but does not want to depend on a woman' (Martin 1980: 93). Women threaten the boundaries of masculinity and femininity, so men want to 'keep women out of patrol work' (Martin 1980: 94). Yet another explanation sees resistance to women as a much deeper issue relating to the contestation of the rights to 'manage' social control and 'own' its mechanisms (Heidensohn 1992). Finally, resistance is explained by the contradiction between the *doxa* of policing – that it is about strength, violence, danger, excitement – and the realities of police work, which are more about providing service and maintaining order. Women represent the 'soft' side of this policing role; this is why their entry into policing threatens to expose police work for what it really is:

> Women undermine the essential core of policework: the emphasis on crimefighting and the masculine image that accompanies it. Because of the association of women with service occupations and with the less desirable 'feminine' service aspects of policing, entry of women into the male world of patrol highlights these 'feminine' peacekeeping and service elements which most policemen prefer to hide from public view and their own consciousness. (Martin 1980: 95).

As a result, the image of policing as a masculine enterprise is under threat (Heidensohn 1992; Martin 1980; Jones 1986)

How do female officers cope with the resistance they encounter? Martin (1980, 1990) describes women's adaptations along a continuum that ranges from the *police*woman to the police*woman*. *Police*women resist sex-role stereotypes and identify with the masculine police culture by 'seeking to be more professional, aggressive, loyal, street-oriented, and macho than the men' (1990: 147), whereas police*women* tend to 'embrace a service-oriented approach to police work, display little initiative or aggressiveness on street patrol, seek personal accept-ance, and obtain non-patrol assignments' (147). These adaptations do not pose any challenge to the *doxa* of traditional policing, which legiti-mates the belief that policing is naturally men's work requiring physi-cal strength and bravery. Like masculine domination in the wider society, the domination of a masculine order in policing is not seen as arbitrary, because the mythic vision of police as crime fighters helps construct the perception that biological differences lead naturally to the sexual divi-sion of labour. Even though biological difference (i.e., 'the manly man and the womanly woman') is a social artefact (Bourdieu 2001: 23), both men and women are trapped by it. Women either accept their biologi-cal inferiority, or they strive to overcome it by becoming the manly policewoman (which requires unlearning the habitus they acquired in sex-role socialization). In contrast, men take to risky behaviour (e.g., high-speed chases, heavy drinking) to prove 'they have balls.' Hence, the 'logic of sexism' associates masculinity with the dangerous 'out-side' work of crime fighting, and femininity with the safe 'inside' work of service and dispute resolution (Hunt 1990, Martin 1999). The 'sym-bolic domination' (Bourdieu 2001) of the mythic vision means that the masculinity of 'real police work' is accepted by both men and women as self-evident and natural, as well as neutral.

Yet this view of how women adapt to policing is premised on as-sumptions about the stability of the field and the relatively limited range of options available to women. It also ignores the social processes and historical mechanisms that are responsible for 'eternalizing' the structure of masculine domination (Bourdieu 2001). A more useful way of understanding the limits and prospects for women in policing is to make visible these processes and mechanisms through which the gendered nature of policing is accomplished. To this end, one promis-ing approach is 'doing gender' (West and Zimmerman 1991), which has recently been applied to the study of policing (Martin and Jurik 1996; S.E. Martin 1996). Briefly, with this approach, gender is 'not a fixed attribute of individuals but an emergent property of social prac-tice'; it is a form of social differentiation *accomplished* by people in their interactions with others, but this accomplishment takes place within the context of larger social structures and institutions: 'as individuals do gender, they simultaneously reflect, reproduce, and sometimes challenge existing social structural arrangements' (Martin and Jurik 1996: 28, 46). Thus, gender is 'both an outcome of and a rationale for various social arrangements and as a means of legitimating one of the most fundamental divisions of society' (West and Zimmerman 1991: 14). Doing gender in policing means creating differences between male and female officers. These differences are not 'natural, essential, or biological'; once established, however, they are used to 'reinforce the "essentialness" of gender' (24):

> Doing gender ... renders the social arrangements based on sex category accountable as normal and natural, that is, legitimate ways of organizing social life. Differences between men and women that are created by this process can then be portrayed as fundamental and enduring dispositions. In this light, the institutional arrangement of a society can be seen as responsive to the differences, the social order merely an accommodation of the natural order ... If we do gender appropriately, we simultaneously sustain, reproduce and render legitimate the institutional arrangements that are based on sex category. If we fail to do gender appropriately, we as individuals – not the institutional arrangements – may be called to account (for our character, motives, and predispositions). (32-3)

Appier's (1998) account of the history of women in policing in the LAPD demonstrates how the gendered division of policing was accomplished. Police work was not always narrowly constructed as masculine: American municipal police in the nineteenth century were often involved with 'nurturing and sheltering activities' such as caring for lost children and homeless people – roles that can be regarded as 'feminine.' However, because all police officers were male at the time, police work was by definition men's work. It was in fact female activists, in their attempts to justify the employment of female police, who created the differences between male and female officers by drawing on 'middle-class gender stereotypes':

> They claimed, for example, that women's inherently compassionate nature would make them better than men at performing some police duties, such as preventing crime, handling female and juvenile cases, and protecting the moral and physical safety of women and girls in public. (Appier 1998: 3)

The unintended effect of this was the beginning of a division of police work based on gender: 'by identifying some areas of police work as feminine and other areas as masculine, proponents of women police imposed gender divisions where none had existed before' (161). This female-gendered 'crime prevention' model of police work never became dominant; instead it prepared the ground for a new, male-gendered 'crime control or militarized' model of police work to take off.

Although the crime control model is still dominant in most police forces, in recent decades it has been challenged by alternative models such as community policing and problem-oriented policing. Also, social movements such as feminism, and legislative changes such as equal employment opportunity laws, have succeeded to some extent in questioning the sexual division of police work, so that women are no longer required to 'account for' their wish to join the police (West and Zimmerman 1991). Women who join the police today expect equal treatment and equal opportunity for promotion and career development; this means that at the organizational policy level, being female is not perceived as negative capital. Yet the gendered nature of the policing habitus seems unchanged. How to account for this? In the following sections we draw on female recruits' experiences to shed light on how individuals and the organization have engaged in 'doing gender' and reinforced the domination of masculinity in policing. We also describe how gender has interacted with other forms of symbolic capital, and analyse how changes in the field may have affected the doing of gender. Our analysis is based on a question we asked of female recruits at the second interview, and asked again at the third and fourth interviews – whether they thought their experience had been different because they were female.[1] As a word of caution, not all interviewees reported differential treatment. At each round, there were women who did not go beyond saying 'no' in response to the question.[2] Some said they personally had not experienced differential treatment, but gave examples of others' experiences. Some differentiated between situations where they were treated differently and situations where they were not treated differently.

Doing Gender Equality

Women in the cohort were attracted to police work for many of the same reasons men were – to work with people, to serve the community, to have a professional career. They also cited job security and the nonroutine nature of police work. However, women were significantly more likely to rate working with people as an important factor for joining (see chapter 3). Nine out of ten recruits in the cohort were born after 1965, the year women gained full status as members of the NSW Police Force (Sutton 1992: 69). By the time they joined the police, the NSW Anti-Discrimination Act had been in force for more than fifteen years and the affirmative action policies in the police force had been in place for more than a decade. So it was not surprising that when female recruits in our cohort first joined the police, they by and large did not expect to be treated differently because they were women. For example, a female recruit cited in chapter 3 expected to be treated 'more equally' than before, even though she recognized that policing was 'still a man's club' (1/25-year-old female).

Female recruits participated in 'doing gender equality' by reaffirming this expectation. When asked at the second round of interviews (after six months of academy training) whether their training experience was different because they were female, respondents told us there were no differences in organizational expectations and thought this was 'good' or 'fair enough':

> The training – no, they taught you as much as what ... the guys do ... You have to do the same amount of push-ups as ... the guys do. You're not allowed to do female push-ups ... Like they don't hassle you 'cause you can't do them, they laugh at you. (2/22-year-old female)

Their responses reflect a determination that women should not be treated any differently by the organization because of their gender. A handful of interviewees were in fact critical of any practices that gave women leniency, and of women who used their gender to gain advantage. One interviewee reported that 'there was others here that didn't make the criteria and I think they got through because they're a woman.' She worried that this 'jeopardizes the opinion that others have of other female officers' (2/20-year-old female). For another, affirmative action negatively affected her sense of personal achievement, and even denigrated her personal gains:

> Like, I just feel that because of the quotas that say that they will have a certain amount of women they want in here, sometimes you feel a bit like you're only here because you're a woman. But I think I deserve to be here just as much as ... anyone else ... My friends ... when I first got in here they

said, 'You'll be right, you're a woman, you'll get in easy' kind of thing. Oh ... that used to make me angry because [I've] got the marks at school. (2/19-year-old female)

Some interviewees commented on the difficulties women were having with the physical training, but none of them argued that the organization should accommodate these differences in the training regime. One interviewee referred to, and rejected, the complaints of other women about the physical training. These women argued that 'it's not fair that we have to do the obstacle course at the same time that the guys do': 'They wanted ... the best of both worlds and you can't do it that way ... I mean this is a job where you can't be female or male as an officer' (2/21-year-old female). She criticized these same women for using their gender to gain advantage, arguing, 'You can't really be a lady if you want to be a policewoman.'

Male staff also did 'gender equality,' and so did the organization as a whole. There seemed to be a heightened sensitivity to EEO principles and practices at the academy. Female interviewees said that at the organizational level, they were not treated any differently in terms of training expectations. At the interpersonal level, their accounts suggest that some male staff at the academy and in the field were also sensitive to gender issues. One interviewee said that lack of differential treatment at the academy was often quite explicit, and even 'patronizing':

[Q: [Did] you find that your training experience was different because you're a female? If so, how?] No, because they really, really plug the fact that we're all the same, and I think that's good. [Q: Have they consciously been saying that?] Yeah, when it suits to, ... Sometimes overall but ... also because they have to. Like they'll say it in a sort of patronizing way ... 'Oh, you can carry that because you're a woman and we have no discrimination,' and that sort of crap, which is fair enough. (2/29-year-old female)

Another interviewee was conscious that male tutors were 'a bit ... more hesitant' around female recruits, implying an underlying concern with EEO and sexual harassment issues (2/21-year-old female). A chief inspector in the field took it on himself to ensure that female students were aware of how they should deal with sexual harassment (2/22-year-old female). During Phase 4, a male senior constable in the field challenged a 'touchy feely' sergeant's behaviour with other female officers by joking about EEO charges: 'A senior constable would be around and he would ... just make a joke like,' I'll have you on an EEO charge if you don't stop,' that sort of thing, just joke around sort of thing' (3/20-year-old female). This interviewee had also had an experience[3] with this sergeant, but she felt she could not say anything at the time:

> I mean, in your first week, telling your sergeant – he would probably turn it around and say, 'No, I wasn't doing anything, I was just being friendly, what are you going on about?' sort of thing and then turn it around into a big deal and then you would look like the idiot.

In summary, the achievements of the women's movement and of equal employment opportunity policies have generated a habitus among women that they do not expect to be treated differently because they are women. This determination is consistent with the 'liberal feminist' perspective that emphasizes equality of treatment for men and women (Martin and Jurik 1996: 24). Once accepted into the police academy, female recruits continued to reinforce this habitus by rejecting any differential treatment, even as some acknowledged physical differences between males and females. This attitude was consistent with organizational policies and reinforced by the practices of some of the male tutors and police officers encountered by female recruits. However, not all female recruits rejected differential treatment, and as recruits commenced field training and experienced operational police work, 'doing gender equality' soon gave way to 'doing gender differences.'

Doing Gender Differences

At the third and fourth round of interviews, the determination that there should be 'no difference' did not come across as strongly. This is partly due to changes in respondents' concerns. In the second round, interviewees' responses to the question of differential treatment had been almost equally divided among issues of organizational expectations, 'performance' (women's difficulties with the physical training), and experience with colleagues (especially male 'joking'). Issues of organizational expectations and performance were not raised nearly as often in the third and fourth rounds. Instead, the focus was on individual experiences. In contrast to the earlier determination not to be treated differently, by this time gender differences were more or less accepted as natural, and differential treatment was not always judged negatively. Gender differences were constructed by some in terms of essential physical differences. For example, women's inferiority in terms of physical strength was not disputed even in the second interviews: 'They [our peers] just joke around about ... females aren't nearly as strong as males ... which is true' (2/24-year-old female).

Other differences were essentialized as 'natural' or in terms of differences in the 'make-up' between the sexes:

> I think that there's always going to be a female and male thing, but I think that's in any job as well – I don't think it's just the police. I think it's just a fact of nature. [Laugh] One's female and one's male. And ... I've never found any problems with that. (4/22-year-old female)

> One thing that I find in this job is the way people drive cars. Males, like you go with male officers they'll always drive the car faster, harder, and you drive with female officers and they don't. And like you might get in with a male and they'll say, 'Oh, you're a girl driver,' all this sort of stuff, whereas I'm not intimidated by that – I'll say 'Oh, that's fine' ... That's why the guys always crash the car or something like that. In that way guys ... always have something to prove to each other ... that they're better or they're faster or they're pissed, whereas females will say, 'I don't care about that, it's not a priority,' and they don't worry about that sort of stuff. But, that's just the female/male make-up, I think. (4/22-year-old female)

These essentialized differences become salient as both men and women accept that physicality – size, strength, endurance – is a central requirement of the job. Thus, being female carries negative capital in 'real police work.'

Physicality

Physicality was a central theme throughout the three rounds of interviews. In the second round, some women were having difficulties with the physical training component of PREP, particularly the obstacle course.[4] These difficulties were most often attributed to the physical differences between men and women. In this round, women maintained their determination not to be treated differently by the organization; no interviewee who raised physical differences as an issue suggested that such differences should be formally taken into account in the training. They referred to the matter simply as a 'difference' they had experienced or, more often, observed. However, not all female recruits in the cohort shared the belief that women should not be given special consideration. Two interviewees referred to tutors who gave extra (informal) help to those who were struggling with the physical training. Neither condemned this practice: 'They [tutors] know the obstacle course is a problem for the girls, the girls just don't have the upper body strength ... We had a lot of tutors spending the time helping the girls' (2/22-year-old female).

Male classmates were less understanding and sympathetic towards physical differences:

> Most guys get [the obstacle course] straight away, but they just don't understand why some females just ... can't do it ... I didn't have any problems at all, but I could relate more when ... some of ... the other girls are having ... major, major problems. But the guys, they were really arrogant and said: 'Oh, why didn't you just do this or do that?' ... Another thing, I personally didn't have any problems, but just with the firearms some girls ... just aren't strong enough to fire them for long periods ... Obviously guys are ... a lot stronger and they're just probably stronger at things like that. But [the] academic side, there's not much difference. (2/ 20-year-old female)

For one female, size and gender contributed to the pressure she felt to prove herself. She said she placed this pressure on herself – it did not come as a message from others:

> Being a female ... I feel that I always will have to prove myself a bit more because, like, I'm ... not very big or muscular or anything ... So most people think that I'm just ... what could I really do to help? Or, I don't know, I just always feel I have to outdo the men all the time. (2/19-year-old female)

'Physical endurance' was the basis of an argument one female interviewee encountered for why women should not be 'in the job':

> Well ... he didn't see it as a woman's job ... They can't look after themselves and ... what if some big seven-foot giant came and attacked them? ... Basically, because of their physical endurance ... [Q: And did that impact on how you worked with him?] No, I just basically ignored it ... That's his

view, but I didn't really say anything to him about it ... I basically had a whinge to the other girls ... But it just annoys me. Because I'm one for ... equal rights and stuff like that. (4/20-year-old female)

Another interviewee said she had not been treated any differently when it came to task allocation (station versus patrol). She wondered whether this might be related to physical stature:

I'm probably lucky myself. I'm ... one of the bigger females anyway, so [whether] that has something to do with it ... If you're a smaller female then ... the attitude might be different again. I don't know. I always hear talk of this: I've never met her, don't know her, [but], apparently there's some really short girl, four foot or something. I always hear stories about her, poor girl, ... so they obviously have different opinions on her than they do on other females. (4/21-year-old female)

This woman's physique, at least during her probationary period, was not on its own sufficient to reduce male concerns for her safety: during Phase 4, a supervisor told her to take care when on patrol with another female. Nor was her size enough to make her feel safe when she was working with another female – she worried sometimes when working with another female.

Implicit in these accounts is the assumption that physicality is central to police work and that in this regard females are in a 'deficit' position. Yet as one interviewee observed, some male officers welcomed women as partners because they had 'other ways of approaching things':

I know there's probably officers that feel that this job is not for women at all, but none of them have ever voiced that opinion to me ... A lot of the male officers that I've worked with ... have always told me that they'd ... rather work with me as a female than with another bloke [Q: Because you're female or because you're you?] Probably because I'm me, yeah. And because ... I always point out what my inadequacies are ... I know that a lot of men feel that this is a job for men [and] there's a lot of physical things that you have to do that only men can do because they're physically strong and physically capable. And I've let them know that, and they'll say, 'Oh, that doesn't matter to me ... because you've got ... other ways of approaching things ... than brawn.' So, yeah, it doesn't matter. (4/ 25-year-old female)

Male Protectiveness

The notion that physicality is an essential part of police work often manifested itself as male protectiveness of females in operational policing. In rounds three and four of the interviews, protectiveness was the most frequently mentioned issue. Some females regarded protectiveness as 'only natural' (4/21-year-old female). According to one interviewee, there is an 'unwritten rule' in operational policing that physical violence toward female officers is anathema: 'They've got this thing out there that anyone that hits a female officer is a no-no, they'll get flogged if they hit a female officer' (3/25-year-old female). Protectiveness, which apparently was not consistent across the service, was mainly displayed on the street in potentially volatile situations:

> I think you notice it when you work with a male and you go to a brawl, in ... our district anyway. I mean, I've got friends that work in busier stations than me, and they're just treated as one of the guys. If we go to a situation where there's a lot of men – I know I went to one, [and] they ... didn't like me being that close. They asked me to step back. (3/25-year-old female)

Being excluded from potentially violent situations was generally perceived as protectiveness, although one interviewee considered the possibility that it might be a reflection of men's uncertainty about women's ability to 'do the job':

> I don't know whether it's them sort of thinking, 'Oh no, you can't do the job,' or sort of a way they want to protect you. I don't know, but that's how I sort of get the feeling that you are pushed to the outer when the shit hits the fan. (3/20-year-old female)

Male protectiveness was especially evident when two females worked together as partners: 'The guys will back you up if you're a female ... Two females on a car crew, they know they'll be there. You can guarantee they're not far away' (4/22-year-old female). The practice of backing up all-female car crews was seen as justified. One female probationer said she would prefer to work with a male partner:

> I mean, they're fair enough to worry. I mean, I worry about it myself sometimes when I'm working out with another female. You sort of think,

some of the jobs you come across, you think, 'Oh, I'd much rather be working with another male.' (3/21-year-old female)

Women, however, 'walk a tightrope' in volatile situations. According to one interviewee, even though the males will be protective, one must at least make an attempt to get involved:

I mean, it's not good to stand back and let the blokes get in. You've got to get in there and do it too, otherwise they may form an opinion about you that you're ... not going to back them up. (3/25-year-old female)

Men would protect women in other ways. One female probationer referred to a supervisor who advised two females rostered together, 'Just be careful when you're out there – don't pull up ... a car with too many people on board.' She thought that the supervisor 'had every right' to give that advice, and she had 'no complaints about him saying it' (3/21-year-old female). In another example, a male officer – a 'guy's guy' – prevented a female constable from seeing a dead body and would not let her drive (4/22-year-old female). One female constable viewed the practice of not rostering two females together as 'shielding' (4/19-year-old female), although this tasking practice was not always perceived as protection.

Though determined not to be treated differently (expressed in the second round of interviews), female recruits by and large accepted male protectiveness of women in the job. Of the ten interviewees who referred to this practice at the third or the fourth interview, only three objected. One of those who objected regarded the practice of excluding females from 'high risk' situations as a potentially reportable matter, but decided not to 'worry about it':

I've been involved in a couple of incidents where we've gone to certain areas of our patrol and arrested people and it's been pretty high risk sort of situation [and] you'll be driving the car and they'll say, 'Oh, you stay in the car and we'll go out ... and deal with it.' It's like, 'Oh, I'm sorry, I'm not a man but I'm still wearing the uniform' ... I mean, I could easily put people on papers for that ... for EEO matters, but I just don't worry about it. But I find you're just better off saying to them ... 'I'm here too, I can do whatever you have to do.' (4/19-year-old female)

Most female interviewees were accepting of, or non-judgmental about,

the practice and were more concerned that women not present themselves as an additional burden to male officers:

> It really doesn't worry me. I mean ... if they're concerned about me being
> there and they're not going to do their ... job because they're fearful of me
> getting hurt ... I mean, I'd rather move away and know that they're not
> going to be worrying about me. (4/25-year-old female)

One interviewee who expressed frustration about this behaviour at the
third interview had become inured by the fourth: 'I wouldn't say it's
something they consciously think about, I'd say it's something they
automatically do, they just do it' (4/20-year-old female).

This change in attitude regarding male protectiveness is supported
by results of the surveys. Respondents were asked in Surveys 1, 2, and
4 to indicate their level of agreement or disagreement to this statement:
'Female police officers need to be looked after in tough situations.'
Although less than 50 per cent of respondents agreed or strongly agreed
with this statement throughout the three surveys, both males and females became increasingly likely to agree with the statement over the
course of the research. This attitudinal change was statistically significant[5] for men by the time they had completed their academy training –
a jump from 11 per cent agreed to 27 per cent between Survey 1 and
Survey 2. Women's attitudinal change took a little longer: the percentage who agreed or strongly agreed with the statement rose from 4 per
cent in Survey 1 to 19 per cent[6] in Survey 4. But it should be pointed out
that at each of the three surveys, over 60 per cent of the males and over
80 per cent of the females in the cohort were either neutral or disagreed
with the statement.

Good Manners and Sexist Jokes

Besides showing protectiveness toward female recruits, male officers
'did gender differences' in other ways. Some exhibited 'good manners' as a way of treating 'the ladies' properly, as one female recruit
observed:

> It's just sometimes, like, boys would ... not say things ... in front of us girls
> which they would say in front of the boys, which is ... good manners,
> which I thought was nice ... That's because our tutor always said 'Make
> sure you treat the ladies in the class properly.' (2/19-year-old female)

This interviewee appreciated the 'gentlemanly' deference to her gender; another interviewee was especially put off by the same thing. She cited the same issue (males opening doors for her) at the third and fourth interviews. By the fourth interview, however, she had grown to accept that the male concerned was being 'just a gentleman,' and she had become 'used to it' (4/22-year-old female). One interviewee who was critical of women's use of gender to gain an advantage thought this was achieved by 'playing' on men's 'gentlemanliness':

> [Q: And did it work?] Most of the time it did, yeah. I think that's because the guys in the class are sort of used to [being] the gentleman – 'Oh, OK, look, she's upset about it so I won't do it,' and things like that. (2/21-year-old female)

Male officers also did 'gender differences' by telling sexist jokes. Some female interviewees reported hearing these both at the academy and in the operational field. These interviewees thought the jokes should be taken at face value and seen as harmless fun. Often both males and females engaged in them:

> There's sexism and there's sexism, and you've got to take a lot of it lightly ... Joking around and garbage and everyone has a good laugh about it, but I think ... if you said to them: 'Look, I don't like it, don't,' they would stop ... No one I've worked with would intentionally make you feel 'Urhh' ... and I mean, the jokes come out of the girls as well. We're just as bad as the boys in some areas. (4/19-year-old female)

One interviewee, however, differentiated between harmless jokes and those that are 'below the belt':

> I was definite that I wasn't going to be treated any differently because of the fact that I was female ... You've still got guys ... that'll be sexist and that sort of thing, but I mean, most of them say it in jest and I can cop that. That's all right, but when it gets to a point where ... it's a below-the-belt hit, ... I'll have something to say about that. [But] I would say generally, on the whole, training-wise, I didn't strike any problems at all. (3/29-year-old female)

Some interviewees encountered negative attitudes towards female officers but did not take them seriously:

[Young males in the class] always bag females – shouldn't be in the job. You just ... laugh at them 'cause you know a lot of them are joking ... or if they're not [it] doesn't worry me ... I really don't care what they think. I mean, we're here and we're here to stay so it doesn't really matter. I mean ... we even wear ... the men's shirts now. (3/25-year-old female)

Few interviewees reported outright resistance by male officers. Some anticipated resistance but did not encounter any. One female thought she was 'missing something' because she had not experienced resistance from a notoriously resistant male:

One male here, I heard, 'Oh, he doesn't like to work with females ... and you have the worst shift with him,' ... I love working with him. I get along fine with him, and the first shift I worked with him ... we did nothing but talk. (4/20-year-old female)

Tasking

Supervisors also participated in 'doing gender differences' in rostering and assignment of duties. The practice of not rostering two females together was rejected by some female constables (4/20-year-old female; 4/21-year-old female). One interviewee (4/20-year-old female) reported that this was the practice of a supervisor who did not believe that women should be 'in the job' because of their lack of 'physical endurance.' Another interviewee saw this as a form of protectiveness exercised by some sergeants:

They shield the females, a lot of them do. They will not put two girls on the truck together. Or ... if they can, they'll put the girls in the Station and the boys out. But a lot of them do think, 'Well, you get the same money, you put up with the same stuff, so you get out there and do it,' and that's fair enough. I don't ask to be shielded in any of that and neither do any of the other girls here, but ... It's just the way some sergeants work, whether you like it or not. (4/19-year-old female)

One interviewee described being assigned 'some horrible job' which she felt happened because of her gender:

At my training [patrol] there's been a couple of blokes who have been a bit, like, sexist, I suppose. [Q: In what way?] Like females in their job sort of thing ... Like, there was one night ... they gave me some horrible job to do ... I don't know if it was just the way they did it, I just really felt like I had been given it to do because I was a female and that really pissed me off ... I didn't appreciate that one bit ... You won't ever completely cut that out, I don't think. (3/22-year-old female)

Some female constables reported that women tended to be used for work with children and female victims (4/19-year-old female), and with sexual abuse cases (4/21-year-old female). Also, female officers were assigned to search females, since males are not permitted to carry out this task (4/21-year-old female). Beyond 'searching females,' one interviewee said she experienced no difference in tasking: 'I've been given shit jobs just like everyone else has' (4/19-year-old female).

Public Attitudes

Members of the public, through their interaction with police, also engaged in 'doing gender differences.' One issue that became more salient as recruits gained experience in operational policing was the way female officers were treated by males from particular ethnic communities. This was mentioned by one female interviewee in the third round, and by four in the fourth round. One constable viewed this as a form of 'discriminatory' experience (4/20-year-old female). Another cited it as a primary reason for her seriously considering, at the time of the interview, leaving the service: 'The last thing they ['ethnic people'] want to see knocking on their front door and giving out orders is a female' (4/19-year-old female). One interviewee described her experience in some detail:

I don't know whether it's because of the area that I'm actually work[ing] in, a very high Moslem community area. I find that ... the men don't like speaking ... to a female police officer. [Q: How do you know that they don't like speaking to a female?] They'll tell you ... when you're actually doing a job, you're the senior officer and you've got a junior officer to you and you might be doing a job, they won't look at you, won't speak to you, they'll only speak to the ... male officer. They don't like it ... when a female is questioning them about something. It's ... really almost like [a] male chauvinistic sort of a thing. They just do not want to speak to you and they'll let you know that. They'll stand there and swear at you and carry on and ... [Q: And they wouldn't do that to a male?] And they would not do that to a male, no. And I know that I'm not the only one that's noticed that because the male officers ... that I have worked with have all commented to me that they've all noticed it. And ... they don't hesitate to try and hit you or assault you in any way ... The guys don't seem to get ... that same sort of treatment. (4/25-year-old female)

Whether this sort of discriminatory behaviour was restricted to male members of certain ethnic communities or a more general phenomenon requires further exploration.

In summary, female interviewees' accounts suggest that 'gender differences' were constructed in terms of essential physical differences between males and females, and were bolstered by the acceptance that physicality is central to police work. Male officers routinely engaged in doing gender differences by showing good manners in front of 'ladies' and by telling sexist jokes, but most significantly by protecting females from dangerous or unpleasant work situations. Supervisors also played a role in doing gender differences through rostering and assignment practices that demonstrated protectiveness of females and that also reinforced the gender division of labour. Some members of the public, too, were complicit in doing gender differences, by bypassing or abusing female officers. As they gained more experience in policing, female recruits in the cohort also participated in doing gender differences, by not challenging the *doxa* that physicality is central to policing and by accepting male protectiveness as 'fair enough.'

The phenomenon of male protectiveness has been well documented in the literature. In Carol Martin's study (1996) of the impact of antidiscrimination laws on female police constables, women referred to 'chivalrous' behaviour on the part of male officers, one element of which was 'protection.' While most did not object to, and indeed liked, chivalry if it did not undermine them, some were concerned when it extended into the working environment and 'perpetuated the stereotype of the "weak link" syndrome, particularly in situations of potential danger or violence' (1996: 10). Similarly, Susan Martin's research (1990) into the status of American women in policing found that there continued to exist a 'cycle of protection.' This protection was in relation to the denial of certain assignments, allocation to 'quiet beats' and 'inside' jobs, and being 'put with partners who tend to take the initiative' (1990: 96). This 'cycle of protection' created a Catch-22 situation for women officers: protection interferes with the opportunity to learn by taking action and results in incompetence, lack of confidence, and demotivation. The protected woman is 'deprived of the opportunity to become [an] effective patrol officer' (96–7). As a consequence, she may hesitate in a potentially volatile situation, be blamed for her incompetence, and be perceived as a potential danger.

The transition from doing gender equality to doing gender differences is resonant of Martin's analysis (1990) of female officers' adaptations to police work: the continuum between police*woman* and *police* woman. The benefit of a longitudinal study is that we are able to observe not only individual differences in adaptation at a given time, but also changes in a group over time. Female recruits' determination not to be treated differently in the second rounds of interviews is consistent with the *police*woman orientation: a striving 'to minimize the effects of their gender on their colleagues' and citizens' perceptions of their competence and commitment' (Worden 1993: 213).[7] By the third and fourth round of interviews, after a year or more of experience in operational police work, female interviewees were focusing more on their experience of *men*, with very few references to their experience of organizational gender practices or gender-based performance differences. Their acceptance of, or refusal to pass judgment on, male protectiveness is suggestive of the police*woman* adaptation: permitting one's 'sexual identity (and traditional sex-role stereotypes) to influence their own and others' perceptions of their performance' (213). The police-*woman* accepts 'the paternalistic bargain' and welcomes or tolerates men's protection (Martin and Jurik 1996: 97).

Gender and Other Symbolic Capital

If the doxa of traditional policing emphasizes physicality, which is then equated with masculinity, female recruits are doubly disadvantaged because as newcomers they also lack expertise and experience. Often it is not easy to disentangle gender issues from training issues, as one female probationer observed:

> I mean, the only thing you'll find is, say, like I'll go to do a shoot or something like that and if I'm having problems they'll help you more. Not because you're female but because you're having problems. I suppose it's attributed to the fact that I'm female and you are a bit weaker and all that sort of stuff. But you're always going to have ... that sort of gender thing, like females always are weaker than males. (3/22-year-old female)

Another interviewee compared the 'jokes' she encountered as a woman with the taunts that all probationers received during training. For her it was not so much about being a woman as about being a rookie. She felt she would be spared once she could demonstrate her ability to 'do the job':

> I mean, you've always got the little ... jokes, but you just brush those off because I expected them. The same as I ... expected things being a probationer whether male or female ... I don't let those sort of things bother me. I think some girls probably would, but I'm just out there to have a good time and to do my job. I think once people ... realize that that's what you're there for, and they admire that you can do the job and you have an understanding of the job, they just let you go. (3/24-year-old female)

At the fourth interview, this same person again referred to the need to 'prove yourself.' While accepting the assumption that being a woman carried negative capital ('the lesser sex'), she was convinced that by accumulating other symbolic capital (proving yourself trustworthy), she would gain respect and acceptance:

> It's, well, always been considered more of a man's job ... and women find it a little bit hard to settle in or be accepted. I think ... it's a trust thing on the side of the males. I think females ... of course are considered the lesser sex, but I really don't have any problems. I ... don't take offence to people, I try and prove myself as being trustworthy and ... if people choose not to respect me, well, then that's their problem. I do the best I can in my job and I've found that most people turn around and they don't have any problem working with me. But I think initially you have to prove yourself. But I think in a lot of circumstances initially you have to prove yourself whether you're male or female ... to be trustworthy. (4/24-year-old female)

Similarly, another interviewee thought that 'proving yourself' was not necessarily a gender issue:

> I think as long as you get out there and do what you're supposed to do. You've got to, just like anyone else. There's a guy that's slacking off or whatever, like, he's not going to have the respect of his colleagues ... It works the same down here. Well, that's been for me anyway. (2/22-year-old female)

We saw in chapter 5 that male probationers expressed similar sentiments about the need to 'prove' themselves. However, being a woman meant that 'you've got to prove yourself a bit more':

> I think you've got to stand up for yourself a bit more ... You've got to show that you ... I think you've got to prove yourself a bit more if you're a female ... I think you've got to show that, not that you're one of the boys, but that you're a good worker and that you'll do things. (4/22-year-old female)

> They [male partners] probably sometimes have a bit more faith in the males. You've got to sort of prove yourself a bit more. More so on the street than, you know, doing all the general paperwork and that sort of stuff. (3/21-year-old female)

As women gained seniority, the issue of rank began to emerge. We saw earlier that for one interviewee, there were times when gender took precedence over seniority in her interactions with the public. Two interviewees relayed similar experiences in their dealings with fellow officers:

> There was a brawl or something like that [at the demonstration patrol], and I was the senior person in the station, and the sergeant chose the male person, who was a junior person, and that gave me the shits. (3/20-year-old female)

> It depends on who you're working with ... If I'm working with a, [probationer] straight out of the academy that's a male, he'll try and boss me around 'cause he thinks I'm a female, and I just don't cop that ... I find that that happens a lot ... or they try to take charge and ... I hate that so much, it's so annoying. 'Cause it's so disrespectful ... Especially younger guys ... about twenty-one-year-olds ... I just feel like, 'Oh you're only a chick,' [laugh] yeah ... There's a lot of girls that probably don't [put them in their place] but I do. (4/19-year-old female)

These accounts suggest that as female constables gain experience and seniority, they return to 'doing gender equality' again. The assumption seems to be that other forms of symbolic capital can make up for the negative capital of being a woman.

Gender and the Doxa of Policing

Underlying the above analysis of female recruits' accounts is the doxa of traditional policing that police work involves dealing with danger and violence and hence requires physical strength and the use of force. No matter that this doxa is contradicted by the empirical fact that the bulk of police work does not involve physical confrontation. As Heidensohn argues, it is the 'myths *about the nature of policing which are critical*' to the perpetuation of the denial of a role and legitimacy to women in policing (1992: 99, emphasis in original). What we have seen in this study is that both men and women seem to be perpetuating this myth. We saw in chapter 4 that many interviewees emphasized the essentially dangerous nature of police work, and were critical of the apparently minor role that safety issues played in academy training. We also saw that training in 'officer safety and survival skills,' 'use of firearms and batons,' and 'weaponless control' was rated as 'highly relevant' by both male and female respondents at Survey 2. This suggests that both sexes perceived the ability to deal with physically dangerous situations as integral to the occupation. During the academy training, the fact that some females encountered difficulties with physical training was considered a problem that 'the girls' had. Many accepted without question the 'fact' that men and women were essentially different, particularly in relation to physical strength. These factors – the perception of danger as an important aspect of police work, women's problems with physical training, the acceptance of 'natural' physical differences, and the importance accorded to physical skills – served to reinforce the notion for both males and females that 'female police officers need to be looked after in tough situations.'

This is not to deny that policing sometimes involves danger and that physical coercion may be required in some situations, or that women are generally less strong physically than men. The point is that the disproportionate emphasis on danger and physicality as hallmarks of police work legitimates male domination of the occupation, while keeping this domination invisible and masked by the appearance of universality. As Bourdieu observes, the 'dominant definition of practice' may be sexed, but no one would see it as such:

> The particularity of the dominant is that they are in a position to ensure that their particular way of being is recognized as universal. The defini-

tion of excellence is in any case charged with masculine implications that
have the particularity of not appearing as such ... To succeed completely in
holding a position, a woman would need to possess not only what is
explicitly demanded by the job description, but also a whole set of proper-
ties which the male occupants normally bring to the job – a physical
stature, a voice, or dispositions such as aggressiveness, self-assurance,
'role distance,' what is called natural authority, etc., for which men have
been tacitly prepared and trained as men. (2001: 62)

The apparently 'universal' recognition that physicality is important
for police work legitimates both physicality and masculinity as positive
forms of symbolic capital. We have seen, however, that other forms of
symbolic capital are also at play. Thus, female police officers, by 'proving themselves' to be competent and trustworthy or by gaining experience and rank in the hierarchy, may be able to convert their deficit to
advantage, as Moi explains:

We cannot assume that femaleness will carry equal amounts of negative
capital throughout a woman's life in all social fields ... In some contexts,
'femaleness' may even be converted from a liability to an advantage. In
general, the impact of femaleness as negative capital may be assumed to
decline in direct proportion to the amount of other forms of symbolic
capital amassed. Or to put it the other way round: although a woman rich
in symbolic capital may lose *some* legitimacy because of her gender, she
still has more than enough capital left to make her impact on the field.
(1991: 209)

We saw that in some situations, gender was a more relevant factor
than rank or experience. For example, the negative capital of femaleness affected tasking to the extent that some supervisors would not
roster two female officers together. In their interactions with members
of the public, some female officers experienced challenges to their
legitimacy as police officers. This, even though being a police officer is
generally regarded as a form of positive symbolic capital, since citizens
'generally defer to police officers, who tend to have higher status than
most citizens they encounter' (Martin and Jurik 1996: 88). For female
officers, these challenges are a reflection of the 'close association of
authority and control with masculinity' (89).

As noted in previous chapters, the crime control model of policing
has been challenged in recent years by alternative models such as

community policing and problem-oriented policing. The reforms in the NSW Police Service in the late 1980s were in fact explicitly linked to the adoption of community policing as the 'principal operational strategy' (Chan 1997). PREP, the recruit training program introduced in that era, was itself intended to be a challenge to the traditional crime-fighting model and its dominant definition of practice. This challenge may not have been entirely successful, given the subsequent organizational shift to the 'firm but fair' variant of aggressive crime-fighting strategy. Even so, there is evidence that for the cohort in this study at least, the new program has succeeded in inculcating definitions of 'good police work' that do not include physicality. Superiority of physical strength and the ability to use physical force were rarely mentioned as examples of good police work in any of the rounds of interviews (chapter 6, Table 6.4). Even though by the fourth round of interviews interviewees were more likely to nominate law enforcement outcomes than communication skills as examples of good police work, the valued attributes of these 'law enforcement outcomes' had nothing to do with physicality. Practices that were highly regarded included alertness to unusual situations, quick response, good investigative skills, preparation of good court briefs, and the proactive use of intelligence reports. Where the ability to assume control or assert authority was mentioned in examples of good police work, the skills that were extolled were the ability to defuse situations using communication skills and the ability to control situations while treating people with respect. In fact, physicality was cited in examples of 'bad police work'; these included entering a situation aggressively, threatening or provoking violence, being violent or abusive, engaging in unnecessary car chases, and aggravating volatile situations.

In chapter 7 we referred to the changing field of policing, not only locally but also globally. Women's increased access to education and employment is one of those global changes. Through equal opportunity and affirmative action policies, the proportion of female police officers in New South Wales has increased from less than 2 per cent of sworn officers in the 1970s to around 11 per cent in the early 1990s (Sutton 1992: 71). In theory, the active recruitment of women into policing should have converted the symbolic capital of being a woman from negative to positive. But as the female interviewees' accounts in this chapter have shown, such a shift has not happened. Most female recruits who entered the police expecting equality of opportunity and equity in treatment eventually contributed to 'eternalizing' masculine domination by accepting the doxa of traditional policing and the 'paternalistic bargain' of male protectiveness. Thus, in spite of organizational policies that encouraged gender equality and a training curriculum that challenged the crime control model of policing, individuals within the organization – both men and women – perpetuated the doxa of masculine domination by doing gender differences. Increasing the proportion of females in policing may perhaps make a difference in the longer term if women seriously challenge the mythic vision and its assumptions about the essentialness of physicality in policing.

9

Conclusion: Learning the Art of Policing

All newcomers to an organization experience a period of adjustment and reorientation before they feel comfortable. The socialization process provides new members with 'knowledge, ability and motivation to play a defined role' in the organization (Van Maanen 1976: 70). In most cases, 'successful' socialization involves individuals taking on new self-images, new involvements, new values, and new accomplishments (Caplow 1964, cited in Van Maanen 1976: 75). Yet as Schein (1968) points out, outcomes of socialization can range from 'rebellion' to total 'conformity.' Neither of these extremes is necessarily beneficial to the organization. The socialization of police recruits is a case in point. Is full conformity to the prevailing organizational mission an indicator of success? Is rebellion against the dominant culture a sign of failure? Or is it more important for recruits to develop into 'creative individualists' (Schein 1968) who accept the 'pivotal demands' but reject certain role behaviours as irrelevant or peripheral to the job? For police recruits, who typically see joining the police as a vocational call rather than an occupational choice, the breaking-in process often represents a *breakpoint* during which 'established relationships are severed and new [ones] forged, old behavior patterns forgotten and new ones learned, former responsibilities abandoned and new ones taken on' (Van Maanen 1977: 16). Yet having made these breaks from their former selves and successfully negotiated their new role as police constables, many also become disillusioned and cynical about their work and their organization. This paradoxical but stable finding in the policing literature forms the starting point of this inquiry into police socialization.

A central concern of this book has been the relationship between organizational socialization and professionalism. We have challenged the conventional wisdom that links formal training to professionalism and police culture to deviant practices by unpacking both 'professionalism' as an ideal and 'culture' as a theoretical construct. We have argued that professionalism is not a pure concept independent of historical and political context; rather, as both an ideal and a normative standard, professionalism is a contested site. Similarly, organizational culture is not homogeneous, all-powerful, unchanging, and independent of human agency and social conditions. It, too, is subject to contestation and negotiation. Hence professionalism is neither an antidote to the 'corrupting influence' of culture nor its alternative: it is in fact *constitutive* of culture and as much a product of historical and political conditions as culture itself is. In other words, it is possible to conceive of a 'professional' police culture. This is why the empirical research on which this book is based focused on the processes by which concepts of police professionalism are developed, transformed, or strengthened. Also, this book has examined how police recruits learn the craft of policing, the types of practice models that they encounter, their experience of 'police culture,' and their adaptations to the new organization.

As we pointed out in chapter 1, traditional models of socialization tend to understate the degree of cultural division within an organization, downplay the active role of recruits in determining their own adaptation strategies, and ignore the sociopolitical conditions within and outside the organization. As a result, they tend to assume a degree of stability and homogeneity in the organizational culture. Thus, organizational socialization is often conceived of as a fairly linear and uniform process of 'fitting in' with the dominant culture. The advantage of reconceptualizing socialization in terms of Bourdieu's schema of field and habitus is that it enables us to accommodate the fluidity and contingency of socialization paths (Manning and Van Maanen 1978) and to account for variations in adaptive strategies and outcomes. Such contingency and fluidity is especially salient for organizations operating in a volatile social and political environment. The New South Wales case study provides a context for examining the utility of this framework for understanding the processes and outcomes of police socialization. It is, in many ways, a significant and theoretically relevant case. The study took place at a time when traditional policing models were being challenged and problems of police misconduct and corruption were once again in the spotlight in a number of countries. The NSWPS was typical of many police organizations – it had undergone many years of reform, only to discover, through the highly publicized investigations of a Royal Commission, that corruption was entrenched and systemic in many parts of the organization. In the following sections, we explore the implications of the case study.

Learning the Craft of Policing

Similar to recruits in earlier studies, the cohort in this one joined the police in order to help people and serve the community. They were attracted to the career prospects of the occupation as well as to what they saw as the varied, non-routine, and exciting nature of police work. They generally had a very high opinion of the occupation, placing it at the top of a list of eighteen occupations in terms of both honesty and professionalism, and only slightly below medicine and the law in prestige. This does not mean they were totally naïve about police work. Before joining the service, most of the recruits had acquired some knowledge about police work, either through members of the family, or through relatives or friends who were police officers, or through direct personal experience with police officers. They had a fairly realistic idea of what the occupation is about. Thus, their anticipatory socialization was moderated by an active search for information (Morrison 1993).

The great majority (86 per cent) of the recruits did not find the discipline at the academy very harsh or at all harsh. This is consistent with Crank's observation (1998: 197) that stress training of the kind described by Van Maanen is disappearing from police training regimes. The recruits in the present study found the academy staff much more friendly and approachable than they had expected. What many of them did feel uncomfortable with – and this became a source of great resentment as they moved through their training – was the Phase 1 curriculum, which was designed to make recruits aware of the social context of policing. This was referred to derisively as 'warm and fuzzy stuff,' and many recruits saw it as taking up too large a proportion of their training, and as in any case irrelevant in terms of preparing them for the practical demands of policing. Interviews with academy instructors suggest that Phase 1 was indeed designed to mould recruits' attitudes – to make them aware of, and hopefully reject, racial and sexual stereotypes – rather than to teach them practical skills. This attempt at 'liberalizing' recruits may have benefited some, but most saw it as an indication that the academy was out of touch with the realities of policing.

These feelings were confirmed and amplified after recruits came into contact with operational policing in the field. Their four weeks of field observation in Phase 2 and their close to a year of field training in Phase 4 brought them into what they regarded as the 'real' world of policing. In contrast, the academy was seen as about 'theory,' 'scenario,' 'play acting,' and 'made up' reality. On the one hand, they were intoxicated with the challenge of 'being out there doing something.' On the other hand, they began to see the gap between the knowledge they had acquired at the academy and the skills they needed to survive in the field. They felt fearful and ill prepared. In all this, the training they received at the academy became an easy target. Complaints ranged from the polite observation that 'everything at the academy is really clinical and sort of staged' to a blunt condemnation that 'the academy is a heap of bullshit' (cf. CARE 1990).

For all the rhetoric of 'professionalism' that formed the basis of PREP, the bulk of recruit training was based on the notion that policing is a craft to be learned 'on the job' (Freidson 2001: 89). Field training remained an apprenticeship arrangement where probationers learned by 'watching, listening, and mimicking' their field training officers and other officers in the field (Van Maanen 1973: 412). Probationers developed a number of strategies for coping with the challenges of the job and for fitting in at their new environment. One of these was to listen, observe, and ask questions but 'not say too much' – and especially not challenge anyone's practice openly. This strategy of 'keep your mouth shut' or 'be seen and not heard' was a demonstration of respect for experience and rank; it was also a survival technique. Judging from field observation and interviews with field training officers (FTOs), this was indeed what was expected of recruits (cf. Van Maanen and Schein 1979).

During their field training, probationers acquired both technical knowledge and various dimensions of organizational cultural knowledge (Sackmann 1991; Chan 1997). At first, probationers hungered for basic technical knowledge (cf. Morrison 1993). They spent their first weeks getting to know the simple, routine procedures. Later, they learned how to satisfy the bureaucratic requirements of 'paperwork.' As they gained experience in the field, they developed routine ways of categorizing their environment and the people they encountered (dictionary knowledge). Also, they began to distinguish between the theoretical knowledge taught in the academy and what they regarded as 'real' knowledge acquired in the field. Part of this 'real' knowledge taught them to be cynical about certain segments of the public – those who lied to police or who refused to 'help themselves' or take responsibility for their own actions. Some probationers developed the view that the public generally did not like police. This heightened the contrast between the support provided by other police and the unfriendly attitudes shown by the public. Having a good relationship with one's workmates became paramount. Probationers also began to admire the practical skills possessed by their buddies and other police, especially people skills, knowledge of how to act under different circumstances, and the ability to take control of difficult situations. They also started to work out 'short cuts' that helped them get through their work more efficiently (directory knowledge). Besides technical skills and practical assumptions, probationers also learned how to survive in the organization by covering themselves at all times (recipe knowledge).

Changes in Habitus

The metamorphosis from new recruit to police constable involved some major shifts in attitudes and values – changes in the habitus. By the end of their field training, most probationers felt they had changed as people. Many thought they had become more mature and more confident, although they had lost some of their idealism and naïvety. The training they received had 'deposited' within their bodies and minds a 'feel for the game' of policing. These changes were perceptual and attitudinal as well as physical. Perceptually, they were more observant, more aware and alert to what went on around them. In terms of attitudes, they were less tolerant, more suspicious of people, and more cynical, although these changes were by no means uniform. Physically, they had taken on the posture and verbal manners of police officers.

Not surprisingly, the cohort had picked up some typical elements of the occupational habitus of street-level policing: cynicism, dislike of paperwork, and distrust of management and outsiders, including the general public (Reiner 1992; Reuss-Ianni and Ianni 1983; Van Maanen 1978a). Most of the probationers we interviewed at the end of their field training expressed a high degree of disillusionment with the job. The most frequently raised complaint was the amount of paperwork required (cf. 'The Paper Burden' in Ericson and Haggerty 1997: 296–302). Frustration was directed at the accountability requirements imposed by managers, Internal Affairs, and outside agencies such as the Ombudsman. Managers were seen as ineffective 'bludgers' who did not support front-line police, in terms of either providing adequate resources or 'backing up' workers in the face of public complaints. Recruits' attitudes toward the community became progressively and significantly more negative over the eighteen months of their training. The vast majority thought they had become more cynical and suspicious, more aware of the negative aspects of society, and more likely to stereotype people. The perceived lack of appreciation by the public for the work police did for them had led some to abandon their ideals of wanting to help people, because people 'don't want to be helped.' Others were disappointed that there were limits to what they were able to achieve. Over the course of their training, recruits developed a more negative attitude toward the criminal justice system. Although there was no significant change in their general attitudes toward corruption, the rule of law, and work practice during the first six months of training, there was a significant and negative change over their period of field training.

Competing Concepts of Professionalism

Throughout their training, recruits encountered competing notions of professionalism and occupational competence. The 'full professional model' on which PREP was based was variously interpreted by academy staff and field training officers. The original ideal was to develop police officers with the ability to analyse problems, empathize with others, reflect on their own values and biases, and take appropriate actions in ambiguous or dangerous situations (see chapters 2 and 4). Our interviews with academy instructors show that interpretations of professionalism can involve things ranging from 'shiny boots and a neat uniform,' doing things 'by the book,' and paperwork that is 'neat and tidy,' to competence and ethical standards. A number of instructors saw Phase 1 as helping raise students' awareness of their own biases and assumptions, as well as moulding their attitudes so that they would show more empathy toward ethnic minorities and disadvantaged groups.

These attempts to 'liberalize' recruits' attitudes were later derided by officers in the field and by the recruits themselves as 'warm and fuzzy stuff' and as irrelevant to operational police work. Our interviews with FTOs show that most had never heard of the 'full professional model' or the 'reflective practitioner.' Their sense of 'professionalism' (not necessarily the term they would use) included a range of qualities such as doing things 'by the book,' the ability to 'suss out' situations, showing consideration toward people, communication skills, and the ability to 'think on your feet.' FTOs were critical of the training that recruits received at the academy; in their view, probationers lacked basic skills. FTOs were also deeply suspicious of what they saw as the academy's attempt to produce a 'new breed' of police officers who were prepared to challenge experienced officers and report on police misconduct.

Recruits' lack of confidence and practical experience when they first entered the operational field made these criticisms especially poignant. Their desire to 'fit in' and be accepted by operational police also meant they would never openly contradict these criticisms. But when we interviewed probationers away from the field, some of them admitted that the negative view of the academy was partly perpetrated by officers in the field – a fact confirmed by our observation during Phase 4, even though most officers in the field would not have kept up-to-date with what was being taught at the academy. A few recruits told us they did not agree with these criticisms of the academy. They thought the academy had provided basic knowledge that they could draw upon later in the field. They felt there was a place for theoretical knowledge, and that academy training was not meant to replace field training, which was where practical training was supposed to take place.

Recruits were not passively shaped by negative role models. As subjects told us in interviews, and as we observed in the field, probationers came across models of 'good' as well as 'bad' police work. In Survey 3, the great majority of respondents (from three-quarters to nine-tenths) thought that their field learning experience varied with the local area command they were assigned to and with the personalities or working styles of the local area commander, the shift supervisors, and their shift partners. Local areas varied in terms of workload, culture, amount of experience, and general attitudes toward work among officers. Local area commanders could be authoritarian, inaccessible, and negative, or they could be friendly, clear in their expectations, and generous in their feedback. These leadership styles had consequences for morale and practice.

Probationers also commented on how they needed to adapt to the inconsistent styles and expectations of different shift supervisors and shift partners. Probationers' adaptations to their work environment did not consist of blanket acceptance of everything they were told in the field. When given the opportunity to express their own views, some probationers were quite willing to criticize and distance themselves from certain practices. Individual probationers formed judgments about police work and the police organization based on their own experiences, and were able to distinguish between 'good' and 'bad' models. Some interviewees felt that having been exposed to different policing styles, they could decide for themselves the type of police they wanted to become. This was true especially of older probationers. Field observation suggests, however, that probationers almost never openly questioned their seniors' actions or judgments. On many occasions, we observed probationers simply keeping quiet while their seniors expressed strong opinions about various issues. At times they felt obliged to defend the seniors' actions and their own tolerance of certain practices. Nevertheless, on a small number of occasions, we heard probationers question their seniors' actions.

An important finding is that contrary to previous stereotypes, not all FTOs were cynical and disenchanted. Most of the FTOs we interviewed seemed motivated by a desire to pass on a version of professionalism down the line – they wanted probationers to learn how to do things properly (procedural correctness), but also efficiently and in a way that satisfied legal and bureaucratic requirements. They also shaped probationers' attitudes – though not always consciously – by encouraging them to 'listen,' to be enthusiastic about the job, and to use their common sense. Some FTOs were careful not to criticize the academy, but the impression we got was that few FTOs were aware of what was being taught at the academy unless they themselves had been through PREP recently. FTOs themselves distinguished between the positive and negative aspects of police culture, and they were not apologists for bad practice. In some sense they saw themselves as protectors of the probationers from their external environments.

Changing Culture

Recruits in the study displayed a high degree of reflectiveness about their own experience. During the fourth round of interviews, they willingly shared their thoughts about police culture with the researchers. From what they told us, police culture is about camaraderie, mateship, and support in the job. It is a common understanding that police share with one another, since they face similar situations as an occupational group. It is also a support mechanism at both a professional level and a personal level in a job that requires trust and teamwork. But these officers were not blind to the negative side of the culture. About half the interviewees readily admitted that police culture can lead to insularity and stereotyping, and noted that when solidarity is used to justify lying to protect one another or to cover up misconduct, 'that's when the culture goes wrong.' They saw police culture as no different from other occupational cultures that arise from unique work situations: police culture develops as a defence mechanism to cope with the working conditions – the shift work, the unpleasant situations police have to attend to, the abuse they get from offenders and from the public, and the widely shared frustration with the organization. According to the interviewees, newcomers to the police are always watched closely and with suspicion. People who are different or deemed untrustworthy are excluded or treated like outcasts. Police who inform on or complain against other officers are considered dangerous and are ostracized.

The interview data suggest that police culture in New South Wales was in a state of flux at the time. Nearly half the interviewees told us that police culture was changing or had changed. They felt that the 'old' culture of heavy drinking and criminal cover-up no longer existed. It was no longer considered taboo for police to complain against other police. A few interviewees told us that they themselves had reported misconduct. One interviewee described an incident where an officer who used excessive force on a suspect was confronted by another officer and reported to a supervisor. He concluded that there had been a cultural change from 'that old school of all stand over and you protect your mates at any cost.' This view was supported by another interviewee who had personally complained to a senior officer against an officer who turned up for work drunk on a number of occasions. He compared this changing culture to changing community attitudes to drink driving. A recruit who had reported some officers for being 'very drunk' on duty said she had 'worn it ever since,' but she never regretted it and felt that other police agreed with her action. Although we did not have access to information that could verify these claims, we had no reason to suspect that these officers were not telling the truth. The stress of informing on another police could be enormous. Officers did not find it easy to 'dob in' other police. Some interviewees said they would be worried about what colleagues would think of them. One constable said he would be very angry if someone put him in that position, but he would still report, because 'you don't need police like that that do things unethical.' Another also felt uncomfortable about dobbing in other police, but thought that the most people would respect the person who had the courage to do so.

These anecdotal reports cannot be taken as indicators of cultural change. Our surveys did detect some shift in attitudes. Responses to eleven ethical scenarios show a general shift between Survey 1 and Survey 3 in terms of a greater willingness to report misconduct *formally* to the police service. This shift is statistically significant for all except two scenarios. Yet there was also an opposite trend – for certain less visible misconduct ('Avoid RBT,' 'Hit youth,' 'Private business,' 'Accept beer'), a higher proportion of respondents would prefer to 'turn a blind eye' and take no action (see chapter 6).

The Changing Field of Policing

We must interpret these results in the context of the changing social, political, and organizational conditions of policing, not only in New South Wales but also in other Western democracies. Some of these changes relate to broader societal trends: globalization, the proliferation of information and communications technologies, and the dominance of 'new public management' discourse. Others are more specific to the immediate concerns of policing: the trend toward militarizing and privatizing policing, the change in the gender and ethnic composition of police forces, the new emphasis on efficiency and accountability, and the rise of new models of policing.

As pointed out in earlier chapters, the field of policing in New South Wales has been changing since the reforms of the mid-1980s. Among the changes introduced in this era, two dimensions are highlighted in this study. The first relates to the total redesign of the recruit training curriculum (PREP) in concert with the ideal of professionalism and the vision of community policing. The second involves the active recruitment of women to join this male-dominated occupation. The adoption of community policing and a 'full professional' model of policing was a challenge to the traditional crime-fighting model. It legitimated a new form of symbolic capital in the field of policing – one based on problem solving, the provision of professional service, and building partnerships with the community. The recruitment of women also posed a challenge to traditional policing – albeit an unsuccessful one, since physical capital still tends to override other forms of symbolic capital (see chapter 7).

The Wood Royal Commission into police corruption led to further radical changes in the field of policing. These included the establishment of a permanent 'watchdog' to investigate serious corruption; the introduction of legal provisions that gave the commissioner power to dismiss incompetent or corrupt police; the authorization of targeted integrity testing and random alcohol testing of police; and the introduction of a performance-based accountability system for local area commanders. Unpopular though some of these new accountability initiatives were, they were party responsible for what was regarded as 'cultural change' in the police service. Police became more conscious of the constraints and risks their job entailed and had to learn how to negotiate this new field, in which a wrong move might bring about complaints, investigations, and disciplinary actions.

We have argued that the complexity and contingency of the socialization process in New South Wales was due to some of these changes in the field of policing. In particular, the reforms that came in the wake of the Royal Commission led to some major shifts in the weights of different types of capital. Both recruits and serving police officers were now aware of the stronger emphasis on integrity and professionalism as forms of symbolic capital and of the economic consequences of being found corrupt or incompetent. As suggested in chapter 1, the success of reforms depends on their ability to change the habitus of police officers, and especially on their ability to change the crime-fighting *doxa* of traditional policing. The available evidence suggests that organizational commitment to change has been perfunctory (HayGroup 2000) and that implementation has been uneven (Moss 1998). The instability of the organizational habitus is likely to continue. As conditions change, both recruits and serving members of the organization are much more conscious and cautious in making adjustments to their habitus. The struggle over the meaning of 'professionalism' – between traditional 'street cops' and those wanting to produce a 'new breed' of professional police who make independent judgments, value integrity above peer solidarity, and take a more compassionate approach to policing – has been partly a consequence of the instability in the field. Recruits in this study were caught between competing notions of professionalism; some of this is reflected in the split loyalty they felt between the academy and operational policing. The Royal Commission and subsequent policy changes served to intensify these conflicts. In the end, most recruits sympathized more with the 'street cops' as they felt the weight of increased accountability and public distrust of police. Nevertheless, the political climate generated by the Royal Commission has shifted the balance of power so that integrity – taught in the academy but devalued in the field – is once again a valued form of capital. The game has changed, and the established culture has become increasingly shaky. Newcomers have learned to adapt and adjust, and in time, through their own practice, they too will contribute to the redefining of professionalism.

Theorizing Police Socialization

The New South Wales case study demonstrates the utility of the theoretical framework adopted by Chan (1997) for understanding police socialization. Bourdieu's concepts of field, capital, and habitus are useful for explaining culture and socialization in terms of the interaction between structural conditions and cultural knowledge in organizations. Habitus is an especially appropriate tool for describing the system of dispositions that individuals acquire, initially through personal history and experience, and later through organizational socialization. For policing, habitus incorporates various dimensions of cultural knowledge, including unexamined assumptions, accepted definitions, tried-and-true methods, and shared values, as well as bodily display and physical deportment. Under normal conditions, police recruits incrementally adjust their habitus to 'fit in' with the dominant culture of their workplace. The acquired habitus then becomes a 'feel for the game' – a stable set of dispositions that generate coherent ways of seeing, thinking, and acting, requiring almost no conscious thought on the part of the actor. Once a recruit has acquired the appropriate habitus, he or she will feel accepted and comfortable, like a 'fish in water.'

But the framework does not assume the existence of a stable, homogeneous organizational habitus that newcomers must learn in order to become accepted. Rather, it allows for the possibility of (a) multiple cultures within one organization – as evidenced by the competing concepts of professionalism taught in the academy and in the operational field – and (b) a changing organizational culture. Here is where Bourdieu's concept of field and the related notion of capital become crucial. The field defines the 'game.' Relative to others within the police organization, recruits are at the bottom of the hierarchy in almost every dimension of capital. Their game, then, is to accumulate as much cultural capital (knowledge, skills, and experience), social capital (good will, cooperation, and camaraderie), and symbolic capital (a favourable reputation among workmates and superiors) as possible. But the values of different types of capital are not constant. External changes – which can be either changes in the position of policing in the 'field of power,' such as a drop of public support as a result of corruption revelations, or changes in preferred style of policing, as in the introduction of community policing – can affect the values of different forms of capital as well what counts as symbolic capital. When the field is changing, the organizational habitus must adjust. As a result, serving members whose habitus is the product of a different field are just as uncomfortable as the recruits. They try to discredit the change (as shown by constant criticisms of the academy by operational police officers in the case study) and hang on to the 'old' habitus. At the same time, they feel like 'fish out of water' in the changed field. Unless they can find an enclave of the organization where change has not occurred, they may have to leave the organization or 'drop out' by abandoning their interest (*illusio*) in the 'game.'

Bourdieu's framework has generally emphasized social reproduction rather than social change. The emphasis on the 'unconscious' or automatic connection between habitus and practice allows little room for rational calculation or conscious thought before action. Yet as we have seen in this case study, recruits can be highly reflective and conscious of the socialization process. At times they reported a degree of strategic calculation that is seldom discussed in socialization studies. In this sense the case study has 'stretched' Bourdieu's framework so as to recognize, as Bourdieu (2000: 163) recently conceded, that people who 'occupy awkward positions' cannot rely on the automatic guidance of their habitus. Instead, they have to watch themselves carefully and correct any inappropriate moves they make as a result of following a habitus from their previous 'life.' In the presence of a stable, homogeneous organizational culture, most recruits will in time adjust their habitus more or less to what is appropriate to their environment, and their actions will be guided unconsciously by the new habitus. But if the organizational habitus is changing or fragmented, recruits will continue to be conscious of their actions, and cautious of them for as long as caution is necessary. Recruits do not simply try to 'fit in,' rather, they take on the habitus of operational policing always with an eye on how the rules of the 'game' may be changing.

The case study also suggests that 'successful socialization' is not necessarily about conformity to a dominant organizational culture, even if a homogeneous, stable culture exists. Just because an occupation or organization has developed ways of seeing, thinking, and acting that have 'worked' in the past does not mean that it is healthy for the organization to eternalize the reproduction of this culture. The assumption that policing is a craft (Wilson 1978: 68) that places a premium on experience and practical skills, and that can only be learned through an apprentice system, has already been challenged by the movement toward a professional model of policing. Where recruits have successfully adjusted their habitus in harmony with the traditional 'street cop' culture, or learned a 'feel for the game' of operational policing, there is a danger that they will become 'locked into' an anxiety avoidance mode of learning rather than a problem-solving one (Schein 1985). It may be that for officers to become creative problem solvers, they will sometimes have to consciously 'fight against' the habitus they have learned. For example, in certain interactions with citizens, 'good police work' may involve a conscious effort to 'fight against' the automatic tendency of the occupational habitus to stereotype, to assume a 'siege mentality,' or to treat everyone with suspicion. The idea of working against one's habitus may seem to contradict Bourdieu's original framework, but a 'creative individualist' (Schein 1968), like other people that 'occupy awkward positions' (Bourdieu 2000) in an organization, is likely to be more conscious and reflective in making his or her moves. This is a technique that artists regularly use to maintain freshness and authenticity in their practice.[1] Indeed, the idea of a reflective practitioner is based on the same principle of elevating practice from the unthinking automatism of the occupational habitus. In this way, successful socialization is not so much about perfecting the craft as about learning the *art* of policing.

The Future of Reform: Challenging the Doxa

The New South Wales case study has shown that reform through training is possible, but also that reform has many obstacles in its path. The new recruit training curriculum (PREP), introduced in the late 1980s, had some success in laying the foundation for a new model of policing and with it a new conception of professionalism. The model was community policing, which emphasizes preventive policing, order maintenance, and local accountability (Chan 1997: ch. 6). It was a direct challenge to the doxa of traditional policing that police work is about crime fighting, crook catching, and physical coercion. PREP set out to subvert the traditional model by raising consciousness about ethics, the social and legal context of policing, and the prejudices recruits bring to the job (see chapter 4). It also constructed a model of good police work based on the ideal of a professional and reflective practitioner.

The academy curriculum stayed fairly close to the objective of implementing this ideal, and had some success in 'liberalizing' or at least containing unprofessional attitudes (Wortley 1992; see also chapter 6, Table 6.7). The same cannot be said of the field training component of PREP. Recruits who joined the police generally brought with them the assumption that policing was about crime fighting (see chapter 3, Table 3.5), and it did not take long for them to start repeating the mantra that Phase 1 of PREP was about 'warm and fuzzy stuff' and quite irrelevant to 'real' policing. Their contact with 'seniors' in the academy and with operational police during Phase 2 no doubt reinforced this criticism at an early stage. One would expect Phase 4 – almost a year of on-the-job training among operational police – to harden probationers' attitudes against the academy training. To a large extent it did just that, especially in relation to Phase 1 (see chapter 4, Table 4.6). Nevertheless, the 'lessons' of the academy were not totally lost. There was still a high degree of identification with communication skills as an important indicator of 'good police work,' at least up to the third round of interviews (see chapter 6, Table 6.4). Partly as a result of the new organizational emphasis on integrity, recruits by the end of their training had become more conscious of corruption issues and were showing – at least in response to hypothetical scenarios – a greater willingness to formally report certain types of misconduct to the police service (see chapter 6).

This suggests that where training curricula are backed up by organizational policies, training objectives are more likely to be realized. The converse is also suggested by the case study: where training curricula are at odds with organizational policies, training objectives are likely to be frustrated. In other words, the police service's move away from community policing in the late 1990s toward a NYPD-inspired style of crime fighting has made it difficult if not impossible for a training curriculum based on community policing to have any lasting impact on recruits. The academy–field divide (see chapter 4) is both an indicator that community policing has not taken hold in operational police work in spite of the Avery reforms (Chan 1997: 204–5) and a reflection of the fact that the organization is no longer committed to that model of policing. The bridging of that divide is therefore a matter not only of linking theory to practice – although that is an important prerequisite – but also of establishing some kind of consensus throughout the organization about 'why things are done the way they are' (Sackmann's [1991] axiomatic knowledge). As Sackmann's research suggests, debating and negotiating axiomatic knowledge is the key to changing organizational culture, because axiomatic knowledge defines the organization's 'purpose, its strategic intention, its design and characteristics of preferred members' (156). Once organizational processes are set up to implement the new axiomatic knowledge, changes in other dimensions of cultural knowledge follow. Nowhere is this point more clearly illustrated than in the case of female police officers. As discussed in chapter 8, the drive to encourage women to join the police in recent decades is unlikely to make a significant difference to the masculine culture of policing unless the *doxa* that equates 'real' policing with crime fighting and physicality is challenged.

Reformers do not have to look far for alternatives to traditional crime-fighting policing. Since the late 1970s, problem-solving and community-policing strategies have been challenging traditional policing strategies on the basis that the latter have been ineffective in controlling crime (see Moore 1992 for an overview). The revival of crime-fighting policing in recent years, riding on the wave of success of the 'New York miracle,' has all but eclipsed any debate about alternative strategies in New South Wales, even though any success in crime reduction brought about by the 'firm but fair' policing strategy was likely to be due to the 'Compstat' type process for managerial accountability and the use of problem-solving techniques such as targeting repeat offenders and 'hot spots' (see Dixon 1999). Though there may be political capital to be made by politicians in portraying police strategies in terms of aggressive crime fighting, the reality is that unless there is a radical change in the role of police in society, the major part of general duties police work will involve the handling of non-criminal or non-serious but potentially criminal matters (cf. CJC 1996a). Any attempt to cling to crime-fighting policing as an ideal is doomed to failure, not only because it ignores the bulk of what most police officers do every day, but also because of the obvious fact that there are many causes of crime over which police can have little control. Once it is recognized that definitions of 'good police work' cannot be divorced from *actual* police work – providing policing service to citizens rather than some heroic vision of crime fighting – it is not difficult to formulate models of best practice. Much work has already been done by the architects of PREP in New South Wales and by reformers all over the world. The production of 'good' police officers, however, requires more than a superior training package. It cannot happen without full organizational commitment and wide community support for a more innovative, effective, and publicly accountable model of policing – one based on what police can realistically do, rather than some mythic vision of what they wish they could do.

Notes

1. Organizational Socialization and Professionalism

1 Research studies carried out in the 1970s or earlier were conducted with predominantly male police officers, although the masculine gender may have been used to represent all police officers, male and female. This comment applies to all such masculine references throughout this report. The cumbersome use of 'sic' in relation to each reference is avoided.

2 Van Maanen and Schein (1979: 230–54) identified six dimensions of socialization tactics: socialization can be collective or individual, formal or informal, sequential or variable, fixed or variable, serial or disjunctive, and investiture or divestiture.

3 Several excerpts from Chan (1997: ch. 4) are integrated into this text without attribution to avoid the use of cumbersome and extended quotations.

2. Research Organization and Methods

1 Some recent longitudinal studies of police recruits exist, but they tend to focus on specific aspects of recruits' attitudes rather than on their socialization processes (see, for example, Wortley 1992).

2 This refers to s181D of the *Police Service Act*, which gives the commissioner power to 'remove a police officer from the Police Service if the Commissioner does not have confidence in the police officer's suitability to continue as a police officer, having regard to the police officer's competence, integrity, performance or conduct.'

3 Information provided by the police service regarding the actual number of students at each stage was not always accurate. For example, we were told that there were only 120 students left in the cohort in Phase 5, but a subse-

quent list showed a total of 139 students (which was more consistent with the survey response for that round: N=134).

4 As it turned out, one of the selected interviewees did not commence PREP training and was therefore not part of the cohort.

5 Two interviewees refused to be taped in Round 1, and one refused to be taped in rounds 2 to 4.

6 Two interviews were abandoned because of logistical problems that could not be overcome in spite of repeated attempts to arrange a suitable time.

7 The term 'police patrol' was used to indicate local police commands. In 1997, 'patrols' were renamed 'local area commands' (LACs). Because this change in terminology occurred during the research project, readers will find both terms being used throughout the book.

8 We noted that some students were sent to training patrols instead of demonstration patrols.

9 One shift was not accounted for because a report was not completed.

10 External validity issues such as the generalizability of findings from one cohort in one police service at one particular period of time are less relevant, as the research is designed as a case study (see Yin 1989) that aimed at furthering analytic understanding in context rather than statistical generalization.

3: Joining the Organization

1 This was slightly below average in class size compared with intakes in previous years: the average class size between 1988 and 1993 was 177.0, with the smallest being 51 and the largest 331 (NSW Police Service 1994: 23).

2 This information was derived from the first questionnaire survey completed by 147 of the 150 students in the first week at the academy: one person never commenced training, and two questionnaires were not returned.

3 The definition of ethnic background in the NSWPS (1994: 41) was based on parents' country of birth.

4 TAFE stands for technical and further education.

5 According to the Australian Bureau of Statistics' 1996 census data, the median household income was $33,000 per annum.

6 For 9 per cent of the respondents, this question was non-applicable, presumably because their parents were deceased.

7 Lower mean ratings represent greater perceived importance.

8 Strictly speaking, it is not necessary to conduct tests of significance on

what amounts to the entire population of the cohort (i.e., not a sample). Nevertheless, statistical tests provide an indication of the probability of Type I error if we treat this cohort as a sample of all recruits in New South Wales.

9 Throughout this book, all interviewee age details refer to age at entry to the academy.

10 Percentages do not add up to 100, since multiple responses were available.

11 Higher School Certificate, the equivalent of matriculation.

4: Learning at the Academy

1 The concept of 'boundaries' was used by Schein (1968b) in an unpublished paper cited by Van Mannen (1976: 78). Career movements in an organization may involve the crossing of different types of boundaries: vertical (e.g., rank), radial (centrality), and circumferential (e.g., duty).

2 NSW Police Board (1992: 2).

3 Ten instructors were interviewed. All were sworn police officers with an average of sixteen years in the police service.

4 This particular dilemma is well illustrated in the cross-examination at the Police Royal Commission of a young police officer who was involved in recreational drug use. See Royal Commission Transcripts 21/1/96 (191) pp. 19033–65.

5 This section was written by Janet Chan originally as part of chapter 5. It has been moved to this chapter and revised.

6 The setting of the debriefing sessions was such that students were more likely to be uninhibited about describing their experiences. However, a fair proportion of the students we interviewed also criticized poor practices they observed.

7 These include practical fingerprint skills, presentation of research on Aboriginal issues, self/mentor assessment (one-on-one interviews between tutor and student), firearms examination and practical assessment, batons exam and practical assessment, fitness assessment and obstacle course, handcuff review, various examinations, case write-ups, a 1500-word assignment on one of the themes from Block 4, a final examination that included material from Phases 1 and 3, debate/presentation, OSPAC (Objectively Structured Simulated Patrol Assessment Centre) major assessment where students were assessed in pairs in a simulated operational situation, and OSPAC minor practical assessment one-on-one with tutor (NSWPS 1995 and personal communication with officer safety staff).

8 This account of the 'passing out parade' was reconstructed from an

audiotape of the event, press report, and the author's own observations of such events.

9 To protect the identity of the cohort, this date was not identified.

10 An exercise carried out in week one of PREP that is designed to explore the effects of power and authority.

11 Spearman's Rank Correlation.

5: Learning in the Field

1 According to the *PREP Course Documentation* (NSW Police Service 1993: 72): 'There are ten designated Demonstration Patrols. These were designated because of their location, the suitability of their Police Stations, and the education and training support structure they possess. All Demonstration Patrols have a specifically designated full-time Patrol Education and Development Officer, and an appropriate number of specially trained Field Training Officers. In the Demonstration Patrols Probationary Constables are supernumerary, that is, they are additional to the normal authorized strength of the Patrols.'

2 The (non-random) sample consisted of fourteen male and four female field training officers. They held the rank of constable (8) or senior constable (10). Their average age was 31, with 22 being the youngest and 41 the oldest. At the time of interview, their average length of service at the NSWPS ranged from 2.8 to 15.5 years (average 8 years), and they had been FTOs for between 3 months and 12 years (average 4 years). The FTOs were nominated by the local education and training officers, and it came as a surprise to us that in fact two of the FTOs were members of the cohort in this study.

3 Responses are drawn from round 3 of the interviews, which took place at the academy after the completion of Phase 4. The total number of interviews conducted was fifty-four.

4 We observed 30 shifts at 13 demonstration patrols and 28 shifts at 25 training patrols. Among 51 shifts where the probationer was part of a car crew, the rank of the senior partner was distributed as follows: constables (23), senior constables (13), not recorded (13), and probationers (2).

5 The vast majority (86 per cent) of first buddies were male. About two-thirds were senior constables, while the rest were constables.

6 Recruits who participated in the interviews were asked at the second, third and fourth interviews: 'Did you see any examples of good (bad) police work? Please elaborate.' These questions were designed to elicit *concrete* descriptions of what respondents considered 'good' and 'bad' police work

at various stages of their training and development. Obviously, respondents who told us they did not 'see' any good or bad police work should still have been able to articulate what they thought good and bad police practices were, but they were not asked to do so. In fact, none of the interviewees told us they had not encountered good police work, but a number of them maintained that they had not seen any examples of bad police work.

7 The observer was a former police officer with eight years of policing experience.

8 Observers experienced 44 instances of the police car driven 'quite fast,' 'very fast,' or simply 'sped to the scene.' In 11 other instances the experience was either described as 'very high speed' or the observer commented on the dangerousness of the driving. Speeds were not consistently recorded. However, speeds that were recorded ranged from 80 km per hour to 170 km per hour. The 170 km per hour ride was described by the (male) observer as a 'terror ride.'

6: Taking On the Culture

1 Third round of interviews – 53 respondents.

2 Five items were discarded following a reliability analysis which indicated that those items did not have a high correlation with the rest of the items.

3 Respondents were given an identical set of statements in Survey 1 and Survey 3 to rate their level of agreement or disagreement on a five-point Likert scale. These items – encompassing statements about the courts, prisons, parole policies, police powers, defence lawyers, victims, and criminal justice processes – were then scored and summed (after appropriate reverse coding and the exclusion of three items found not to correlate well with the others) to form an aggregate score. A higher score represents a more positive attitude toward the criminal justice system.

4 As part of the third round of interviews (N=50), we asked probationers whether their views had been affected by the Royal Commission. Instead of answering the question directly, interviewees had tended to use the occasion to express their own views of how the commission had affected policing.

5 Three respondents said they didn't know what the commission's impact was or gave some vague answers.

6 Respondents were asked to rate their level of agreement or disagreement to a series of statements along a five-point scale. After reverse-coding the appropriate items and discarding one that did not correlate well with the

rest of the items, we constructed a composite score by summing thirteen items, with a high score indicating a more 'ethical' attitude, and vice versa.

7   Although mean scores were presented to summarize differences, tests of significance were based on non-parametric Mann-Whitney U tests at the 0.05 level.

8   Mean 'justified' scores were 4.84 for males and 3.78 for females.

9   Mean 'justified' scores were 2.09 for males and 1.50 for females; mean 'corrupt' scores were 5.95 for males and 7.28 for females.

10   We divided respondents into two groups: those under twenty-one and those twenty-one and above at the time of Survey 1. We then compared their responses. Only statistically significant results are reported here.

11   Mean 'serious' scores were 6.98 for the older group and 7.88 for the younger group. Mean 'corrupt' scores were 5.47 for the older group and 6.44 for the younger group.

12   Mean 'corrupt' scores were 3.75 for the older group and 4.73 for the younger group for 'Private business,' and 6.06 vs 7.04 for 'Racist language.'

13   Mean 'serious' scores were 8.61 for the older group and 7.59 for the younger group.

14   For 'take cigarettes,' the mean 'serious' scores were 6.38 vs 7.51 and the mean 'corrupt' scores were 5.89 vs 7.12. For 'Fabricate report,' the mean 'serious' scores were 6.68 vs 7.62. For 'Steal/lie,' the mean 'justified' scores were 1.55 vs 2.65.

15   There was a slight variation in wording of the options presented between Surveys 1 and 3. The categories 'Report matter to a senior officer' and 'Report matter to Internal Affairs or Professional Responsibility Branch' in Survey 3 were merged and compared with 'Report matter to NSW Police Service' in Survey 1 under the new heading 'Formal report within the NSWPS.' The category 'Informally raise with a trusted officer' in Survey 3 was compared with 'Informally raise with a trusted Senior Officer' in Survey 1. 'Other' options were nominated by 1 to 4 per cent in Survey 1 and 1 to 6 per cent in Survey 3. They included a number of qualifications and comments about the conduct, or indications that they would 'speak to' a particular officer without indicating whether it was formal or informal reporting.

16   Although female respondents in Survey 1 were generally less likely than males to take 'no action,' and more likely to take informal action or raise the matter directly with the officer involved, there were only two instances where the differences were statistically significant. In relation to the 'Private business' scenario, female respondents were significantly *less likely*

to take no action (21 per cent vs 42 per cent), and in relation to the 'Lie in court 1/steal' scenario, male respondents were significantly *more likely* to report the matter to the Ombudsman (13 per cent vs 0 per cent). By Survey 3, however, these differences were no longer significant. The only statistically significant difference between males and females in Survey 3 relates to the scenario 'Take cigarettes,' where 62 per cent of male respondents said they would make a formal report within the NSW Police Service, compared with 43 per cent of female respondents who nominated this option.

17 Very few significant differences due to age were found in Survey 1. Older respondents were *more likely* than younger ones to take informal action with a trusted officer in the 'Take cigarettes' scenario (51 per cent vs 33 per cent) as well as the 'Threaten violence' scenario (52 per cent vs 34 per cent). Younger respondents, however, were *more likely* than older ones to make a formal report to the Police Service (28 per cent vs 10 per cent) or to report the matter to the Ombudsman (6 per cent vs 0 per cent) in relation to the 'Fabricate report' scenario. By Survey 3, none of the differences were statistically significant.

18 University education made little difference to what actions recruits would take in response to the scenarios. In Survey 1, the only significant differences were in relation to two scenarios. In the 'Take cigarettes' scenario, respondents with some university education were *less likely* than those without university education to take informal action with a trusted officer (30 per cent vs 52 per cent). In the 'Accept beer' scenario, respondents with some university education were *more likely* than the others to take no action (78 per cent vs 59 per cent), but were *less likely* to take informal action with a trusted officer (8 per cent vs 26 per cent). By Survey 3, these and other differences between the two groups were no longer statistically significant.

7: Negotiating the Field

1 A total of 53 constables were interviewed.

8: Doing Gender

1 Of the 75 interviewees selected at the commencement of the study, 27 (36 per cent) were female. While 27 females were selected for interview, not all attended each round of interviews.

2 The number of interviewees who did not go beyond saying 'no' were: 5 of

19 in round 2, 4 of 16 in round 3, and 2 of 18 in round 4. In addition, the question regarding female experience was inadvertently omitted at a small number of interviews. The figures here represent those who attended interviews, and those who were asked the question about female experience.

3 It was not clear what the 'experience' was, but the 'touchy feely' reference implied physical contact. No other interviewee referred to 'physical contact' experiences or experiences of a sexual nature.

4 The obstacle course has since been removed from the recruit training program.

5 Mann-Whitney U test, $p < 0.05$

6 In Survey 4, 33 per cent of male respondents agreed with the statement.

7 Worden's (1993) interpretation of Martin's adaptations is the choice here. Martin's definitions create an image of the 'butch' versus the 'beauty queen.' It was the image created by Worden's definitions that more accurately describes the women and their adaptations in this study.

9: Conclusion: Learning the Art of Policing

1 The famous Australian artist Sidney Nolan explained his constant change of mediums as a way of 'fighting against' the bodily hexis of a master painter: 'It's very important – to me, anyway – to change, especially as one gets older and masters the technicalities of painting. You see, even the muscles learn tricks. It's like an actor; the gestures become habitual and he walks through the lines. Well, in the same way, the muscles learn through the movements that go on with a painter, until finally he learns and his arms learn, more or less, to produce a certain thing. It's like a trick shot in billiards or tennis. Yes, you must fight against it because I suppose if a painting is worth anything it is supposed to come from some place inside yourself that you cannot get to through any other means' (Barber 1964: 99).

Bibliography

Abbott, A. (1988). *The System of Professions: An Essay on the Division of Expert Labor*. Chicago: University of Chicago Press.

Adkins, C.L. (1995). 'Previous work experience and organisational socialization: a longitudinal examination,' *Academy of Management Journal* 38(3): 839–62.

Alexander, J.C. (1995). *Fin de Siècle Social Theory: Relativism, Reduction and the Problem of Reason*. London: Verso.

Appier, J. (1998). *Policing Women: The Sexual Politics of Law Enforcement and the LAPD*. Philadelphia: Temple University Press.

Ashforth, B.E., and A.M. Saks (1996). 'Socialization tactics: Longitudinal effects on newcomer adjustment.' *Academy of Management Journal* 39(1): 149–78.

Ashforth, B.E., A.M., Saks, and R.T. Lee. (1998). 'Socialization and newcomer adjustment: The role of organizational context.' *Human Relations* 51(7): 897–926.

Australian Law Reform Commission (1992). *Multiculturalism and the Law*. Report No. 57. Commonwealth of Australia.

Avery, J. (1981). *Police: Force or Service?* Sydney: Butterworths.

Babbie, E. (1992). *The Practice of Social Research*. Belmont, CA: Wadsworth.

Baldwin, R., and R. Kinsey (1982). *Police Powers and Politics*. London: Quartet Books.

Barber, N. (1964). *Conversations with Painters*. London: Collins.

Bayley, D., and H. Mendelsohn (1969). *Minorities and the Police*. New York: The Free Press.

Becker, H., B. Greer, E.C. Hughes, and A. Strauss (1961). *Boys in White*. Chicago: University of Chicago Press.

Bittner, E. (1978). 'The functions of the police in modern society.' In P. Manning and J. van Maanen, eds., *Policing: A View from the Street*. Santa Monica, CA: Goodyear.

Black, D. (1971). 'The social organization of arrest.' *Stanford Law Review* 23: 1087–111.

Bourdieu, P. (1977). *Outline of a Theory of Practice*. Cambridge: Cambridge University Press.

– (1987). 'What makes a social class? On the theoretical and practical existence of groups.' *Berkeley Journal of Sociology* 32: 1–18.

– (1990a). *In Other Words: Essay towards a Reflexive Sociology*. Cambridge: Polity Press.

– (1990b). *The Logic of Practice*. Stanford: Stanford University Press.

– (2000). *Pascalian Meditations*. Cambridge: Polity Press.

– (2001). *Masculine Domination*. Stanford: Stanford University Press.

Bourdieu, P., and L.J.D. Wacquant (1992). *An Invitation to Reflexive Sociology*. Cambridge: Polity Press.

Bradley, D. (1996). 'Contemporary police education in Australia.' In D. Chappell and P. Wilson, eds., *Australian Policing: Contemporary Issues*. 2nd ed. Sydney: Butterworths.

Bradley, D., and P. Cioccarelli (1989). 'Chasing Vollmer's fancy: Current developments in police education,' in D. Chappell and P. Wilson, eds., *Australian Policing: Contemporary Issues*. Sydney: Butterworths.

Brogden, M., T. Jefferson, and S. Walklate (1988). *Introducing Policework*. London: Unwin Hyman.

Brogden, M., and C. Shearing (1993). *Policing for a New South Africa*. London: Routledge.

Brown J.M. (1998). 'Aspects of discriminatory treatment of women police officers serving forces in England and Wales.' *British Journal of Criminology* 38 (2): 265–82.

Brown L.M., and F. Heidensohn (2000). *Gender and Policing: Comparative Perspectives*. London: Macmillan.

Calhoun, C. (1993). 'Habitus, field and capital: The question of historical specificity.' In Calhoun et al., eds., *Bourdieu: Critical Perspectives*. Cambridge: Polity Press.

Caplow, T. (1964). *Principles of Organization*. New York: Harcourt, Brace and World.

Centre for Applied Research in Education (CARE), University of East Anglia. (1990). 'The New South Wales Police Recruit Education Program: An Independent Evaluation.' Unpublished report.

Chan. J. (1996). 'Changing police culture.' *British Journal of Criminology* 36(1): 109–34.

– (1997). *Changing Police Culture: Policing in a Multicultural Society*. Melbourne: Cambridge University Press.

– (1999). 'Governing police practice: Limits of the new accountability.' *British Journal of Sociology* 50(2): 249–68.

– (2000a). 'Globalisation, reflexivity and the practice of criminology.' *Australia and New Zealand Journal of Criminology* 33(2): 118–35.

– (2000b). 'Backstage punishment: Police violence, occupational culture and criminal justice.' In T. Coady, S. James, S. Miller and M. O'Keefe, eds., *Violence and Police Culture*. Melbourne: Melbourne University Press.

– (2001a). 'Negotiating the field: New observations on the making of police officers.' *Australia and New Zealand Journal of Criminology* 34(2): 114–33.

– (2001b). 'The technological game: How information technology is changing police practice.' *Criminal Justice* 1(2): 139–59.

Chan, J., D. Brereton, M. Legosz, and S. Doran (2001). *E-Policing: The Impact of Information Technology on Police Practices*. Brisbane: Criminal Justice Commission.

Chan, J., S. Doran, and C. Devery (1999). 'Learning the craft of policing: Police training, occupational culture and professional practice.' Final Report to the NSW Police Service and the Australian Research Council.

Christie, G., S. Petrie, and P. Timmins (1996). 'The effect of police education, training and socialisation on conservative attitudes.' *Australian and New Zealand Journal of Criminology* 29(3): 299–314.

Corns, C. (1992). 'Inter-agency relations: Some hidden obstacles to combating organised crime.' *Australian and New Zealand Journal of Criminology* 25(2): 169–85.

Crank, J. (1998). *Understanding Police Culture*. Cincinnati: Anderson Publishing.

Criminal Justice Commission (1993). *Recruitment and Education in the Queensland Police Service: A Review*. Brisbane: Criminal Justice Commission.

– (1995). *Ethical Conduct and Discipline in the Queensland Police Service: The Views of Recruits, First Year Constables and Experienced Officers*. Brisbane: Criminal Justice Commission, Research and Coordination Division.

– (1996a). 'The Nature of General Police Work,' CJC Research Paper Series 3(2), May.

– (1996b). 'Gender and ethics in policing.' CJC Research Paper Series 3(3), October.

Cullen, F., B. Link, T.T. Lawrence, and T. Lemming (1983). 'Paradox in policing: A note on perceptions of danger.' *Journal of Police Science and Administration* 11: 457–62.

Cunneen, C., and T. Robb (1987). *Criminal Justice in North-East New South Wales*. Sydney: Bureau of Crime Statistics and Research.

Davids, C., and L. Hancock (1998). 'Policing, accountability, and citizenship in the market state.' *Australian and New Zealand Journal of Criminology* 31(1): 38–68.

Dixon, D. (1993). *Report on a Review of Police Powers in Queensland.* Vol. 1. Brisbane: Criminal Justice Commission.

– (1997). *Law in Policing: Regulation and Police Practices.* Oxford: Clarendon Press.

– , ed. (1999). *A Culture of Corruption.* Sydney: Hawkins Press.

Ericson, R.V. (1981). 'Rules *for* Police Deviance.' In C. Shearing, ed., *Organizational Police Deviance.* Toronto: Butterworths.

– (1982). *Reproducing Order: A Study of Police Patrol Work.* Toronto: University of Toronto Press.

– (1993). *Making Crime: A Study of Detective Work.* 2nd ed. Toronto: University of Toronto Press.

– (1993). 'The division of expert knowledge in policing and security.' *British Journal of Sociology* 45(2): 149–75.

Ericson, R., P. Baranek, and J. Chan (1987). *Visualizing Deviance: A Study of News Organization.* Toronto: University of Toronto Press; Milton-Keynes: Open University Press.

Ericson, R.V., and K. Haggerty (1997). *Policing the Risk Society.* Toronto: University of Toronto Press; Oxford: Clarendon Press.

Ericson, R.V., and N. Stehr, eds. (2000). *Governing Modern Societies.* Toronto: University of Toronto Press.

Etter, B. (1992). 'The future direction of policing in Australia.' Paper to the Australian and New Zealand Society of Criminology Annual Conference, Melbourne, 30 September–2 October, 1992.

Fielding, N. (1988). *Joining Forces: Police Training, Socialization, and Occupational Competence.* London and New York: Routledge.

Finnane, M. (1999). 'From police force to police service? Aspects of the recent history of the New South Wales police.' In D. Dixon, ed., *A Culture of Corruption: Changing an Australian Police Service.* Sydney: Hawkins Press.

Fitzgerald Report. (1989). *Report of the Commission of Inquiry Pursuant to Orders in Council dated (1) 26 May 1987; (2) 24 June 1987; (3) 25 August 1988; (4) 29 June 1989.* Brisbane: Queensland Government Printer.

Freidson, E. (2001). *Professionalism: The Third Logic – On the Practice of Knowledge.* Chicago: University of Chicago Press.

Giddens, A. (1984). *Constitution of Society.* Cambridge: Polity Press.

Goldsmith, A. (1990). 'Taking police culture seriously: Police discretion and the limits of law.' *Policing and Society* 1: 91–114.

Goldstein, H. (1979). 'Improving policing: A problem-oriented approach,' *Crime and Delinquency* (April), 236–58.

Hage, G. (1994). 'Pierre Bourdieu in the nineties: Between the church and the atelier.' *Theory and Society* 23: 419–40.

Harris, R. (1978). 'The police academy and the professional self image.' In P. Manning and J. van Maanen, eds., *Policing: A View from the Street*. New York: Random House.

HayGroup (2000). *Qualitative and Strategic Audit of the Reform Process (QSARP) of the NSW Police Service: Report for Year 1 (March 1999–March 2000)*. Sydney: HayGroup.

Heidensohn, F. (1992). *Women in Control? The Role of Women in Law Enforcement*. Oxford: Clarendon Press.

Holdaway, S. (1983). *Inside British Police*. Oxford: Basil Blackwell.

– (1995). 'Constructing and sustaining "race" within the police work force.' Paper to the British Criminology Conference, Loughborough, July.

Hughes, E.C. (1958). 'The study of occupations.' In Merton, R.K., L. Broom, and L. Cotrell, eds., *Sociology Today*. New York: Basic Books.

Huon, G., B. Hesketh, M. Frank, K. McConkey, and G. McGrath (1995). *Perspectives of Ethical Dilemmas: Ethics and Policing – Study 1*. Payneham, South Australia: National Police Research Unit.

Hunt, J. (1990). 'The logic of sexism among police' *Women and Criminal Justice*. 1: 3–30.

Illich, I. (1977). 'Disabling Professions.' In I. Illich, I.K. Zola, J., J. McKnight, Caplan, and H. Shaiken *Disabling Professions*. London: Marion Boyars.

IPETAC (1986). *Interim Police Education and Training Advisory Council Second Report, Incorporating the First Report*. Sydney: Police Board of NSW.

Johnson, R. (1993). 'Editor's introduction.' In P. Bourdieu, *The Field of Cultural Production*. Cambridge: Polity Press.

Jones, S. (1986). *Policewomen and Equality: Formal Policy v Informal Practice?* London: Macmillan.

Jones, G.R. (1986). 'Socialization tactics, self-efficacy, and newcomers' adjustments to organizations.' *Academy of Management Journal* 29: 262–79.

Leishman, F., B. Loveday, and S.P. Savage, eds. (1996). *Core Issues in Policing* London: Longman.

Lusher Report (1981). *Report of the Commission of Inquiry into the New South Wales Police Administration*. Sydney: NSW Government Printer.

Manning, P. (1978a). 'The police: Mandate, strategies and appearances.' In P. Manning and J. Van Maanen, eds., *Policing: A View from the Street*. Santa Monica, CA: Goodyear.

– (1978b). 'Lying, secrecy and social control.' In P. Manning and J. Van Maanen, eds., *Policing: A View from the Street*. Santa Monica, CA: Goodyear.

- (1978c). 'Rules, colleagues, and situationally justified actions in
  P. Manning and J. Van Maanen, eds., *Policing: A View from the Street*. Santa
  Monica, CA: Goodyear.
- (1997). *Police Work: The Social Organization of Policing*. 2nd ed. Prospect
  Heights, IL: Waveland Press.

Manning, P., and J. Van Maanen, eds. (1978). *Policing: A View from the Street*.
Santa Monica, CA: Goodyear.

Manning, P.K. (1992). 'Information technologies and the police.' In M. Tonry,
and N. Morris, eds., *Modern Policing*. Chicago: University of Chicago
Press.

Mansfield, B., and I. Bernard (1986). 'A brief history of police education in
NSW, 1981–1995.' Report to the Ministerial Advisory Council on the Police
Academy.

Martin, C. (1996). 'The impact of equal opportunities policies on the day-to-
day experiences of women police constables.' *British Journal of Criminology*
36(4): 510.

Martin, S.E. (1980). *Breaking and Entering: Policewomen on Patrol*. Berkeley:
University of California Press.
- (1990). *On the Move: The Status of Women in Policing*. Washington, DC: Police
  Foundation.
- (1994). '"Outsider within" the station house: The impact of race and gender
  on black women police.' *Social Problems* 41(3): 383–400.
- (1996). 'Doing gender, doing police work: An examination of the barriers to
  the integration of women officers.' Paper to the First Australasian Women
  Police Conference, Sydney, 29–31 July.
- (1999). 'Police force or police service? Gender and emotional labor.' *Annals,
  AAPSS* 561: 111–26.

Martin, S.E., and N.C. Jurik. (1996). *Doing Justice, Doing Gender*. Thousand
Oaks, CA: Sage.

Mastrofski, S.D., R.B. Parks, A.J. Reiss, Jr, R.E. Worden, C. DeJong, J.B. Snipes,
and W. Terrill (1998). *Systematic Observation of Public Police: Applying Field
Research Methods to Policy Issues*. Washington: National Institute of Justice.

McBarnet, D. (1979). 'Arrest: The legal context of policing.' In S. Holdaway,
ed., *The British Police*. London: Edward Arnold.

McConkey, K.M., G.F. Huon, and M.G. Frank (1996). *Practical Ethics in the
Police Service*. Payneham, S.A.: National Police Research Unit.

Merton, R.K. (1957). *Social Theory and Social Structure*. Rev. ed. Glencoe, IL:
Free Press.

Moi, T. (1991). 'Appropriating Bourdieu: Feminist theory and Pierre
Bourdieu's sociology of culture.' *New Literary History* 22: 1017–49. Reprinted

in T. Lovell, ed. (1995) *Feminist Cultural Studies*, Vol. 2. Aldershot: Elgar Reference Collection.

Mollen Report (1994). *Commission Report: Commission to Investigate Allegations of Police Corruption and the Anti-Corruption Procedures of the Police Department.* New York: The Commission.

Moore, M. (1992), 'Problem-solving and community policing.' In M. Tonry and N. Morris, eds., *Modern Policing*. Chicago: University of Chicago Press.

Morgan, D.H.J. (1994). 'Theater of war: Combat, the military, and masculinities.' In H. Brod and M. Kaufman, eds., *Theorizing Masculinities*. Thousand Oaks, CA: Sage.

Morrison, E.W. (1993). 'Newcomer information seeking: Exploring types, modes, sources, and outcomes.' *Academy of Management Journal* 36(3): 557–89.

Moss, I. (1998). *Police Adversely Mentioned at the Police Royal Commission.* A Special Report to Parliament under section 31 of the Ombudsman Act. Sydney: Office of the NSW Ombudsman.

Muir, W.K. (1977). *Police: Streetcorner Politicians*. Chicago: University of Chicago Press.

NSW Ombudsman (2002). *Improving the Management of Complaints*. Sydney: Office of the NSW Ombudsman.

NSW Police Board (1992). *Presentation to the Premier: Community Based Policing.*

NSW Police Service (1988). *Annual Report*. Sydney: NSWPS.

– (1989). *The Police Profession: Role of Education and Training.*

– (1992). *New South Wales Police Recruit Education Program: Course Documentation, Transition 1990–1991.* New South Wales Police Service, November 1991 / March 1992.

– (1993). *PREP Course Documentation*. Sydney: NSW Police Service.

– (1994). *Transition. Report of the June–November 1994 Working Party Review of Changes to Recruitment Policy and Practice.* Sydney: NSW Police Service (Unpublished).

– (1995). *PREP Phase 3 Study Guide* January 1995 Edition.

– (1996). *Initiatives in Education and Training*. Sydney: Education and Training Command, NSWPS.

NSW Police Service Field Training Directorate (n.d.). *PREP Phase IV Review* (unpublished).

O'Malley, P., and D. Palmer (1996). 'Post-Keynesian policing.' *Economy and Society*. 25(2): 137–55.

PARC. (1994). *Report of the Police Academy Review Committee to the NSW Police Board.* Sydney: NSW Police Board.

Powell, W.W., and P.J. DiMaggio, eds. (1991). *The New Institutionalism in Organizational Analysis.* Chicago: University of Chicago Press.

Price, B.R. (1977). *Police Professionalism: Rhetoric and Action*. Lexington, MA: Lexington Books.

Reiner, R. (1978). *The Blue-Coated Worker: A Sociological Study of Police Unionism*. Cambridge: Cambridge University Press.

– (1992). *The Politics of the Police*. 2nd ed. London: Harvester: Wheatsheaf.

Reiss, A. (1971). *The Police and the Public*. New Haven, CT: Yale University Press.

Reuss-Ianni, E., and F. Ianni (1983). 'Street cops and management cops: The two cultures of policing.' In M. Punch, ed. *Control in Police Organization*. Cambridge, MA: MIT Press.

Ryan, P. (1998). 'New South Wales Police Service: The Next Stage in Reforming the Service.' Paper prepared for Paul Whelan, Minister for Police.

Sackmann, S. (1991). *Cultural Knowledge in Organizations*. Newbury Park, CA: Sage.

Sacks, H. (1978). 'Notes on police assessment of moral character.' In P. Manning and J. Van Maanen, eds., *Policing: A View from the Street*. Santa Monica, CA: Goodyear.

Saks, A.M., and B.E. Ashforth (1997). 'Organizational socialization: Making sense of the past and present as a prologue for the future.' *Journal of Vocational Behavior* 51: 234–79.

Sarantakos, S. (1993). *Social Research*. South Melbourne: Macmillan.

Schein, E. (1968a). 'Organizational socialization.' *Industrial Management Review* 2: 37–45.

– (1968b). 'The Individual, the organization and the career: A conceptual scheme.' Unpublished paper.

– (1985). *Organizational Culture and Leadership*. San Francisco: Jossey-Bass.

Shearing, C.D., and R.V. Ericson (1991). 'Culture as figurative action.' *British Journal of Sociology* 42: 481–506.

Shearing, C. (1981). 'Deviance and conformity in the reproduction of order.' In C. Shearing, ed. *Organizational Police Deviance*. Toronto: Butterworths.

Sheptycki, J.W.E. (1998). 'Policing, postmodernism and transnationalization.' *British Journal of Criminology* 38(3): 485–503.

Skolnick, J.H. (1966). *Justice without Trial: Law Enforcement in a Democratic Society*. New York: John Wiley and Sons.

Skolnick, J., and J. Fyfe (1993). *Above the Law: Police and the Excessive Use of Force*. New York: Free Press.

Smith, D. (1994). 'The political and social constraints to reform.' In K. Bryett and C. Lewis, eds. *Un-Peeling Tradition: Contemporary Policing*. Melbourne: Macmillan.

Sparrow, M.K., M.H. Moore, and D.M. Kennedy (1990). *Beyond 911*. New York: Basic Books.

Sturma, M. (1987). 'Policing the criminal frontier in mid-nineteenth century Australia, Britain and America.' In M. Finnane, ed., *Policing in Australia: Historical Perspectives*. Kensington: UNSW Press.

Sutton, J. (1992). 'Women in the job.' In P. Moir and H. Eijkman, eds., *Policing Australia: Old Issues, New Perspectives*. Melbourne: Macmillan.

Sykes, G. (1989). 'The functional nature of police reform: The myth controlling the police.' In R. Dunham and G. Alpert, eds., *Critical Issues in Policing: Contemporary Readings*. Prospect Heights, IL: Waveland Press.

Tomlinson, J. (1999). *Globalization and Culture*. Cambridge: Polity Press.

Van Maanen, J. (1973). 'Observations on the making of policemen.' *Human Organisation* 32(4): 407–18.

– (1974). 'Working the street: A developmental view of police behavior.' In H. Jacob, ed. *The Potential for Reform of Criminal Justice*. Beverly Hills, CA: Sage.

– (1975). 'Police socialization: A longitudinal examination of job attitudes in an urban police department.' *Administrative Science Quarterly* 20: 207–28.

– (1976). 'Breaking in: Socialization to work.' In R. Dubin, ed., *Handbook of Work, Organization and Society*. Chicago: Rand McNally.

– (1977). 'Experiencing organization: Notes on the meaning of careers and socialization.' In J. Van Maanen, ed., *Organizational Careers: Some New Perspectives*. London and New York: John Wiley.

– (1978a). 'Kinsmen in repose: Occupational perspectives of patrolmen.' In P. Manning and J. Van Maanen, eds., *Policing: A View from the Street* Santa Monica, CA: Goodyear.

– (1978b). 'The asshole,' in P. Manning and J. Van Maanen, eds., *Policing: A View from the Street*. Santa Monica, CA: Goodyear.

– (1983). 'The boss: First-line supervision in an American police agency.' In M. Punch, ed., *Control in Police Organization*. Cambridge, MA: MIT Press.

Van Maaner, J., and E. Schein (1979). 'Toward a theory of organizational socialization.' *Research in Organizational Behavior* 1: 209–64.

Vollmer, A. (1971). *The Police and Modern Society*. Montclair, NJ: Patterson Smith.

Wacquant, L.J.D. (1992). 'Toward a social praxeology: The structure and logic of Bourdieu's sociology.' In P. Bourdieu and L. Wacquant, *An Invitation to Reflexive Sociology*. Cambridge: Polity Press.

Waddington, P.A.J. (1999). 'Police (canteen) sub-culture: An appreciation.' *British Journal of Criminology* 39(2): 287–309.

Walker, S. (1977). *A Critical History of Police Reform: The Emergence of Professionalism*. Lexington, MA: Lexington Books.

Weick, K. (1979). *The Social Psychology of Organizing*. Reading, MA: Addison-Wesley.

West, C., and D.H. Zimmerman. (1987). 'Doing gender.' *Gender and Society* 1: 125–51.

Westley, W.A. (1970). *Violence and the Police: A Sociological Study of Law, Custom and Morality*. Cambridge, MA: MIT Press.

Wilson, J.Q. (1978). 'The police and crime.' In P. Manning and J. Van Maanen, eds., *Policing: A View from the Street*. Santa Monica, CA: Goodyear.

Wimshurst, K. (1995). 'Anticipating the future: The early experiences and career expectations of women police recruits in post-Fitzgerald Queensland.' *Australian and New Zealand Journal of Criminology* 28 (3): 278–97.

Wood Report (1997). *Royal Commission into the NSW Police Service: Final Report*. Sydney: NSW Govt.

Worden, A.P. (1993). 'The attitudes of women and men in policing: Testing conventional and contemporary wisdom.' *Criminology* 31(2): 203–39.

Wortley, R.K. (1992). 'Police prejudice, discrimination and socialization: An attributional perspective.' PhD thesis, School of Behavioural Sciences, Macquarie University.

Wortley, R.K., and R.J. Homel (1995). 'Police prejudice as a function of training and outgroup contact: A longitudinal investigation.' *Law and Human Behaviour* 19(3): 305–17.

Yin, R.K. (1989). *Case Study Research: Design and Methods*. Applied Social Research Methods Series, Vol. 5, Newbury Park, CA: Sage.

Young, M. (1991). *An Inside Job*. Oxford: Clarendon Press.

Index